Help Starts Here
The maladjusted child
in the ordinary school

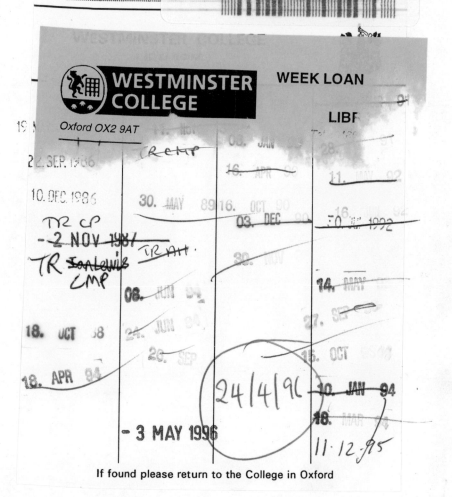

Help Starts Here

The maladjusted child
in the ordinary school

ISRAEL KOLVIN

ROGER FORBES GARSIDE

ARTHUR RORY NICOL

ANGUS MACMILLAN

FRED WOLSTENHOLME

IAN MUIR LEITCH

TAVISTOCK PUBLICATIONS

London and New York

First published in 1981 by
Tavistock Publications Ltd
11 New Fetter Lane, London EC4P 4EE

Published in the USA by
Tavistock Publications
in association with Methuen, Inc.
733 Third Avenue, New York, NY 10017

Photoset by Rowland Phototypesetting Ltd
Bury St Edmunds, Suffolk

Printed in Great Britain by
Richard Clay (The Chaucer Press) Ltd
Bungay, Suffolk

British Library Cataloguing in Publication Data

Help starts here.
1. Child psychotherapy   2. Problem
children – Education
I. Kolvin, Israel
371.94   LC4801
ISBN 0-422-77380-8

Library of Congress Cataloging in Publication Data

Main entry under title:
Help starts here.

Bibliography: p.
Includes index.
1. Problem children – Education.
I. Kolvin, Israel.
LC4801.H44   371.93   81-14184
ISBN 0-422-77380-8 (U.S.)   AACR2

Contents

Foreword   *page* vii
Preface and acknowledgements   ix

Part One
Introduction

1 General introduction: basic concepts   3
2 Some basic problems in evaluation   16

Part Two
Method and background

3 Aims and method   35
4 The children, their schools, families, and therapists 54

Part Three
Treatment approaches

5 Behaviour modification approach   83
6 The nurturing approach – a teacher-aide
   programme   139
7 Parent counselling-teacher consultation   172
8 Group therapy for children   217

Part Four
Results and conclusions

 9   Final analysis: junior and senior schools   265
10   Summary and conclusions   299

Part Five
Technical appendices

1   Evaluative measures used   335
2   Method   342
3   Results   350
4   School and therapist effects on outcome   380

References   385
Name index   424
Subject index   431

Foreword

The study of children's development and wellbeing has a tradition in Newcastle upon Tyne which dates back to just after the Second World War.[1] The work reported in this book continues the tradition. It is a sustained enquiry carried out by a team of psychiatrists, psychologists, and social workers in a representative group of schools in Newcastle upon Tyne and Gateshead between 1972 and 1979. A thousand junior schoolchildren, aged seven, and 3300 seniors, aged eleven, were screened and as a result 265 juniors and 309 seniors were studied in detail. The aims were to identify and characterize psychiatric and educational difficulties in these children and to compare different ways of helping the children overcome these difficulties. The whole intention was practical from the beginning.

The starting initiative was unusual. Aware of the country-wide alarm at the increase in unruly behaviour in the classroom, the present Prime Minister, Margaret Thatcher, then Secretary of State for Education and Science, asked her advisory committee for special education to look for the causes and to suggest remedies. Newcastle upon Tyne's record of research in social paediatrics and psychiatry, and more recent developments in child psychiatry, made the city an obvious choice for this new project, and so the committee invited the principal author and his colleagues to accept the task of research.

With their long involvement with children and families in the communities chosen for study, the authors naturally describe their approach and interpret their findings in terms of child development, educational progress, and family background. They begin with their

[1] Spence, J., Walton, W. S., Miller, F. J. W., and Court, S. D. M. (1954) *A Thousand Families in Newcastle upon Tyne*. The Nuffield Foundation, Oxford: Oxford University Press.

definition of psychiatric disorders in children, accepting that in different parts of the UK, between 7 and 25 per cent of children under 16 are affected by them, and review from previous studies the natural history of these disorders and the extent to which they may undergo spontaneous remission.

As a guide to the choice of management, they record in the introductory chapters a wide-ranging critique of previous methods, with an estimate of their validity. The methods finally selected were: a 'nurturant' approach, through the use of teacher-aides, behaviour modification, parent counselling-teacher consultation, and group therapy, through playgroups and discussion groups. The authors did not limit their approach to severe examples that were the cause of national concern, but considered the complete range from incipient to established disorders. This was because the development of these disorders is such that a mild, early disturbance can become a severe disability in later childhood.

To consider the conclusions they reach would be to destroy the mounting excitement of the reader as he or she follows the findings and arguments of the study.

Who then should be the readers? First, and foremost, teachers, in training and in the classroom, child psychologists and psychiatrists, paediatricians, educational administrators, politicians, and thoughtful men and women who are concerned with education in their communities.

Two comments on the conclusions are justified in this introduction. The findings show the rich potential of the ordinary school for preventive psychiatry, providing a unique opportunity to reach a large number of children in difficulty and distress. It is also necessary to realize that the treatment programmes were directed to the return of well-adjusted behaviour, as well as to improved academic achievement.

As we hold a book between its containing covers, we tend to consider it complete in itself. To speak adequately to the reader the book should be rooted in the tested experience of the past, explore the present with precision, and point reliably to the future. This report has all these qualities and should lead to new understanding and new practice. This will depend on those responsible accepting that the methods shown to be effective are professionally practicable, are educationally appropriate, and make good commonsense.

I hope this book will be widely read and boldly applied.

NEWCASTLE UPON TYNE 1981   S. D. M. COURT

Preface and acknowledgements

In modern society all children attend school, and school has a powerful socializing influence in child development. Not only are children expected to acquire knowledge; they must also learn to adapt their behaviour and their interpersonal relationships in accordance with socially acceptable norms. It seems probable that if difficulties over this adaptation are not recognized and dealt with, a lasting sense of inferiority, failure, and poor adjustment will arise: this book is about finding children with difficulties in school and exploring ways of helping them.

The data we provide in this book could be dealt with adequately only by fairly complex statistical methods, but the details of these are not necessary for an understanding of our conclusions and how they were reached. They are, though, included in the Appendices for the specialist reader.

The six key members of the team who have been with the project from beginning to end are: I. Kolvin, the Research Director; R. F. Garside, the Deputy Director; A. R. Nicol, who spearheaded the playgroup and group therapy approaches; F. Wolstenholme, who organized the nurture work programme; A. Macmillan, who was responsible for the behaviour modification approach; and I. M. Leitch, who undertook the mammoth task of handling the computerization of the data.

A research project of this extent needed the co-operation and collaboration of many individuals besides these few. The contributions of others were many and varied. First, and foremost, we need to thank Heads and staffs of the many schools in Newcastle upon Tyne and Gateshead who have been so helpful in the project. We also have to thank the Directors of Education and the Directors of Social

Services of these two cities. We are indebted, too, to the devoted group of mental health professionals who carried the research project into the individual schools. Our sincere thanks are offered to Mrs M. Blackburn for administrative help and to Mr J. Maxwell (previously of Moray House) and Professor R. Davies (previously of the National Children's Bureau) for help with the choice of educational and psychological measures.

The planning committee

In a similar way, we are indebted to our local planning committee which, in addition to the six authors, included the following experts from the area: Mr A. Arnot, Dr K. F. Bailey, Mr J. Ford, Miss M. McLaren, Dr L. Mills, Mr C. A. Norman, Mr A. Pears, and Mr R. Stansfield.

The steering committee

We have not yet mentioned the important subject of financial support. This was based on a long-term project grant from the Department of Education and Science.

The Department of Education and Science steering committee made an invaluable contribution over a period of seven years. Given this lengthy duration of the research, there were a number of changes on this committee. We list here those who made a regular contribution for at least one year:

Previous Chairman: Mr M. A. Walker, Department of Education and Science (June 1972 to September 1976)
Current Chairman: Professor Sir John Walton, University of Newcastle upon Tyne (June 1977 to June 1980)
Director: Professor I. Kolvin
Deputy Director: Dr R. F. Garside
Representing the University of Newcastle upon Tyne:
Mr A. Arnot, Professor D. Child, Professor D. Eccleston, Professor Sir Martin Roth, and Professor J. K. G. Webb;
Representing the Department of Education and Science:
Mr J. G. Bagley, Miss J. D. Dawkins, Mr G. H. N. Evans, Mr J. R. Fish, Mr J. A. Humphreys, Mr D. McLaughlin, Mr C. A. Norman, Mr M. J. Rabarts, Mr V. M. Stevens, and Dr K. Whitmore;
Representing the National Health Service:
Dr L. Brierley, Dr M. Sackwood, and Dr D. L. Wilson;

Representing the social services:
Mr G. T. Lythe and Mr B. Roycroft;
Representing the local education authority:
Dr K. F. Bailey and Miss M. A. Sproat.
Honorary Secretary: Mrs M. Blackburn

Some others who, because they moved posts, were only able to attend for a brief period; they included Professor S. D. M. Court, Dr P. Mason, and Dr F. Tait.

The project team

From 1972 to 1980 a host of workers contributed to the research for this study. Some stayed for only brief and others for longer periods, some joined at the beginning of the research, others at a later stage, and the number of those contributing varied from time to time. Except for the authors of the current monograph, all members of the project team are listed below in alphabetical order (those with asterisks after their names helped with planning or supervision):

Mrs M. Bailey (teacher-aide)
Mrs M. Bell (social worker)
Mrs M. Blackburn (administrator)
Dr W. Brough* (psycho-therapist)
Miss L. Cox (secretary)
Mrs M. Davidson (senior secretary, typing manuscript)
Mrs M. Evans (secretary)
Mrs D. Fadden (research interviewer)
Dr L. Gabor* (psychotherapist)
Miss L. Harvey (social worker)
Mrs L. Hepplewhite (teacher-aide)
Mrs M. Howitt (computer programmer)
Mr C. Hulbert* (senior psychologist)
Mr S. Iveson (psychologist)
Miss S. Jackson (social worker)
Mrs A. Jones (teacher-aide)
Mrs E. Kennedy (computer programmer)
Mrs E. Khangure (social worker)
Mrs J. Kirby (teacher-aide)
Mrs P. Kitchen (teacher-aide)
Miss M. McLaren* (lecturer in social work)
Mrs L. Mein (senior secretary)
Miss L. Midgeley-West (psychologist)
Dr L. Mills* (principal educational psychologist)
Mrs L. Mullin* (social worker)
Mrs N. Nelson (research interviewer)
Mrs L. Palframon (secretary)
Mrs J. Parker (social worker)
Dr M. Place (child psychiatrist)
Mrs H. Russell (technical editor)
Miss E. Schlater (social worker)

Mrs I. Smith (research interviewer)

Mr R. Stansfield* (Head-teacher)

Miss L. Walker (psychologist)

Mrs M. Westwood (teacher-aide)

Miss N. Whitehead (psychologist)

Mrs J. Wood (teacher-aide)

Dr R. Wrate* (child psychiatrist)

Mrs M. Wright (research interviewer)

General acknowledgements

We are indebted to the editors of the following journals and books for their permission to reproduce copyright material: *British Journal of Guidance and Counselling*; *British Journal of Psychiatry*; *Educational Research* (NFER Publishing Company Ltd); Graham, P. (Ed.) *Epidemiological Approaches in Child Psychiatry* (Academic Press Inc. London); *Journal of the Association of Workers for Maladjusted Children*; *Journal of Child Psychology and Psychiatry*; Laing, A. F. (Ed.) *Trends in the Education of Children with Special Learning Needs*; *Psychological Medicine*; *Special Education: Forward Trends*.

We are also indebted to the following for their permission to use tests: Dr E. Cowen for making his training manual available; The Devereux Foundation for the availability of their school behaviour scales; and Professor Michael Rutter for his parent and teacher behaviour scales.

We would like to thank, too, the following authors for permission to reproduce material from their papers: Professor C. L. Barrett, the University of Louisville, USA; Dr P. Sainsbury, Graylingwell Hospital, Chichester.

Part One
Introduction

1 General introduction: basic concepts

Summary

The main object of the research project described in this book was to find ways of developing mental health services in the community, particularly in ordinary schools, in an attempt to counteract the modern society's high incidence of psychological problems. Essentially, we were concerned with finding ways of identifying maladjusted children in ordinary schools and, more important, evaluating the effectiveness on them of different types of treatment, administered from within the school.

Because the developmental stage of the child is relevant to the type and nature of the problem experienced, two age groups of children were selected for study – seven-year-old juniors (265) and eleven-year-old seniors (309), ranged over six junior and six senior schools. We tested four treatment approaches – behaviour modification, nurture work, parent counselling–teacher consultation, and group therapy. Our research necessitated the development of techniques for the detection of disturbance at both early and late stages, for assessment of the results of treatment, and for evaluation of different approaches.

In this chapter we start by setting our work in the context of current discussions about types of treatment. We consider that effective results may depend on where the therapy takes place and the qualities of the therapist. Also of great importance is the type of problem in evidence. Common childhood psychiatric disorders can be classified as either neurotic or conduct disorders, both of which differ from normal patterns of behaviour in a quantitative rather than a qualitative sense. Both these disorders are defined in this chapter, and their high prevalence in the community is stressed. We also examine some studies that maintain that psychotherapy is ineffective. The differences between therapy in the clinic and in the community are discussed, together with the advantages and disadvantages of the latter. The concept of 'cure' is also considered in this context. The reasons for using ordinary schools as a frame of reference are discussed in detail, and the potential of the school to influence child development is stressed throughout.

We go on to discuss the classification and our choice of therapies. Approaches may be classified in a number of ways, such as direct or indirect – according to whether the therapist sees the child face-to-face or not; or as psychodynamic or behavioural – according to whether the therapist works with inner thoughts and feelings or confines him- or herself to observable behaviour.

The background to our research project

Alarming research findings over the 1960s and 1970s have forced mental health clinicians to review their approach to their work. In various parts of the UK, for example, between 7 and 25 per cent of schoolchildren are handicapped by frank psychiatric problems (Rutter, Tizard, and Whitmore 1970; Rutter et al. 1975; Kolvin et al. 1977; Macmillan et al. 1980). Many have educational difficulties that may be related to their own and their families' adverse attitudes to, and experience of, the educational system. In these circumstances, approaches to mental health that advocate prolonged, highly special-ized treatment of a few children have become impossible to defend – but what is to take their place? Faced with what is a major public health problem with implications for so many aspects of human effectiveness, what can be achieved by a 'treatment' service? Do we, in fact, have to sit back and wait for broad changes in social policy? Or can we adapt our services to meet real, immediate needs?

Many clinicians have responded to these concerns by moving into the community. They have started meeting teachers and children in schools and visiting homes. In doing so they have encountered those who are involved in the bringing up of children with whom they themselves only have brief contact. They have had to ask again how clinical skills can fit into the long-term projects of care, parenting, and education. What adaptations are needed? How can brief yet relevant interventions be carried through with the same rigour and attention to detail that has characterized the best of traditional therapy approaches? How can the 'dilution' of skill, which many clinicians fear, be avoided?

In the early 1970s, in Newcastle upon Tyne, UK, we started to study these questions, as have others on both sides of the Atlantic (e.g. Bower 1969). We were attached to a clinical base, reputable both in terms of paediatric and of psychiatric services, in a city with an excellent educational and school psychological service. Not only were we looking for complementary ways of extending services into the community but, most important, we were attempting to *evaluate the effectiveness* of the services we set up.

An important aspect of our approach, and one that we will emphasize repeatedly, is that we were approaching the child within the context of the school. This was because, right from the outset of our research, we recognized the important socializing influence of the school (Power *et al.* 1967; Rutter *et al.* 1979) and the unique opportunities that school provides as a background for therapeutic intervention. In the British educational system the compulsory age of school entry is five years, although many local education authorities admit children who are approaching their fifth birthday. The common pattern is for the child to move at seven years from infant to junior school, where the curriculum is more academic and formal. At this stage the child will usually have made a start at basic school subjects. Next, at the age of eleven years, the child usually moves from a smaller, neighbourhood, junior school, to a larger, secondary school, which is able to provide a much broader curriculum for all ability groups. At this stage the child will be expected to have a firm grasp of the basic subjects of writing, reading, and arithmetic. There are variations of the above, for instance certain local education authorities favour a middle school pattern, but none applied to our schools.

It seemed to us that we could make maximum use of the school background if we started working with the children at an early point in their long, settled period in the school. For this reason, we selected our younger children at the age of seven years, after they had settled in the junior school, and the older children when they were eleven years old and had settled in the secondary school. We thought that younger children were in a plastic, undifferentiated stage of development, including development of their problems. For this reason we sought to identify a spectrum among them – from those who showed early signs of difficulties to those with quite severe disorders. Among the eleven-year-olds we identified those with more established disorders. In this way we sought to help the younger children with a wide spectrum of severity of problems, whereas with the older children we found we were only concerned with the treatment of established disorders.

In both age groups we tried to develop a range of treatment approaches that complemented each other in their theoretical bases and the levels of training of the staff involved.

During this research work we pioneered many techniques and expanded, developed, or modified others in order to detect disturbance both in its early and in its more deeply developed stages. We also developed techniques for the evaluation of improvement and outcome (which are not necessarily the same – see Chapter 3) and for assessing the effectiveness of the different approaches from as many points of view as possible: these are described more fully in subsequent chapters.

The fields both of mental health and of education abound with contrasting theories, some of which were useful to us and require careful elaboration, while others were of less service. It was our hope that the research project would enable us to test out the various theories as applied in practice.

The traditional approach to treatment and its current status

Since the start of our research project a widespread and often impassioned debate has developed over the organization of mental health services. The 'Aunt Sally' of these discussions has often been the so-called 'traditional child guidance approach'. Considering that the whole child guidance movement is only about seventy years old, it seems unlikely that there has ever been a clearly identifiable traditional approach. Nevertheless, characteristics that are generally associated with the term may include: a team of psychiatrist, psychologist, and social worker who work together on all cases; prolonged treatment with intensive psychoanalysis as the only 'real treatment', other approaches being considered to be inferior and makeshift; long waiting lists, which restrict admission; finally, the ivory tower image created by restricted community involvement for all except the educational psychologist in his or her capacity in the school psychological service.

These characteristics are now generally associated with outmoded practice. Reports from both the USA (Long, Morse, and Newman 1971) and the UK (Rehin 1972), for example, suggest increasing disenchantment. In the UK a series of professional reorganizations (Seebohm Committee 1968; NHS Reorganization Act 1973; DES 1974) together with further proposals for change (Court Report 1976; Warnock Report 1978) have led to a great deal of experimentation and intermingling of roles. In addition, the emergence of new concepts and techniques of treatment, and of stronger individual professional identities, has added to the ferment.

A difficulty is that, too often, new work patterns have been moulded by strongly held opinion, fashion, and interprofessional rivalry, rather than by well-considered ways of providing services of proven effectiveness for children. Very seldom have heuristic questions been asked; too often, answers have been prematurely provided. In connection with this Garside *et al.* (1973) have posed a series of crucial questions. For instance, is the team approach the most effective and sensibly economic use of the highly skilled members of such a psychiatric clinic? For what types of cases does it work best? Do all cases merit the triple-team assessment? These questions highlight the need to examine what type of treatment works best for what type of disorder, under what conditions, and with what type of therapist (Strupp and Bergin 1969). Organizational relationships should stem from such knowledge rather than from competing whims and fashions in treatment.

The effectiveness of treatment as a whole has been considered by various reviewers (Eisenberg 1969; Robins 1970, 1973; Levitt 1971). The major conclusion has been that results of psychotherapy, and in particular one-to-one psychotherapy, are unimpressive. For instance, in his early review, Levitt claimed that treated patients and untreated controls improve at the same rate (Levitt 1957). Eisenberg (1969) also came to the conclusion that traditional psychotherapy has not been proved to be effective. The most quoted study in this area is that of Shepherd, Oppenheim, and Mitchell (1971). They compared fifty emotionally disordered children, who were neither delinquent nor psychotic, with an untreated control group matched for type and severity of disorder. Two-thirds of each group improved markedly, so that treatment appeared to make little different to outcome. The issue of spontaneous improvement is a major one and we will return to it in Chapters 2 and 10, together with a more detailed review of previous studies that have cast a somewhat more optimistic light on psychotherapy.

Why community intervention?

This question is particularly relevant in view of the strictures of the previous sections: if we are so unsure of treatments given by the clinic, why complicate the issue still further by giving services on a community basis? The answer is that community interventions and therapies are in many ways quite different from clinic therapy, and thus cannot be evaluated by extrapolation from clinic-based studies

(Hulbert, Wolstenholme, and Kolvin 1977; Wolstenholme, Hulbert, and Kolvin 1976; Nicol 1979).

The first difference is that many of the community-based therapies have an educational component. Children with educational problems frequently have overlapping problems, both at home and at school, consisting of psychiatric disorders, minor physical problems, visuo-motor difficulties, antisocial behaviour, and 'deprivation'. Robins (1973) pointed out that, in these circumstances, educational therapies make sense, whether the educational problems are considered to be primary or secondary to such handicaps. Robins saw such therapies, based on 'traditional educational techniques or behaviour modification techniques, which are educational methods more precisely designed and more self-consciously related to learning theory' (1973:111), as constituting a major movement in child psychiatry in the USA in recent years.

The second point is that the community base allows the therapist to gauge the general social climate that is impinging on the child. Hobbs (1966) has pointed out that most concepts of child disturbance demand an understanding of the way the wider systems of family, neighbourhood, and school support have been broken down. This is where notions of 'cure' can be seen to be inapproriate – a more realistic aim is to assist the wider support systems to 'cure sometimes, relieve often and comfort always' (Garside *et al.* 1973:149). The clinician is likely to find that the child is part of a destructive web of social interactions in which his or her own difficulties in social relationships are complicated by understandable but less than helpful responses from the wider systems of family and school.

A third, and most important, difference is that the school base (for example) is a familiar environment for the child, where the established pastoral system of the school may help in familiarizing the child with therapeutic procedures; this particularly influences the tendency of clients to continue therapy (Holmes and Urie 1975).

As well as giving help to children within their familiar setting, school-based therapy may help teachers to be involved more actively in treatment. This is its fourth difference from clinic-based treatment and it is particularly relevant to so-called 'indirect' treatment approaches (see p. 14). Despite contact with colleagues in the staff room, teachers can become very professionally isolated and the presence of a mental health worker who can talk to them about classroom difficulties can be a great support. The professional isolation of teachers is reported by Knoblock and Goldstein (1971).

A fifth difference is that, in working in the community, one is able to contact children in need of help who, through poor motivation or family disorganization, would never appear at a clinic. Related to this is the controversial issue of whether one should 'treat' children who have not specifically come for help. We will return to this theme in Chapter 10, where we discuss ethical issues.

A sixth difference is that community intervention allows us to reach *large* numbers of children in need.

Despite these advantageous factors, we were aware of several possible disadvantages of community-based work. For instance, the first was the potential lack of confidentiality when away from the formal clinic with its 'medical' component. Also, community institutions, such as the school, are powerful social systems with established hierarchies demanding conformity to norms. The community worker is always in danger of serving institutional needs that perhaps conflict with a child's needs or, alternatively, of siding with a child against community demands. The implications of these possibilities are discussed in Chapters 6 and 7, where we talk of the importance of the clinic base in community mental health work.

The ordinary school as a frame of reference

Throughout this book, the term 'ordinary' school covers all state schools that are not 'special' schools for the physically, emotionally, or mentally handicapped. We have already touched on several of the reasons that influenced our decision to make the school our frame of reference: the recent diversification of treatments; the fact that the prevalence of disturbed children is so high; the advantages of community intervention. Much more important is the fact that the school is second only to the home in its potential for influencing child development. This has recently been demonstrated persuasively in studies that show different schools produce different results, as measured by school behaviour, achievement, attendance, and delinquency (Power *et al*. 1967; Finlayson and Loughran 1975; Reynolds, Jones, and St Leger 1976; Rutter *et al*. 1979). In addition, there are suggestions that these results are associated with different aspects of the atmosphere and curriculum of the schools (Rutter *et al*. 1979). Thus, there are trends in the school that may be working for or against any treatment efforts. We will return to this theme in Chapter 10 and Appendix 4.

A second factor making a move into the school particularly relevant at present is a shift in emphasis in educational philosophy. This shift is well illustrated in the UK by the findings of a recent committee of inquiry into the educational needs of handicapped children (Warnock 1978). This report recommended that the concept of handicap be replaced by one of special educational need. Traditional thinking has seen children either as handicapped or non-handicapped. Special educational need is a more positive concept, one in which children are not seen in the light of their particular handicap, but rather in terms of everything about them, their abilities as well as their disabilities. This change of emphasis has profound implications, both for bringing more flexibility into the school curriculum, and also for introducing therapeutic techniques where indicated.

While some believe that teachers have an important role in managing social and behavioural problems of children, there are many who would see this neither as part of their task, nor one for which they have been equipped. Thus, despite the fact that some of their most crucial tasks involve handling difficult, unsettled, and disruptive children, student teachers are usually given very little training in coping with such problems, but are, instead, left to 'sink or swim'. There is thus a great diversity of attitudes, and of ability to cope with behavioural problems (Kounin 1970). While the central theme of our research was to test specific techniques, we were acutely aware that, among teachers, there were often very polarized opinions about whether they could, or should, make any contribution towards solving the behavioural or emotional problems of children.

In addition, we were often aware of a deep-seated suspicion between home and school. Often, in their formative years, parents have had unfortunate experiences at school which they carry over into adult- and parenthood without appreciating that the climate within schools has changed, and is generally more permissive and humane than in the old days. Teachers nowadays are often receptive to the idea that parents should have some kind of link with the school. Unfortunately, ways of developing these links have yet to be adequately developed.

The role of the ordinary and the special school in helping disturbed children

Although our aim in this project was to help disturbed children in ordinary schools this should not be construed as a denigration of the important role of the special school.

We have already stressed that teachers in ordinary schools do not necessarily see coping with the problems of disturbed children as part of their job. The management of emotional problems in school demands a high degree of skill and, as Gropper *et al.* (1968) pointed out, there should be programmes to train teachers to recognize social and emotional problems. This is being actively developed at the present time (Jeffery *et al.* 1979). The enhanced skills and awareness of the teachers must be a necessary background to the more specific treatment efforts embodied in intervention programmes.

Some of the concepts deriving from work carried out in the USA have, so far, been ill-digested in the UK. For example, Redl (1949, 1966) has suggested that if the disturbed child is retained in an ordinary class the other children may, by a form of contagion (germophobia), become disturbed. Empirical research by Kounin, Friesen, and Norton (1966) has led to the conclusion that teachers who are successful as classroom managers are also likely to be successful in coping with the behaviour of emotionally disturbed children in the classroom. In addition, they reported that those teachers who proved successful at coping with disturbed behaviour also produced a climate that prevented such disturbance from disrupting the behaviour of other children. Such conclusions have been supported by subsequent research. For instance, in an American study, Saunders (1971) reported that elementary schoolchildren who were exposed to an emotionally disturbed child for a period of three months did not appear to be affected by the experience. However, he agreed that the length of the exposure may not have been long enough to provide conclusive results and, further, he only studied the effects of disturbance of an acting-out variety and not of the withdrawn, neurotic type. The implication of this research is that the disturbed behaviour of one or two distressed children in the classroom does not necessarily give rise to generalized disruption. In conclusion, the policy of retaining emotionally disturbed children in ordinary classes is an important one but, at the same time, it has yet to be properly evaluated.

As we were introducing treatments of as yet unknown effectiveness we thought it essential on ethical grounds that we did not influence the normal processes of referral among the children and schools who were in our study. On occasions we fully anticipated that this might mean that children in the study would be referred to child guidance or child psychiatry units for further assessment, treatment and, if appropriate, placement in a special school.

The problems of troubled children

Our concept of psychiatric disorder is based upon that outlined by Rutter, Tizard, and Whitmore (1970) who defined it as marked and prolonged abnormalities of behaviour, emotions, or relationships sufficient to give rise to handicap which might affect the family, community, or child. For instance, the problem could manifest itself as a handicap in the areas of emotional or social adjustment and educational progress.

One of the many facets of work with children is that they are developing organisms: behaviour that is quite common at one age may give rise to great concern at another. For example, enuresis is so common at the age of four years that it is not usually regarded as worth treating, whereas this would not be the case with a fifteen-year-old. Conversely, preoccupation with sexual matters may be quite appropriate in a fifteen-year-old, but would be regarded with concern in a seven-year-old. For this reason, it is important to be sure of the developmental stage of the child when assessing his or her symptoms.

What types of psychological disorders do children suffer from, and how long do they last? These questions about natural history must be answered before one can begin to discuss treatment sensibly.

There are a variety of types of childhood disorder that differ in their clinical features and outlook. Some of these are rare, such as infantile autism and adolescent schizophrenia, in which the children show behaviour that is quite different from that of normal children. In this community-based study we did not come across any cases of this degree of disturbance. Much more common were neurotic and conduct disorders, which represent less extreme degrees of departure from normal and in which the exaggerated feelings and types of behaviour involved represent basically a *quantitative* rather than a *qualitative* deviation from normal (Kolvin *et al.* 1975a).

NEUROTIC AND CONDUCT DISORDERS

Population and follow-up studies of the common handicapping disorders of childhood have confirmed the clinical impression that there are good grounds for distinguishing between those disorders that are characterized mainly by neurotic problems and those that are characterized by problems of conduct. Many disturbed children, of course, show varying mixtures of neurotic and conduct problems but we found it convenient to use a simple dichotomy based on the predominant type of problem.

A *neurotic* disorder is one in which there is an abnormality of the emotions but no loss of reality sense. Neurotic disorders in this category include states of disproportionate anxiety or feelings of depression, obsessions, compulsions, phobias, and hypochondriasis. These disorders can be extremely incapacitating and, while many of them appear to improve with time and not progress to disorders in adult life, it seems that some of the earlier estimates of 'spontaneous remission' were unduly optimistic. The theme of spontaneous remission is discussed in Chapters 2 and 10.

A *conduct* disorder can be contrasted with an emotional disorder in that it gives rise to disapproval and distress in *other people*. It overlaps legally defined delinquency, but also includes non-delinquent disorders of conduct, such as bullying and disruptive classroom behaviour. The main point is that the behaviour is abnormal in its sociocultural context and its association with other symptoms, such as abnormal social relationships. Behaviour typical of an individual with conduct disorder would be truancy and stealing. Conduct disorders usually become manifest in middle childhood and the outlook is generally much worse than that for neurotic disorders (Robins 1966; Robins, West, and Herjanic 1975); they may precede life-long behaviour and personality disorders and, in addition, may be associated with deviance in subsequent generations.

The distinction into these two major types of behaviour has not only been of clinical value but has regularly emerged from multivariate statistical studies of child behaviour, irrespective of whether the samples studied were younger or older children, or of whether they were a random sample of the population, a delinquent sample, or a child psychiatric clinic sample (Kolvin *et al.* 1975a). There is evidence to support this distinction, from studies of aetiology, sex ratios, responses to treatment, long-term prognoses, and educational progress (Rutter 1965, 1970).

We should emphasize that these are merely the major crude groupings of disorders, which may vary and overlap from case to case. A full assessment of a disturbed child would include not only a description of the disorder but also a comprehensive assessment both of the child's functioning and the pressures to which he or she might be subjected within the family and other settings. Specific assessments would also be needed to explore the applicability of the various treatment approaches (Graham 1974).

We were aware that there are fundamentally different ways of approaching children's emotional problems to the one we adopted. One might, for example, have contrasted sociological approaches (Rock 1973; Hargreaves, Hester, and Mellor 1975), the approach of practical educationalists (Clegg and Megson 1968), or psychoanalytic approaches (Freud 1922). We regarded each of these as important in their own context but chose our approach as being the most useful for our purpose.

Different types of therapy – those chosen for our project

The treatment approaches currently available are most easily differentiated by consideration of the theory on which they are based, and it is usually at this level that protagonists of different therapies argue most passionately. How do the theoretical differences of the various schools of therapy, whether psychoanalytical, existential, behavioural, or transactional, influence what actually happens between therapist and patient? This is a question that may be investigated at many levels, right down to a fine-grain analysis of interaction within the session – a task of the utmost complexity and sophistication (Kiesler 1973).

DIRECT AND INDIRECT THERAPIES

We were seeking a crude classification of therapies that would, none the less, reflect fundamental differences in approach and we therefore selected two dichotomies. First, as did Robins (1973), we drew a distinction between direct and indirect therapies. Direct therapies are ones in which work takes place face-to-face with the child; with the indirect therapies, the work is with significant figures in the child's environment who, in turn, undertake some intervention or modify their behaviour towards the child. In trying to sample a wide spectrum of therapies, therefore, it seemed sensible to include both direct and indirect methods for comparison.

In choosing a direct therapy we had the problem of limited skilled treatment resources. For this reason group therapy approaches seemed to be most useful. On reviewing the literature (Ginott 1961; Ohlsen 1973) we concluded that for the seven-year-old children a playgroup approach would be most appropriate, whereas for the eleven- to twelve-year-old children a talking group would be most in line with current practice. We review these techniques more fully in Chapter 8.

Indirect therapies have the potential advantage that mental health expertise can be channelled through other professionals who have an ongoing relationship with the child, or through parents who can work directly with the child (Becker *et al*. 1967; Patterson 1972); these persons are not necessarily mental health experts (Caplan, 1964). Such an approach was incorporated into our research as parent counselling-teacher consultation (see Chapter 7).

For some of our therapy programmes the direct-indirect classification was less appropriate. For example, we used a behaviour modification programme with the eleven- to twelve-year-old children that involved special training for teachers, and a nurture work programme with the seven- to eight-year-olds that involved a group of specially trained teacher-aides.

In Chapter 10 we discuss further the theme of directness in the light of our own findings.

PSYCHODYNAMIC AND BEHAVIOURAL APPROACHES

In distinguishing between consultation and behaviour modification approaches we come to the second major dichotomy in our classification of therapies. This was according to whether the emphasis was on psychodynamic or behavioural approaches. In psychodynamic approaches, of which mental health consultation and group counselling are examples, the therapist is concerned with internal events and nuances of feeling within his or her client, whereas, in behavioural approaches, the therapist concentrates on observable behaviour as his or her focus of intervention. We sought to employ a behavioural emphasis in both the behaviour modification and the nurture work regimes.

Another, and overlapping, way of distinguishing types of therapy is by the skills and experience of the professional therapists. Many authorities have recently realized the important part that may be played in mental health programmes by people who are not traditionally associated with the mental health services, such as parents (Patterson 1972), teacher-aides (Hulbert, Wolstenholme, and Kolvin 1977), and teachers (Becker *et al.* 1967; Macmillan and Kolvin 1977b). This is in addition to a wide range of mental health professionals with diverse patterns of training.

The identification of disturbed children

From our discussion of the variety of problems, circumstances, and treatments available, it will be clear that uncovering problems of maladjusted children is a very complex process. In our research project we had to develop rapid and effective ways of identifying children in need (see Chapter 3). We should emphasize that our screen was a research enterprise that may not always be best for ordinary practice. Part of putting our research into context will be a discussion of how children should be identified in the normal day-to-day work of the school. In complex cases of multiple psychological handicap the combined expertise of many professionals may be needed to assess the child and decide what will be, for him or her, the most appropriate programme of management and the most helpful type of placement.

2 Some basic problems in evaluation

Summary

In this chapter we review some of the ways in which investigators have tackled fundamental problems pertaining to the complex task of evaluation of psychotherapy.

The three basic components of psychotherapy have been described as (a) the patient and his or her problems; (b) the therapist, his or her personality, style and technique; (c) the period of therapy and its aftermath. To these we added a fourth – the psychosocial environment in which treatment takes place. In the following pages we examine each of these components and their impact on the treatment of maladjustment in children in ordinary junior and senior schools.

Under the heading 'children and their problems' we discuss the following in relation to treatment: the severity and type of disorder; educational issues; and the age and developmental stage of the child.

We consider the controversy about the relative importance of the therapy technique and the child's personal relationship with the therapist. We discuss therapists' styles (directiveness, warmth, empathy, genuineness, activity level) and the effect these qualities may have on the child. Evidence is presented that points to other people, such as teachers, parents, nursery nurses, and teacher-aides, being able to make a worthwhile contribution to treatment.

With regard to the effect of time in psychotherapy, we stress the need for protracted follow-up studies after treatment has ended, and show that their timing may be crucial. We present the rationale for short-term therapy, in which it is argued that brief and intensive treatment may be more effective than long-term approaches.

The psychosocial environment (both home and school) has a

profound effect on a child's behaviour and development, and thus on any psychotherapeutic regime. We consider that it may be one of the factors influencing spontaneous remission.

We draw attention to the different types of control groups, and the importance of assessing whether or not the members of these groups are receiving some form of 'treatment'. We also examine the concept of spontaneous remission.

Introduction

Whatever his or her origin, be it the field of practical psychotherapy or academic psychology, the newcomer to psychotherapy research is likely to be overwhelmed by the complexity of the task of evaluation as there seem to be so many subtle and shifting variables that may be important, and so many conceptual as well as practical logistic problems to overcome. This chapter selectively reviews some of the ways in which psychotherapy research workers have tackled some of these basic problems.

The early approach, in the USA, used by Eysenck (1952) for adults and by Levitt (1957) with children, was simply to ask, 'Is psychotherapy effective?' Both authors pooled the results of previous studies and came to the conclusion, now much discussed and criticized, that there was no evidence that psychotherapy was effective. We now examine in some detail the criticisms that have been made of these reviews, particularly of Levitt's work because this concerns children.

One important criticism is that the question asked by these early workers was too general. As outlined at the start of the chapter, psychotherapy has three basic ingredients, each of which is almost infinitely variable and must be considered when developing and testing theories of psychotherapy (Kiesler 1971). To reiterate, these ingredients are (a) the patient and his or her problems; (b) the therapist, his or her personality, style, and technique; and (c) the period of time over which the therapy occurs and over which its effects may become manifest. Our community-based approach led us to add a fourth ingredient, the psychosocial environment in which treatment takes place. Levitt (1957) was, in fact, aware of the need to differentiate some of these ingredients. He tried in his review to include only those studies in which the patient population suffered from emotional and neurotic problems and he distinguished between measurements made at the end of treatment and after a follow-up period. However, the types of treatment used in the studies he pooled were heterogeneous, and the suggestion that he added together the results of quite dissimilar studies is further supported by the fact that *within* his treatment group the reported outcomes were quite different.

A more sophisticated method has been used with adults. This consisted of combining the results of different studies, a task undertaken by Glass and Smith (1976) and Smith and Glass (1977) in a survey of 375 controlled studies with differing patient groups, treatments, and follow-ups. These authors calculated the results of each study in a way that was statistically comparable with the others (they calculated the mean difference on outcome measures between control and treatment groups divided by the standard deviation of the control group). They were able to show that the 'average' client receiving therapy was better off than 75 per cent of the untreated controls. It would be interesting to repeat this analysis for the results of child psychotherapy studies, as it failed to support Eysenck's pessimistic conclusions. We return to Smith and Glass's work in Chapter 10. Meanwhile, as both Gottman and Markman (1978) and Kiesler (1971) pointed out, we are more likely to gain an understanding of psychotherapy by looking at its key ingredients separately rather than in combination with one another. We will now look at these components in terms of their affect on our own research.

The children and their problems

The first ingredient mentioned by Kiesler is the characteristics of the patients and their problems.

THE SEVERITY OF DISORDER

We defined a disturbed child as one in whom there was some *demonstrable* abnormality of behaviour, emotions, or social relationships. The simplest dichotomy of characteristics was, therefore, between disturbed and non-disturbed children. Caplan (1964) has suggested that all disorders are present at the outset in an undiagnosable form and that they develop from this into manifest disorders. In his concept of 'secondary prevention', he argued that it may be advantageous to take action very early in the development of a disorder. In our community study we were in a good position to examine Caplan's concepts.

The first difficulty we faced was that of identification. Escalona (1974), in a discussion of intervention programmes for children at psychiatric risk, pointed out that there is a range of minor neurological abnormalities and, particularly, social adversities which is associated with a raised incidence of psychiatric disorder and, as such, can be seen as a risk factor. The problem is that, unless we undertake generalized and massive efforts to alter the life experience of young children, it is only when minimal but overt deviations of development occur that any specific interventions become possible. Among young children who are in the process of development it seems important to offer help to a wider group than just those with established disorders. The detection of less severe abnormalities seemed to us to offer a way of doing this. We postulated that children with both established and less severe disorders are 'at risk' in terms of the extension or progression in severity of such difficulties (Kolvin *et al*. 1977). All these children should therefore be offered help early on. Our view was that there was already evidence of an association between educational, emotional, and relationship difficulties, and that study of the processes of treatment in an at-risk group comprised of children with both established and less severe disorders would help us to decide which children respond best to intervention.

There is another sense, however, in which treating mild disorders is important. Because some of the children we see have such serious handicaps, we assume that these cases must have absolute priority in treatment. On the other hand, there seems little point in mounting complex treatment unless the treatment is effective. We also need to study the impact of treatment on milder disorders, because it is important to know whether treatment is effective for them.

THE TYPE OF DISORDER

We have referred to the need to consider the type of disordered behaviour that a child is showing. The type of disorder affects the choice of treatment because there is no reason to think that the same therapy will be effective for all types of disorder. As the field is so large, we will give only a brief didactic account of the evidence of effectiveness of psychological and educational treatments on various types of disorders.

Neurotic disorders
Although we would have expected numerous attempts to evaluate the effectiveness of psychotherapy in neurotic disorders, the available literature was, in fact, very sparse. In a series of studies, Eisenberg and his colleagues (Cytryn, Gilbert and Eisenberg 1960; Eisenberg *et al*. 1961) compared the effects of drugs and psychotherapy on various diagnostic groups. As might be expected, judging from the results of other follow-up studies, the neurotic-disordered group showed greater improvement under both treatment conditions than did the conduct-disorderd group, but psychotherapy showed no advantage over drug treatment. It should be noted, though, that the psycho-

therapy given in this study was rather ill-defined and attenuated.

One major study on evaluation of treatment of phobic children was the important work of Miller *et al*. (1972). This study involved random allocation to treatment and control groups using time-limited treatment (eight weeks at three sessions per week) and same-sexed therapists; ratings at pre-, post-treatment, and follow-up (fourteen weeks, one, and two years) undertaken by independent raters; control of initial values by covariance; and the use of multiple outcome measures. The two treatments studied were psychotherapy and systematic desensitization. Only forty-four children were treated and there were twenty-three waiting-list controls. The results of the treatments did not differ, but both differed from the results of the waiting-list controls, on the basis both of the evaluating clinician's ratings of severity and of behaviour scales completed by the parents. Follow-up two years later showed that children who were successes at the end of treatment continued to be successes. The rates of improvement were more impressive for younger than for older children, as shown in *Table 2(1)*. However, sex, IQ, socioeconomic status, and chronicity were not related to outcome. The only other relevant finding was that children of highly motivated parents were more likely to succeed.

Table 2(1)   *Treatment of phobic children* (from Miller *et al*. 1972)

	under ten years				over ten years				total			
	treated		controls		treated		controls		treated		controls	
	n	%	n	%	n	%	n	%	n	%	n	%
successful	23	96	8	57	9	45	4	45	32	73	12	52
unsuccessful	1		6		11		5		12		11	

Conduct disorders

These problems give rise to more social distress and concern than neurotic disorders and carry a worse prognosis (Robins 1966). A review of relevant treatment studies had to include some studies of delinquency, as the chronic offender is very likely to fall into the category of conduct disorder. Many of the studies, both of counselling (Powers and Witmer 1951) and residential programmes (Clarke and Cornish 1977), yielded negative results. Nevertheless, the studies described below yielded positive results and may augur well for future work in this area.

Adams (1970) evaluated a counselling programme for delinquents in a custodial setting (the PICO Project). The study compared the reconviction rates for two sorts of offender (both of whom had a counselling experience) with those of comparable control groups. The first type of offender showed awareness of problems, verbal ability, high anxiety, and a desire to change; offenders in this group were termed 'amenables'. The second type ('non-amenables') did not show these characteristics. After release on parole the amount of time spent in any kind of custody was recorded. It was found that the non-treatment controls of both 'amenables' and 'non-amenables' had spent a similar time in custody, whereas the treated 'amenables' had fared considerably better. The treated 'non-amenables' had done worst of all. This study illustrated to us the importance of examining separately children with different characteristics.

Some institutional programmes have operated on the basis of psychodynamic theory. For example, at Northways House (Miller 1964) some severely disadvantaged delinquents were selected, following Borstal training, and were offered a residential treatment. The boys were expected to go out to work and the establishment was run along the lines of a normal residence for boys of their social group, with the inclusion of psychoanalytic components. Although numbers were small, there were encouraging signs, when compared with a control group, that the Northways boys were functioning better at follow-up in that they had lower reconviction rates, more settled marriages, and better employment records than control boys with similar Borstal records and background characteristics.

More recently, encouraging findings have been published on the effectiveness of behaviour modification in conduct disorders. Patterson and his colleagues (Patterson, Cobb, and Ray 1973; Patterson 1974) developed a home-based treatment programme for children with problems of conduct. This complex, four-staged programme involved instruction to the parents about behaviour modification principles, followed by analysis and modification of behaviour. These workers have reported very significant reductions in the rates of particular types of rowdy behaviour over the course of treatment. Alexander and Parsons (1973) compared family behavioural treatment of delinquents with other approaches and reported that the behavioural regime was the only one that led to a significant reduction in recidivism.

Behaviour modification techniques have also been used with notable success in residential settings. In the Achievement Place Project the assumption was that the boys lacked social skills. These were inculcated by a comprehensive curriculum of training in such skills, which was linked with a token economy system (tangible rewards for achievement). There was a self-government system and relationships with staff were informal (Willner *et al*. 1978). Objective evaluation has shown this to be an effective form of management.

Table 2(2)   *Outcome of treatment in different categories of psychiatric disorder* (Barrett, Hampe, and Miller 1978, from data by Levitt 1963)

improvement	neurosis n = 230	special symptoms n = 213	mixed n = 697	acting out n = 349	psychosis n = 252	total n = 1741
	%	%	%	%	%	%
much	15	54	20	31	25	26
partial	46	23	48	24	40	39
none	39	23	32	45	35	35

Barrett, Hampe, and Miller (1978) reorganized Levitt's data (which relates to the USA) to compare the progress of different categories of disorder. *Table 2(2)* is an adaptation from the 1978 work and shows the different outcomes. The neuroses in this table appeared to be the type more commonly found in adults than children and, therefore, were likely to be of a deeply ingrained or intractable type, with only a small percentage showing impressive improvement. The mixed category, which apparently consisted of general child guidance cases, gave rise to a similar picture. On the other hand, it was not unexpected that the category of special symptoms, which included a number of conditions known to improve spontaneously with time, such as enuresis, tics, and phobias, showed impressive results. The acting-out category, which was likely to contain a large number of children with antisocial behaviour, had a high percentage of cases that showed no improvement. By British criteria, it is unlikely that one in seven cases treated in child psychiatry would be considered psychotic – nor indeed would such high rates of improvement be expected with psychoses. We therefore suspected that these cases would be placed in a mixed category in the UK.

Educational problems
Many approaches to educational problems involve components that might reasonably be called psychotherapeutic. Two examples are early intervention (Head Start) programmes and special educational settings (Project Re-Ed). There is likely to be an overlap between educational problems and conduct disorders and many of the projects were designed to deal with both.

The Head Start projects have been reviewed by Bronfenbrenner

(1974). This is a most important review because, instead of giving a depressing 'thumbs down' to the whole Head Start movement, Bronfenbrenner has tried to co-ordinate aspects of the various evaluation projects that did give positive results and to integrate them into a picture of what could constitute success. The picture he presented was briefly as follows:

(i)   When compensatory stimulation is provided for the pre-school child there are substantial IQ gains while the programme lasts but, after a year, this trend reaches a plateau, with gains becoming rapidly eroded once the help ends (DiLorenzo 1969; Gray and Klaus 1970; Weikart, Deloria, and Lawson 1974). Deutch (1971) saw this erosion of gains of an enrichment programme, even when it was still continuing, as being determined by social and family factors beyond the school, citing the fact that the children whose response was poorest came from the poorest environments.

(ii) The hope that programmes started early in life would produce the greatest and most enduring gains has not been fully sub-stantiated (Braun and Caldwell 1973). Children involved in pre-school programmes, joined before the age of three years and *not directly involving mothers*, did no better than those who entered later, although their programmes were of equal duration.

(iii) Hays and Grether (1969) found that the lack of stimulation experienced by the disadvantaged child over the long summer holidays appeared to be responsible for much of the loss incurred in the areas where gains had previously been made. This is a strong argument in favour of home-based programmes which are, obviously, not subject to this problem.

(iv) Indeed, home-based intervention has led to dramatic and en-during gains, three or four years after help was stopped. There is, however, one important qualification – maternal interest and participation in the scheme are essential, as shown in (ii) above. A one-to-one interaction between a motivated mother and her child, around a common educational-type activity, was found to be crucial (Levenstein 1970; Schaefer and Aaronson 1972). The earlier the interaction began, the greater the gains appeared to be Karnes *et al.* 1968; Gilmer, Miller, and Gray 1970; Levenstein 1970): they were negligible if interaction started late. It is essential that such home-based educational programmes be reinforced when the child's dependency on his or her mother is greatest, that is, in the second year of life (Bronfenbrenner 1968; Levenstein 1970). So impressive were these findings that Radin (1972) suggested parent education is an essential adjunct to any compensatory pre-school programme if the child is to continue to benefit cognitively.

(v) The optimal time for parental involvement seems to be in the first three years of the child's life. Nevertheless, there is considerable evidence to show that parental involvement thereafter continues to be an important factor in the educational progress of the child (Smith 1968). Some families (especially psychologically vulnerable families) are so socially disorganized that the parents are unlikely to be able to participate. In such circumstances a more radical solution has been attempted – the separation of infant and mother during the waking day, the provision of compensatory stimulation for infants (Heber *et al*. 1972), and the training of mothers in child-rearing and basic domestic skills. Such radical intervention would appear to be intellectually, educationally, and morally justifiable only when home conditions appear to be totally detrimental to child development. However, not only are the costs of such projects prohibitive but, of equal importance, we know little about their social and emotional consequences.

At least four important conclusions relevant to preventive child psychiatry have emerged from educational research. First, with disadvantaged children greater educational gains are likely to result from more, rather than less, structured educational programmes. Second, there seems to be an overriding need for the involvement of the mother and child in a common educational task. Third, erosion of gains after help has stopped must be recognized as a problem. Finally, Bronfenbrenner (1974) stressed the need to improve the total living conditions of disadvantaged families in the community. It is unfortunate that the Head Start projects concentrated almost entirely on educational and cognitive measures. Behaviour ratings were often made, but were generally so diverse that no general conclusions could be drawn.

Other educational evaluations have been linked to special educational projects of various sorts. Quay *et al*. (1972) reported the effects of a part-time resource room run within the ordinary school. After one year of this special regime the experimental group had made significant gains in academic achievement. There were very marked differences between the children's behaviour while in the special and then ordinary classes, measured concurrently. Another widely known educational treatment is Project Re-Ed (Weinstein 1969). This consisted of a short-term residential educational treatment programme. Measures were made before and after the programme by the referring school, parental reports, and achievement tests. In the early reports there was, unfortunately, no control group, but it is interesting that the most spectacular improvements were those reported by parents.

Neurotic disorders, conduct disorders, and educational problems constitute the three most relevant types of problem that children are likely to have. There are, however, many other important ways in which children may differ. .

THE AGE AND DEVELOPMENTAL STAGE OF THE CHILD

It is an index of the early and primitive state of child psychotherapy research that so few studies have seriously looked at the effect of psychotherapy on children of different ages. An exception is the Miller (1972) study quoted above (p. 20). This demonstrated that not only was the outcome of phobic states better in younger than older children, but also that treatment was more effective amongst the former.

The therapist: his or her personality, style, and technique

There is some controversy as to whether or not the therapist is more important than the therapeutic technique.

THERAPISTS' STYLE

A great deal has been written about therapists' styles and their relationship to other factors in therapy. It seemed obvious to early researchers (e.g. Fiedler 1950) that practitioners from different theoretical schools of psychotherapy would show differences in the way that they approached their patients. Different theoretical schools do, indeed, suggest very different approaches to the patient. For example, Rogers's (1952, 1959) non-directive therapy is extremely brief and passive compared with the prolonged treatment recommended by psychoanalysis. Sullivan's (1953, 1956) technique, influenced as it is by the view that the self is made up of others' views of the individual, might be expected to be very different from the psycho-analysts' view that biological drives are of fundamental importance in personality development. It must have come as a surprise, then, to these early workers to find that the theoretical school of the practitioner was fairly unimportant compared, for example, with the differences between inexperienced and experienced therapists from the same school (Luborsky *et al.* 1971, 1975). Strupp (1958) carried out detailed studies of interaction in psychoanalytic and Rogerian therapies. He confirmed that differences existed between the approaches, and that these were very much in line with what might be expected on theoretical grounds. More recent work has been reviewed by Pope (1977). He concluded that theoretical orientation is one of several influences on therapist style. In factor analytic studies, various main characteristics of style have been identified: for example, nurturance, a non-judgemental approach, an analytic approach, etc. Little has been done to relate these to reactions in the client or indeed to the outcome of therapy. Unfortunately, no one has examined how a particular treatment style is modified by different treatment settings, for example, psychoanalytic therapy applied to groups compared with casework. It is just such comparisons that would have been of the greatest relevance to the present research.

Therapist directiveness
The first of the more specific elements of the therapist style is therapist directiveness. This is defined slightly differently from study to study, but generally consists of the extent to which the therapist leads the interaction and is prepared to introduce themes or to make interpretations ahead of the client and in areas of which the client is unaware. It also includes advice-giving. Ashby *et al*. (1957) undertook a study with six therapists, three of whom were trained to be 'directive' and three 'reflective' therapists. Psycho-neurotic patients were randomly assigned to the therapists. The most striking result of this study was that certain types of patient seemed to respond better to the directive therapists, while other types preferred the reflective therapists. Those patients who had been the most defensive before treatment behaved more defensively with a leading (directive) therapist than did those who manifested a need for autonomy before treatment started. The latter group reported feeling less defensive during directive therapy than during reflective treatment.

More recent studies have confirmed this differential effectiveness of directive and reflective therapist with different types of client. For example, in two studies (Abramowitz *et al*. 1974; Friedman and Dies 1974) clients were assessed as internally directed or externally controlled on a locus of control categorization (Rotter 1966). As expected, the externally controlled group were best with directive therapy and the internally controlled one preferred the non-directive treatment.

Warmth, empathy, and genuineness
These are the most intensively studied therapist qualities, and several extensive reviews have been produced. Truax and Carkhuff (1967) claimed unequivocally that these three qualities, which may be measured from brief tape-recorded segments of therapy sessions, were necessary for the success of therapy with a wide range of client groups. There has been a great deal of discussion as to what the

qualities actually constitute – particularly because accurate empathy is concerned with unobservable phenomena. A more recent review (Mitchell, Bozarth, and Krauft 1977) acknowledged that results of the early studies had not always been replicated. With different types of therapies and different client groups there may be major variations in the importance of these qualities.

Another point that gives rise to uncertainty is the absolute level of the therapist qualities. Mitchell, Bozarth, and Krauft (1977) commented that if the therapists are generally below an absolute cut-off level of empathy, warmth, and genuineness the conditions fail to operate and no correlation with outcome can be expected.

Considering the importance attached to these qualities in research with adults, it is surprising that they have not been studied to a larger extent in research into child psychotherapy. Siegel (1972) found that improvement among children with learning disabilities in both verbal and behavioural spheres related to length of time in play therapy and to therapist levels of empathy, warmth, and genuineness. Truax *et al.* (1973) found more mixed results. However, parents' perceptions of improvement were related to the therapeutic qualities of the therapists.

Therapist activity level

This has been studied by Lennard and Bernstein (1960) and very extensively by Matarazzo and colleagues (Matarazzo *et al.* 1965; Matarazzo *et al.* 1968). Interviewer activity in these studies was measured by the *amount* of therapist or interviewer activity, regardless of its *content*. There is no evidence that therapist activity measured in this way directly affects outcome: however, an active therapist is more likely to be seen by the patient as warm and be able to put the patient at his or her ease than is a more detached therapist. In one study there were significantly fewer missed appointments with active therapists (Lennard and Bernstein 1960). Both warmth and patient attendance are important variables in the success of therapy.

THE EFFECTIVENESS OF NON-SPECIALIST HELP

Adams (1975) wrote disparagingly of the extent to which children are treated, not directly by highly trained mental health professionals as adults might be, but by other workers such as teachers, parents, nursery nurses, and teacher-aides. Nevertheless, there is evidence that such people can make a considerable contribution to treatment projects. Carkhuff has undertaken a number of studies and has reviewed the field (Carkhuff 1968; Anthony and Carkhuff 1977). Three studies in the mental health area suggested that non-professionals can be as effective as fully qualified professional workers (Poser 1966; Zunker and Brown 1966; Truax and Lister 1970). While there have been some criticisms of the methodology of these studies – particularly the dissimilarity of the professionals and non-professionals on criteria other than that of their qualifications – there is no evidence to contradict these findings.

In the educational field, both teachers (Aspy and Roebuck 1971) and teacher-aides (Cowen *et al.* 1975) have been used in treatment projects. Again, there is evidence of the positive impact on student mental health of the teachers' skill in human relationships. These results are discussed more fully in Chapter 6.

The dimension of time in psychotherapy

The effects of psychotherapy may increase or decrease with time, they may be seen only after a latent period (even after treatment has stopped), and may cease altogether after a while. It is therefore very important to have short, intermediate, and long-term follow-up studies.

DURATION OF TREATMENT

Strupp (1978) offered the following reasons for asserting that short-term psychotherapy would receive increasing attention from therapists and researchers:

(i)   Most forms of psychotherapy, whether or not they are specifically designated as short-term are, in fact, time-limited. For instance, it has been found that in clinical work, because of practical considerations, the average length of therapy is only a few sessions (Garfield 1978).

(ii) The evidence suggests that time-limited psychotherapy is as good as unlimited or long-term therapy (Luborsky, Singer, and Luborsky 1975).

(iii) In terms of patients' expectations, resources, motivations, and practical considerations, it is essential to develop psychotherapies that yield significant returns in the shortest possible time with the least expense.

Garfield (1977), too, has pointed out that short-term therapy should be the treatment of choice for practically all patients. On the basis of many reports (e.g. Harris, Kalis, and Freeman 1963) it would seem that about two-thirds of patients respond positively to such intervention; hence, if indicated, the remaining one-third can continue to receive therapy, can be referred elsewhere or, if the patients are considered to be unsuitable for the type of therapy currently available, treatment can be discontinued. One can compare the same type of treatments of different duration, or one can compare different types of treatment of different duration. Miller and colleagues (1972) compared different treatments of the same duration in children and found that the treatments gave similar results.

FREQUENCY OF CONTACT

There is recent evidence that more frequent sessions of psycho-therapy are more effective than less intensive therapy. Heinicke and Strassman (1975) compared psychoanalytic psychotherapy adminis-tered to nine-year-olds once a week, with similar therapy given to them four times a week. They reported impressive results for the latter on one- and two-year follow-ups when studying clinical data and reading ability. However, the samples were of small sizes and the evaluations appeared not to be blind. There were only few comments on the nature of the conditions being treated, their severity and duration, and no information was given about the characteristics of the therapists used in this study.

TIMING OF FOLLOW-UPS

Until recently this topic attracted only minimal interest, but it is, in fact, of the utmost importance that follow-up studies should be carried out at the right time if subtle therapy-induced changes in behaviour are to be detected. Recent advocates of detailed single-case studies using time series analysis have emphasized the importance of repeated measures over time in understanding the process as well as the outcome of therapy.

An interesting example of the importance of timing in follow-ups is given in the review, by Wright, Moelis, and Pollack (1976), of previous studies of individual child psychotherapy: they reported a consistent trend for improvement to be more pronounced at follow-up than at termination of treatment.

The psychosocial environment

This is a component of psychotherapy that has been almost entirely ignored in the literature on adult psychotherapy but that is less easy to pass over with children. It is now abundantly clear that children's environments at home (Rutter 1971; Birch and Gussow 1972) and school (Reynolds, Jones, and St Leger 1976; Rutter *et al*. 1979) have a profound effect on their behaviour and development. Any specific intervention occurs against the background of this development and is likely to interact with it in numerous ways (see the section on spontaneous remission later in this chapter (p. 31)).

Control groups in evaluative research

Intimately related to the questions of timing and psychosocial environment is that of control groups. In any study the control group must be selected with the object of the study clearly in mind. Even so, it is not always possible to select the perfect control group. There have been many accounts of the advantages and disadvantages of various control groups (e.g. Campbell and Stanley 1966), and some of these are discussed briefly below.

NO-CONTACT CONTROL GROUPS

This type of control necessitates the collection of data on subjects without their having knowledge of the proceedings, so that there is minimal experimental bias involved (Mitchell and Ingham 1970). There has been some research to demonstrate that most other control groups, including waiting-list control groups, show significantly more improvement than the no-contact control group.

NO-TREATMENT CONTROL GROUPS

There is evidence (Bergin 1966, who cites other studies) that subjects who do not receive psychotherapy seek help elsewhere: from friends, clergy, relatives, and professionals other than psychotherapists. This sometimes occurs in over 50 per cent of 'untreated' patients (Saslow and Peters 1956). For this reason a review of spontaneous recovery rates (Bergin 1971) suggested that such rates may be considerably lower than the 67 per cent suggested by Eysenck (1952). Bergin estimated the average spontaneous recovery rate for neurosis at 22.4 per cent, and he also pointed out that the rates reported by Levitt may have been inflated by including slightly improved cases.

Perhaps the most important work is that of Lambert (1976), who has demonstrated that testing sessions, or even one interview, may be of therapeutic benefit for the client: thus, the clients in no-treatment control groups may, in fact, be receiving some 'treatment'. Indeed, in some studies there were clients who attributed their improvement to the initial interview. Other studies have also shown that initial testing and initial contact have positive effects on clients, but, unfortunately, we can have no idea of how much help was being sought, nor of the extent to which these control subjects changed their behaviour in relation to the help that was being given. We can only surmise that some amount of treatment may be more effective than none, but, at the same time, it is difficult to visualize a situation where there really is no treatment being received at all.

WAITING-LIST CONTROL GROUPS

There are many advantages in using such clients as they are a common-place aspect of many clinics and thus form a natural control group; they are also motivated to complete the post-assessment programme by the guarantee of subsequent therapy. Unfortunately, though, like the 'no-treatment' control group, they may be seeking treatment elsewhere.

ATTENTION-PLACEBO CONTROL GROUPS

These groups comprise individuals who regularly meet the therapist for a chat, or for play, but who do not receive any proper treatment. The group may serve to control such factors as frequency of contacts, expectations of improvement, and therapeutic interest. In one study (Paul 1966) the attention-placebo group improved more than the no-treatment controls and, at the end of a two-year follow-up, this pattern re-occurred.

OTHER TREATMENT GROUPS

The groups that drop out from treatment are sometimes called 'terminator controls'; they are inadequate as controls because there is some unknown selection factor operating in termination. However, they can teach us some useful things about the therapy programme. It has been shown (Shapiro and Budman 1973) that clients from individual and family therapy who terminated against professional advice disliked the therapists because the latter were inactive, detached, and uninvolved, and the therapy did not have a clear direction. Those who remained in treatment tended to appreciate an active therapist who presented a programme with clearly articulated goals and direction.

CONTAMINATION OF CONTROLS

The problem of contamination arises when controls have contact with treated cases, as such contact allows for the possible transmission of treatment's beneficial effects. A similar situation occurs where contamination is transmitted through teachers or other workers, a matter of the greatest importance to the present study (see Chapter 10).

SPONTANEOUS REMISSION

So-called 'spontaneous improvement' is mentioned in many reviews of treatment outcome (e.g. Levitt 1971). This is a sensible recognition of the fact that just because improvement in a disorder follows treatment it does not necessarily mean that the treatment was effective – a control group is necessary against which to compare the extent of improvement.

It is most important to recognize the statistical phenomenon of regression. If a group of individuals is selected by an extreme score on any assessment procedure that group will inevitably give a less extreme score if this procedure is repeated. In our research adjustments were made to allow for regression effects; these are more fully described in Chapters 3 and 9 and Appendices 2 and 3.

Second, many factors, apart from treatment, have been shown to be predictors of a good or bad outcome. For example, Richman (1977), in a one-year follow-up study of disturbed three-year-old children, found that a problem was more likely to persist if it was initially severe, if the child's parents had a poor marital relationship, if his or her mother was depressed, or the child had been subjected to poor housing conditions or stress during the previous year. These findings suggested that there are many mechanisms involved in whether a disorder improves or not: indeed, it may be that the treatment itself is a relatively weak change agent compared with the child's other social circumstances.

A third point to consider is that, in the light of recent research findings, it seems possible that professional psychotherapists do not have a monopoly of 'natural' therapy skill. Families do not only, or even usually, come to professionals for advice. Instead, friends or relatives with the right personality attributes (Truax and Carkhuff 1967) may effectively give counsel and advice, thus adding their contribution to the child's 'spontaneous' improvement (Bergin 1971).

Part Two
Method and background

3 Aims and method

Summary

As mentioned in our introductory chapter, the main aims of our research project were to identify maladjusted children in ordinary schools and to evaluate the effectiveness of different treatment approaches applied to them. In comparing these approaches, seven hypotheses were tested. We describe these below (p. 36) and outline how we tested them.

A total of almost 600 children were selected to take part in the study by a series of screening methods (involving approximately 4300 children) that identified those with signs of disturbance. These methods detected junior schoolchildren, aged seven to eight years, who showed some signs of having social or psychiatric disturbance or learning problems. These we have described as being 'at-risk' children. With the senior schoolchildren, aged eleven to twelve years, only those who showed relatively clear-cut psychiatric disturbance were included. The screening tests, then, differed for junior and senior children but, basically, they relied on a classroom multiple criterion screen.

Subsequently, additional information was gathered on those identified, from the teacher, the child, and his or her parents. The data were used to place each child's disturbance into the category of either conduct or neurotic disorder, and to rate the degree of severity of the problem.

The children thus selected as being 'screen-positive' were randomly allocated to various treatment or control regimes. Each regime was mounted in each of the six junior schools; a similar plan was adopted for the senior children. To ease the impact on the schools, different regimes were studied in two consecutive years. We summarize the elements of the treatment programmes, and outline how the effects of these treatments were evaluated, taking into account various initial differences between the groups. We also touch on the problem of missing data, which was not, however, found to affect the conclusions drawn.

Aims and hypotheses

In aiming to identify maladjusted schoolchildren and compare ways of treating them we mounted two programmes of treatment – one for younger children (aged seven to eight years) and one for older children (aged eleven to twelve years). Each programme consisted of four regimes – three treatment regimes and one no-treatment regime (the controls). The regimes for both programmes have been outlined in Chapter 1 and are summarized in *Table 3(1)*.

Table 3(1)   *Basic design of research project*

school	type of therapy and year of treatment			
	at-risk controls (ARC)	parent counselling-teacher consultation (JPC)	group therapy/ playgroups (PG)	nurture work (NW)
junior (total n = 270)	(project year 1) n = 67	(project year 1) n = 69	(project year 2) n = 74	(project year 2) n = 60)
	maladjusted controls (MC)	parent counselling-teacher consultation (PC)	group therapy/ senior groups (SG)	behaviour modification (BM)
senior (total n = 322)	(project year 1) n = 92	(project year 1) n = 83	(project year 2) n = 73	(project year 2) n = 74

Note: both the junior and senior school programmes took place within six schools.

The precise aims of the research were to test the following hypotheses, which applied both to the younger and the older children.
(1) The four regimes (which include the no-treatment regime) differ in effectiveness in reducing maladjustment; that is, some forms of management are better than others.
(2) One or more of the three treatment regimes is more effective than the no-treatment regime (the controls) in reducing maladjustment; that is, any treatment is better than no treatment at all.
(3) Regimes differ in effectiveness according to the diagnostic category into which the child falls; that is, some regimes are more effective in helping children with neurotic disorders than those

with conduct disorders, and vice versa. This hypothesis relates to mutually exclusive categories of children, whereas hypothesis (5) refers to different patterns of behaviour which may co-exist in the same child.

(4) Regimes differ in effectiveness according to the sex of the child; that is, some regimes are more effective for boys, others for girls.

(5) Regimes differ in effectiveness according to patterns of behaviour co-existing in any one child; that is, some regimes are more effective in reducing the neurotic component of a child's behaviour and others in reducing his or her antisocial behaviour, so that a child's neurotic behaviour may be reduced while his or her antisocial behaviour remains unchanged.

(6) Irrespective of treatment regime, improvement is related to diagnostic category; that is, children with conduct disorders differ from those with neurotic disorders in relation to degree of improvement.

(7) Irrespective of treatment regime, improvement is related to the sex of the child; that is, boys differ from girls in relation to degree of improvement.

Method of testing hypotheses

Our first task was to detect suitable cases, which we did by screening, as subsequently described. We then assessed and classified these screen-positive children and randomly allocated them by school class into one of four regimes, ensuring that every regime was represented in each school. Assessments of the children were undertaken at the baseline and on two and three subsequent occasions for the juniors and seniors respectively (see *Table 3(5)*). Data analysis involved comparisons of the effects of the four regimes.

TIMING

At the outset we were aware that the project would make heavy demands on school staff over and above their normal duties so, to lessen the impact, intervention was spread over two consecutive years, involving children of the same age and general characteristics in both years. During the first year the control regime and one specific treatment regime (parent counselling-teacher consultation) were studied in both the junior and senior schools. The remaining treatments (nurture work and group therapy for the juniors and behaviour modification and group therapy for the seniors) were studied in the second year (see *Table 3(1)* and *Figs 3(1)* and *3(2)*). It was not practicable to randomize the treatment methods within both years of the study for two main reasons – first, insufficiency in numbers of screen-positive cases in a single year and, second, insufficiency of resources to carry out all treatments simultaneously.

Screening – general considerations

Several basic principles guided the design of our screening method with both junior and senior schoolchildren. First, because we were interested primarily in intervention in school settings we sought screen measures that could be applied in the schools. Had we been interested in, for example, prevalence of psychiatric disturbance, this would have demanded a different type of screening, including the home. Second, as we felt that as little energy as possible should be deflected from the main object of the study – getting special help to the children – we wanted the screen to be conducted as rapidly and economically as possible. Disruption of school routine had to be minimized, particularly because of the value of ensuring staff co-operation in a follow-up project of this nature. Third, as we wanted to explore the many ways in which disturbance may manifest itself within the school, we considered it preferable to develop a screen battery that would draw upon three sources of information – teachers, peers, and the children themselves.

The schools in which we worked – six junior schools and six junior high or comprehensive schools (the senior schools) – were broadly representative of those in the Newcastle upon Tyne and Gateshead area; the social class distribution of the area is slightly below the national average (Neligan, Prudham, and Steiner 1974).

Screening was conducted with children entering the first year of junior or senior schooling in the academic year beginning September, 1972, and then again one year later with the new intake (see p. 37).

Screening – junior schoolchildren

THE POPULATION

Taking the two cohorts together, approximately 1000 children were screened. A description and analysis of the screening method are provided elsewhere (Kolvin *et al.* 1977). The mean age of this population of children was seven years and nine months and the sex distribution was about equal (52 per cent were boys and 48 per cent girls).

DESIGNING THE MULTIPLE CRITERION SCREEN

A child must make three major adjustments at school. First, there are the formal educational and academic demands; second, there must be accommodation to requirements for behavioural control; and, third, appropriate social relationships with peers have to be established. We proposed that signs of failure, whether mild or severe, in any one of these areas may have repercussions in any of the others: also, mild disorders may progress to more serious behavioural or educational problems over time. We therefore described these children as being 'at risk'. With these points in mind, we felt that for our purposes a multiscreen model (e.g. that of Bower, 1960–69) was preferable to one that relied on a single measure. We scanned the literature for screen measures that could be applied in schools and were likely to be reliable, valid, and reasonably efficient predictors of disorder.

We eventually decided to use five screen criteria, which were as follows:

(i) and (ii) The sociometric criteria of *isolation* and *rejection*. Each child in a class was asked to choose three classmates they would like to sit beside in class, and three they would like to play with at playtime; in addition, they were asked which they would *not* like to sit beside or play with. This procedure yielded two scores: isolation, which is defined as a lack of positive choice, and rejection, which is defined as receipt of a large number of negative choices. In a class of approximately thirty children, a child was considered to be isolated if he or she scored nought, or one positive choice, and to be rejected if he or she received fourteen or more negative choices. Each of these cut-off scores was intended to identify about 6 per cent of the population, judged by the pilot study data, but in practice we found that the yield was higher than 6 per cent; in other words, there were more isolated and rejected children than we expected. The sociometric criteria are described more fully elsewhere (Macmillan *et al*. 1978). Test-re-test reliability was assessed for two age levels. First, administration on two occasions (four-and-a-half weeks apart and involving a total of fifty-eight seven-year-old children in two primary classes) yielded a correlation of 0.64 for isolation and 0.87 for rejection. A similar exercise with sixty-one eleven- to twelve-year-olds yielded correlations of 0.72 for isolation and 0.87 for rejection.

(iii) *Reading*. In the Isle of Wight study (Rutter, Tizard, and Whitmore 1970), the definition of educational backwardness was reading accuracy or comprehension twenty months or more below the child's chronological age, and this included 7.9 per cent of the population. Some of the children in our study (i.e. those who were just seven years old) were too young for a similar definition to be used with any degree of confidence, so we selected a cut-off of a reading quotient (RQ) of seventy-five or less on the Young (1968) group reading test. This meant that, at seven to eight years of age, the selected children were non-readers on this test. We appreciated that this would produce a higher yield than the Isle of Wight study. In fact, it led to an inclusion of 12.2 per cent of of the population.

The Young Group Reading Test was developed to provide a group measure of reading ability that permitted easy application and quick marking. Two parallel forms are available, each comprising forty-five items. The first fifteen of these require the child to select which one of between three and five words matches a given picture. With the remaining thirty items the task is to identify synonyms in a multiple-choice sentence-completion format. The two sections are timed, with four and nine minutes respectively being allowed. Young's standardization sample consisted of 7400 children in an urban area, aged six years and six months to twelve years and eleven months. However, because 50 per cent of the scores of children over ten years were above the test ceiling, the number of results making an effective contribution to the tables of norms was about 5600.

Young reported satisfactory reliability of 0.95. Validity data showed correlations of 0.88 with Neale's Analysis of Reading Ability (A) accuracy score, 0.88 with Vernon's Graded Word Reading Test, and 0.88 with the National Foundation for Educational Research (NFER) Sentence Reading Test (1) (n = 80 in all cases).

(iv) *Behaviour – the Rutter teacher scale B2.* This is a well-known and established scale completed by teachers regarding children's behaviour in school. It yields a total, a neurotic, and an antisocial score. Rutter (1967) and Rutter, Tizard, and Whitmore (1970) found that a cut-off of nine or more on the total score had discriminative value. In their Isle of Wight study it selected about 10 per cent of the boys and 4 per cent of the girls – an average 7 per cent. This cut-off produced nearly 30 per cent of children in our pilot study in Newcastle upon Tyne, and over 20 per cent of the children studied overall. We decided, therefore, to use a slightly more rigorous criterion, and raised the cut-off to ten. At this level 17 per cent of the population were included, more than double the rate reported by Rutter (Kolvin *et al.* 1977).

(v) *Absenteeism*. This is item 'N' on the Rutter B2 scale – 'tends to be absent from school for trivial reasons'. Children were selected on this criterion if the rating 'certainly applies' was made.

IDENTIFICATION OF 'AT-RISK' CHILDREN

Identification by any one or more criteria was taken as indicating that the child might be 'at risk'.

Screening – senior schoolchildren

THE POPULATION

Taking the two consecutive years of screening together, approximately 3300 children were screened. The sex ratio was about equal and the mean age was eleven years and eight months. Again, a more detailed description and analysis of the screening methods are provided elsewhere (Macmillan *et al.* 1980).

DESIGNING THE MULTIPLE CRITERION SCREEN

With the senior children we sought measures that reflected the perceptions of the child, his or her peers, and the teacher. We felt that the most commonly used screening technique – teachers' ratings – might be inadequate if teachers' views were not supplemented by other information. For example, teachers may overlook quiet, passive, but potentially disturbed children (Garner and Bing 1973) and may not be sufficiently attuned to the interpersonal difficulties that some children may be experiencing. We thought that sociometric data might supply more accurate information on social functioning and that self-ratings, in complementing teacher- and peer-derived data, might reveal the personal unease and concerns that both other sources of information may bypass.

   We employed, then, three screen measures yielding six criteria contributing to identification:

(i) *Teachers' ratings*. The scale used here was the same as that employed with the younger children – the Rutter B2 scale. As mentioned previously, as well as a total score it yields two sub-scale scores, one for neurotic, the other for antisocial behaviour. To increase the reliability of the two sub-scales the number of items contributing to them was enlarged in the present study; this was following an inspection of Rutter's data (1967), bearing on discrimination of the two types of disorder. Items were added on the basis that they (a) differentiated the psychiatric group from the controls and (b) differentiated the diagnostic groups. The revised sub-scales therefore consisted of the following items concerning neurotic behaviour: G, H, J, K, N, Q, R, V, and W; and concerning antisocial behaviour: A, B, D, E, O, P, S, T, and Z. Details are provided elsewhere (Macmillan *et al.*, 1980).

(ii) *Sociometry*. The sociometric instrument was the same as that employed with the junior children, but it was used in a slightly different way, as explained in the following section on cut-offs.

(iii) *Self-rating*. The measure employed here was the Junior Eysenck Personality Inventory (JEPI) (Eysenck 1965). This is a sixty-item questionnaire yielding an extroversion-introversion score, a lie score, and a neuroticism score. It was with the last of these dimensions that we were particularly concerned. The high scorer on neuroticism is likely to be 'moody, touchy, anxious, restless, rigid' (Eysenck 1965:3). These are the characteristics associated with instability; the stable person (a low scorer on neuroticism) is likely to be calm, carefree, easy-going, and reliable.

ESTABLISHING CUT-OFFS AND ASSIGNING WEIGHTINGS

It was decided to take extreme scores, on each of the screen measures, as indicators of maladjustment (Macmillan *et al.* 1980). The actual scores used as cut-offs were decided in most cases by examining published data on the characteristics of the instrument. For the sub-scales of the Rutter questionnaire and sociometry, however, cut-off scores were decided on the basis of a pilot study of 200 cases. With a multiple criterion screen one can weight each extreme score equally or, alternatively, assign additional weightings to very high scores on particular measures. With the former system, there is the pitfall that it is theoretically possible for a child to obtain a very deviant score on one specific measure only, but to, nevertheless, be excluded because his or her *summed* weighted score is not sufficiently high. To avoid this we adopted a weighting system that allowed children with markedly deviant teacher- or self-ratings to be selected on that basis alone.

With the Rutter B2 scale a cut-off of nine has been regarded as providing the best discrimination between children attending child guidance clinics and a normal sample (Rutter, Tizard, and Whitmore 1970). We retained this cut-off, assigning it a weighting of one point towards the deviance classification. In addition, we gave the more extreme score of fifteen or over a weighting of two. This was arrived at by adding one standard deviation to Rutter's original cut-off. A cut-off of nine identified about 12 per cent of the sample, while a cut-off of fifteen identified 2 per cent. These cut-offs were different from those used for the junior schoolchildren.

Cut-offs were assigned on the neurotic and antisocial sub-scales which gave rise to a yield closest to that of the total score. A score of four on the neurotic and antisocial sub-scales identified 11 and 14 per cent respectively, and hence was assigned a weighting of one. We should emphasize that our use of the sub-scales as providing weighting scores was different from the use by Rutter, Tizard, and Whitmore who used the two sub-scales for diagnostic purposes. The three Rutter weighted scores were added together to contribute to the total screen score. The use of the two sub-scales ensured that important specific aspects of behaviour were taken into consideration.

With the sociometric criteria our decisions about cut-offs were guided by our findings with the Rutter scale. Cut-offs were adjusted so that percentages similar to that identified by the Rutter total cut-off were selected. For isolation a cut-off of one positive choice or less was selected; this picked out 14 per cent of the pilot children. For rejection, twelve or more negative choices were taken as the cut-off and this also selected 14 per cent. Scores on or beyond these cut-offs were each weighted one point.

Cut-offs of one-and-a-half and two standard deviations above the mean for neuroticism were taken for the JEPI, with the scores being averaged so as to be equivalent for both sexes. These scores were twenty and twenty-three respectively: 17 per cent of the pilot sample scored one-and-a-half standard deviations above the mean. Children with scores of twenty to twenty-two were allotted two points, and those with more extreme scores of twenty-three or twenty-four, three points.

The screen tests used for both junior and senior children are shown in *Table 3(2)*.

Table 3(2)   *Screen tests used in Newcastle upon Tyne Action Research Project*

source of information	junior school	senior school
peers	sociometry	sociometry
teacher	Rutter teacher scale B2 absenteeism	Rutter teacher scale B2

child	reading assessment
	  (Young group
	  reading test)
		Junior Eysenck
		  Personality
		  Inventory

The children's scores on each of the screen measures were summed. Those obtaining a total of three or more points were regarded as screen positives; those scoring below this total were viewed as screen negatives. From the summary of cut-offs and weighting scores in *Table 3(3)* it can be seen that children could be selected as screen positives on the basis of extreme scores on either the Rutter B2 scale or JEPI neuroticism alone, or by various combinations of scores from the three instruments (sociometric, JEPI, or Rutter B2 scale). The maximum weighted score that could be obtained was nine. The weighted score could therefore yield information concerning not only the presence or absence of disturbance, but also its level of severity.

Table 3(3)   *Weighting system used to identify children in senior schools*

instrument	scores used		weighting
Rutter teacher scale B2	total score	9–14	1
		15 or more	2
	neurotic sub-scale (Newcastle modification)	4 or more	1
	antisocial sub-scale (Newcastle modification)	4 or more	1
sociometry	isolation	0 or 1	1
	rejection	12 or more	1
Junior Eysenck Personality Inventory	neuroticism	20–2	2
		23–4	3

Note: children with a weighting score of three or more were regarded as screen positive.

Additional data (see Appendix 1)

The baseline data provided by the screening techniques were supplemented by information obtained from interviewing the parents (on family and social conditions and the child's behaviour), from completion, by the teacher, of more detailed classroom behaviour checklists, and from some group and individual psychological tests (*Table 3(4)*). For screen purposes the Young Reading Test was used, with the Holborn Test used as an additional baseline measure. For all subsequent assessments the Holborn Test was used. The correlation between these tests was 0.9. All the data amassed were then studied by a psychiatrist in order to arrive at a diagnosis (conduct or neurotic disorder) on each child and also to rate them according to the degree of severity of the problem. In a very small number of cases it was not possible to arrive at such a clear-cut diagnosis.

Rutter, Tizard, and Whitmore (1970) managed to classify 90 per

Table 3(4)   *Additional assessments used*

source of information	junior school	senior school
child	reading verbal and non-verbal IQ	ability tests school attitude questionnaire
teacher	classroom behaviour scale	classroom behaviour scale
parent	social data parent attitudes child behaviour and temperament	social data parent attitudes child behaviour and temperament
clinical staff	clinical assessment	clinical assessment

cent of their cases into conduct, neurotic, and mixed categories. However, they reported that their mixed group had much in common with their pure, conduct group. We therefore decided to split our cases into neurotic and conduct disorders by combining the conduct and mixed groups, thereby forming an expanded conduct-disorder group. Previously we had found that there was high agreement between clinicians in such a classification (kappa = 0.9). In addition, the clinicians rated all cases according to the extent of disturbed behaviour on four-point scales, namely: 1 = nil; 2 = dubious; 3 = moderately severe; and 4 = markedly severe. For this research's purposes three scales of disturbed behaviour were employed: *overall severity*, *antisocial* behaviour, and *neurotic* behaviour. The sources of information upon which the ratings were based were the behaviour and temperament scales derived from parental interviews and the behavioural information available from assessments in the school.

Allocation to treatment or control groups

The children who had been selected according to the criteria outlined above, i.e. the screen-positive children, were allocated by school class, at random, to various treatment or control regimes. The use of untreated controls for evaluation of treatment effects may be ethically justified where resources are inadequate to meet the very basic needs of the community, when it is acceptable to allocate randomly rather than to allow selective factors to determine which children are helped. Controls are certainly justified where there are doubts about treatment effectiveness; in fact it is from such controlled studies that we obtain evidence not only of ineffectiveness but also of the possible

Table 3(5)   *Timing of assessments after baseline assessment (in months)*

treatment regime	end of treatment: limited assessment of seniors only	midline follow-up: senior and junior programmes (approximate)	final follow-up: senior and junior programmes
juniors			
at-risk controls	–	18–22	36
parent counselling-teacher consultation	–	18–22	36
nurture work	–	17–19	36
group therapy/playgroups	–	18–20	36
seniors			
maladjusted controls	15–18	15–18	36
parent counselling-teacher consultation	15–18	15–18	36
behaviour modification	7	15–18	36
group therapy	7	15–18	36

Note: for the majority of cases the midline follow-ups were completed over a narrower band of time than was the case with the other assessments.

adverse effects of certain forms of psychotherapy (California Youth Authority 1970).

There were two types of controls in operation: first, control groups in the schools in which treatment programmes were being undertaken (within-school controls) and, second, controls in schools where no treatment was being given (between-school controls). Subsequently, we discovered that the differences between schools were such that it would have been inappropriate to rely on between-school controls and, therefore, data relating to these are not presented in this book. One problem of having the control pupils in the same school as the treated pupils was the possibility that the beneficial effects of treatment may have spread to the former. While we were aware of this possible contamination of the within-school controls, it was noted that this contamination would tend to *reduce* differences between treated and control regimes, rather than exaggerate them.

Within certain practical constraints, we tried to ensure that the schools used were reasonably representative of state-run schools in the cities of Newcastle upon Tyne and Gateshead. These cities are fairly typical of the large, industrialized conurbations in the north of England, with their attendant economic and social problems. Indeed, this area has traditionally been associated with severe economic difficulties, and we believe that this is one of the major reasons for the relatively small-scale influx of immigrants.

Figure 3(1)   Flow chart of study: junior school programme (this programme took place in each of six junior schools)

Entry of first cohort at age 7–8 years

at-risk controls

parent counselling–teacher consultation

undertaken by six social workers

1st year of project

2nd year of project

3rd year of project

4th year of project

Entry of second cohort at age 7–8 years

nurture work

undertaken by seven teacher-aides

playgroup regime

undertaken by six therapists (social workers)

Key:

⊞ = period during which assessment was taking place

▨ = period during which treatment was taking place

▨ = continued treatment at family request

Figure 3(2) Flow chart of study: senior school programme (this programme took place in each of six senior schools)

1st year of project | 2nd year of project | 3rd year of project | 4th year of project

maladjusted controls

parent counselling-teacher consultation

undertaken by six social workers

behaviour modification

undertaken by psychologist and teachers

senior group therapy

undertaken by six therapists (social workers)

Entry of first cohort at age 11–12 years

Entry of second cohort at age 11–12 years

Key:

= period during which assessment was taking place

= period during which treatment was taking place

= continued treatment at family request

Summary of elements of treatment programme

In our project four forms of treatment were evaluated: parent counselling-teacher consultation in both junior and senior schools; group therapy with children in both junior and senior schools; nurture work with junior children; and behaviour modification with senior schoolchildren. For each treatment regime the senior members of the project team (who comprised mainly the authors of this book) organized training programmes for therapists and other personnel involved. Detailed training documents were also drawn up, where necessary. *Table 3(1)* shows the number of children selected for each treatment and control regime, and a full account of the types of treatment is provided in Chapters 5–8. A summary of the elements of the treatment programmes is given below.

BEHAVIOUR MODIFICATION

Used:	in senior programme
Duration:	approximately two school terms
Personnel involved:	directed by a psychologist, implemented by teachers
Training:	introductory training manual followed by seminars
Programme:	defining and establishing goals; main technique of social reinforcement; individual behaviour prescriptions; continuous consultation with supervisor

NURTURE WORK

Used:	in junior programme
Duration:	five school terms
Personnel involved:	carefully selected non-professional teacher-aides; teachers; mental health professionals
Training:	teacher-aides – some training but retention of natural style teachers – explanatory seminars
Programme:	compensatory and enrichment activities; emphasis on healthy interaction experiences; some behavioural shaping; individually tailored help recommended for treated children, *plus* regular discussions and support from mental health professionals

PARENT COUNSELLING-TEACHER CONSULTATION

Used:	in both junior and senior programmes
Duration:	three school terms
Personnel involved:	school-based social workers; teachers; back-up team of senior social workers and psychiatrists
Training:	social workers having special training for their role in an educational setting
Programme:	school-based activities – consultation with teachers of the identified children; attempts to link home and school
	home-based activities – planned short-term case-work with families (averaging six sessions), *plus* back-up support for social workers from psychiatric team

GROUP THERAPY/PLAYGROUPS

Used:	in both junior and senior programmes
Duration:	one school term – ten sessions
Personnel involved:	social workers ignorant of information from any previous assessments of the children's problems
Training:	introductory training programme followed by continuous supervision by psychotherapist and child psychiatrist
Programme:	small groups – withdrawal from classes utilizing principles derived from Axline (1947a); Rogers (1952), and Ginott (1961)
	juniors – play and reflection of feelings
	seniors – more traditional therapy

Evaluation of the effects of treatment

A series of follow-up assessments were undertaken at specified intervals, which included the end of the treatment (senior children only) and two main further assessments – the first being eighteen months and the final three years after the baseline assessment. We planned the intervals so that the time between assessments was brief enough to have been sensitive to any changes that occurred and yet, we hoped, long enough to allow changes to occur. The different initial levels of severity of psychological disorder between the regimes had also to be taken into account in the analysis because initial levels inevitably affect the results. As well as the objective assessments shown in *Tables 3(2) and 3(4)* some more subjective views of improvement were gathered and used to provide descriptive comparisons, but were not used in the main statistical analysis.

Fuller accounts of how we dealt with theoretical and technical problems of classification, definition, measurement, and details of treatment are provided in subsequent chapters and have already been described, in part, elsewhere (Garside *et al*, 1973; Harvey *et al*. 1977; Kolvin *et al*. 1975a; Nicol and Bell 1975; Hulbert, Wolstenholme, and Kolvin 1977). Full details of our method are provided in Appendix 2.

OUTCOME

We used two methods to compare the effects of the different regimes (including the no-treatment regime). The first, more simple method was to calculate the outcome (as defined by Sainsbury (1975) and described in Appendix 2) for each child and then find the number who showed good, moderate, and poor outcome for each regime. This was done for three global ratings: general, neurotic and anti-social behaviours. Significance between groups was tested using the well-established chi-squared test. It should be pointed out that outcome ratings tended to be more reliant on data collected at home than at school.

IMPROVEMENT

The second, more complex method was to compare regimes by using analysis of covariance. By this method average improvement scores for each regime were compared for every measure separately at each subsequent follow-up. The special feature of analysis of covariance is that differences between regimes in initial severity and other factors which may affect improvement are taken into account. In our research project we took initial score, general severity of maladjust-ment, non-verbal IQ, and an index of social functioning of the family into account; we used these 'covariates' because preliminary analysis suggested that these were the most important of a larger number studied. In addition, an index of family history of psychiatric illness was used as a covariate in the junior regimes. On some of these factors the children in the four regimes (both junior and senior) differed, even though we had allocated the children to regimes on a random basis. While these differences were probably due to chance rather than being systematic, we thought they should nevertheless be allowed for. This was the justification for the use of analysis of covariance (see Appendix 2).

In addition, we summed certain measures and carried out analysis of covariance on these. Measures were summated on the basis of the results of factor analyses. For example, with the junior children it was found that there were five variables that measured neurotic disturbance, and these were added together (equally weighted) to provide a 'neurotic' score. Five other variables measured antisocial behaviour and likewise, these were added together to give an 'antisocial' score.

Analyses of covariance were carried out on the four regimes as a group (separately for junior and senior children) and we also compared each regime with every other, taking into account the number of regimes (see Appendix 2 for details).

Numbers of cases, losses, and missing data

We selected more cases than were necessary for our purposes in order to leave a reasonable safety margin for coping with unexpected losses. Kolvin *et al.* (1977) and Macmillan *et al.* (1980) have provided detailed discussions of the number of cases selected by screens. In the junior school programme we allocated 270 children to our treatment and control regimes but, for various reasons, five of these were not used, and 265 children entered the project. In the senior school programme we allocated 322 children; thirteen were not used, and 309 children entered the project. At the end of the follow-up period, three years later, we remained in contact with at least 95 per cent of cases in both junior and senior school programmes. However, contact does not necessarily imply that complete information was obtained. As we had anticipated, more problems occurred with missing data than with missing cases. This was because extensive data were collected from multiple sources, which meant that information could have been available for a child on one particular assessment but not on another. This problem of missing data occurred across time (i.e., assessment points), between the main sources of information (namely the home and the school), and within these main sources. One way of depicting it was to compare key data across time: for instance, while *full* 'screen' data were, of course, available at base, they were not available for 4 per cent of the juniors at the mid-point and 8 per cent at the final follow-up; nor were they available for 5 per cent of the seniors at the mid-point and 14 per cent at the final follow-up.

Information from home was always more difficult to collect than school data. Another problem was encountered when children moved school, in which case we did not consider it reasonable to ask the new school to allow us to undertake sociometry for a single child. Yet another involved the self-completion instruments, where difficulties arose with children who persistently failed to attend school or were unpredictable in their attendance. Key home data were not available for 11 per cent of the juniors at the mid-point and 15 per cent at the final follow-up, nor for 11 per cent of the seniors at the mid-point and 16 per cent at the final follow-up.

We were particularly concerned with missing cases, and those cases where data were missing. We studied these in terms of all school and home data available at the baseline and, perhaps surprisingly, no evidence was found that the missing cases differed to any extent from those who remained in the study. The more complex statistical analyses utilized data both across time and assessments and, therefore, reduced the pool of cases with complete data available (see Appendix 3). We checked our results in various ways, and found that this reduction made no difference to the conclusions of the research project. For instance, on certain key variables we studied improvement on all cases available at each follow-up and found the differences between the two methods (i.e. common data as compared to all data) were trivial. In the less sophisticated analyses cases were not debarred by minor absences of data and therefore the pool of cases was more complete (see Appendix 3).

4 The children, their schools, families, and therapists

Summary

There are many influences on child development and for this reason, we describe not only the children themselves but also their environments, particularly their schools and families.

Background information was amassed regarding the schools selected for the study. As we point out, the evidence suggested that these schools were reasonably representative of those in Newcastle upon Tyne and Gateshead.

The characteristics of the families of the pupils involved in this study (family composition, child and family health, social hazards, social conditions, family relationships, attitudes towards each other, and attitudes towards other members of the community) are outlined in this chapter.

Also, we discuss the overall picture of the children's handicaps at the outset of the research project. This was obtained by means of parental reports (on behaviour and temperament) and school measures (on behaviour, peer relationships, self-assessment, ability and attainment, and attitude to school).

In addition, we point out that the therapists involved were fully trained professionals, but differed in their therapeutic characteristics.

In order to assist in our descriptions, we will refer in this chapter to the normal control groups who acted as a comparison to screen-positive study children. (The former were randomly selected from the screen negatives as outlined in Kolvin *et al*. (1977) and Macmillan *et al*. (1980).)

The children's schools

Six junior and six senior schools were selected as being roughly representative of those in the two adjacent cities of Newcastle upon Tyne and Gateshead. In addition, one senior and one junior school were used for pilot purposes. In this section we provide an account of two types of information about these fourteen schools. First, we list simple factual information about them and, second, detail more fundamental characteristics of teacher management, qualities of interest and care, etc.

FACTUAL DATA – SENIOR SCHOOLS

The pupils
A high percentage of the children in the seven schools studied received free school meals. Without going into detail, free school meals are made available to children coming from poor or under-privileged homes and therefore the percentage of such children in a school tends to reflect the type of neighbourhood in which the school is located. In only one school was the number receiving free school meals under 10 per cent, and in three schools it was over 30 per cent, with the other schools falling between these extremes.

Turning to school attendance of pupils we obtained information relating to the previous school year. The average rate of attendance was 87 per cent and the differences between schools ranged from 79 to 95 per cent.

We also enquired about whether the schools suffered from vandalism in the previous year and asked the Headteachers to rate this as marked, moderate, or little. Two of the schools were considered to have suffered extensive vandalism, two moderate vandalism, and the other three little vandalism. We tried to obtain some estimate of the amount of vandalism by calculating the cost per pupil to the school, though details were difficult to obtain as some of the schools did not keep a record of this type of information. From what we could ascertain, the range was from as little as 64 pence per pupil (averaged) to as much as £9 per pupil per annum.

We obtained some additional information about the school in general, such as the number of pupils excluded in the previous academic year. In three of the schools no pupils were excluded, in another two schools two or three pupils were, and in the remaining two there were slightly higher rates – one had excluded six pupils and the other eight in the previous academic year.

We produced a child movement index based on children moving schools. Their reasons for doing so were varied, ranging from, for example, moves due to family change of home address, their having been excluded by school due to behaviour problems, or their current placement having been inappropriate. We then obtained a total score of movement and from there a child movement index in relation to the number of children in the school. This averaged about 3 per cent with 6.6 per cent at the highest level in the previous school year.

The teachers
Our next set of data covers the senior school teachers. It was interesting to note that the percentages of married teachers ranged from 63 to 83 per cent with an average percentage of 76. We calculated the number of young teachers compared to older ones, defining young teachers as being under forty and older ones as being over that age. We found that the number of young teachers ranged from 48 per cent at one extreme through to 83 per cent at the other. On average, about two-thirds of the teachers in the secondary schools were under forty.

We also looked at the percentage of teachers who had recently joined the schools and noted that this was quite high in some schools with as many as 42 per cent of teachers having joined over the two academic years previous to the start of our project. In other schools there was much more stability in the sense that over the same period only 17 per cent of the teachers were newcomers. The average percentage of staff joining the schools over the previous two academic years was about 28 per cent. This period proved to be a time of considerable staff movement in all the senior schools and was subsequently followed by considerable staff stability. We tried to obtain information about teacher absenteeism but this was only available for five of the seven schools studied. We converted the information to an index in relation to the number of part-time and full-time teachers, but because this was a conversion formula rather than a provision of raw data, it is not worthwhile reporting it here. Perhaps, though, it is useful to comment that it corresponded quite closely with the underprivilege index reported below.

Neighbourhood support
Information was gathered about the neighbourhood support for the school, as perceived by the Headteachers who rated it in terms of much support, moderate support, and relatively little support. Additional information was requested if the support was described as particularly good or particularly poor. In no school was there marked neighbourhood support, in four there was some or moderate support, and in three relatively little.

Finally, we developed an index of underprivilege based on the

number of children having free school meals, the amount of neighbourhood support for the school, and the extent of vandalism
experienced. Using this index we found that it was immediately clear
which schools had high and which had low rates of underprivilege.

FACTUAL DATA − JUNIOR SCHOOLS

Again we have information on seven schools, one of which was a
pilot school, the other six being included in the main research project.

The pupils
There were no schools with under 10 per cent of children having free
school meals; one school had over 10 per cent, two had over 20 per
cent, and four over 30 per cent.

The school attendance rate was higher than in the senior schools;
the average percentage of pupil attendance for the previous academic
year ranged between 88 and 95 per cent. As was the case with the
seniors, very few of the schools had immigrant children − the
numbers being between 1 and 2 per cent.

The extent of vandalism in the junior schools was very low, with
only one school having what the Headteacher regarded as a moderate
problem; all the others reported little in the way of vandalism.

The percentage of children moving from our schools to others
averaged about 6 per cent with 10.9 per cent at the highest level in the
previous school year.

The teachers
The percentage of married teachers was as low as 45 per cent in one
school and as high as 78 per cent at the other end of the range, with
the average of those married being 60 per cent. The presence of
young teachers ranged from 42 to 80 per cent, with an average of 67
per cent.

Staff who joined the school over the two years previous to the start
of our project ranged from 7 per cent at one extreme to 50 per cent at
the other. In relation to staff joining, the average was 26 per cent. The
teacher absenteeism or illness rate was calculated as an index as was
teacher training and teacher experience. As these were indices there
is no great merit in describing them here, except to say that there
were considerable differences between the schools.

Neighbourhood support
In comparison with the senior schools there was much more neighbourhood support for the junior institutions, two of them being
described as having considerable neighbourhood support, two others

as attracting it to a moderate extent, and the other three reporting little support.

Finally, moving to the underprivilege score we found that there was a wide range of underprivilege, but that it was not so great as in the senior schools.

Figure 4(1)   Comparison of senior schools (the mean on the vertical axis represents the local mean based on fifteen schools)

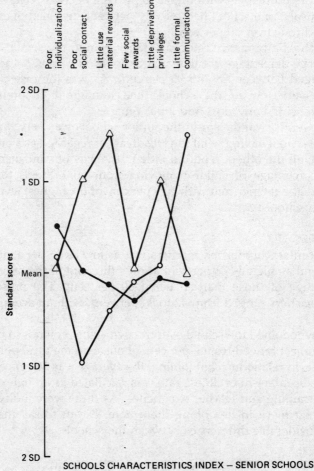

SCHOOLS CHARACTERISTICS INDEX – SENIOR SCHOOLS

LEGEND   O   Profile of a school with high scores
         △   Profile of a school with low scores
         ●   Mean profile of six schools

NOTE: *Most profiles lie with 1 SD either side of mean*

CHARACTERISTICS OF THE SCHOOL ENVIRONMENT

We used an interview technique to provide measures of characteristics of schools – the Schools Characteristic Index, which is described elsewhere (Mullin 1979).

The graphs that we present (*Figs 4(1)* and *4(2)*) are profiles of some of the schools in comparison with the 'norms', the latter being based on

Figure 4(2)   Comparison of junior schools (the mean on the vertical axis represents the local mean based on fourteen schools)

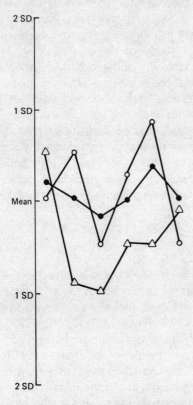

SCHOOLS CHARACTERISTICS INDEX – JUNIOR SCHOOLS

LEGEND   ○ Profile of a school with high scores
△ Profile of a school with low scores
● Mean profile of six schools

NOTE: *Most schools lie within 1 SD either side of mean*

fifteen senior and fourteen junior schools. In each graph we present the mean for either the six junior or six senior schools in the study and for two schools that appeared to have rather different profiles from the others. Of the latter, at the senior school level, one school had little in the way of social contact between the staff and pupils, and the teachers made very little use of either material rewards or deprivation of privileges in their management of the children. The scores for this school were seen to digress about one standard deviation from the mean on these particular scales. In the second school the picture was rather different: there was good social contact between staff and pupils and the school did not use an extensive amount of formal communication. The average profile of the six senior schools showed how little the schools, as a group, deviated from the mean profile of all the schools studied.

At the junior school level, there is little in the way of variations, though there were some differences worth reporting – for instance, the graph shows how in the two slightly unusual schools there was poor social contact. Furthermore, a study of the use of deprivation of privileges, showed this approach was more readily applied in one school and less in the other, but the difference was not great. It was further noted that an average profile of the six schools did not deviate very much from the mean profile of all the schools studied.

These profiles tended to suggest that each of the six sets of senior and junior schools selected for our research were reasonably representative of the total population of schools studied. Nevertheless, the differences demonstrated very strongly supported the decision to use a method that allowed for disparities between schools to be taken into consideration throughout.

The children and their families

The characteristics of the families of the pupils involved in the study are outlined in this section. Further details about the population from which the study children were selected, including background characteristics, are provided elsewhere (Kolvin *et al*. 1977; Nicol *et al*. 1981), where they are compared with those of the normal controls.

In the junior age range (seven to eight years) there were 265 first-year pupils (60.4 per cent were boys and 39.6 per cent were girls). The older pupils (eleven to twelve years) were in their first year of senior school and, again, boys outnumbered girls (55.5 per cent to 44.5 per cent respectively). There were 309 senior pupils assigned to the various regimes at the start of the study.

Although the inclusion criteria for the two age ranges were different (and harsher in the case of senior pupils) there was a surprising similarity between the family characteristics of both groups. Hence, for the purposes of presentation, the family details of the two sets of pupils are considered together, though occasions where differences arose are discussed.

FAMILY COMPOSITION

In some of the following descriptions we compare the rates of various features found in the screen-positive study children with those of the groups of normal controls, thereby illustrating the abnormal characteristics of the screen-positives.

Intact families
The type of family situation that study children were experiencing is shown in *Table 4(1)*. Proportionately fewer of the senior pupils than the junior ones lived with both their natural parents, 17 per cent of the former coming from single-parent families. Further, for both age groups the rate of single-parent families in this study easily exceeded the 10 per cent rate reported for children of all ages (Finer Report 1974) and the 6 per cent rate found amongst seven- and eleven-year-olds in the National Child Development Study (NCDS) (Wedge and Prosser 1973). Irrespective of age, four of the study children had been adopted, three were fostered on a long-term basis, and the remainder were living with their parents or relatives.

The living arrangements of the children largely reflected the civil state of the parents. The proportion of children who had experienced the break-up or dissolution of their parents' marriage was very similar (18.3 per cent of seniors and 15.7 per cent of juniors).

Table 4(1)   *Family situation*

child living with	seniors		juniors	
	n	%	n	%
both natural parents	224	73.7	201	77.3
natural mother alone	44	14.5	30	11.5
natural father alone	7	2.3	2	0.8
natural parent and step-parent	23	7.6	17	6.6
living away from both natural parents	6	1.9	10	3.8
total (available data)	304	100	260	100
missing data	5		5	

National origins
The national origins of fathers were more varied than those of mothers. 93.5 per cent of the fathers of junior pupils were born in Britain and of

the remainder the largest sub-group were of Asian origin (3 per cent); even fewer of the fathers of senior children came from abroad. There were only eight mothers from the two age groups who were not British-born, and of these all but three were of Asian origin. Thus, the demographic characteristics of these families were similar to those reported in previous studies undertaken in the north-east of England (Kolvin *et al.* 1981).

Parental age
The average age of mothers of junior pupils was thirty-five years and five months, and thirty-eight years and ten months for fathers. Not surprisingly, the parents of the senior pupils were slightly older (thirty-nine years and five months in the case of mothers, and forty-two years and four months for fathers).

Family sizes and ordinal positions
Table 4(2) gives the distribution of children per family. The average size of families was slightly higher in the case of senior pupils than of junior ones (4.25 and 4.1 children respectively). Large families, i.e. those with five or more children, were marginally more common in the senior pupil group (41 per cent). The proportion of large families amongst the junior children was still double that reported in the NCDS for a similar age cohort (Wedge and Prosser 1973). The mean number of children was higher in the screen-positive than in the normal control groups (p < .05) (see Kolvin *et al.* 1977; Nicol *et al.* 1981).

Table 4(2)   *Number of children in family*

number of children	seniors		juniors	
	n	%	n	%
single children	19	6.2	14	5.4
two	46	14.9	47	18.1
three	62	20.1	57	21.9
four	55	17.9	48	18.4
five	62	20.1	34	13.1
six or more	64	20.8	60	23.1
total (available data)	308	100	260	100
missing data	1		5	

FAMILY HEALTH
Child health
Circumstances at birth. Each family was questioned as to the presence of the following health problems during the perinatal period: haemorrhaging or high blood pressure during the pregnancy; prolonged

labour (more than thirty-six hours), a breech or emergency Caesarian operation; a premature birth (before the thirty-sixth week); a birth-weight of less than five-and-a-half pounds; breathing difficulties, fits or severe jaundice in the infant.

Any of these difficulties could occur singly or in combination with one another. Approximately one-third of the study children had experienced one or more of the perinatal problems and a tenth of them had experienced at least two of them. The high rates of such problems were probably a reflection of the high loadings of adverse social experiences of these families.

Developmental history of the child. There are a number of problems associated with retrospective accounts of child behaviour and development: first, there is the difficulty of recall (Yarrow 1963); second, the wide range of normal variations for achieving milestones. Nevertheless, three simple questions are frequently relied upon to provide information about a child's development: when did the child take three steps unaided?; at what age did the child use two- or three-word phrases?; when was night-time bladder control achieved? Such questions are likely to provide valid information concerning only gross delays in development.

By the age of eighteen months only a minority of the study children (2.3 per cent of juniors and 4.3 per cent of seniors) had failed to take three steps unaided and only seventeen had not used three-word sentences by the time they had reached their third birthday. These figures were within the range of expectation of such delays in a Newcastle upon Tyne population of school children (Neligan, Prudham, and Steiner 1974; Fundudis, Kolvin, and Garside 1979).

Delays in achieving consistent bladder control at night were quite common amongst the study children and 17 per cent of junior pupils had not achieved control – i.e. bed-wetting occurred more than once a month – by the age of four-and-a-half years. The figure for senior pupils was 15 per cent. In addition, 11 per cent of the juniors were still wetting the bed at the age of seven, and 7 per cent of the seniors were still doing so at the age of eleven. Again, on the basis of earlier population studies in Newcastle upon Tyne, these rates were quite within our expectation (Kolvin, MacKeith, and Meadow 1973; Miller 1973), though the rate at seven years was double that described in a national study (Blomfield and Douglas 1956). However, significantly more of the senior screen-positive children had bowel/bladder problems than did the normal controls.

Child illness: physical. Again, there was a similarity in the rate of mild handicap at both age levels amongst the study children. The major exception was, however, in the number of visual problems (including

squint). Especially notable were the numbers of children who required spectacles. Senior pupils were twice as likely to wear glasses as
the younger children (17 per cent as opposed to 7 per cent). This may,
however, not be a true difference, but merely a reflection of the age at
which pupils are screened for such problems.

Only seven of the study children had been diagnosed as suffering
from some form of deafness, but 9 per cent had some form of ear
trouble, the most common complaint being repeated or chronic ear
infection. A surprisingly high percentage of them (9 per cent) had
received a head injury that had involved either loss of consciousness,
hospital contact, or fracture.

The sequelae of these accidents and health difficulties were reflected
in the number of reported hospital admissions for these children.
Admissions were marginally more common among senior pupils of
whom one-quarter (24.4 per cent) had undergone an operation requiring a general anaesthetic and of whom a further 23 per cent had
been admitted to hospital but not required an operation. For junior
pupils, the rates were 21 and 20 per cent respectively.

Mothers were asked if their child had any chronic disability or
physical disorder that had necessitated more than a term's absence
from school, involved either regular attendance at a clinic or the use of
special facilities at home. Overall, 7 per cent of the study children had
been affected in some such way. We should point out that while all
illnesses occurred more frequently in the screen-positive children than
the normal controls, this difference did not prove to be significant.

Child illness: emotional. It was reported that 7 per cent of both senior
and junior study children were seeing a GP for an emotional disorder. An additional 7 per cent of senior and 4 per cent of junior
pupils had been in touch with their family doctor for emotional
problems at some time prior to the preceding six months. More of the
older pupils than the junior ones had a history of psychiatric help.
Amongst the former, 6 per cent fell into this category whilst only 3 per
cent of the juniors did so, but this was likely to be a function of age.
Again, such medical contact was significantly higher in the screen-
positive children than in the normal control groups.

Family health
Physical health. A number of studies have shown that certain types of
child psychiatric problem are associated with parental physical and/or
emotional ill-health (Rutter 1966; Wolff and Acton 1968).

In our study children's families both physical and emotional problems were much in evidence. One-third of the families had at least one

member affected by a chronic or recurrent physical illness that had lasted continuously or intermittently for more than a year, and that had substantially impaired a parent's work capacity. In 6 per cent of families illness affected more than one member, but most often illness was confined to one of the parents.

Emotional health. Many studies have shown that complaints of 'nervousness' in children correlate with psychiatric disorder in their parents (e.g. Hare and Shaw 1965). Wolff and Acton (1968) correlated the response to a simple question about 'nerves' with other indices of maternal psychiatric disorder. They found that the response correlated significantly with psychiatric illness, treatment for psychological conditions, hostility scores on the Foulds Hostility Scale (Foulds 1965), and ratings of personality disorder made after an extensive parental interview.

Parents were asked the simple and useful question 'Do you suffer with your nerves?' (Nicol *et al.* 1981). Mothers of senior pupils answered positively in 46 per cent of cases and fathers in 12 per cent. The figures for parents of junior pupils were 42 and 10 per cent respectively. A second measure of maternal health that we used was the Goldberg Health Questionnaire (Goldberg 1972). The scores of mothers of our study children were compared with those of the mothers of the normal control groups and the comparisons are described in other publications (Kolvin *et al.* 1977; Nicol *et al.* 1981), but to summarize, the mothers of senior pupils who were screen-positive had significantly higher scores than the mothers of the normal controls; the mothers of screen-positive junior pupils also obtained higher scores than their counterparts in the normal control groups, but here the difference was not statistically significant.

A harsher but more reliable estimate of the presence of parental emotional problems was obtained by recording those with a psychiatric history. Evidence of previous or current outpatient and inpatient psychiatric help was found in 14 per cent of the parents of senior pupils and in a similar percentage of parents of the juniors.

With so many parents experiencing psychiatric difficulties, other children in the families, apart from the study children themselves, may be at risk. In fact, 8 per cent of both senior and junior pupils had brothers or sisters who had been referred to a psychiatrist. A further 6 to 7 per cent had siblings who had received advice from GPs for emotional difficulties.

SOCIAL HAZARDS

Child experiences
Parent-child separations are accepted as a potential cause of short-

term distress but, in themselves, play only a minor part in the causation of persistent psychiatric disorders (Rutter 1971; Rutter and Madge 1976). It is when separations involve unpleasant experiences, or when they reflect longstanding family disturbance, that longer-term problems are more likely to occur.

Two features of *Table 4(3)* are immediately evident. First, the study children were more likely to have experienced paternal rather than maternal separations in their first five years, with two-thirds of these paternal-child separations lasting for more than six months. Second, the number of separations, both paternal and maternal, were highest among the senior pupils. In previous publications we have shown these separations among the study seniors to be significantly higher than in the case of seniors in the normal controls (Kolvin *et al*. 1977; Nicol *et al*. 1981).

Of the study children at both age levels separated from one or both parents for more than a month in their first five years, thirty-five (i.e. 6 per cent) stayed at home, twenty-four (4 per cent) were with relatives, nineteen (3 per cent) were in hospital, and twenty (3 per cent) were 'in care'. One further child had been fostered privately. Some of these separations were temporary in that family members were reunited at a later date; however, just as many were examples of the permanent disruption of a family, the result of divorce or marital break-up.

Table 4(3) *Parent–child separations of over one month in the five years of life*

length of separation	from mother		from father	
	seniors $n = 308$	juniors $n = 259$	seniors $n = 307$	juniors $n = 259$
	%	%	%	%
no separations over 1 month	84	89	71	76
1–2 months	8	2	6	4
3–6 months	3	5	4	3
over 6 months	5	4	19	17
total (available data)	100	100	100	100

The events surrounding the death of a parent are also known to be associated with the presence of psychiatric problems in children (Rutter 1966). The mothers of five and the fathers of seventeen study children had died. No child had experienced the death of both parents.

Involvement with the police was reported by the parents of twelve (4.6 per cent) junior study children; in these cases no action had been taken. The rate was three times higher for the eleven-year-old group however, with thirty-nine (13 per cent) study children having had some contact with the police; sixteen of these had been referred to the local authority for advice, action, or court proceedings.

Again, disproportionately more of the senior pupils (6.5 per cent compared with 1.5 per cent of juniors) had been involved in compulsory contact with social welfare agencies. The level of voluntary contact, at 7 per cent, was almost identical for both age groups.

Family experiences

Detailing of hazardous events affecting family members other than the study child was restricted to problems with alcohol and contact with social welfare agencies.

Problems of excessive drinking amongst parents or siblings that resulted in social disruption (violence, absenteeism, loss of job, marital difficulties, separations) or damage to health (hospital admissions) were reported in the case of 11 per cent of the study children, with identical rates for the families of both junior and senior groups.

Contact with social welfare agencies was again dichotomized according to the compulsory or voluntary nature of the involvement. Over a quarter of all the families had some contact (13 per cent voluntary and 15 per cent compulsory contact in the case of the families of senior pupils and 15 and 7 per cent respectively for the families of juniors). Again, members of the families of both of the study groups had experienced greater contact than had those of the normal controls.

SOCIAL CONDITIONS

Social class

The occupational group of the breadwinner was classified according to the Registrar-General's *Classification of Occupations* (1951). It is apparent from *Table 4(4)* that there was a marked downward social class gradient amongst the study families and an under-representation of white collar workers. A second feature of the table is the high level of unemployment reported in this sample, affecting nearly one-quarter of the families. The unemployed category was only used for breadwinners who were long-term unemployed (i.e. those who had not worked for at least a year). With few exceptions, the majority of the long-term unemployed were from the unskilled and semi-skilled

Table 4(4)   *Social class distribution of the study families*

occupational group of breadwinner	seniors		juniors	
	n	%	n	%
I & II	13	4.2	18	6.9
III	144	46.8	110	42.3
IV & V	83	26.9	70	27.0
unemployed	68	22.1	62	23.8
total (available data)	308	100	260	100
missing data	1		5	

members of the community. Again, the percentage of families in the middle and upper social strata was lower in the study groups than in their respective normal controls but the differences only proved statistically significant in the case of the seniors.

Work records of the breadwinners
An unsatisfactory work record was one where the breadwinner had been out of work continuously for the last year or had not held a job for a continuous year in the preceding three (*Table 4(5)*). This definition was designed to take into account the employment prospects in the area at the time of the study. From the details available, it would appear that almost a third of the study children came from families for whom unemployment was a recent or continuing experience.

Table 4(5)   *Category of work record of breadwinner*

work record	seniors		juniors	
	n	%	n	%
satisfactory	215	69.8	177	68.1
unsatisfactory	35	11.4	55	21.2
no effective breadwinner	58	18.8	28	10.7
total (available data)	308	100	260	100
missing data	1		5	

Mothers working outside the home
There are many factors that influence the effects a mother has on her children when she is employed outside the home, yet few investigations have attempted to control for these. Thus, this issue continues to provoke controversy in professional and lay circles alike. Two recent reviews have tended to suggest that maternal employment outside the home generally appears to have no harmful effects on the

school-age child's adjustment (Wallston 1973; Etaugh 1974). Just under half the study children's mothers were working at the time of the original assessment. Of the mothers of senior and junior pupils, 29 per cent were working part-time and 15 per cent full-time.

Housing conditions

There can be little doubt that the quantity and quality of accommodation available to the residents of Newcastle upon Tyne has improved since the Second World War (Miller *et al.* 1974). Nevertheless, our investigation found conditions of overcrowding (i.e. more than 1.5 persons per room) were experienced by the study families of 19 per cent of junior school pupils and 12 per cent of senior pupils. In addition, almost 5 per cent of the study families did not have an indoor toilet. Overall, the housing conditions were significantly poorer in the case of our study children than in the normal controls (Kolvin *et al.* 1977; Nicol *et al.* 1981).

The condition of the home was assessed at the initial interview and, whilst the majority of homes were well-cared for, 12 per cent of study families' homes showed signs of a definite neglect of basic standards by the householders.

FAMILY RELATIONSHIPS AND ATTITUDES

Parent-child relationships

In previous publications we have compared patterns of discipline for our study children with those for normal controls (Kolvin *et al.* 1977; Nicol *et al.* 1981). We report here the significant comparisons, which are based on parent interview data.

Some 15 per cent of the parents of junior study pupils and 13 per cent of the senior ones reported using high rates of physical punishment, i.e. spanks more than once a week or slaps most days. The corollary of this was that well over half of the parents (57 per cent of juniors' and 63 per cent of seniors') said they rarely spanked their children and that an occasional slap (not exceeding once a month) was their limit. A comparison with the respective normal controls revealed a significantly greater exposure to physical punishment among the senior study pupils ($p < .01$), but not among the juniors.

The technique of depriving a child of privileges was used by only a minority of the parents of the study children (7 per cent), irrespective of the age of the child. Isolation procedures, i.e. sending a child from the room or to his or her bedroom, were used more frequently by the parents of senior pupils (14 per cent) than by those of junior pupils (9 per cent). In neither case was it significantly different from the normal controls.

On the positive side, the parents of 56 per cent of study children of both ages said they used reasoning methods in disciplining their children, i.e. they frequently explained their requests or demands. A further 23 per cent, though, said they rarely used this mode of approach. According to this measure study children at both age levels were less likely to have parents who reasoned with them than were the normal controls ($p < .05$ for juniors and $p < .01$ for seniors).

The marriages
Seventeen to 20 per cent of the study children had parents who had divorced or separated. In almost half of these cases a parent had remarried or was involved in a stable cohabitation. Where there was a marriage or cohabitation, mothers were asked about it, and in particular whether there had been any separations, serious rows, or fights.

In the case of the junior pupils thirty mothers and two fathers lived alone and were therefore excluded from the analysis. So, too, were the fifty-one single parents of senior pupils. There were, then, 228 intact 'marriages' among the families of junior pupils and 254 among those of senior pupils. The percentages in the following account refer to these two totals.

For the younger age group thirty-eight mothers (17 per cent) said they had considered separating from their partners, although this had never occurred, whereas forty mothers (18 per cent) had followed this intention through, but had later returned to continue the marriage. In the case of parents of the older children, forty-five (18 per cent) had considered separating and forty-two (17 per cent) had separated for a short period.

Mothers were also asked about disagreements that became heated arguments or rows. Frequent rows, i.e. more than once per week, were reported in 10 per cent of the families of both age groups. In 10 to 13 per cent of households these arguments became violent, that is to say blows were struck or property was destroyed.

For each family an index of marital difficulties was created by combining the rate of separations, rows, and fights into a single rating. The parents of senior study pupils had significantly more problems with their marriages than did the parents of the respective normal controls ($p < .05$). This was not the case with the parents of the junior study children.

Attitudes towards and contact with the community
School relations: parental involvement. At the beginning of the study parents were asked how often they had visited their child's school in the previous year. In general, parents of the junior study children had visited their child's school more often than had those of senior study children, although 19 per cent had not been in touch with the school for over a year. A further 23 per cent had made just one visit. Almost half of the parents of senior pupils had not visited the school over the previous year, whilst 19 per cent had made one visit. This was very different from the parents of the normal controls (p < .01). It was rare for parents and teachers of the study children to see one another more than once in a year, even though there were opportunities at open days or parent evenings. Our data also suggested that educational difficulties were common in other family members, though the rates did not exceed those found in the corresponding normal controls. These difficulties may have contributed to a generally poor view held by the families of the educational system.
School relations: children's problems and their attitudes toward school. Parents reported that 8 per cent of junior children and 12 per cent of senior children disliked school very much. A further 14 to 15 per cent of pupils expressed moderate dislike of school. We have shown that dislike of school was reported very much more frequently by the study children than by the normal controls (p < .01).

Mothers of 27 to 30 per cent of pupils thought it possible that their children had some difficulties at school. A further 19 to 24 per cent of mothers described 'definite' problems with schooling. Again, when compared with same-age normal controls, reported problems were significantly higher in the study children (p < .01).
Community involvement. Using a simple measure of the number and type of social contacts a family enjoyed (Wallin 1954) the families of junior pupils were found to be more isolated than normal control families (p < .05) (Kolvin *et al.* 1977).

The children's initial social and emotional adjustment, intelligence, and educational achievements

THE PARENTAL REPORTS
Two types of parental interview were used: these were the behaviour interview (Kolvin *et al.*, 1975b), which tapped aspects of children's behaviour, and the temperament interview (Garside *et al.* 1975), which aimed to tap the style of children's behaviour. The development of these interviews was reported in Nicol *et al.* (1981).

The behaviour interview

The results from the behaviour questionnaire showed that the most commonly occurring neurotic symptom was sensitivity, which was present to a handicapping degree in 22.7 per cent of the junior school and 27 per cent of the senior school sample. Anxiety was also common, occurring in 9.2 per cent of the junior sample and 13 per cent of the senior sample. School resistance, to at least the extent where persuasion was needed to get the child to school at minimum once a week, occurred in 6.8 per cent of the junior sample and 9.4 per cent of the senior sample.

Of the antisocial symptoms tantrums were the most common. These were reported as occurring at least once a day in 13.5 per cent of the junior sample and 18.5 per cent of the senior sample. Pilfering of a chronic type, where the family had to be careful not to leave things lying about, occurred in 0.8 per cent of the junior and 4.2 per cent of the senior sample. Truanting was reported as a major problem in 1.2 per cent of the junior and 4.6 per cent of the senior sample.

Somatic symptoms of major proportions were also common. Abdominal pain occurring several times a week was a feature of 3.9 per cent of the junior and 3.2 per cent of the senior sample; headache of similar frequency occurred in 2.7 per cent of the juniors and 4.2 per cent of the seniors. There were also sleep problems in 15.8 per cent of the juniors and 12.1 per cent of the seniors.

Overall, the senior children seemed to show higher rates of behavioural disturbance except in those areas that may represent developmental delays, such as enuresis.

The temperament interview

The temperament interview was designed to reveal temperamental characteristics in a variety of life areas, including mealtimes, playtime, sleep, and dressing. Despite the fact that this was a disturbed population, marked overactivity occurred in only 12.4 per cent of the sample, even in play. Irritability of mood was particularly a feature of dressing in the morning, where it occurred in 11.4 per cent of the seniors, but only 4.2 per cent of the juniors. Shyness and withdrawal were more common in the study children when they were confronted with adults than when facing other children or new situations. Extremes of dependency were only slightly more common in the junior children (8.1 per cent) than in the seniors (7.5 per cent). This may be a further reflection of the fact that the seniors were a more disturbed group. The latter showed poorer concentration than the juniors: parents reported that 10.8 per cent of the seniors, but only 5.4 per cent of the juniors, had very poor attention spans.

Trends in the data

In order to get an insight into any important trends in the data derived from the behaviour interview the children from separate diagnostic groups were compared on three dimensions – neurotic, conduct, and somatic-developmental. The same was done with the temperament data but in this case there were four dimensions – withdrawal, activity, irregularity, and mood.

The junior children showed no differences in symptomatology between the boys and girls *within* the groups diagnosed either as conduct disorder or neurotic disorder. On the other hand, there were differences *between* the diagnostic groups. As one would expect, the conduct-disordered children showed the highest scores on the conduct dimension and the neurotic-disordered children had the highest scores on the neurotic one. For the boys only the conduct-disordered group also showed significantly higher scores on activity and irregularity than did the neurotic-disordered group.

In relation to the senior children the picture was somewhat different. First, there were some quite marked differences with regard to the behavioural and temperamental dimensions between the boys and girls within the diagnostic groups. The boys showed higher average scores than did the girls on the conduct dimension, both in the conduct-disordered and the neurotic-disordered groups. The neurotic boys also showed a higher score than the neurotic girls on the somatic-developmental dimension. Sex differences were also apparent on the temperamental dimension, with the conduct-disordered boys showing higher scores than the girls on the mood and withdrawal dimensions (i.e. the boys tended to be more moody and withdrawn than the girls). The differences between the diagnostic groups were not as clear-cut as with the junior children. Thus, among the boys in both groups, none of the differences between behavioural and temperamental dimensions achieved significance. Among the girls, though, the neurotic group showed higher scores on both the neurotic and the somatic-developmental dimensions, and also on the temperamental dimensions of activity and mood.

THE SCHOOL MEASURES

The Rutter B2 behaviour scale reflected the high rate of disturbance in school among both the junior and senior pupils. In the juniors slightly under one-third and in the seniors over one-third of the children exceeded the cut-off score on the Rutter total scale. In the juniors nearly 10 per cent of the sample showed a marked degree of absenteeism from school.

The scores derived from the Devereux Classroom Behaviour Scale were, in general, high compared with published norms. Thus, in both the junior and senior schoolchildren more than 25 per cent scored more than one standard deviation above the mean in the areas of classroom disturbance, impatience, disrespect, external blame, achievement anxiety, external reliance, inattention/withdrawal, irrelevant responsiveness, inability to change, quitting, and slow work. In contrast, low scores were noted in the areas of comprehension, creative initiative, and the need for closeness.

The sociometric measures revealed the extent to which the children experienced difficulties in peer relationships. Among the juniors 31 per cent of the children were not chosen as a friend by more than one child in the class (many by none), whereas 22 per cent were rejected by fifteen or more children in the class. With the seniors the situation was slightly worse: 34 per cent of the children were isolated and 29 per cent were rejected. In addition, the senior children completed the self-report Junior Eysenck Personality Inventory. Eleven per cent of them scored more than one and a half standard deviations above the mean on neuroticism.

Regarding ability and attainment there was a downward skew in the juniors in comparison with national norms. On the Moray House Picture Test 62 per cent of the children sampled scored an IQ of below 100 on the non-verbal test and 79 per cent on the verbal test. Eighty-two per cent of the children scored below 100 on the reading quotient derived from the Holborn Test, and 85 per cent on that derived from the Young Group Reading Test. In the case of the senior children we used an ability for which there are no published norms, but this was not important as they were used solely as change measures.

Only the senior children were given the Barker Lunn School Attitude Scale. Again, there were very definite trends in the results when compared with available norms. More than 25 per cent scored more than one standard deviation below the mean on attitude to school, interest in school work, relationship with teacher, anxiety in class, and social adjustment, whereas the normal control groups, as a whole, scored high on attitude to class and academic self-image.

THE CLINICAL PICTURE

In the case of both junior and senior pupils clinical measures of overall severity and assessment of severity on the conduct and neurotic dimensions of behaviour usually revealed similar patterns (see *Figs 4(3)–4(8)*, pp. 76–9). There were, however, some clear-cut differences and these constituted good reasons for the use of statistical techniques of evaluation that made allowance for such initial differences in the case of both outcome and improvement.

The therapists

A most important group of people, who should not be overlooked, were the therapists who participated in the various aspects of the study. This group comprised six social workers, who took part in the parent counselling-teacher consultation, and in group therapy, and playgroup programmes, and the seven teacher-aides who took part in the nurture work programme. The teacher-aides are described in Chapter 6.

The social workers were all university graduates who had additional general social work training. Their previous experience varied: two had just completed courses; two had experience in probationary work; one had already carried out some research on school social work; one had general social work experience.

As the level and type of experience was diverse and only relevant to the study in a general way, a specific programme of training was set up for the social workers. Part of this programme consisted of looking at the school as an organization, and also at various ways of approaching the problems of maladjustment. For these sections of the training programme, clinical cases were taken on for assessment and treatment under the supervision of clinical psychiatrists, psychologists, and social workers. There was also a programme of seminars on various aspects of the literature, and the social workers attended a course of sensitivity groups conducted by Dr W. Brough and colleagues. There were also other specific areas of training and these are dealt with in more detail in the appropriate chapters.

During the course of the project a series of measures were made of the therapeutic qualities of the social workers. (a) During the senior group counselling programme external observers sat in on one of the sessions of each of the seventeen groups. They made ratings of the therapist qualities of accurate empathy, non-possessive warmth, and genuineness. The scales were modifications of those used by Truax and Carkhuff (1967). They also rated the group characteristics of cohesiveness and openness of discussion. (b) Supervisors made ratings of seventeen characteristics thought to be pertinent to the social workers' therapeutic effectiveness. It was found that these characteristics could be reliably assessed by different raters (Nicol et al. 1977). The characteristics were confidence, persuasiveness, warmth, empathy, relationships with colleagues, relationship to authority, clinical judgement, social judgement, openness, charm, friendliness, neuroticism, genuineness, extroversion, non-partisan approach, positive attitude to psychotherapy, and assertiveness.

We have already reported (Nicol *et al*. 1977) that the direct ratings of therapist qualities correlated highly with the supervisor ratings and that there were persistent differences between the therapists on the ratings. The correlations between the therapist ratings and those of the counselling groups (i.e. cohesiveness and openness of discussion) were, on the other hand, rather low. This supported the contention that we were measuring qualities attributable to the therapists themselves, rather than to the interaction or to the children.

Further measures were made of the therapists' reactions to the children in their groups. It was found that those who scored low on measures of empathy and warmth viewed their young clients in a more negative and pessimistic way than those who had high scores.

We can conclude that, although all were fully competent professionally, there were stable differences between the therapists. Such a conclusion makes it possible to identify those qualities of therapists that are related to outcome. This topic has been dealt with in Chapter 2 and Appendix 4.

Figure 4(3)   Current state as clinically assessed: juniors: parent counselling-teacher consultation

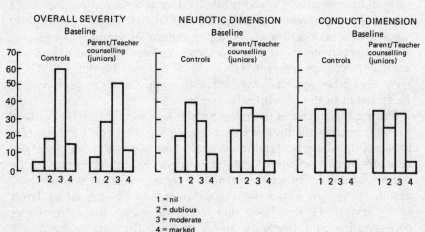

Figure 4(4)   Current state as clinically assessed: juniors: nurture work

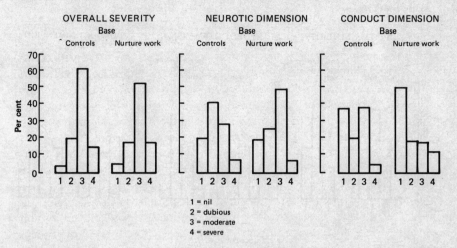

1 = nil
2 = dubious
3 = moderate
4 = severe

Figure 4(5)   Current state as clinically assessed: juniors: playgroups

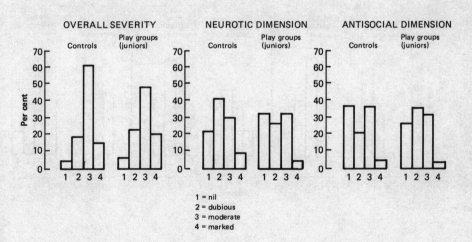

1 = nil
2 = dubious
3 = moderate
4 = marked

Figure 4(6)   Current state as clinically assessed: seniors: parent counselling-teacher consultation

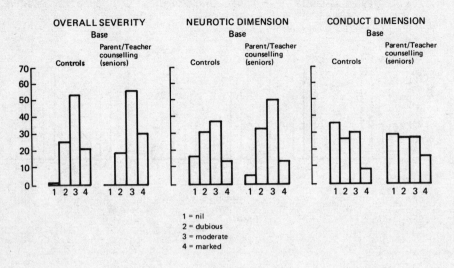

1 = nil
2 = dubious
3 = moderate
4 = marked

Figure 4(7)   Current state as clinically assessed: seniors: behaviour modification

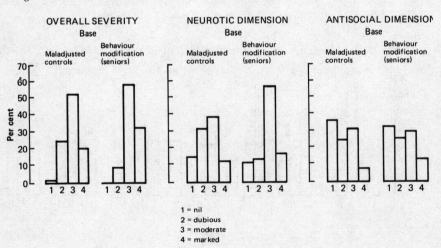

1 = nil
2 = dubious
3 = moderate
4 = marked

Figure 4(8)   Current state as clinically assessed: seniors: group therapy

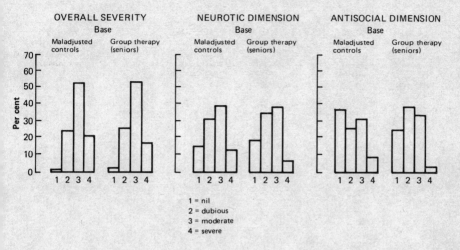

1 = nil
2 = dubious
3 = moderate
4 = severe

Part Three
Treatment approaches

5 Behaviour modification approach

Summary

We review the literature describing previous work on modification of behaviour in the classroom and through this see that it may be necessary to encourage and train teachers to change their style of classroom management, so that they emphasize praise for good behaviour, rather than disapproval of bad behaviour. In some cases rewards such as sweets and toys may be necessary in addition to praise and attention from the teacher. Improved academic achievement is often, but not necessarily, correlated with improved classroom behaviour. Children's interpersonal relationships may also be improved by behaviour modification techniques. It must be remembered, though, that classroom conditions in this country are not equivalent to the model settings in which much of the successful American research work has taken place.

We go on to discuss related issues, such as whether changed behaviour is maintained after treatment and in different settings, and whether types of behaviour other than those specifically treated may also change.

We describe five main components in training teachers to modify children's behaviour in the classroom. These are: instructional methods; feedback; social reinforcement; token reinforcement; and modelling. In order to have the best effect on the behaviour of the children in their classes it is important that teachers maintain their new techniques.

We go on to describe the methods used in our own behaviour modification programme, which were designed to illuminate some of the issues mentioned above. The project took place over a twenty-week period in ordinary secondary schools – the 'natural environment' as opposed to an artificial research setting. Relatively large numbers of children and teachers were involved: the seventy-two children were roughly representative of the range of problem children in the school population, and the thirty-nine teachers were also fairly representative. Unlike most previous workers in this area, we used multiple measures of behaviour change and carried out long-term follow-up assessments in order to determine the persistence of treatment effects. A further important feature of our study was an attempt to reduce teacher training and consultation time to an absolute minimum.

The treatment methods in our project made extensive use of techniques of social reinforcement – praise, attention, and approval from the teacher were encouraged rather than the use of material rewards, although these were given in a few cases. We were careful to define the types of problem behaviour being treated, to specify successive steps through which a child might be expected to progress, and to pinpoint ultimate objectives closely allied to observable behaviour. Teachers were also encouraged to identify causes and effects of misbehaviour. In the hope that the effects of treatment would be maintained, written reports and suggestions for each child were provided for the teachers at the end of the programme. Efforts to involve parents were unsuccessful.

We attempted to test the importance of the neurotic/conduct disorder classification in relation to children's changes in behaviour as evaluated by teachers. We looked at the child's social and personal adjustment, academic progress, and academic motivation. In a substantial percentage of cases improvement was noted in each of these four dimensions. While no firm conclusions could be drawn concerning the relevance of the diagnostic categories in this context, those comparisons in which significant differences or trends were found favoured girls and also neurotic children of either sex.

Assessment of teacher motivation suggested that children taught by well-motivated teachers had the best results. Direct observation in the classroom suggested that children's task-related behaviour improved as a result of treatment, although no change in teachers' behaviour was demonstrated by this method of observation.

Independent evaluations comprised: (a) psychiatric ratings of outcome; (b) covariance analysis of improvement; and (c) comparison of selected sub-groups of children. These comparisons, drawn at the three follow-up stages, showed that there were some changes in responses in areas that were not specific targets of treatment. Second, the effects of behaviour modification could be detected up to two-

and-a-half years after the end of treatment. Third, the effects of treatment were ultimately apparent in the home, as well as at school. Fourth, changes were apparent to the child, to his or her peers, teachers, and parents.

Introduction

Research into behaviour modification in the classroom has mushroomed in recent years, as it has in other settings with a wide range of child and adult problem behaviours. There are several reasons for this. The first, and probably the most cogent reason, is the effectiveness of behavioural techniques in classroom management in influencing different types of social and academic behaviour. Second, the techniques can easily be used by teachers, not only in one-to-one or small group situations, but also with the more typical classroom size of thirty or so children. Third, not only do behavioural techniques complement regular teaching activities, they can also be seen to have an affinity with basic educational principles – many of the teacher's concerns, such as specifying objectives for learning, arranging for these to be gradually and systematically approached, and harnessing pupils' motivation, are also those of the behaviour modifier.

With the early applications of behaviour modification, as with most new fields of therapeutic endeavour, successes tended perhaps to be exaggerated and magnified. While research continues apace, the early over-optimism has been tempered and the real difficulties that confront behavioural applications in natural settings, away from the rarefied atmosphere of the laboratory or well-funded research projects, are being confronted. Many questions are still to be answered. For example, how can change procedures be designed to provide the best opportunities for maintaining improvement and ensuring that it transfers across settings? Which types of behaviour are the most appropriate targets for intervention? What is the most effective way of teaching the application of behavioural techniques? Once taught, how can continued application be ensured? Can programmes be developed that will fit readily into regular educational settings where the availability of professional manpower and consultation is minimal? In such settings how does a school's organization and administration impinge on an intervention programme? These are some of the difficult issues that face current workers, and to which answers must be provided if the promise of behaviour modification is to be fulfilled.

A review of the literature

In this review we discuss previous results of behavioural intervention for inappropriate classroom behaviour, academic behaviour, and problems of social interaction, and then we examine some critical current issues in research. The review is not intended to be exhaustive and will highlight issues pertinent to the current study. Comprehensive reviews are available in Sherman and Bushell (1974); O'Leary and O'Leary (1976); Nietzel *et al.* (1977), and O'Leary (1978).

For a full description of the form taken by classroom behaviour modification programmes see Macmillan (1976), Meacham and Wiesen (1974), Macmillan and Kolvin (1977a), and the descriptive account of our own programme in this chapter. The essence of classroom behaviour modification lies in the precise and unambiguous definition of types of behaviour to be changed, the specification of objectives and how they are to be approached, and the restructuring of environmental influences, both antecedent and consequent, in order to bring about the desired modification of behaviour.

INTERVENTION FOR PROBLEMS OF INAPPROPRIATE CLASSROOM BEHAVIOUR

Probably the most widely used technique in classroom behaviour modification has involved changing the ways in which teachers make use of praise, disapproval, and the withholding of attention. This is not surprising, given that all teachers use some such elements of social reinforcement, even though the procedures are not always used adequately or appropriately.

Some researchers have characterized the classroom as a

'barren wasteland when one compares it with other normally reinforcing interactions. Most of the reinforcers in the system are highly formalized, such as grades and test scores. The control of social behaviour is achieved more as a function of threatened or applied aversive consequences than by positive social reinforcers.'

(Patterson *et al.* 1969:15)

White's (1975) results suggested that, after the first and second grades, the use of teacher approval diminishes and is consistently exceeded by the use of disapproval. Similarly, a large survey of public school teachers in Florida showed that 77 per cent of their interactions with children were negative while only 23 per cent were positive (Madsen *et al.* 1970). A common explanation of these findings is that disapproval and reprimands, by tending to stop misbehaviour immediately (although temporarily) have become popular techniques with the teacher. This seems to be an unfortunate trap because, in the long run, continued use of high disapproval rates may be quite ineffective in management and attention to undesirable behaviour may have quite the opposite effect to that intended (Madsen *et al.* 1968a; Thomas, Becker, and Armstrong 1968). For example, in the former study, with a teacher trying to control out-of-seat behaviour, an increase in 'sit-down' commands actually led to an increase in out-of-seat behaviour.

It seems, then, that a shift to more positive forms of control, with emphasis on increased use of approval, may require a major change in teacher behaviour. The technique of social reinforcement may appear deceptively simple, but the extent of change required, on the teacher's part, should not be minimized – teachers have their own established patterns of behaviour, their own reinforcement history, and these cannot be easily discarded and laid aside (Hall *et al.* 1968b, in the USA; Ward 1971, in the UK). However, many studies are now available that point to the benefits, for both teachers and children, that may accrue from the skilled and sensitive use of social reinforcement. Many of the early pioneering studies were conducted in pre-school settings, and illustrated the use of reinforcement (for example, praise, attention, or verbal approval) following desired or appropriate behaviour, or the delivery of a reprimand following undesirable behaviour. These studies suggested that social reinforcement techniques could be employed effectively in the reduction of crying (Hart *et al.* 1964) and in the development of more active motor skills (Johnston *et al.* 1966).

Early work of this nature provided a stimulus and a model for subequent investigators: similar techniques both continued to be applied in pre-school settings (e.g. Brown and Elliott 1965; Buell *et al.* 1968; Allen, Turner, and Everett 1970) and were extended to include applications with older children in ordinary primary and secondary schools. Madsen, Becker, and Thomas (1968b), for example, working in a public elementary school in the USA, chose two children with problem behaviour from two separate classrooms, one with twenty-nine children, the other with twenty. After a baseline phase, three experimental components – rules, ignoring disruptive behaviour, and praise for appropriate behaviour – that had been found effective in combination in an earlier study (Becker *et al.* 1967) were introduced sequentially. It was found that rules alone were ineffective, and the rules and ignoring phase was associated with increased disruption. When praise for appropriate behaviour was added to the two other elements, inappropriate behaviour fell from a 70 per cent baseline level to about 30 per cent. Reversal to baseline conditions produced a corresponding increase in inappropriate behaviour, whereas re-instatement of all three experimental components restored satisfactory levels, thus demonstrating their effectiveness. Although the authors pointed to the success of combined praising and ignoring procedures and suggested that praise for appropriate behaviour is probably the key to effective classroom management, it must be stressed that their experimental design, by cumulatively combining procedures, rather than using them separately, made drawing clear-cut conclusions difficult. Nevertheless, this was a seminal study. Numerous subsequent projects have successfully exploited the systematic use of teacher attention to increase study, on-task behaviour, and desirable social behaviour (e.g. Hall, Lund, and Jackson 1968a; Hall *et al*. 1968b; Wasik *et al*. 1969; Broden *et al*. 1970; Breyer, Calchera, and Cann 1971; Peterson, Cox, and Bijou 1971). Other studies have focused on the reduction of disruptive conduct, such as noisy behaviour or talking in class, tantrums, and aggression (Thomas, Becker, and Armstrong 1968; Ward and Baker 1968; McAllister *et al* 1969; Hall *et al*. 1971; Lates, Egner, and McKenzie 1971).

As O'Leary and O'Leary (1976) have pointed out, the effectiveness of experimentally manipulated teacher attention has been demonstrated with a wide range of subject populations in a variety of contexts, ranging in age from pre-school (Schutte and Hopkins 1970) to twelfth grade (*c.* seventeen years) (McAllister *et al*. 1969), from classes of three children (Zimmerman and Zimmerman 1962) to classes of thirty-nine (Hall, Lund, and Jackson 1968a), and from normal classes (Madsen *et al*. 1968b) to classes for the retarded (Hall *et al*. 1971). Some studies focused on only one child in a class (e.g. Kirby and Shields 1972), while others included the behaviour of an entire group (Hall *et al*. 1968b).

We have already mentioned the possible undesirable effects of teacher disapproval: nevertheless, some of the studies cited above demonstrated its effectiveness when used in conjunction with praise and approval. Ignoring a child may not always be sufficient action to extinguish inappropriate behaviour, and stronger intervention may be necessary. McAllister *et al*. (1969) for example, achieved significant improvement in children's talking-out and turning-around behaviours with a combination of praise to the class as a whole for appropriate behaviour and disapproval to individuals every time they talked out of turn or turned around. Thus, selective use of disapproval may be beneficial and, indeed, such negative forms of intervention clearly cannot be ruled out when learning is being disrupted, or when a child may be hurt by another's aggressive behaviour. In this connection, Madsen *et al*. (1970) have suggested that it is the ratio between positive and negative methods that is important. They advised a 4:1 positive to negative ratio as the optimum, although no data were presented to support this recommendation. Given that disapproval is necessary and inevitable, studies by O'Leary and Becker (1968) and O'Leary *et al.* (1970) suggested that soft reprimands, audible only to the offending child, are more effective in reducing disruptive behaviour than loud ones audible to the whole class. The latter may well give the miscreant an undesirable spot in the limelight, or create a 'ripple effect' (Kounin 1970) where surrounding children are affected by the scolding.

Most intervention involving social reinforcement has been in primary schools, and there is a relative dearth of studies with secondary schoolchildren. However, the behaviour of the secondary-school-age child is equally modifiable, as studies by McAllister *et al.* (1969), Atkinson, Davis, and Sanborn (1972), and Cormier and Wahler (1973) have demonstrated.

What is it that makes teacher attention so effective? Apart from its reinforcement or incentive value for children it may also have an informational function in cueing the child to behave in a particular way, especially when it is specific ('I'm pleased that you are asking more questions in class, Billy') rather than vague ('You've been a good boy today'). There is also the opportunity for observational learning by other children, so that the child who is praised acts as a 'model' of desired behaviour in the classroom (Broden *et al.* 1970). Much work remains to be done in identifying accurately the critical ingredients of social reinforcement. In addition to the suggestions above, other factors that need consideration are the proximity of the teacher, and the general effect of reducing disruption in the classroom. We have suggested earlier that the apparent simplicity of applying social reinforcement may be deceptive; it is equally clear that theoretical questions remain.

One fundamental drawback in the use of social reinforcement is that it may not be sufficiently powerful with some children. Teacher praise may, in fact, be aversive in some cases. In such situations the use of token procedures (rewarding with points or tokens exchangeable for a range of attractive reinforcers – sweets, access to preferred activities, choice of toys, etc.) in addition to the systematic use of teacher attention is likely to be more effective. It is worth stressing that it is desirable to make use of tokens in addition to and not instead of teacher praise and attention. Tokens, and the rewards to which they lead, are essentially props that facilitate behaviour change. The intention of such a programme, and the task facing the person administering it, is to bring the resulting behaviour change under the control of natural variables in the child's environment, and appropriate use of teacher attention has a critical role here that must not be dismissed.

That token programmes are potentially more powerful than teacher attention alone was demonstrated in a study by O'Leary *et al.* (1969). Working in a second-grade class with seven problem children, aged about seven years, who were prone to wander around hitting other children and making a noise, they found that a combination of rules, altered classroom structure, and praise-and-ignore techniques were generally ineffective in reducing disruptive behaviour. Significant improvements were recorded with the introduction of a token programme. Many other reports are available that support the impact of token procedures in increasing task attention (Bushell, Wrobel, and Michaelis 1968; Broden *et al.* 1970; Sulzer *et al.* 1971; Ferritor *et al.* 1972) as well as reducing negative, disruptive, and deviant behaviour (O'Leary and Becker 1967; Carlson *et al.* 1968; Kuypers, Becker, and O'Leary 1968; Walker and Buckley 1968; Wolf *et al.* 1970). A number of classroom token programmes have taken the form of the 'good behaviour game', which employs groups rather than individuals (Barrish, Saunders, and Wolf 1969; Harris and Sherman 1973). The 'game' consists of dividing the class into groups that earn or lose points according to their behaviour. The group that earns most points (or loses least) wins the reinforcing event.

The use of token procedures in the ordinary classroom may seem alien and irrelevant to many (see Kuypers, Becker, and O'Leary 1968; O'Leary and Drabman 1971). However, in a useful recent review, McLaughlin (1975) has suggested that token systems can be readily adapted to regular classrooms. He pointed to the importance of such aspects as ease of implementation and management, low costs, compatibility with school and community attitudes, and pupil satisfaction in determining the viability of programmes.

It is possible that the behaviour of secondary-school-age children is more readily modified by token reinforcement than by the use of teacher praise and attention (Nolen, Kunzelmann, and Haring 1967; Meichenbaum, Bowers, and Ross 1968: Lovitt and Curtiss 1969; Williams, Long, and Yoakley 1972; Blanchard and Johnson 1973; Main and Munro 1975). Heaton *et al.* (1976), in a recent intervention with junior-high-school students, demonstrated the effectiveness of a token reinforcement programme (by comparing treated children with a control group in traditional schooling) in reducing misbehaviour and suspension from school, as well as in increasing academic achievement. Possibly the largest-scale application of token procedures was that undertaken in the USA by Rollins *et al.* (1974), which incorporated secondary-school-age as well as elementary-school-age children. This was an ambitious study, involving over 700 subjects in sixteen experimental classes and fourteen control classes. Children in the experimental classes received tokens (exchangeable for sweets, toys, school supplies, and activities) for attentive classroom behaviour, and over the several months of the programme measures of disruptive and on-task behaviour showed their superiority over the controls in improvement of conduct. They also gained more than the controls on measures of IQ and academic achievement.

A further technique used to control inappropriate and disruptive behaviour is time-out, which involves placing the child in temporary social isolation following misbehaviour. Theoretical and ethical issues in its use were discussed by Macmillan, Forness, and Trumbull (1973) and Gast and Nelson (1977).

INTERVENTION FOR PROBLEMS OF ACADEMIC BEHAVIOUR

There are comparatively few studies demonstrating the effectiveness of teacher attention on academic achievement, which has more commonly been promoted through the introduction of token procedures. A rare exception is Stromer's study (1977) which successfully employed praise, with correctness feedback and modelling, to modify letter and number reversal difficulties in children from regular and special education classes.

Most classroom studies that focus on academic behaviour have employed some form of token reinforcement system. An early venture into the classroom by Wolf, Giles, and Hall (1968) showed the effects of token procedures in an after-school remedial programme for sixteen fifth and sixth graders (ten and eleven years of age) who were at least two years below reading norms and who were chronic low achievers. These children gained 1.5 years on the Stanford Achievement Test, while a matched comparison group gained 0.8 years in the same time. Similar impressive gains have been reported in remedial settings by Clark, Lachowicz, and Wolf (1968) and Kaufman and O'Leary (1972).

Hewett, Taylor, and Artuso (1969) rewarded an experimental classroom group of emotionally disturbed children with check marks (leading to tangible rewards like sweets, prizes, and extra time in arts and crafts) for being on time, following directions, and correctly completing assignments, and obtained significant gains in mathematics, but not in reading and spelling. In addition to improvements in basic reading and arithmetic achievement, gains in quality of handwriting, creative writing, and vocabulary have been reported (see O'Leary (1978) for review).

Token reinforcement systems can have as strong an effect on secondary-school-age children's academic behaviour as they had on their social behaviour (e.g. Glynn 1970; Chadwick and Day 1971; Kirby and Shields 1972). Sherman and Bushell (1974) suggested that no clear line can be drawn between investigations of classroom social and disruptive behaviour and those that concentrate on academic performance. However, much discussion has been directed at the question of whether it is best to modify social behaviour such as task attention, compliance, listening to instructions, etc., with the expectation that this will generate academic gains, or attempt to reinforce academic behaviour directly. This question is part of a wider debate within behaviour modification as to the appropriateness of behaviours selected as targets (Winett and Winkler 1972; Emery and Marholin 1977).

A number of workers have documented the extent to which academic achievement and social behaviour are correlated. Thus rating-scale behaviour such as attention, persistence to task, compliance with teacher demands, and ability to follow directions has been found to correlate highly with various achievement measures and teacher grades (Davidson and Greenberg 1967; Swift and Spivack 1968, 1969). Longitudinal studies have demonstrated the utility of teacher ratings of 'attention' and 'co-operation' in predicting later achievement (Meyers, Atwell, and Orpet 1968) and the extent to which aggressive and disruptive behaviour can forecast academic failure (Feldhusen, Thurston, and Benning 1970). Attention and attending behaviour are repeatedly highlighted as important to academic success (Lahaderne 1968; Bryan 1974). Cobb and his colleagues (Cobb 1970, 1972; Hops and Cobb 1973) argued that these are 'not academic behaviours per se, but rather, the first components in a chain of correct academic responding' (Hops and Cobb 1973:196). They view them as 'survival skills', necessary, though not sufficient, for successful academic functioning. If these survival skills can be improved and strengthened, academic gains will follow. This hypothesis has been supported for reading achievement (Cobb and Hops 1973; Hops and Cobb 1973) and maths (Walker and Hops 1977).

Evidence also exists, however, to show that increasing attentive or reducing disruptive behaviour does not necessarily have an effect on academic performance (Ferritor et al. 1972; Harris and Sherman 1974; Marholin et al. 1975). If one wishes to modify academic behaviour it may be best to reinforce academic behaviour directly in the form of gains on tests or achievement measures. This has been found to not only improve academic behaviour but also to increase attentive and decrease disruptive conduct (Ayllon, Layman, and Burke 1972;

Winett and Roach 1973; Ayllon and Roberts 1974). While the evidence here is conflicting, it is clear that the selection of target behaviours for modification must be carried out with care and with consideration of their potential value, if improved, for the child, as well as for the teacher.

INTERVENTION FOR PROBLEMS OF SOCIAL INTERACTION

In addition to coping with academic requirements and demands for behavioural control in their school life, children also have to acquire the skills that make for effective interpersonal relationships in their peer group. Poor peer relations predict subsequent disturbance (Combs and Slaby 1977; Macmillan *et al.* 1978) and it is therefore important to cope with these difficulties at an early stage.

Dissatisfaction has been expressed with methods in this area, which rely heavily on adult-administered techniques. Strain, Cooke, and Apolloni (1976) suggested that the methods require continuous teacher presence if the effects are not to disappear, and, additionally, that effects are liable to be beneficial only inconsistently as children move around a variety of classroom environments. Adults intervening to provide reinforcement for interaction may well interfere with and disrupt the interaction (O'Connor 1972) and considerable skill may be called for in providing sensitive reinforcement (Roedell, Slaby, and Robinson 1977). Some approaches depend on the occurrence of desired behaviour, or approximations to it, which can then be reinforced and gradually shaped. If relied on exclusively, these methods may be excessively time-consuming, or with extremes of isolated or aggressive behaviours, unfeasible. They are also limited where new or complex social skills need to be taught, such as the skills involved in initiating interaction or solving social conflict. Finally, adult-dependent methods disregard the critical contribution of peers in social interaction and the central role of the reinforcement that they provide.

A number of studies are available that overcome some of these difficulties. Modelling and shaping methods have been used successfully (O'Connor 1972; Evers and Schwarz 1973) but their results have not been consistently replicated (Gottman 1977).

Gottman, Gonso, and Schuler (1976) elaborated the modelling method by adding a social skills training package. This programme sought to teach skills that were found to play an important part in the discrimination between popular and unpopular children and that contributed to effective social functioning. Nine weeks after the intervention significant changes in sociometric position were reported for the subjects.

Allen *et al.* (1975) undertook behaviour modification in groups of sociometric isolates, meeting on a weekly basis about thirteen to seventeen times for sessions lasting fifty minutes each. The programme proceeded in three phases: (a) simple interactive games; (b) games emphasizing poise and flexibility within a social group; and (c) social play outside the group, in the playground. Children were reinforced with tokens for appropriate behaviour. Sociometric measures at the end of term and at follow-up five months later showed significant gains for the twenty-three treatment children, while untreated controls showed only minimal changes.

The value of taking the role of peers into account and stressing the reciprocal nature of interaction is apparent in the work of Walker and Hops (1973). Working with isolated children, they showed that interaction could be increased by rewarding (with points exchangeable for back-up reinforcers) both the withdrawn child and his or her classroom peers.

There are a number of procedures, not central to the concerns of the present study, that are receiving increasing research attention. These involve: (a) the use of group contingencies (Litow and Pumroy 1975); (b) the use of children as agents of change in the classroom, to modify both peer behaviour (e.g. Drabman 1973; Solomon and Wahler 1973) and teacher behaviour (e.g. Sherman and Cormier 1974); and (c) efforts to teach children methods of self-control, self-evaluation, and self-reinforcement (see Nietzel *et al.* 1977 for review).

The foregoing review demonstrated the potential impact of a variety of behavioural procedures in altering children's behaviour in the classroom. While the capacity of treatment to change behaviour is not in doubt, there are a number of issues in the literature on behaviour modification that deserve further attention and these are discussed below.

GENERALIZATION

The question of generalization is a major one for all applications of behaviour modification. It involves three basic issues. First, can changed behaviour be maintained after treatment ends? Second, can it transfer to settings other than the treatment setting? Third, can change be observed in behaviours that were not the specific targets of treatment?

Although a number of studies have demonstrated persistence and transfer of behavioural changes these are in the minority and reversal to pre-intervention levels has been the more typical pattern (Kazdin and Bootzin 1972; Marholin, Siegel, and Phillips 1976; Stokes and Baer 1977). Paradoxical as it may sound, generalization failures are quite consistent with operant theory. If behaviour is a function of its consequences, then it will adjust to the influences prevailing in a given situation. If supportive reinforcement is withdrawn (as with termination of treatment or transfer to an unprogrammed setting) then the behaviour in question will probably decrease in strength.

MAINTENANCE

It is clear that there is a dearth of studies of maintenance in classroom work. Kauffmann, Nussen, and McGee (1977) surveyed 152 separate experiments conducted in classroom or educational settings between 1968 and 1974, and found that 72 per cent reported no follow-up data whatsoever. In the other 28 per cent, follow-up data were based on verbal reports (28 per cent), behavioural observations (54 per cent), or standardized testings (18 per cent). For studies relying upon verbal reports the average follow-up duration was 107 days, but only eighteen days for studies in which behavioural observations were employed. Thirty-six of the forty-two experiments in which follow-up data were reported showed effective maintenance. Less encouragingly, though, follow-up data were included in a greater percentage of studies published before 1971 than in those published subsequently. The paucity of follow-up studies is not restricted to classroom projects in behaviour modification but is prevalent to an equal extent in other areas, too (Cochrane and Sobell 1976; Keeley, Shemberg, and Carbonnel 1976).

The importance of securing control group data when maintenance is assessed was shown in an important study by Kent and O'Leary (1976). A standardized twenty-hour treatment programme involving the child, his or her parents, and teachers was evaluated, emphasizing social reinforcement from the teacher and special home-based rewards and privileges contingent upon school performance. Relative to no-treatment controls, the treated children had improved significantly on observational and rating measures by the end of treatment, but at the nine-month follow-up gains by the control group wiped out these differences. However, treated children showed better achievement scores and grades at follow-up than did the controls, though this was not maintained to the end of the study. Despite this long-term effect, it has been found in many classroom programmes that, once reinforcing contingencies are withdrawn, behavioural gains tend to dissipate (Birnbrauer et al. 1965; Kuypers et al. 1968; O'Leary et al. 1969) and behaviour change may not persist even into times of the day when programmes are not in effect (Kuypers et al. 1968; Meichenbaum, Bowers, and Ross 1968; Wolf, Giles, and Hall 1968).

TRANSFER

Few studies have been designed to find out whether a change in behaviour in one setting results in a similar change in other settings where a programme is not in operation. In educational environments it is important to know if programmes in one classroom have implications for children's behaviour in others, if gains in 'special' class or school settings transfer to regular settings, and if improved behaviour in school transfers to the home. As with maintenance, training effects have been found to tend not to transfer across settings (e.g. Kuypers *et al*. 1968; O'Leary *et al*. 1969; Broden *et al*. 1970). These discouraging findings are hardly surprising in view of the situation specificity of behaviour (Mischel 1968). Where problem behaviour exists in two settings, intervention may be necessary in both. Thus, Wahler (1969), working with two boys showing deviant behaviour in home and school, found that modifying behaviour in the home did not result in corresponding changes in school. Change did not occur in the classroom until procedures of differential attention similar to those applied in the home were extended to the school. Even with less dissimilar settings transfer may not occur. Glavin, Quay, and Werry (1971), in the USA, employed a token system to reduce disruptive behaviour and increase task-related behaviour in a special classroom for elementary children. The improvements obtained in this setting were not observed on return to the regular classroom, and behavioural and academic gains were not maintained at the two- to three-year follow-up (Glavin 1974).

CHANGES IN BEHAVIOURS OTHER THAN SPECIFIC TARGETS
OF TREATMENT

The optimist who looks for maintenance and transfer of treatment effects also looks for a spread of effects to responses other than the ones targeted during a programme. Behaviour modification has perhaps been excessively concerned with measuring only responses that have been the focus of treatment; the need for greater attention to multiple response evaluation has been expressed recently (McNamara 1975). As well as being concerned with positive transfer to other behaviours we should also, of course, be aware of the possibility of negative side effects. Prompted by the latter concern, Ward and Baker (1968) found neither positive nor negative effects in the Wechsler Intelligence Scale for Children (WISC), projective questionnaire, and Draw-a-Person scores following a programme involving changes in teacher attention. However, Twardosz and Sajwaj (1972) obtained gains in social interaction when reinforcing in-seat behaviour. The studies examined earlier in this chapter, which show achievement of IQ gains following reinforcement of attentional or task-related behaviour, have provided evidence on the wider effects that may ensue from treatment, but these results are not always obtained. In a rare attempt to measure children's attitude changes associated with participation in a classroom behavioural programme, Buys (1972) found that children perceived their teachers as liking them more, became more positive in their own attitude towards the teachers, but evaluated being good in class in a more negative manner.

PROGRAMMING FOR MAINTENANCE AND TRANSFER

The message here seems to be clear, and it is conveyed in the frequently quoted but less frequently implemented suggestion that 'generalization should be programmed rather than expected or lamented' (Baer, Wolf, and Risley 1968:97). The picture is not entirely bleak, however, and with the growing concern with these issues methods for promoting maintenance and transfer have multiplied. Some positive findings are emerging, and these can be considered in the light of the particular techniques employed.

The first of these techniques involves the development of types of behaviour that are likely to be maintained by the natural environment, as reflected in the suggestion by Baer and Wolf (1972) of a 'behavioural trap': if behaviour can be developed, even through artificial or contrived means, it may then be naturally supported and maintained by the consequences (for example, praise and attention) it elicits. Allen *et al.* (1964), for example, found that after increasing a withdrawn child's interactions, removal of attention did not result in relapse – the behaviour may have been maintained as a function of the 'trap' of social interaction.

Second, attempts can be made to substitute one programme for another. For instance, Walker, Hops, and Johnson (1975), returning children to a regular class setting from a special education, token economy classroom, compared a substitute programme having natural reinforcers (praise, grades) with a control condition with no programme in effect. Children with the substitute programme maintained their behaviour better than did those without one and, when all programming was withdrawn, the former group's superiority was evident at the four-month follow-up. Substitution of one programme for another is not strictly a maintenance strategy – the programme still only showed that its implementation altered behaviour in the subsequent setting.

A third measure for promoting maintenance and transfer is to gradually remove or thin out the reinforcement being provided. After controlling disruptive behaviour in an adjustment class with token reinforcement procedures, Drabman, Spitalnik, and O'Leary (1973) gradually faded out the teacher rating by which point-earning was determined. During a final phase in which no checks were made by the teacher – unfortunately a brief twelve days – appropriate levels of behaviour were maintained. Similarly, Turkewitz, O'Leary, and Ironsmith (1976) faded out back-up reinforcers and found maintained behavioural improvement after the reinforcers were completely withdrawn, albeit for the relatively short period of five days. Greenwood, Hops, and Walker (1977) obtained substantial maintenance over a nine-week period following cessation of formal intervention procedures by phasing out the specific behavioural programme materials, the classroom rules, and a class bar graph indicating daily progress. Phasing out may, to some extent, involve periods of intermittent or irregular reinforcement, a technique that is traditionally recommended where maintenance is sought. It may also be implicit in the fourth strategy of delaying delivery of reinforcement. Greenwood *et al.* (1974) gradually increased the number of sessions before reinforcement could be earned, and maintained appropriate behaviour at the three-week follow-up.

A fifth method for seeking maintenance of treatment effects, and one that is gaining in popularity, is the use of self-reinforcement. Theoretically, if a child can become relatively independent of external reinforcement and can control his or her own behaviour, gains may not disappear once programmes come to an end. However, when attempts are made to replace external reinforcement by self-reinforcement, excessive leniency in self-reward may result (Santogrossi *et al.* 1973). This is not always the case, however. In the study already cited, by Drabman, Spitalnik, and O'Leary (1973), children had complete control over reinforcement administration in the successful twelve-day phase when teacher management was eliminated. Bolstad and Johnson (1972) showed that self-administered points were superior to teacher-administered points in controlling disruptive behaviour, but the maintenance period was of only seven days' duration.

Finally, the involvement of parents seems essential if it is intended that effects of classroom-based programmes transfer into the homes. The extent to which parents control reinforcers for their children (for example, access to toys, play activities, TV, pocket money, etc.) underlines the potential impact of their involvement for generality of effect. Many studies have successfully involved parents to buttress school-based intervention (see Atkeson and Forehand (1978) for review), although they have not directly addressed maintenance/

transfer issues. These studies have commonly involved conveying information to parents concerning their child's behaviour in school, and then making available contingent rewards in the home. A great deal has been written about parental involvement, and the subject has been reviewed by Johnson and Katz (1973), O'Dell (1974), and Graziano (1977); its potential for the prevention of later problems, as well as for the support and enhancement of intervention conducted elsewhere, is enormous. As with other parent programmes (Chilman 1973), problems in enlistment, maintaining interest, and modifying attitudes and behaviour remain.

TEACHER TRAINING

We know that a number of techniques exist that may be successfully employed by teachers to modify children's behaviour in the classroom: the important question centres on how teachers may be most effectively trained to apply these techniques. Methods of training teachers have been reviewed recently by a number of workers (e.g. Sherman and Bushell 1974; Copeland and Hall 1976; Kazdin and Moyer 1976). While many training approaches have adopted multi-faceted procedures, a number of components that have been isolated in certain studies may be identified. Kazdin and Moyer (1976), for example, detailed five dimensions: (a) instructional methods; (b) feedback; (c) social reinforcement; (d) token reinforcement; and (e) modelling.

Instructional methods
Instructional methods, which include lectures, discussions, and course work – all generally didactic in format – are perhaps the most widely employed approach, and their popularity is reflected in the large numbers of instructional manuals now available for teachers. However, there appears to be no reliable evidence that an instructional element leads to application of behavioural techniques rather than merely permitting acquisition of knowledge of such principles and methods (Bowles and Nelson 1976).

A number of training programmes have been reported that rely heavily, although some not exclusively, on an instructional format. The Consulting Teacher Model, for example, emphasizes behavioural principles, measurement procedures, and the systematic use of reinforcement techniques (McKenzie et al. 1970).

A similar programme is the Responsive Teaching Model for graduates that usually takes the form of ten, weekly, three-hour sessions (Hall and Copeland 1972; Hall, Copeland, and Clark 1976). Graduate students lead discussion groups of about ten people and content covers recording and measurement procedures, experimental designs, the examination of learning principles and research studies, and supplementary lectures and films. Students are encouraged to apply what they have learnt by conducting experiments in their classroom and subsequently discussing them in the group sessions. It was in this way that Hall hoped students would incorporate Responsive Teaching procedures into their actual teaching situations. There is a clear awareness of the need to translate knowledge into practice in this model and, indeed, to provide the combination of practical, theoretical, and research skills that enable teachers to build on what they have learned during the course. The model's effectiveness is attested indirectly by the large number of studies that have flowed from it – Copeland and Hall (1976) reported that some sixty Responsive Teaching studies had been published, and some 2000 educators had been trained since the programme began. Both this and the McKenzie model utilize relatively traditional academic practices that are generally assumed to assist the development of rather generalized skills. In studies on neither, though, was there any analysis of specific changes in teacher behaviour as a result of their training experiences.

However, didactic procedures may be effective if supplemented with training in the situation in which the techniques are to be applied. Thus, McKeown, Adams, and Forehand (1975) found that disruption in the classroom was lessened following participation in a laboratory group, but not when only written instructional material was provided. The laboratory group afforded opportunities for supervision and reinforcement of attempted applications, feedback as to the quality of performance, shaping of teachers' behaviour, and modelling of described performance by the experimenters.

Feedback
The use of feedback is implicit in some of the models already discussed, in the context, for example, of discussion of experimental applications of procedures and selective reinforcement of teachers' efforts. In this section it will be taken to refer to the provision of information about the adequacy of performance or knowledge of results.

Feedback in training exercises usually takes the form of verbal or written reports of behaviour. Cooper, Thompson, and Baer (1970), for example, used verbal comments to one teacher and written notes to a second, referring to the teacher's frequency of praise and failure to praise appropriate child responses. Feedback was given every ten minutes and successfully increased the percentage of time both teachers spent attending to the children's appropriate behaviour. The teacher who received written notes postponed reading them until the end of the day and, interestingly, the procedure was less effective with her than with the teacher who received immediate verbal reports, possibly because of the delay in feedback. After feedback was eliminated, appropriate teacher behaviour began to decline, but data on maintenance were not collected. That the immediacy of feedback may be critical was also suggested by the failures reported in studies where graphical or verbal feedback was given at the end of the day (Rule 1972; Saudargas 1972; Cossairt, Hall, and Hopkins 1973) or every other day (Breyer and Allen 1975).

Social reinforcement

While classroom behaviour modification literature is replete with successful examples of the use of social reinforcement techniques with children, there seems to have been a remarkable reluctance to consider the experimenter's or consultant's relationship with the teacher in terms of the principle of reinforcement theory. These principles operate at *all* levels in the consultant-teacher-child interaction.

Few studies are available in which conscious use has been made of social reinforcement to enhance the effects of training. Cossairt, Hall, and Hopkins (1973) found that systematic changes in teacher behaviour were not produced by merely telling teachers after each class how often the students attended and the amount of praise given. However, praise for the teachers' performance markedly increased their use of praise in the classrooms, and student attending behaviour increased under this condition. McDonald (1973) contrasted the effect of praising teachers for their selection of certain behaviour change strategies with that of simply telling them which strategies to employ. Teachers who received praise tended to show more 'supportive' behaviours and use fewer reprimands or commands ('desist' behaviours) than those who received consultation without praise.

These studies suggested that explicit use of social reinforcement can be a potent influence on teacher behaviour. What is surprising is that so little use has been made of it.

Token reinforcement

As with social reinforcement, examples of the use of token reinforcement are somewhat limited. McNamara (1971) compared the effect of token reinforcement (points were exchangeable for cans of refreshment) with that of a response cost procedure (withdrawal of tokens) in altering teacher attention to appropriate and inappropriate child behaviour. The contingent delivery or removal of points was effective in altering teacher behaviour.

Modelling

Modelling has not been evaluated extensively in teacher training. This is despite its potential impact in conveying explicit behavioural requirements, an impact at its most forceful (Ringer 1973) when modelling is conducted in the classroom where the teacher actually functions. In Ringer's study, an investigator (model) initially took major responsibility for the administration of verbal and token reinforcement, while the teacher observed. The teacher was gradually introduced and given progressively more responsibility for administering reinforcement, while the experimenter was phased out.

Kazdin and Moyer (1976) concluded that it may be necessary to employ a variety of procedures in teacher training rather than to rely on a single approach. Modelling or role-playing may ensure implementation more readily than didactic methods. Provision of reinforcement is important in maintaining changed teacher behaviour as well as in its initial modification. Brown, Montgomery, and Barclay (1969) and Cooper, Thomson, and Baer (1970) have shown that withdrawal of reinforcement for teachers leads to their behaviour reverting to pre-training levels; this, of course, has predictable consequences for the children's conduct.

RESEARCH ENVIRONMENTS VERSUS NATURAL SETTINGS

Despite the numerous successes reported in the predominantly American literature on behavioural modification, concern has been expressed that the almost exclusive research framework of the studies makes it difficult to reproduce their results in ordinary schools (e.g. O'Leary and Kent 1973; Rollins et al. 1974). Specifically, it has been suggested by Kent and O'Leary (1976) that features such as course credits, joint authorships in publications, opportunities to work for a higher degree, and frequent monitoring of progress by research personnel, constitute advantages for teachers that are not usually available in natural settings but that may contribute substantially to positive outcomes. In addition, ready availability of research funds gives more flexibility in the choice of reinforcers for children and, in turn, increases the opportunity of maximizing motivation.

An equally critical aspect of the published literature is the extent to which studies have been designed as demonstration models. In other words, the concern has been to show that behaviour modification, or a specific technique within the behavioural umbrella, actually works, and this has been mostly achieved not by models that closely replicate 'natural environment' conditions, but by ones that, to a considerable extent, depart from them. What are the 'natural environment' conditions? In the UK, at least, they are frequently characterized at the general level by inadequacy of professional manpower relative to the numbers of children in need of help (Kolvin *et al.* 1975a) and, from the behaviour modification perspective, by limited teacher training and consultation time, and limited funds. In addition, psychologists working in schools often have to work with teachers who are not hand-picked for the task and whose motivation is less than ideal. They also frequently have to forego the luxury of independent observers who can provide the sort of data that is the cornerstone of the behaviour modification approach.

EXPERIMENTAL DESIGN

As already pointed out, the effect of reinforcement procedures in classroom behaviour modification has been assessed predominantly by reversal or ABAB designs (alternating periods of treatment and no treatment). There are a number of important research questions that these designs cannot answer adequately, and control group designs are increasingly recognized as being important in clarifying issues such as the relative efficacy of different treatments and the magnitude and persistence of behaviour change attributable to particular treatments, and in providing controls where there is multiple treatment interference (Kazdin 1973, 1975; O'Leary and Kent 1973). The latter authors have argued cogently that behaviour modification research may have more social impact when designed in the form of large-scale projects with control groups, than even numerous, successful reversal studies with small numbers of subjects.

Methods used in our behaviour modification programme

IMPORTANT THEMES IN THE PROGRAMME

Our behaviour modification programme had a number of features that were designed to take into consideration and clarify certain critical issues. First, the intervention took place in regular classrooms in ordinary junior high or comprehensive schools, so the project was firmly based in the natural environment. The secondary school population has been relatively neglected in classroom behaviour modification research (Heaton *et al.* 1976; Macmillan and Kolvin 1977a). This reduced the need to make inferences as to the applicability of behaviour modification from work in special settings or with younger children.

Second, relatively large numbers of teachers (n = 39) and children (n = 72) were involved. With few exceptions (e.g. Rollins *et al.* 1974) previous studies have dealt with limited numbers of both teachers and children (two or three teachers dealing with up to a dozen children is fairly typical) with attendant doubts as to general applicability. The children in our study exhibited a range of problem behaviour and were not selected purely for disruptive conduct: they could be described as roughly representative of the range of problem children found in the school population. Similarly the teachers, although certain selection criteria were applied (see p. 105), comprised a fairly representative sample.

Third, multiple measures of behaviour change were employed, supplementing the direct observations of behaviour that are the most frequently employed measures in classroom research. Very few workers (e.g. Buell *et al.* 1968; Chadwick and Day 1971; and Mulligan, Kaplan, and Reppucci 1973) have used multiple measures in this area. The issue of response generalization in behaviour modification research is an important one that has been neglected, possibly as a result of narrowness of focus in choice of target behaviours.

Fourth, an important part of the study design, in addition to the use of maladjusted controls and comparison with other treatment regimes, was the provision for follow-up. Recent studies have begun to pay more attention to the need to assess persistence of treatment effects (Patterson 1974; Allen *et al.* 1975; Kent and O'Leary 1976) reversing the tendency to ignore the problem completely or to conduct a follow-up after such a short period that the results are of very little clinical significance (Turkewitz, O'Leary, and Ironsmith 1976). While some behaviour modifiers would aver that what happens after their intervention 'is a function of chaotic or unfortunate programs of contingency . . . that are out of (their) control' (Willems 1974:160), we would agree with Willems's rejoinder that this may be construed as an evasion of responsibility and that behavioural interventions might unwittingly disrupt good things or set bad things in motion that become clear only after long periods of time'.

The fifth significant feature of the study, and one that has considerable bearing on the ability to reproduce the method in ordinary educational/clinical psychological practice, was the attempt to reduce teacher training and consultation time to an absolute minimum. Some reports of the amount of professional time required to set up programmes are rather discouraging for the psychologist with a heavy caseload, who can devote only part of his or her time to intervention. Abidin (1971), for example, reported that thirty hours of a psychologist's time is required to establish an individual behaviour modification programme with a teacher who has no previous experience of the approach, and 150 hours is needed to establish a token economy programme. Such demands on professional time seem quite prohibitive and unrealistic, and more typical of the traditional analytical therapies. Tomlinson (1972) conducted a more feasible exercise, reducing consultant time to 2.4 hours per child referral and 4.2 hours per token economy, by consulting with groups of teachers, concentrating consultation time during early stages of the programme, and limiting data collection. Intensive workshops offer another alternative in reducing training time, and these have been extensively employed (e.g. Madsen and Madsen 1973; Rollins *et al.* 1974) but are not always administratively or practically possible. Limiting professional time devoted to training and consultation is an important consideration when setting up a behaviour modification programme in ordinary schools, but should not put the quality of the project at risk. Training teachers in the principles of behaviour modification and ensuring that procedures are adequately implemented are not easy exercises that can be achieved by a simple series of instructions, but ones that require careful planning and monitoring.

THE SELECTION OF TEACHERS

In each of the six schools the Headteacher was asked to 'sound out' a group of about six to eight teachers whom he or she thought (a) might be favourably inclined towards involvement in the treatment programme and (b) had substantial teaching contact with the classes concerned. A discussion was then held with each of these groups in order to explain more fully the techniques to be employed and the role and extent of commitment anticipated for the teachers. At the end of this discussion the teachers were each given a copy of a document introducing the concepts, principles, and techniques of behaviour modification (Macmillan and Kolvin 1977b) and were invited to attend a series of three, weekly, group sessions dealing with this treatment approach. While there was no obligation to attend these seminars, the group of thirty-nine teachers who started the sessions were not regarded as volunteers because their nomination by the Headteacher must inevitably have created a sense of commitment, although this no doubt varied in extent from person to person. This was an important issue in view of its implications for co-operation and motivation in implementation of the programme. The group consisted of twenty-four female and fifteen male teachers. All but eight had more than five years of teaching experience.

TEACHER TRAINING

As mentioned earlier, we felt that, in order for our method to be replicable, training and consultation time should be kept to a minimum. Training was in three phases and was directed by a consultant, in this case a psychologist. First, the teachers were expected to read and assimilate the basic document referred to above. Second, three, weekly, one-hour group meetings were held with each set of teachers, either during the lunch-break or after school hours, whichever was more suitable. In these sessions, there was discussion of the content of the document, some relevant studies from the literature were described, and some time was devoted to discussion of how one or two of the selected cases might be handled in a behavioural framework. There was a limited amount of role-playing, for example to demonstrate the use of combined praise-and-ignore techniques. In the third phase, consultations with individual teachers were begun, once the group sessions had been completed. In these meetings discussion was initially geared to the organization of individual behavioural programmes for the selected children taught by that teacher. While all available information was drawn upon in the preparation of a treatment strategy, the emphasis was always on behavioural functioning and how the child could be helped in the classroom, as opposed to other settings. Detailed personal prescriptions were given to the teacher for each target child. Once treatment strategies had been prepared and implementation begun, the content of these sessions changed to discussion of practical difficulties and progress in the application of techniques. These sessions were continued throughout the duration of the programme, lessening in frequency with time and as teachers were considered to be capably handling the treatment requirements. 'Training' was therefore considered to be an ongoing process; the consultation phase was extremely important, because it offered some hope of bridging the gap between acquisition of knowledge and actual implementation, which the document/seminar phases alone would have been unlikely to achieve. In addition, these individual sessions presented an opportunity for the consultant to reinforce the efforts of the teacher in applying the techniques, and to provide specific and focused feedback on the observational data.

The average number of consultations conducted per child in the course of the programme was nine (range four-thirteen). The total time taken up by the seminars and the consultations in the six schools was eighty hours, with a mean of 13.3 hours per school (range 11.6–15.7 hours). This refers to on-site time only and does not include

time spent travelling and preparing material for seminars and consultations, or written prescriptions.

PROGRAMME DESIGN

After a three-week baseline period, during which the seminars were
held and baseline observations were collected, the intervention
programme ran in each school for twenty weeks. The introduction of
the programme to the schools was staggered: the six schools were
taken in three pairs, so that, as the baseline phase ended for the first
pair and they proceeded into treatment, the second pair began the
baseline and so on.

TREATMENT METHODS

We decided at the outset to emphasize techniques of social reinforcement – relying upon the systematic and contingent use of teacher
praise, attention, and approval – rather than techniques based upon
the use of material or concrete rewards. As was anticipated, however,
we found that children differed in their response to social reinforcement: for this reason, material rewards were, in fact, given in a
limited number of cases.

There were several reasons for emphasizing social reinforcement.
One of these has already been discussed: this is the difficulty that
might be experienced in the transition phase at the end of a
programme where concrete rewards were employed. Social reinforcers, on the other hand, occur more 'naturally' in the child's
environment than do material rewards and may therefore be more
conducive to generalization and maintenance of behaviour change
obtained in the treatment phase.

Second, the natural-artificial dimension of proposed rewards is a
very significant one in an educational context, with continuing debate
about the merits of extrinsic rewards and whether or not the
emphasis should instead be on 'intrinsic motivation', with children
being rewarded for 'learning for its own sake'. While we personally
favoured the use of material rewards (Macmillan and Kolvin 1977a)
our role in this exercise was not one of crusade and conversion, but
one that clearly had to accommodate the ideals and philosophies of
the schools, represented by Headteachers and the various teachers
with whom we worked. There were, in fact, wide differences in
attitudes on this issue, some teachers openly favouring concrete
rewards and welcoming their applications, others rejecting them out
of hand. Our decision to minimize the use of concrete rewards was,
finally, as much dictated by their artificiality in the regular, natural
classroom setting as by objections raised by teachers.

Lastly, because in the majority of cases we were dealing with one or two problem children within a large group (usually around thirty), it was considered invidious to make material rewards openly available to these few children and not the others. Teachers were quick to point out that this would be unfair and possibly lead to counter-productive rivalry and jealousy. Consideration of cost precluded the extension of such schemes to the entire class. Although the social reinforcement techniques recommended were intended to function as a general classroom-wide management strategy, it was inevitable that slightly more attention was paid to target children than to others by the teachers concerned. However, this was generally considered to be less obtrusive than administration of material reinforcers to the select few. Some teachers were openly opposed to the notion that certain children should receive extra attention at the expense of others, despite the fact that, even in the absence of a systematic intervention strategy, they tended to give more attention to these children anyway.

DEFINING PROBLEMS AND ESTABLISHING GOALS

Our first task when confronted with a problem child was to attempt to describe and define the areas requiring change, in observable terms. Thus 'nuisance', 'troublesome', 'unruly', might be translated into 'keeps talking out of turn', 'gets out of his or her seat and wanders around', or 'pinches other children'. This sort of specific definition is essential if there is to be a precise focus for reinforcement, and it facilitates direct and relevant assessment of problem behaviour. Once the behaviour has been defined in this way, it is equally important to apply the same stringent criteria in defining goals and objectives for treatment. Targets such as 'well-adjusted' or 'self-actualizing' are too vague and nebulous.

Accordingly, in the early phases of consultation, much time was devoted to clarifying concepts of problem behaviour, and encouraging precise initial definitions, clear specification of successive steps through which a child might be expected to progress, and statements about ultimate objectives that were closely tied to observable behaviour. The notion of developing behaviour through successive steps was considered to be crucial to the success of a programme, both in modifying teachers' unwarranted expectations of change, and in conveying the need for gradual 'shaping' of behaviour towards the specified goal.

Teachers were also encouraged to view behaviour in an environmental context, for example, by identifying possible causes and effects. What happened before John hit Bill? Was he teased? What were the consequences of hitting? Did Bill cry, or stop teasing? This kind of approach to the events or circumstances associated with behaviour is known as a 'functional analysis' – an attempt to identify what is functionally related to the occurrence of the behaviour (Yule 1977). It involves postulating a relationship between the problem behaviour and environmental events as a prelude to altering these conditions. Teachers were encouraged, in particular, to observe their own behaviour *vis à vis* the child in terms of its possible functional role, to vary it according to the treatment prescriptions, and to monitor its effects. There are obvious constraints, of course, on the extent to which a teacher can carry out such experimental variations in the classroom.

A major theme in the area of problem definition and setting of objectives was identifying the range of problems that could come within the ambit of the programme. Teachers' interpretations of what constitutes 'disruption' inevitably vary, and it is clearly impossible to establish absolute uniformity in this area. However, the basic types of behaviour detailed (see *Table 5(5)*) were discussed with all the teachers as a means of achieving some common basis of understanding. One of the basic objectives of the programme was to increase the amount of time that children spent 'on-task' or engaged in learning, and this aim could be pursued with most of the children to be treated. Teachers were encouraged to provide reinforcement not only for task attention and studying behaviour, but also for increased/improved output and achievement. In pursuing these goals, one is automatically engaged in reducing disruptive behaviour or activities that interfere with learning.

The screen measures (see Chapter 3) disclosed a variety of behavioural problems, creating the task of evolving ways in which these could be tackled within the framework of the classroom. For example, although the Rutter B2 scale is not a measure that focuses solely on classroom behaviour, nevertheless much of its content reflects conduct that could be modified in the classroom. For example, restlessness, difficulty in settling, disobedience, worrying about things, complaining of aches and pains, and unresponsiveness, are all behaviours on which reinforcement techniques can be brought to bear.

JEPI neuroticism is somewhat different in that the contents of the items of this scale are rather general, and not necessarily focused on the classroom (for example, 'Do you sometimes feel cheerful and at other times sad without any good reason?' 'Are you touchy about some things?' 'Do you worry about awful things that might happen?'). This generality proved less of a difficulty than was anticipated, in that teachers readily found, in children with high neuroticism scores, worries and anxieties that they could work with in the classroom – this applied even in the case of seven children selected solely by the neuroticism criterion. These children showed behaviours such as shyness and excessive sensitivity, and tendencies to worry about performance, marks, homework, and so on. Again, these were responses within the 'reach' of a teacher prepared to use gradual shaping, modelling, and prompting techniques to encourage such children.

Sociometric screen data are concerned with success and failure in social interaction and these are probably determined to a greater extent by behaviour in the playground than in the classroom. Nevertheless, there are several methods relating to social interaction that can be explored in the classroom:

(i)   shaping procedures for withdrawn children to encourage interaction where classroom activities allow it;

(ii) the creation of special groupings in, for example, project work, craft work, etc. so that desired behaviours can occur (drama activities in two schools created some excellent opportunities);

(iii) seating with compatible peers;

(iv) reinforcing peers for interaction, or for initiating contact;

(v)   with rejected children, reinforcing their co-operative behaviour or friendly approaches, to encourage these to take the place of conduct that usually tends to elicit rejection in others, for example, boasting, teasing.

With all these strategies, of course, opportunities for intervention were to be seized by the teachers wherever they presented themselves – in or out of the classroom.

In addition, the reading measure among the second-level tests enabled poor reading and associated responses to be targets for reinforcement. There was thus an effort in the programme to confront the spectrum of presenting problems rather than to focus narrowly on one or two limited types of response.

THE APPLICATION OF SOCIAL REINFORCEMENT TECHNIQUES

In the implementation of social reinforcement procedures we were guided by the established findings of workers such as Becker *et al.* (1967), Hall *et al.* (1968), and Madsen *et al.* (1968), although their subjects were younger than those selected for our programme. Comparable work with secondary-school-age children was rare (McAllister *et al.* 1969).

The social reinforcement applied took the form of directed attention, of comments of praise or approval, smiles or a nod, or physical contact such as a hand on the shoulder or a pat on the back, whichever suited the teacher's personal style and abilities. It is quite clear that some people experience marked difficulty in using social reinforcement techniques, whether in normal or therapeutic situations, and with some teachers considerable encouragement and support were required. It was also pointed out that what was reinforcing for any particular child could not be defined *a priori* – for example, physical contact from a teacher of the opposite sex might embarrass some children; similarly, the class bully might regard the teacher's approval as highly undesirable in view of his or her projected 'hard' image. Accordingly, teachers were encouraged to experiment with different forms of social reinforcement if no success was immediately apparent. It was also possible that the reinforcement might vary or wane in effectiveness over time with any one child. For example, the comment 'good girl/boy' might be effective initially, but would soon lose its effect if repeated excessively without variation – so the need for flexibility in this respect was also stressed.

When developing specific aspects of behaviour, reinforcement was to be made available following particular responses. For example, a highly distractible child might be given comments of approval when observed attending to task; a shy, inhibited child might be given comments of encouragement and a smile when he or she made an assertive response in a group situation. It was considered desirable that comments of approval should convey clearly to the child *why* he or she was receiving such positive attention (for example, 'I'm pleased that you kept on working on these sums, John') rather than being vague, non-specific statements (for example, 'You've been a good boy today'). The requirements for a programme such as this are described more fully elsewhere (Macmillan and Kolvin 1977b). To encourage teachers to make frequent use of positive social reinforcement they were asked to look actively for specific aspects of behaviour that could be rewarded: to try, in the case of badly behaved children, to 'catch the child being good' (Madsen *et al.* 1968a). Where possible, teachers were to attempt to reinforce behaviour that was incompatible with the conduct they were trying to eliminate. For example, a child given to talking to neighbours might be praised for reading a book quietly, or an aggressive child might be given approval for co-operative responses.

Directing comments of approval at a child implicitly conveys information or cues to other children as to how they ought to behave. The child who receives approval may thus function as a 'model' for the others. Teachers were encouraged to use this 'modelling' opportunity: for example, in situations where a target child was behaving badly, an adjacent child who was behaving well could be praised.

Minor instances of disruptive or deviant behaviour were to be ignored, on the assumption that attention directed to such behaviour, even of a critical, disapproving variety, might tend to reinforce and unintentionally increase it (Madsen *et al.* 1968a). The use of disapproval was not ruled out, however, and was recommended where it was impossible to continue ignoring misbehaviour, such as when the learning situation was being disrupted, or when any child was put in physical danger. An important consideration here was the balance achieved between positive and negative controls, and a heavy emphasis on the former was recommended. Where disapproval was employed, soft, private reprimands were considered preferable to loud, public ones, which may have an adverse effect by creating the very situation that a wrongdoer desires – publicity and a spot in the limelight (O'Leary *et al.* 1970).

APPLYING A BEHAVIOURAL CONTRACT SYSTEM

In a handful of cases, where social reinforcement was insufficiently powerful to effect changes in disruptive behaviour, behavioural contracts giving access to a variety of concrete rewards or preferred activities were employed. The initial step was to discuss with the child why such a system was being developed. This involved examining the implications of disruptive behaviour for the child's own learning and for the functioning of the class in general. The contract was presented as a means of helping the child to plan his or her own behaviour consciously and of affording greater control over its consequences. The arrangement was regarded as a private one, between child, psychologist, and the particular teachers involved. The confidential nature of the exercise was essential if the administration of concrete rewards on an individual, rather than a whole-class basis, was to be viable.

A list of positive and negative types of behaviour was drawn up, these being tailored to the needs of the individual case. Points values were attached to each of these, with points being earned for positive behaviour, and deducted for negative behaviour. A card bearing these details was given to the child, so that there was no doubt about which types of behaviour would be considered positive, and which negative. Teachers awarded or deducted points on the basis of behaviour during lessons, informing the child of the details at the end of the lesson. Points totals were recorded on another card, which the child could keep.

The first points target was always easy to achieve, so that the child could make a good start, but subsequent targets became progressively more difficult, so that back-up rewards became more distant in time and were gradually faded out. Points targets were always decided upon in discussion with the child.

Rewards were administered by either the psychologist or a teacher, and were made available as soon as conveniently possible after a target had been reached. They usually took the form of items such as pencils, rulers, felt-pen packs, notepads, or small toys such as plastic animals or soldiers. Activities were sometimes structured as rewards and, as far as the timetable allowed, children would be allowed extra time in favoured activities, such as reading magazines, cooking, or caring for laboratory animals.

PROVISIONS FOR MAINTENANCE OF TREATMENT EFFECTS

It is evident from reports in the literature that unless specific steps are taken to facilitate and encourage the maintenance of treatment effects, the changes obtained may not persist once the programme has ended (O'Leary and Drabman 1971; Levine and Fasnacht 1974; Walker, Hops, and Johnson 1975). This consideration was one that determined, to a great extent, how the reinforcement programme was developed and applied, because the most appropriate time for planning for maintenance is not when a programme is over but rather when it is being designed and constructed. The decision to emphasize social reinforcement was perhaps the most important element in this consideration.

In those few cases in which material rewards were given they were always accompanied by comments of approval and praise, and were gradually phased out towards the end of the programme. In fact, with all forms of reinforcement there was a reduction in frequency and intensity towards the end of the programme. This was guided by previous findings that behaviour may be more effectively maintained by intermittent rather than continuous reinforcement (Bijou and Baer 1978) and by a desire to lessen the contrast between treatment and post-treatment environmental conditions.

When the consultation programme ended, further written prescriptions for follow-up management were made available to the teachers, with written feedback on the children's progress in treatment. Because the end of the consultation programme coincided with the end of the school session, it was inevitable that, in the new session, most of the treated children would no longer have teaching contact with any of the core of teachers involved in the programme. Although this presented a serious difficulty as far as maintenance was concerned, it was unfortunately one that we were precluded from tackling effectively because of lack of resources.

Our attempt to involve the parents of treated children in group discussions of behavioural management was a venture designed to achieve a spread of treatment effects as well as their maintenance. Apart from encouraging the transfer of gains obtained in the school setting, parental involvement was also considered to be of potential value in providing continuity of reinforcement against the background of frequent change and inconsistency of management in the school. There were not enough team members to enable the parental exercise to take place at the same time as the school-based programme, so its feasibility was not explored until near the end of the consultation phase. Lack of resources also prevented a personal approach or home visit to the parents to explain the nature of their possible involvement and seek their co-operation. The approach was made by letter, with pre-paid reply cards but, although initial non-responders were sent a second card, only 12 per cent of the parents showed interest, so the project was reluctantly abandoned.

Assessment of the behaviour modification programme by teachers and project team

In addition to the more objective assessments that afford comparisons between the children in the various treatment regimes and the maladjusted controls, we obtained some other perspectives on change solely in relation to the behaviour modification regime. Thus, we (a) obtained teachers' evaluations of change in various aspects of child behaviour; (b) examined the relation of teacher motivation to outcome; and (c) took observational measures of child and teacher behaviour before and during treatment.

CLINICAL EVALUATIONS OF IMPROVEMENT IN BEHAVIOUR MODIFICATION CASES

Behaviour modification programmes in schools frequently involve a three-level or 'triadic' model as described by Tharp and Wetzel (1969). In this approach, adopted in the present study, behaviour modification techniques are applied by a 'mediator' or 'change agent', a teacher who has substantial day-to-day contact with the problem child. This mediator is advised by a consultant, who does not deal directly with the child. Evaluations of this model have concentrated on measures of change in observed behaviour in child and teacher but these can be usefully supplemented by assessments that are more subjective in nature – evaluations of change made by teachers themselves. These are useful for a number of reasons. First, the efficacy of behaviour modification is critically dependent upon its delivery by such people and the evolution of a flexible and sensitive system of management must be guided by change agents' views. Second, the findings of observational measures alone, although statistically significant, may be discounted as trivial and irrelevant by teachers if their perceptions have not correspondingly changed. Their evaluations shed light on the clinical relevance of the intervention. Third, despite the conspicuous success of behaviour modification in educational settings, this approach does not always meet with general approval, and, in fact, often gives rise to controversy. Hence, feedback from teaching staff can yield invaluable accounts of emergent problems, thus influencing the manner in which techniques are subsequently introduced and implemented.

NEUROTIC/CONDUCT DISORDER AND SEX OF CHILD IN
RELATION TO IMPROVEMENT

In the analysis of teachers' evaluations there is interest not only in the overall improvement, if any, of the children, but also in whether certain types of children improve more than others.

Despite the well-established findings from long-term follow-up studies that children with neurotic disorders respond better to treatment than those with conduct disorders (Shepherd, Oppenheim, and Mitchell 1966; Robins 1972; Kolvin et al. 1977), such diagnostic classifications have previously been considered of little relevance to outcome in behaviour modification. This neglect of previous findings stems largely from behaviour modifiers' views that diagnosis involves theoretical categories and explanations that are often far removed from actual behaviour and that explain behaviour in terms of sub-surface dynamics – what a person is rather than what he or she does (Stuart 1970). Even more important than the possible disparity between diagnosis and actual behaviour, for the behaviour modifier, is the perceived lack of relevance of diagnosis for a functional analysis of problem behaviour and for the manner in which a behavioural programme may be implemented.

Nevertheless, it may be worthwhile for research to address itself to the crucial question of whether different kinds of disorder respond differentially to behavioural treatment. The aim of the present section is to describe an attempt at testing the relevance of the neurotic/conduct disorder classification, and a child's sex, to outcome as evaluated by teachers. The relationship between diagnosis and independent measures will be dealt with in Chapters 9 and 10.

Method of testing improvement
We were concerned with four areas of potential change in child behaviour:
(i)   social adjustment as expressed in relationships with peers and teachers;
(ii) personal adjustments as expressed in the child's own personal well-being, in so far as this could be judged independently of interpersonal functioning;
(iii) academic progress – achievement evinced by general classroom performance or test results;
(iv) academic motivation – task-directed effort and interest.

The final consultation session with the teachers was devoted to discussion of these four areas in relation to each child in the programme with whom the teachers were in contact. An attempt was made to get a consensus view of the child's progress on the scale shown below. It was not always possible to see all the teachers involved with one particular child at the same time, so some teachers were seen individually, but all the teachers involved in the pro-gramme were consulted. Different evaluations had to be reconciled by the consultant. The following rating scale was used:

0: no problem in this area prior to treatment and remains no problem;
1: marked improvement – no longer recognizable as a problem in this area;
2: moderate improvement – considerable improvement but not to the extent of 1;
3: somewhat improved;
4: no improvement;
5: worse.

It was not possible to rate maladjusted control children on these dimensions, so the present analysis was restricted to within-group changes. As not all of the children had problems in each of the four areas being evaluated the number of cases relevant to the comparison was noted. Children rated 0 were excluded from calculations.

Results
Table 5(1) shows the number and percentage of children who fell into each change grade for the four areas of functioning. For social adjust-ment it can be seen that by summing grades 1–3, fifty-six out of sixty-nine children (81 per cent) appeared to derive at least some benefit from the programme. For personal adjustment the figure was sixty out of seventy-one (85 per cent). The relative figure for academic progress was thirty-four out of sixty (57 per cent) and, for academic

motivation, forty-eight out of fifty-seven (84 per cent). These summed improvement rates nevertheless gave a rather rosy picture of outcome as the 'somewhat improved' category on each dimension contained the bulk of cases.

Table 5(1)   *Distribution of teacher ratings of change on four dimensions (end of treatment)*

rating of change	social adjustment (n = 69)		personal adjustment (n = 71)		academic progress (n = 60)		academic motivation (n = 57)	
	n	%	n	%	n	%	n	%
marked improvement	7	10.1	8	11.3	0	0	2	3.5
moderate improvement	16	23.2	19	26.8	11	18.3	22	38.6
somewhat improved	33	47.8	33	46.5	23	38.3	24	42.1
no improvement	11	15.9	9	12.7	26	43.3	9	15.8
worse	2	2.9	2	2.8	0	0	0	0

Comparisons of boys and girls, and of children with conduct and neurotic disorders, focused on cases falling in categories 1 and 2 as against those in categories 3 and 4.

For academic motivation, girls improved significantly more than boys (p < .05) and there was a trend for children with neurotic disorders to do better than those with conduct disorders (p < .10). With academic progress there was a tendency for girls to do better than boys (p < .10). No significant results emerged from the comparisons for personal or social adjustment.

With mixed groupings, for example for girls with conduct disorders, the samples were too small to permit an adequate comparison. For academic motivation there was a trend for neurotic boys to do better than boys with conduct disorders (p < .10). Tendencies of the same order were evident for personal adjustment, with neurotic boys showing greater improvement than boys with conduct disorders and girls with conduct disorders tending to do better than similar boys.

When we examined the relationship between clinical ratings and teacher consultation data, we found a significant tendency for greater improvement on social adjustment and personal adjustment to be associated with a higher number of consultations (correlation significant at p < .02 for both). The corresponding correlations for academic progress and academic motivation did not reach significance.

DISCUSSION

It was encouraging that for each of the four dimensions a substantial percentage of cases was considered to have improved – over 80 per cent in the cases of social and personal adjustment and academic motivation. The lower improvement figure for academic progress (57 per cent) and its disparity with academic motivation may be due to a number of reasons: (a) the scope for observed improvement in academic achievement may not have been adequate where frequent assessments were not employed; (b) motivation may genuinely have improved without a concomitant change in actual progress; (c) increased motivation may have been more apparent than real; or, as the more cynical may prefer, (d) academic progress may be less open to subjective interpretation than the other dimensions.

Improvement rates above 80 per cent compare favourably with traditional estimates of remission in the absence of treatment, which are usually estimated as two-thirds (Rachman 1973), and even more favourably with the recent analysis by Bergin and Lambert (1978) indicating a median spontaneous remission rate of 43 per cent (see Chapter 10). The fact that the present improvement figures were obtained in such a short period is also encouraging.

The finding that girls' academic motivation improved significantly more than that of the boys, and the trend for girls to show greater academic progress, possibly reflects the well-established tendency for girls to be quieter, more conforming, and superior in performance to boys, especially in reading and verbal skills (Maccoby 1966; Blom 1971). In addition, teachers' tendencies to hold lower expectations for boys (Brophy and Good 1974) may also have made some contribution to the finding.

With regard to the comparisons for neurotic and conduct disorders only trends have been obtained; these favoured neurotic children on academic motivation and personal adjustment. A more stringent assessment of the relevance of diagnostic category, allowing comparison with maladjusted controls, is discussed in Chapter 10. To summarize, the comparisons yielding significant differences or trends favoured girls, and neurotic children of either sex.

It must be acknowledged that the evaluations of change discussed here were subject to bias from a number of sources. First, it is possible that the teachers could have 'faked good' in their reports of change to the consultants. This could have stemmed from dissonance-reducing motives (a need to see a favourable rather than an unfavourable outcome from their investment of time and effort in the programme) or from a desire to respond in terms of what they perceived to be consultants' expectancies. On the other hand, though, some of the teachers may have had no such motivation, or even an opposite one. The teachers were not, strictly speaking, volunteers for the programme, having been recruited by their Headteachers. Although they were all given the opportunity to drop out before the programme began in earnest, the Headteachers' 'recruitment' to some extent implied that their choice was not an entirely free one. Because motivation for the programme varied considerably, some teachers may indeed have been motivated to 'fake bad' in these evaluations.

A further source of bias was that the consultants themselves, having no less an investment in the programme and in trying to achieve a consensus with the teachers, may have influenced their views in a more favourable direction. The writers were aware of these possible distortions and sought to represent the teachers' perceptions as faithfully as possible. These qualifications apply to the overall judgements of change of behaviour and the sex comparisons, but not to those comparisons involving diagnosis, because diagnostic status was not known by the consultants at the time of evaluation.

Teacher motivation

THERAPIST VARIABLES IN BEHAVIOUR MODIFICATION RESEARCH

There has been a certain reluctance in behaviour modification research to deal with, or in some cases even to acknowledge, the potential contribution to treatment of factors relating to therapist characteristics, motivation, and role in therapy. Although such issues have been subject to considerable exploration in psychotherapy research (Parloff, Waskow, and Wolfe 1978), behaviour modifiers have avoided this area, possibly because of a reluctance to deal with the 'intangibles' of therapy (Wilson, Hannon, and Evans 1968) and a conviction, bolstered by demonstrations of the effectiveness of automated procedures (Lang, Melamed, and Hart 1970), that the techniques are effective in their own right. In recent years the importance of therapist variables has been increasingly recognized in the behaviour modification field and these aspects are attracting greater research interest than in the past (Devoge and Beck 1978).

TEACHER MOTIVATION IN CLASSROOM BEHAVIOUR MODIFICATION

Behavioural methods in the classroom invariably involve the training of teachers, whether intensively or superficially, to adopt the role of the 'therapist' who administers the requisite procedures. The question of teacher motivation for such an approach is of immediate concern in such ventures, especially where teacher motivation is not manipulable by direct rewards or credits, or where the management intervention takes place in regular school settings rather than in research or 'laboratory' classes. We have discussed issues of teacher motivation elsewhere in some detail (Macmillan and Kolvin 1977b) and have considered how enthusiasm for a behavioural approach and willingness to change one's own behaviour and responses *vis-à-vis* pupils may be affected by a number of factors already elaborated in previous sections of this chapter. We can reiterate briefly. First, whether a teacher has volunteered or been recruited for a programme may crucially affect his or her commitment to it. Unwilling recruitment into such ventures may well generate resistance to the demands being made. Second, if a teacher regards teaching as his or her primary responsibility, with pastoral functions as a secondary concern, the active involvement required in behaviour modification may not be viewed as a relevant activity. Third, if the teacher's view of behaviour aetiology and influence does not correspond with the current environmental theory of behaviour modification, attempts at environmental reprogramming may not be seen as a useful therapeutic activity. Fourth, punitive and disciplinarian attitudes to child management may be quite incompatible with reinforcement principles. These are issues that may affect the teacher's motivation for behavioural intervention, that may limit his or her interest in and enthusiasm for such an approach, and, in extreme cases, may prejudice the entire intervention.

In a therapeutic model that calls for *active, consistent*, and *sustained* involvement from the person mediating the intervention procedures, it would seem that the person's characteristics that bear upon his or her involvement could be critically related to observed outcomes. We describe here a method of rating aspects of the motivation of teachers involved in the behaviour modification programme, and examine the relationships between these ratings and clinically rated changes resulting from treatment.

METHOD OF RATING ASPECTS OF TEACHER MOTIVATION

A number of dimensions that were considered to have a bearing on teacher motivation were constructed. For purposes of analysis, the three that were considered to have the greatest relevance to involvement in a behavioural programme were selected. These were: (a) teacher's attitude towards behaviour modification; (b) teacher's willingness to change own manner of responding to children; (c) teacher's implementation of techniques. The anchor points of these scales are shown in *Table 5(2)*. To obtain an indication of inter-rater reliability the teachers in one school, where two consultants were

Table 5(2)   *Teacher motivation dimensions*

(A)   *Teacher's attitude towards behaviour modification*
1   seems very interested to develop this part of his/her work – a major part of teaching role
2   good interest – makes some effort to work in this way
3   some interest – shows some reluctance or inability to develop this role
4   no interest – disagrees with principles

(B)   *Willingness to change manner of responding to children*
1   very willing – enthusiastic about change
2   favourably disposed to idea of changing own behaviour
3   willing to change but needs much persuasion and continued support
4   unwilling – opposed to attempts to change behaviour

(C)   *Implementation of techniques*
1   good evidence of implementation (from observer/feedback/concrete examples of discussion)
2   moderate evidence of implementation/occasional implementation
3   slight evidence of implementation
4   little or no evidence of implementation

---

involved consecutively, were rated and correlations computed. A similar rating exercise was conducted by two consultants engaged in a separate programme and the pairs of correlations were averaged by the customary method as described by Fisher (1941). The outcome, as shown in *Table 5(3)*, indicated moderate agreement. About four weeks before the end of treatment all the teachers were rated on the three dimensions by the consultants.

Each child was allocated a 'teacher motivation score' with reference to the score of the teacher who took his or her class, or an average score if the child had exposure to more than one teacher. These scores were then correlated with the clinical evaluations.

Table 5(3)   *Teacher motivation dimensions: inter-rater reliability (n = 32)*

dimension	inter-rater reliability
(A) attitude towards behaviour modification	0.77
(B) willingness to change manner of responding to children	0.70
(C) implementation of techniques	0.69

RESULTS

Table 5(4) shows the correlations between clinical evaluation of positive change and teacher motivation scores. All correlations but one (willingness to change/academic progress) were significant.

Table 5(4)   *Correlation between clinical evaluation of positive change and teacher motivation scores*

dimension	social adjustment (n = 69)	personal adjustment (n = 71)	academic progress (n = 60)	academic motivation (n = 57)
(A) attitude towards behaviour modification	0.36**	0.46***	0.30*	0.39**
(B) willingness to change manner of responding	0.33**	0.35**	0.22	0.28*
(C) implementation of techniques	0.42***	0.41***	0.33**	0.32*

Note: *p < .05; **p < .01; ***p < .001.

COMMENTS

While these results indicated that favourable motivation on the part of teachers was associated with better outcome, the possibilities of bias in the data must be considered. The consultant who was responsible for collating teachers' clinical evaluations also provided the motivation ratings. While the latter were completed before the clinical evaluation exercise, the extent to which *both* ratings reflect aspects of the consultant's own perceptions cannot be determined. Thus, factors such as the consultant's own perception of child improvement and liking of teachers may have played a part in determining the results.

Observational measures in the classroom

Obtaining direct measures of behaviour has been of high priority in the development of behaviour modification. This reflects the concern to focus on problem behaviour that is capable of measurement and, also, the need to provide a basis for evaluation of intervention. Continued monitoring of behaviour following the pre-treatment or baseline assessment affords ready detection of changes, and treatment strategies can be modified accordingly.

It has been stressed elsewhere that we sought to shape the behaviour modification programme in the light of perceived constraints in the 'natural environment' of the ordinary school setting, rather than trying to create an artificial 'research' or 'laboratory' model of limited general applicability. Our placing of an independent observer in the classrooms, however, was a concession towards research and measurement requirements, and we accepted that such personnel are rarely available in ordinary school settings alongside teachers who are keen to apply behavioural methods. (If such teachers are concerned with measurement and evaluation they have to evolve recording procedures that are compatible with day-to-day teaching activities and that they can apply themselves). Given this departure, we acknowledged that our resources and the size of our sample could not allow us to match the concentrated coverage in observation achieved by other classroom researchers.

METHOD OF OBSERVATION

The observer, a female psychology graduate, gained experience in the use of the recording system before the beginning of the study, in pilot work conducted in a school not involved in the main research exercise. She was instructed not to interact with any of the children, and to try to merge into the background as much as possible. To allow the children to get used to her presence her first exposure to each classroom did not involve systematic collection of data. The children were told that she was a student who would be sitting in for a number of sessions to observe teaching methods.

The behavioural coding categories employed for children and teachers are shown in *Tables 5(5)* and *5(6)* respectively. The observer had a clipboard, rating sheets, and a stop watch. An illustration of the rating sheet is given in *Fig. 5(1)*, on p. 126. Child categories were precoded down the left-hand side of the page. The recording procedure required the observer to observe a child for ten seconds and then in the next five seconds record both the child's behaviour and the teacher's response to it (in terms of the categories for teacher behaviour). Thus each cell represented ten seconds' observation and conveyed information about the behaviour of both teacher and child. It was hoped that this manner of recording would illustrate the nature of typical interactions between them. Having recorded one child's behaviour in this way, the observer would then move on to the next child for the following ten seconds, then the next, and so on. Having covered all the target children, the cycle would begin again, and continue until the end of the lesson.

Observation was conducted for treated children only, in classes taken by teachers involved in the research programme. It was also restricted to the baseline and intervention phases. As the observer completed her contract at the end of the treatment period no follow-up data were collected. Had such measures been available, their interpretation would have been complicated by the transfer of the bulk of the children, by that time, to new teachers in the following session.

Table 5(5)   *Direct observation: pupil categories*

symbol	category	definition
X	gross motor behaviour	getting out of seat; standing up, moving around out of chair; rocking in chair; disruptive movement without noise
N	disruptive noise with objects	tapping pencil or other objects; clapping, stamping feet; rattling or tearing paper; banging books on desk; (rate only if noise can be heard with eyes closed; do not include accidental noise, or noise made while performing X above)
A	disturbing others directly and aggression	grabbing others' work/materials; knocking neighbour's book off desk; destroying others' property; kicking; hitting; shoving; pinching; slapping; striking or poking with object; throwing object at another person; pulling hair; tripping
L	looking around, distraction (non-task)	turning head or head and body more than 90° to look at another person, or the back of the room; showing objects to another child; attending to another child; looking into space; (exclude when turning or attending to another child occurs when under teacher's instructions, or in academic context)
V	blurting out, commenting, and vocal noise	answering teacher without raising hand or without being called on; making comments or remarks when no question has been asked; calling teacher's name to get attention; crying; screaming; singing; whistling; laughing loudly; negative comments towards teacher; (must not be directed to another child but may be directed to teacher)
T	talking	carrying on conversations with other children when it is not permitted; (must be directed to a particular child or children)
D	unresponsive	no response to teacher when asked questions or to make a contribution to the lesson
R	task-relevant behaviour	on-task, e.g. writing answers, answering questions, listening, raising hand; other behaviours clearly permitted by the teacher in the carrying out of an academic task

Arranging for the observer to see all the children in the treatment regime, in six different schools, proved no easy matter. Timetable clashes, absenteeism, school outings, travelling time from one school to another, and so on, all posed problems, and led to the adoption of a flexible schedule for observations rather than a rigid and unchangeable one. It became apparent that the demands on the observer to cover all the target children in six schools were excessive. Accordingly, one school was omitted from the observational exercise.

Baseline data could not be gathered on one child because of absenteeism; fifty-five children were ultimately involved.

Two twelve-minute blocks of observation were available for analysis for each child in the baseline period, and six twelve-minute blocks in the intervention phase. Percentages were computed for the time 'spent' in each behavioural category as a function of total time observed. The category of particular concern for purposes of analysis was task-relevant behaviour. Having similarly computed percentages for teacher behaviour, ratios were calculated for approval/disapproval, in line with the thrust of the training programme. In view of the relative shortage of data for some teachers, for purposes of analysis these ratios were calculated for schools rather than for individuals.

RELIABILITY OF THE OBSERVATION PROCEDURE

The reliability of the observation procedure was examined by our bringing in another observer who was using the same schedule in a separate project. The two observers simultaneously rated behaviour in a number of classrooms. Unfortunately, this could not be done before the beginning of the study, and took place during the

Table 5(6)   *Direct observation: teacher response categories*

symbol	category	definition and examples
O	other response	calling on a child for an answer; probing for a response; non-critical instructions: one that does not imply disapproval
1	no response	the teacher makes no classifiable response to the behaviour observed
2	approval	(i) contact: positive physical contact such as patting, holding arm or hand (ii) praise: verbal comments indicating approval, commendation, or achievement, e.g. 'that's good', 'you're doing fine', 'you are studying well' (iii) facial attention: smiling at a child (iv) feedback: giving feedback for academic correctness
3	disapproval	(i) holding the child: forcibly holding the child; putting him or her outside; grabbing; hitting; slapping; shaking (ii) criticism: critical comments of high or low intensity; yelling; scolding; raising voice, e.g 'don't do that', 'stop talking', 'quiet!' (iii) threats: consequences mentioned by the teacher to be used at a later time: 'if . . . . then . . . .' comments (iv) facial attention: frowning, scowling, or grimacing at a child

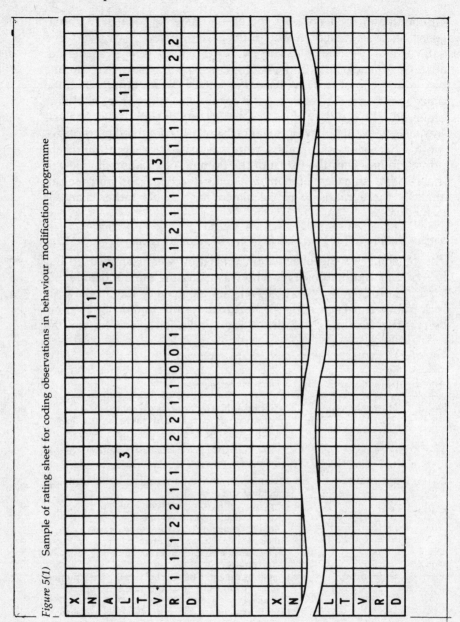

Figure 5(1)   Sample of rating sheet for coding observations in behaviour modification programme

intervention period. It involved observation of thirty-three children in eleven sessions, across the six schools, and a total of eight and a half hours' recording. Reliability proved highly satisfactory, ranging from 80 to 98 per cent agreement, using the formula:

$$\frac{\text{no. of agreements}}{\text{no. of agreements} + \text{no. of disagreements}} \times 100$$

RESULTS OF THE OBSERVATION PROCEDURE

The analysis of children's behaviour focused on changes in task-relevant behaviour. Rather than compare baselines figures with 'treatment' viewed in a global fashion, an attempt was made to detect changes within the treatment period itself. Thus, the treatment period was divided into three equal time-phases. Two observation blocks were available for each of these, and they were averaged to provide one value for task-relevant behaviour for each phase. The two baseline values were similarly averaged. Approval/disapproval ratios were also available for these separate phases.

A comparison of baseline task-relevant behaviour values and the three subsequent treatment values (phases 1, 2, and 3) was carried out by analysis of variance for repeated measures, for (a) all cases; (b) cases classified as 'conduct disorder'; (c) 'neurotic' cases, (d) boys; and (e) girls (see *Table 5(7)*). Where the analysis of variance proved significant the question of *which* means differed significantly was examined. (The statistical test used was the studentized range statistic q (Winer 1971).)

The above-mentioned values for each of the three phases of treatment and the baseline were compared, using the same statistical test as just described. The only pairs of means where significant differences occurred were as follows: when taking into account all

Table 5(7)   *Observational data – task-relevant behaviour: significant differences between pairs of means*

cases analysed	significant comparisons	significance level
all cases	1 > B	p < .05
	3 > B	p < .05
neurotic cases	1 > B	p < .01
	2 > B	p < .01
	3 > B	p < .01
boys	3 > B	p < .05

Note: B = Baseline; 1 = treatment phase 1; 2 = treatment phase 2; 3 = treatment phase 3; the significance levels were derived by using the studentized range statistic q; > means 'better than' in this table.

available cases both the first and third phases of treatment differed from the baseline; for neurotic cases only, all three phases differed significantly from the baseline; and generally, in the case of boys only the third phase differed significantly from the baseline. There were no other significant differences.

Similar analyses were carried out for approval/disapproval values for the five schools. Again, comparing baseline and the three treatment phases, there were no significant differences.

DISCUSSION

The analysis of changes in task-related behaviour for the total group suggested encouraging gains as a function of treatment. In the absence of data on maladjusted controls, or a reversal analysis, this conclusion had to remain tentative. (Too many teachers had expressed concern about the successive application and withdrawal of treatment in a reversal design to make such an analysis possible, nor, indeed, had it been intended.) The trend of the means showed a pattern of rise, fall, then a rise in the final phase, with the first and last treatment phases, but not the second, being significantly higher than the baseline level. A possible explanation for this trend was that the teachers, or the consultant, or both, may have slackened off their efforts after the early phase of treatment, but, once it became evident that early gains were being lost, restored the previous level of commitment. Other explanations included short-term wash out of improvement subsequently compensated for by some longer-term learning process. The same pattern was not evident in the other significant analyses (for girls and neurotic cases) although, in both, the final phase was similarly superior to baseline. It is of interest that the trends reported in the discussion of clinical ratings (pp. 117–19), favouring girls and neurotic cases, were reflected more strongly here in observational data. The data suggested that the neurotic/conduct classification is of relevance to outcome in behavioural work, and it may be of value to workers to examine their respective behavioural referents in the classroom.

The gains in task-related behaviour were all the more encouraging, given that the baseline level was fairly high – 77.5 per cent. It was possible that this level was inflated because the teachers' seminars were being conducted during the baseline and they may have begun experimenting with procedures before the beginning of the treatment phase proper.

The most disappointing feature of the results was the failure to demonstrate change in teacher behaviour, via the approval/disapproval ratios, as a function of training. It may be that teachers' behaviour did not change in the forecasted direction, although the observer's anecdotal reports, and the consultant's impressions, suggested otherwise. On the other hand, it was possible that the observational procedure, perhaps by inadequately sampling teacher behaviour and not being sufficiently representative of it, was not sufficiently sensitive to detect changes.

This brings us to a consideration of other possible sources of error in the observational data reported here. Several reviews of the sources of difficulty in observation are now available (Lipinski and Nelson 1974; Kent and Foster 1977) and a number of critical issues have been identified. First, distortions may be produced by expectations on the part of the observer. Thus, O'Leary, Kent, and Kanowitz (1975) showed that data can be 'shaped up' by the observer when favourable comments are made by a consultant when shown data presenting the expected effect. Detailed and precise definitions of behavioural categories may help to reduce such expectation effects (Kent et al. 1974). In the present study the observer was fully aware, of course, that particular changes were desired in children's behaviour, so some degree of expectation bias may have been present. However, no discussions of data change took place between observer and consultant.

A second source of error is the reactivity of observational procedures – the possible effects on those observed of having a person present who is monitoring their behaviour. The nature of these effects is not clear: thus, for example, Surratt, Ulrich, and Hawkins (1969) suggested that the observer's presence leads to more on-task behaviour in the classroom, but Mercatoris and Craighead (1974) presented data showing no change in levels of appropriate student behaviour. We hope that the time allowed for habituation in the present study reduced unfavourable effects.

Third, 'observer drift' or 'instrument decay' may pose difficulties (Taplin and Reid 1973). These terms refer to deterioration in measurement attributable to changes in the observer, such as gradually changing definitions of behaviour, missing episodes of behaviour, adopting short cuts by collecting only parts of the data, etc. Random or covert checks on observer agreement help to control this. These were not possible in the present study, but definitions were regularly reviewed.

Finally, inter-rater reliability checks may produce inflated agreement scores when observers are aware that their data are being checked (Romanczyk et al. 1973). Checking agreement at unpredictable or unknown times may produce more representative data.

There is a growing awareness that direct observation is not necessarily a reliable, objective, non-reactive form of data gathering, immune from the problems of other kinds of measurement. Observers are fallible too. While sources of observer error have probably not been eliminated in the present exercise, they were taken into account and controlled, as far as resources allowed.

Independent evaluation

In this section we detail three different examinations of how children given behaviour modification treatment compared with maladjusted controls. First, outcome was based on clinical assessment of psychiatric status, yielding comparisons for base to midline, and base to final assessment. Second, we considered improvements on a wide range of behavioural and cognitive measures. These were assessed by covariance techniques which allowed for initial baseline differences between maladjusted control and behaviour modification children. Third, we focused on selected sub-groups within the treatment and control regimes, to make comparisons for which the total group method was not appropriate.

OUTCOME *(see Figs 5(2)–5(5))*

Considering first of all the global rating of severity, no difference was found between children in the two regimes in terms of good outcome for the base to midline comparison, but a striking difference in favour of behaviour modification was apparent for the base to final comparison ($p < .01$). The same picture emerged for antisocial behaviour, though the differences were less marked ($p < .05$). The controls were completely static on this measure. With neurotic behaviour, the behaviour modification children showed superior outcome for both comparisons (base to midline, $p < .05$; base to final, $p < .01$). These results reflect good maintenance effects for behaviour modification across time.

IMPROVEMENT – COVARIANCE ANALYSES

Covariance analyses of improvement for the behaviour modification and maladjusted control children will be considered for data relating to (a) the school and (b) the home. Only significant differences are reported here.

School-based measures
Baseline to end of treatment asessment. On measures relating to classroom behaviour significant differences were present for two Devereux

factors. The behaviour modification children showed greater creative initiative (p < .01) than did the maladjusted controls, scores that Spivack and Swift (1967) suggested were positively related to achievement, measuring 'the degree to which the child exhibits active personal involvement in and positive motivation to contribute to the classroom learning situation' (Spivack and Swift 1967:17). The treated children also showed an increased need for closeness to the teacher

Figure 5(2) Overall severity: seniors: per cent outcome (good and poor categories only)

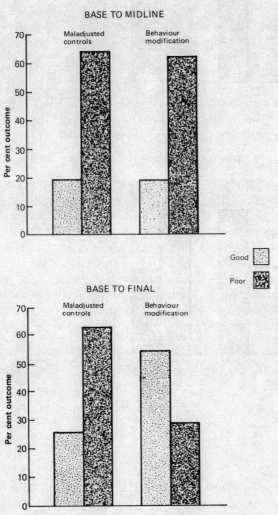

132   Help Starts Here

Figure 5(3)   Antisocial behaviour: seniors: per cent outcome (good and poor categories only)

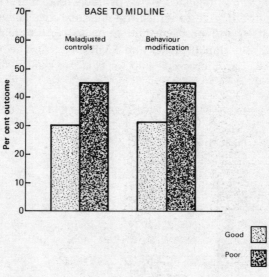

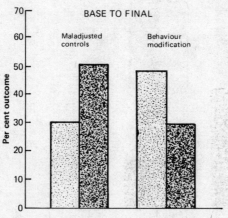

Figure 5(4)   Neurotic behaviour: seniors: per cent outcome (good and poor categories only)

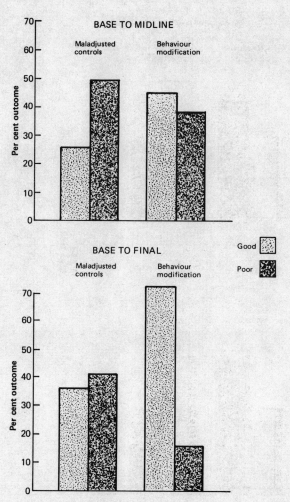

Figure 5(5) Seniors: per cent outcome (good and poor categories only)

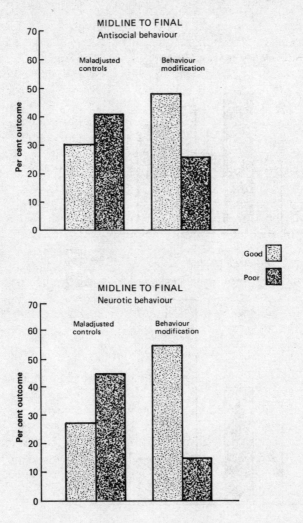

(p < .01). This factor reflects the extent to which children like to be close to, seek out, and offer to do things for the teacher – high scores suggest the teacher is positively valued by the child.

The behaviour modification children also became less isolated (p < .05) as indicated in sociometric measures, and improvement in attitude was also apparent, with the treated children showing a more positive attitude to school (p < .05) on the Barker Lunn scale (item 1) than did the maladjusted controls.

Baseline to midline assessment. None of the significant differences observed at the end of treatment was present in the midline comparisons. However, the behaviour modification children showed decreased neuroticism on the JEPI (p < .01), and also had significantly better scores than the maladjusted controls on Barker Lunn data, indicating decreased anxiety in the classroom (p < .05) and generally in relation to school (p < .05). Finally, changes on cognitive data favoured the treated children, with differences on verbal (p < .01), non-verbal (p < .05), and total (p < .01) ability scores.

Baseline to final assessment. Again, with this set of comparisons the pattern of differences changed. Behaviour rating scores showed significant improvement for the behaviour modification children on the Rutter B2 total score (p < .05), the neurotic sub-score (p < .05), and a decrease in JEPI introversion (p < .05).

Home-based measures

Baseline to end of treatment assessment. The only significant difference to emerge here was on the Rutter A behaviour rating total score, where the maladjusted controls did significantly better than the treated children (p < .05).

Baseline to midline assessment. Maladjusted control superiority was still evident here on the Rutter A total score (p < .05) and a further difference in favour of them was apparent on the Rutter A antisocial sub-score (p < .05).

Baseline to final asessment. The only significant comparison here was on antisocial behaviour (B), and this favoured the behaviour modification children (p < .05).

Aggregate measures (baseline to final assessment)

Comparisons on the global maladjustment score and the neurotic behaviour score were significantly in favour of the behaviour modification children (p < .05 and p < .01 respectively).

Improvement – sub-group analyses

Where specific kinds of intervention were developed for particular children, the total group comparison methods previously described may not be thought the most sensitive way of showing the effects of treatment. Given the multiple criterion method of selecting cases it was possible, for example, for a child to be selected solely on the basis of high teacher ratings, and to obtain scores indicating high popularity on sociometry. No intervention for peer difficulties would therefore be required, yet the total group comparison method included such cases, possibly obscuring changes in the core group with peer problems to which help was conveyed.

This comparison was therefore focused on children in the treatment regime who obtained extreme scores on the screen criteria – scores by which they would have been picked out from the total group as needing special help. They were compared with children selected from the maladjusted control regime in the same way. Scores were those above the cut-offs: Rutter, 9 and above; JEPI – N, 20 and above; Isolation, 0 or 1; Rejection, 12 or above. For teachers' ratings on the Rutter B2 scale, 't' tests showed the behaviour modification children to do significantly better than maladjusted controls between baseline and midline ($p < .05$) and between baseline and final follow-up ($p < .01$). For JEPI – N, behaviour modification was superior at the end of treatment ($p < .01$) and at the final follow-up ($p < .01$), but not at the midline. For the two sociometric indices, although changes at all comparison points were in a favourable direction, none reached statistical significance.

DISCUSSION

These comparisons at the three follow-up stages (end of treatment, midline, and final follow-up), while showing a shifting pattern of changes that makes an overall summary difficult, pointed to some interesting effects. First, there was evidence of changes in responses that were not the specific targets for treatment (for example, aspects of attitude to school, the personality dimension of neuroticism, and home behaviour). Second, there was evidence for the effects of treatment, not only at the midline follow-up but also, more impressively, two-and-a-half years after the end of treatment. Third, effects of treatment were apparent in settings other than those in which intervention was conducted. Thus the school-based programme produced some positive effects in the home, although not until the final follow-up. Fourth, in examination of sources of the measures – self, peers, teachers, and parents – there were no domains in which change was not reported at some stage. Fifth, it was only at the final follow-up that there was improvement on aggregate measures of maladjustment.

The emphasis in the present study on using multiple measures of change and conducting long-term follow-up, sets it apart from most previous studies of behaviour modification in the classroom. The spread of treatment effects, and their apparent long-term effects, were a strong argument for this change in emphasis. It is pertinent to ask whether previous research has failed to identify important changes, either by not measuring them, or by not measuring them for long enough. The long-term effects were particularly encouraging in view of the fact that, at the points at which these data were gathered, the majority of the children were no longer in contact with the teachers involved in the programme, and provision for maintenance was minimal: new teachers had access only to written feedback on children's progress as a result of treatment, and brief written pre-scriptions for management were added to these. While these positive findings for generalization were encouraging, a price had to be paid, in that, having carried out the experiment in a natural setting, many questions about the specific factors controlling the process of general-ization had to remain unanswered.

It is interesting that long-term changes tended to reflect 'sleeper' effects. In other words, effects appeared late, rather than at the end of treatment and being maintained over time. This indicated a need to re-examine the prevalent notion that changes in behaviour modifica-tion are very treatment-specific. In terms of teacher-report measures, this sleeper effect helps to rule out alternative explanations of change in terms of 'demand' factors (teachers being encouraged to report favourable change as a function of their involvement and investment in the programme, or in line with what the consultant might view as desirable.) Thus, while the end-of-treatment rating scales were filled in by teachers involved in the programme (yielding two significant results on the Devereux and on the Rutter B2 total for the sub-group analysis), the significant Rutter B2 results two-and-a-half years later came from teachers, the great majority of whom had had no involve-ment in the programme. Demand effects again seemed an unlikely explanation of parent ratings at the final follow-up, in that there was no convincing reason why they should have operated at this moment, not earlier. In general, the implication of demand effects is that change is being reported where none, in fact, actually occurred. However, if one takes the interactional view that children's problem behaviour is behaviour that comes into conflict with the environment, so that, in this context, teachers' and parents' perception of behaviour as deviant or problematic is a critical factor, then a treatment programme that leads teachers and parents to perceive the child as improved has achieved some success.

It is intriguing that a favourable change in the parental reports of the children's behaviour at home did not emerge until the final follow-up, and that at the two earlier assessment points treated children were faring less well than the controls. How can this effect of poor progress at home, alongside beneficial changes at school, be explained? Other workers have found similar 'contrast' effects, with gains in one setting set against negative results in another (Meichen-baum, Bowers, and Ross 1968; Johnson, Bolstad, and Lobitz 1976). One possible explanation is that the children realized certain types of behaviour led to reinforcement in the school setting and they were accordingly motivated to continue this state of affairs; at home, reinforcement may have been absent and the children may have been disinclined to improve their behaviour, or, if frustrated by the lack of reinforcement, they may have increased their misbehaviour.

One of the most encouraging aspects of the positive results reported here was that they were achieved by low-key intervention, emphasizing natural forms of reinforcement, and applied within the constraints of regular secondary school settings (Macmillan and Kolvin 1977a). A major constraint concerned the 'reach' of the teachers' intervention. In the context of the present programme this had to be classroom-bound and tailored to be compatible with the teachers' primary task of teaching. To have had greater impact, more flexible intervention might have been necessary, allowing more individual approaches, and extending from the classroom to the playground, a significant arena in children's learning. Whether these developments could be achieved on the basis of resources similar to those of the present project is a question that will have to await further study.

6 The nurturing approach –
a teacher-aide programme

Summary

The nurturing approach is a way of attempting to *prevent* the
continuation or deterioration of behavioural and social disturbance
and educational failure in junior schoolchildren. We describe different types of preventive activities (primary, early secondary, late
secondary, tertiary), our teacher-aide programme being an example of
secondary prevention.

We discuss the origins of the teacher-aide programme, the rationale
for basing preventive programmes in schools, and that for the use of
non-professionals in mental health work.

In our scheme, seven non-professional, part-time teacher-aides
each worked directly with seven to ten selected junior schoolchildren
while under the supervision of the class teachers in the six schools
involved. The object was to provide, over the five-school-term
duration, the type of interaction characteristic of a healthy mother-
child relationship, which includes warmth, interest, and acceptance,
together with the ability to be firm when necessary. This is the
essence of a nurturing approach. As well as this nurturing component, we used a *behaviour-shaping* technique. In this, improved
behaviour is achieved through a learning sequence of small, progressive approximations to that behaviour. In some minor respects,
therefore, the teacher-aide programme was similar to the behaviour
modification programme employed with the older children.

We give a detailed account of how the teacher-aide programme was
planned and introduced into the schools involved. The teacher-aides
were selected, from a large number of applications, on the basis of
personality traits, positive family and community functioning, and

other relevant characteristics. The panel was unanimous in the final choice of aides.

The teacher-aides had six main functions: (a) to develop nurturing relationships with the treated children (and sometimes with others in the class); (b) to provide these children with a warm, supportive figure who, we hoped, would constitute a model for them; (c) to assist the teacher by helping individual children in difficulty; (d) to help the treated children with behavioural difficulties by means of behavioural shaping; (e) to help the teacher in the day-to-day running of the classroom; (f) in addition to working under the teacher in the classroom, to spend time outside the classroom, with in-dividuals or groups of children undergoing treatment, involved in activities that would give them additional encouragement and support.

We describe how the teacher-aides received a course of training and were gradually introduced into the schools. An introductory seminar course for the teachers involved was held and any anxieties felt by the teacher or teacher-aides were discussed. We attempted to involve parents in our project, but this plan was restricted by lack of staff.

We discuss some of the potential and actual problems we faced with this treatment approach. These concerned: divided authority and dual loyalties; difficulties of communication between project staff, teachers, and teacher-aides; the fact that the teachers involved were *not* volunteers, and that they differed in teaching experience and style, and in their attitude to the children and the programme; continuity of a child's contact with the teacher-aide throughout five school terms; the relationship between teacher and teacher-aide in the classroom setting; space and timetabling; the responses of the other children in the class. This discussion has led us to suggest improvements detailed in the body of the chapter.

In a subjective evaluation of the programme, we discuss the teachers' and teacher-aides' impressions of the scheme. Overall, the responses were very favourable: the programme seems to have been beneficial for both groups.

We next discuss whether or not the children also benefitted from the teacher-aide programme. We tried to assess this by objective measurements of outcome and improvement. The outcome of this treatment for the treated children was significantly better than for the at-risk controls in terms of overall severity of disturbance at the final follow-up. As far as improvement was concerned, the main changes occurred in aspects of classroom-related behaviour. Consistent im-provement occurred both in reduction in antisocial behaviour (as reported by the parents) and in certain items of classroom behaviour (as reported by teachers). There were similar trends for neurotic and antisocial behaviour as rated clinically.

We believe that a preventive approach in schools constitutes a unique opportunity to reach large numbers of children in difficulty. In addition, our experience with this project has convinced us that there are many lay and professional people in the community who, in conjunction with school staff, can make an important contribution to the prevention of maladjustment.

A review of the literature

PREVENTION OF MALADJUSTMENT

Over the last decade mental health workers have become increasingly aware of the potential value of preventive approaches, both in their primary and secondary forms (Caplan 1964), and such slogans as 'Cure is costly – prevention is priceless' have been used (Lamb and Zusman 1979). Modifications of these approaches have been described by Cowen (1973). So far, one of the main foci of preventive work has been the optimizing of school environments (Allinsmith and Goethals 1962; Cowen *et al.* 1972; Boxall 1973). In theory, such a prevention model has far greater mental health potential than any hospital- or clinic-based treatment programme.

PREVENTIVE ACTIVITIES

Primary preventive activities in child mental health focus on those environments that have a major influence on children's development, especially the home and the school. Such activities attempt to prevent the development of subsequent disorder by attacking what are assumed to be its origins, and simultaneously promoting psychological adjustment (Sandford 1965). Such approaches do not directly focus on individual distress.

Secondary preventive activities can be considered under two broad headings. The first, early secondary prevention, tries to identify children who are considered to be at grave risk of developing abnormally, whether intellectually, socially, or emotionally, and to prevent dysfunction from becoming severe or overt. Late secondary prevention tries to identify children with relatively mild or moderate disorders and is followed by attempts to reduce the duration and severity of the disorders, to prevent them becoming chronic, and to minimize repercussions in other areas of functioning (Bower 1969). Tertiary prevention is directed at entrenched disorders and its main aim is to reduce misery, discomfort, and impairment to a minimum (Cowen 1973). We take the view that the terms 'late secondary prevention' and 'tertiary prevention' are misleading because these approaches are not essentially preventive – we suggest that they should be viewed primarily as forms of treatment.

Most of the glamour of preventive research is attached to primary prevention, which commonly suggests better child-rearing practices or mental health education. However, the present position of primary prevention is distinctly unsatisfactory, with progress being impeded by a lack of clarity of basic assumptions and concepts, and inadequate specification of precise objectives and types of illnesses to be avoided. Secondary prevention (which is the approach that we have used in the teacher-aide programme) has less obvious initial appeal but is, in fact, a considerably more attractive proposition because it focuses on early diagnosis of reasonably specific problems and the prevention of further developments by specific treatment. Nevertheless, claims that preventive endeavours in early childhood will reduce the likelihood of emergence of psychiatric disorders in later childhood and adulthood so far remain unproved.

THE TEACHER-AIDE PROGRAMME – A PREVENTION MODEL

While all three of the intervention programmes used in the junior schools (parent counselling-teacher consultation; playgroups; nurture work) can be considered to have both therapeutic and preventive components, the nurture work (teacher-aide) programme, which attempts to compensate for inadequate stimulation and adverse early life experiences by direct intervention within the school and which uses few traditional psychotherapy approaches, can be considered to be more essentially preventive of the three. A similar view has been advanced by the Rochester University group in the USA (Cowen *et al.* 1971a).

The origins of a teacher-aide programme
This is by no means a recent innovation. Since 1958, the Rochester University group (Zax *et al.* 1968; Cowen and Zax 1969; Cowen 1971a, 1971b, 1973; Cowen *et al.* 1971a, 1972, 1975a; Cowen, Dorr, and Orgel 1971b) has been developing methods of identifying and preventing emotional disorders in children by providing immediate help as soon as difficulties are noticed. This help has been given through a variety of approaches, the non-professional approach being a major one. Cowen demonstrated this with a group of junior schoolchildren who were identified as having some behavioural or social disturbance. These children did *not* receive special help and after a three-year

period they performed significantly less well on 70 per cent of the measures used than a control group of 'normal' children (Cowen, Dorr, and Orgel 1971b). When the 'disturbed' children were provided with child-guidance support they did significantly better (on a number of cognitive and adjustment measures) than an untreated at-risk control group. This was also the case when a teacher-aide service was provided. By current standards these experiments are suspect because of the small size of the samples and the subjectivity of many of the evaluatory criteria. Furthermore, the experiments provided little evidence of long-term effects; nor did the findings suggest what types of disorder responded to what kinds of help. Nevertheless, as hard evidence is scarce, the series has provided valuable empirical pointers that cannot be ignored.

In the UK the Plowden Report (1967) recommended that classroom auxiliaries, placed under the supervision and direction of a teacher, should help individual children. The report proposed that auxiliaries should be trained for employment throughout the junior stage of education and that this training should equip them for wider functions than those of welfare assistants. As we describe later, we have interpreted those wider functions in terms of mental health care.

Rationale for school-based preventive programmes
In a series of papers Cowen and his group have outlined the advantages of locating a preventive programme within the school (Cowen et al. 1971a, 1975a). There are three main points. First, during the school term children spend approximately half of the waking day with their teachers who are, in theory, strategically poised to provide immediate and essential help. Second, if children can be helped at school, rather than at a special institution they are less likely to be perceived or labelled as different and thus can avoid acquiring a social stigma. Third, if children remain in close contact with their existing school and community environment during treatment they will not be confronted with the problems associated with the transition back to normal education, which would occur if they were taken from the ordinary school system for treatment.

Rationale for use of non-professionals
In terms of mental health work in schools different bodies in the USA have become increasingly interested in the use of non-professionals in the application of widely differing approaches. The reasons for such interest are described elsewhere (Grosser, Henry, and Kelly 1969; Sobey 1970); here we will merely consider the rationale for using non-professionals in the school setting.

There is undoubtedly a grave shortage of mental health professional manpower; if alternative ways of helping disturbed children could be provided this would release such professionals for more specific or complex tasks (Cowen *et al.* 1971a), and immediate help could be made available from both professional and non-professional sources at times of crisis. Second, there are important economic considerations. Employing teacher-aides is relatively inexpensive and the amount of time they could spend with a child is far more than any professional could offer. Third, the characteristics of maturity and enthusiasm, a sense of devotion, maternal warmth, an ability to stimulate children, natural wisdom and skills in child-rearing, which are the main ingredients of the help we would like to see provided, are not the prerogative of trained professionals, being apparent in many lay people. Fourth, there are some quantifiable personal characteristics (so-called psychotherapeutic characteristics) that are thought to be associated with the ability to help or counsel others and, again, these are not confined to the trained professional (Truax and Carkhuff 1967). Many people with emotional problems have reported that they obtained satisfactory help from non-professionals (Gurin *et al.*, Veroff, and Feld 1960; Sobey 1970). Fifth, it is possible that traditional psychotherapeutic approaches may not be particularly applicable to the underprivileged, whose needs are greatest (Mayer and Timms 1970) and that they may benefit to a greater extent from less orthodox approaches. Sixth, people may be more likely to model their behaviour on someone whose social background is not too different from their own.

Some comment is necessary about the potential conflicts that might arise from 'cooking in the same kitchen'. These have been described by one set of authors (Zax *et al.* 1966) and, more recently, a list of six 'teacher doubts' has been presented in a paper describing the use of auxiliaries in the classroom (Kennedy and Duthie 1975). The 'doubts' are as follows: that teachers would be inhibited by the presence of another adult in the class; that auxiliaries might engage in teaching; that the funding of auxiliaries would prevent money being spent on employing teachers in order to reduce class size; that auxiliaries would create friction between pupils and teachers; that auxiliaries were not necessary; and, finally, that the time spent in preparing and planning for an auxiliary would outweigh the advantages of his or her presence.

There can be no doubt that the introduction of a teacher-aide into the classroom would produce changes, primarily that the teacher would no longer be working in isolation and that he or she would have to take on the additional activity of supervision of the teacher-aide (Natzke and Bennett 1970). In our opinion, though, the advantages cited earlier outweigh the disadvantages and we therefore argue strongly for the use of non-professionals in early secondary prevention. In addition, there are several (admittedly debatable) arguments for having more than one adult in the classroom. For example, there is evidence that, in the disadvantaged areas of a city, a teacher can spend from 50 to 80 per cent of the time in non-teaching activities, such as discipline and classroom organization (Deutch 1960). A second adult can help release the teacher from these activities, thereby allowing him or her to dedicate more time to teaching activities and to work individually with a greater number of children. With an additional person in the classroom the problems of control and discipline become less conspicuous (O'Leary 1972), provided that there is a good working relationship between the teacher and teacher-aide.

The teacher-aide programme in action

INTRODUCTION

The main objective of this approach is to provide, in ordinary school classrooms, compensatory nurturing for disturbed, disadvantaged, and deprived young children (Hulbert, Wolstenholme, and Kolvin 1977). The concept of compensation is a familiar one to teachers and is similar to that underlying the enrichment programmes characteristic of the Head Start projects in the USA. The Rochester University group in the USA spearheaded the introduction of non-professional personnel into schools (Cowen 1971a, 1973; Cowen *et al.* 1971a, 1975b). In the UK the nurturing component of this scheme was developed in the Woodberry Down Child Guidance Clinic in London (Boxall 1973). Both Cowen's and Boxall's contributions were invaluable in planning the Newcastle upon Tyne teacher-aide programme.

The role of the traditional classroom aide/auxiliary in British schools has been perceived mainly as that of a domestic helper. More recently, recommendations from the Plowden Report (1967) and the Scottish Educational Department (Duthie 1970; Kennedy and Duthie 1975) have suggested the need for a classroom aide with a much wider role than was previously envisaged.

Our scheme, which we have designated a 'teacher-aide programme in ordinary schools', involved seven non-professional, part-time teacher-aides each working directly with the seven to ten selected children while under the supervision of one of the fifteen teachers involved. They were attached to the six junior schools involved from January until July of the following year; one school had two aides.

We were more concerned with the emotional and behavioural aspects of the child's life than with academic progress. The essence of a nurturing approach is to provide the type of interaction characteristic of a healthy mother-child relationship, which includes maternal warmth, interest, and acceptance, together with firmness when necessary.

The teacher-aides were carefully selected and, although given some training, they were encouraged to retain their natural style of relating to the children (Hulbert, Wolstenholme, and Kolvin 1977). Regular consultations between teachers, teacher-aides, and mental health professionals from the project team (a clinical psychologist and a psychiatric social worker) were the bases for the implementation of treatment objectives which were tailored to individual children. The teacher-aides were involved in direct management and care of children, in addition to the usual domestic duties. As well as emphasizing nurturing skills, their training included the use of child-management techniques. These were designed to promote in the child a greater ability to accept personal behaviour limits and to facilitate in the teacher-aide greater consistency in child handling. However, behavioural shaping did not predominate in the programme. In order to determine the long-term effects of the programmes, pupils were followed up for three years after the introduction of the scheme and regular assessments provided the basis for the evaluation described later in this chapter.

THE NURTURING AND BEHAVIOUR-SHAPING COMPONENTS

Boxall's work at Woodberry Down, mostly with West Indian schoolchildren, suggested that the nurturing approach described on page 139 is a viable method for helping children to cope with, and adjust to, some of the demands of school life and the problems characteristic of multiple deprivation. Boxall suggested that such disadvantaged children cannot cope when they are suddenly catapulted into an orderly and structured school situation. She argued that they do not learn the personal controls necessary for behaving in a socially acceptable way and that the achievement of these controls is inhibited by socially and psychologically disorganized home backgrounds. She based her approach on the concept 'what a good mother does is right' and, by studying the skills of mothers, she attempted to define the processes by which socially important behaviours are acquired, such as the ability to wait, share, be co-operative, delay satisfaction, and feel concern for others. From the results of her analysis, she tried systematically to build into her treatment programme these essential elements. Her workers started by concerning themselves more with what the child could actually achieve (the development level reached by the child), than with age-related expectations. Thus, mother-child interactions that might be thought appropriate for younger children were important aspects of her scheme.

The behaviour-shaping component was a supplementary theme, applied in order to achieve complex behaviour through a learning sequence of small, progressive approximations to that behaviour. Boxall used this to encourage the acquisition of personal controls, such as improving a child's ability to wait for gratification, for instance, in sharing food.

In the Newcastle upon Tyne scheme, our aims were similar. While a nurturing approach is essential to further the achievement of such long-term aims as helping the child towards personal and social adjustment, it also aims at developing an intrinsic motivation towards learning. There are, in addition, the important short-term goals of helping the child to cope better with stress, and adapt to the demands of the school and classroom by developing healthy relationships with peers and adults. Such goals are facilitated by improving the class-room atmosphere, by increasing the frequency of acceptable be-haviour, and by decreasing the frequency of inappropriate behaviour.

Many educationalists would challenge the long-held maxim that learning is its own reward (Montessori 1964; Hodges 1972). However, forms of external reward are inherent in every teaching situation. Not even the simplest exchanges between teacher and child are free from the reinforcing influences of gaze, tone, and gesture (Pines 1967; Brophy 1972). When appropriate reinforcement is used in a sys-tematic manner it can help to achieve desired changes in social behaviour and classroom learning. An account of the efficacy of such techniques is provided in Chapter 5 where, in a review of the literature, we describe how various experimentally controlled changes in the teacher's behaviour are followed by changes in the child's behaviour. The teachers implemented classroom rules, offered praise and approval of appropriate behaviour, and ignored inappropriate behaviour. The researchers found that whereas the introduction of rules did not appreciably reduce the frequency of inappropriate behaviour, and that ignoring inappropriate behaviour produced inconclusive results, in contrast, praise for appropriate behaviour and indifference towards inappropriate behaviour were the key tech-niques for improving classroom management. Many workers have indicated that contingent praise is an essential part of successful classroom management.

Operant conditioning procedures, designed to complement the nurturing component, were employed by both teachers and teacher-aides under the guidance of the project team. Such programmes were tailored with the needs of individual children and total classroom management in mind. In some respects, therefore, the teacher-aide programme was similar to the behaviour modification programme employed with the older children.

SELECTION OF THE TEACHER-AIDES

A single advertisement for teacher-aides was placed in a local newspaper and attracted 120 replies. Therefore, we in Newcastle upon Tyne found, like Cowen in the USA, that there are large, untapped resources in the community with the potential to help children in distress. Perhaps one reason for the good response to the advertisement was that mothers prefer working outside the home during, rather than outside, school hours.

In selecting suitable staff Cowen *et al.* (1971a) looked for applicants with warmth and an interest in people, who had successfully reared their own children. The supporting criteria were the talent, interest, and time to be involved in socially useful activities, evidence of a liking for children, a flexible approach to child-rearing, freedom from any emotional complaints, and an appreciation and acceptance that the successful candidate would take a secondary role in the class-room.

Our criteria, which were broadly similar, are listed below. They are not in any order of importance but indicate those characteristics we considered essential in prospective teacher-aides:

(i)   a personality displaying adequate degrees of those therapeutic qualities identified by Truax and Carkhuff (1967) namely, warmth, empathy, and genuineness; in addition we sought evidence of stability and maturity;

(ii)   experience of positive family functioning, including an ability to cope successfully with the normal problems of child rearing, a flexible approach to child management, and evidence of an active interest in undertaking this kind of work;

(iii) experience of positive community functioning, including signs of being the kind of person whom others approached with their problems, an ability to be discreet and be respectful of the con-fidences of others, and enthusiasm for, and experience of, work-ing with children.

Other important pointers that were taken into consideration were the applicants' ability to appreciate the day-to-day difficulties con-fronting teaching staff, and their acceptance of the idea of supervision and training. We also looked for working-class origins, in that the applicants, or their parents, were not too far removed in occupational class from the community in which they were to work. Although this last point is still debatable, some studies have suggested that a person who has experienced a working-class environment is likely to be able to understand and deal more sympathetically and effectively with the problems encountered in such environments (Riessman and Popper 1968; Grosser, Henry, and Kelly 1969).

Screening of teacher-aides by selection panel
The selection panel consisted of a psychiatrist, a social worker, a clinical psychologist, the Headteacher of the school to which the teacher-aide would be attached, and a senior representative of the local education authority. Initial screening, on the basis of application and references, reduced numbers so that we eventually interviewed, for each of the seven available posts, seven to ten candidates. Contrary to our expectations, the decisions about appointments were unanimous in every case, despite the diverging views between the project team and the eductionalists about selection criteria. We discuss the qualities of the teacher-aides more fully later in this chapter.

THE ROLE OF THE TEACHER-AIDE

The teacher-aides in the Newcastle upon Tyne project were involved with the management and care of the child, and had six main, and often overlapping, functions. We carefully took into consideration the teacher-aides' 'natural' way of relating to children, which we regarded as very important and which was to remain, for the most part, unhindered. The functions were:
(i)   to develop with the 'target' children (and sometimes with other children in the class) relationships that fulfilled their assumed needs for nurturing, adopting both a maternal role and supplying the 'vital ingredients' of warmth, security, and firmness;
(ii) to provide the target children with a warm and supportive figure who, it was hoped, would, in addition to the teacher, constitute a model for them;
(iii) to assist the teacher by helping individual children who were in difficulty or who had asked for help with a task; these were essentially non-teaching duties which Duthie described as 'supervision duties', examples being 'checking that the pupils are following their work cards in order; . . . helping pupils with minor problems in the *uses* of material' (Duthie 1970:8);

(iv) to help the target children with their behavioural difficulties by use of behavioural shaping;
(v) to help the teacher in the domestic running of the classroom, preparation of craft and educational material, first aid, and so on; Duthie (1970) described these as 'housekeeping duties' since they comprise those duties which have to do with the day-to-day running of the non-educational aspects of the school;
(vi) in addition to working under the teacher in the classroom, to spend time with the target children, either individually or in small groups, outside the classroom, engaged in discussion, project work, and craftwork (and any other activity that would provide these children with additional encouragement and support).

TRAINING THE TEACHER-AIDES

Again, we were able to benefit from the Rochester experience. We abbreviated, modified, and selected from the Rochester teacher-aide training manual according to our needs, and added a section on behaviour modification. Like Cowen, we offered this manual to the teacher-aides as a resource to be used as a broad guide, rather than as a 'book of rules'.

A fifteen-hour seminar course was also provided. The course covered such areas as:
(i) a review of the aims and methods of our programme, including the philosophy of the preventive approach;
(ii) the employment of non-professionals in mental health work;
(iii) the school – implications of working within a school, the school structure and type of communications;
(iv) the handling of disturbed children – this included an account of the broad types of problem behaviour encountered in childhood, discussion of their management, and also the principles of behaviour modification; it is important to emphasize that these management themes were broached at an introductory level, as we wished to promote, and not to inhibit, the teacher-aides' own natural way of relating to and managing children;
(v) behaviour – the essential principles of observing and describing behaviour were discussed (this was necessary because the teacher-aides were expected to keep a diary and to record events);
(vi) the contentious subject of confidentiality, emphasizing that frank exchanges of information, which are often necessary in such work, should remain confidential to the helping team.

A video tape-recording of adult-child interaction provided the focus for two three-hour discussions on child management, and later there were informal discussions (for about three hours) focusing on individual children with whom the teacher-aides were working. After this introductory course at the research department the teacher-aides were gradually introduced into the classrooms over a two-week period.

A fortnight later the class teachers met as a group for two three-hour sessions to discuss similar topics, but with particular emphasis on the behaviour-shaping element.

By consensus of opinion the teachers elected for the teacher-aides to work for the second half of the school day only, as this was a time when less formal teaching activities were undertaken. Each of the seven teacher-aides were responsible for seven to ten children over the five-term period of treatment.

Teacher involvement

INTRODUCING THE PROGRAMME INTO SCHOOLS

As the teacher-aide programme was part of a larger experimental preventive mental health programme the seven classes in this part of the scheme were chosen randomly; consequently, the teachers involved were not volunteers. The approach to the schools was initially made through the Headteachers, who then introduced the idea to those teachers whom we hoped to involve in the programme. From then on, the project team met the teachers concerned and discussed more fully the implications and functions of the teacher-aide. In the beginning, everyone involved felt anxious about, for example, the possibility of the teacher-aides seeing themselves, or being seen, as able to function autonomously or of usurping the authority of the class teacher, and of the children not knowing who was in charge of the class. The educational content of the teacher-aides' tasks was also of concern. Many of these anxieties were openly discussed before the scheme started in the schools. For instance, it was agreed that it would prove impossible for every task to be completely free of educational content, but such content was to be kept to a minimum and was entirely at the teacher's discretion.

The introduction of the teacher-aides to the classroom was staggered throughout the six experimental schools for practical reasons; during this period, the above-mentioned introductory seminar course for teachers was held. It was stressed at this time that no one could foresee all the possible problems and, as the scheme was evolving, a number of operational decisions would have to be made. Hence, a certain amount of flexibility was required of each teacher/teacher-aide pair. Liaison between project team and each teacher/teacher-aide pair was arranged on a regular fortnightly basis, and took the form of thirty- to forty-minute discussions on the management of individual children and emergent problems concerning the project in general. It was stressed that the project team was available between these times, if required, and we found that the teacher-aides consulted the team more than did the teachers. During the project period teachers were asked to meet as a group at least once a term to discuss problems and to share ideas. The project team would have liked these meetings to occur more frequently but time-tabling problems prevented this.

THE WORK OF THE TEACHER-AIDES

The daily duties of the teacher-aides and how they worked obviously varied. Each teacher-aide kept a diary, and we include two extracts, from different diaries, to illustrate some aspects of their work.

Diary 'A'

'Maureen always used to avert her eyes when I smiled at her, now she gives a quick smile back then immediately looks away. A pity she is absent from school so often as I seem to get back to square one in gaining her confidence. She comes quietly to ask if I'll hold her hand to the library on a Monday.

She will request help for spellings, reading, etc. only after I have made the first approach to her.

She appears to be friendly with another girl in the class; I suspect it may be that Maureen always has sweets for playtime, but at least she is with someone in the playground and not on her own.

Mrs. M. (teacher) will praise Maureen for any effort shown and tells her to come and show me her good work. Once Maureen is praised for something she goes back to her desk and proceeds to continue her work but is soon back to show what else she has done. It is apparent she is delighted.'

Diary 'B'

'Waited for children to go along to classroom, chat with children as we go. Headmaster wanted a word with the teacher. Looked after the children, talking to them until the teacher came to take them into classroom.

Teacher gave them a lesson about Canada; I had brought Canadian coins for the children to examine. As soon as teacher had finished explaining what she wanted from the children I started to help children with their lessons, mainly in the way of helping them to find the answers themselves by talking to them and leading them to find the answers; sharpened a pencil for one child who was having trouble. Helped children with spellings and work generally. At all times helping the target children with encouragement and whichever way they needed help, i.e. spelling, finding answers, etc. Very busy period until break.

  2.45 p.m. Teacher finished story she wanted children to write about. 3 p.m. Took Alan along to another teacher's room to work quietly. Seemed to settle and quiet him and he worked quite well. Colin came along about 3.20 p.m. and both boys worked until 3.30 p.m. Assembly in the hall at this time, helped all the children to get into line and marched into hall to see older children receive swimming certificates. Took children back to classrooms for them to get their coats and to see them off home. A large number of children always kiss me when they leave.'

Parental involvement

THE PARENTAL SCHEME

To complement the school-based work, a parallel parental scheme was organized at a later stage, i.e. in the third term of this treatment. These contacts with parents were spread over two terms. This had three basic aims. The first was to describe more fully the work of the teacher-aide programme to the parents of the target children. The second was to provide guidance and support to parents in coping with the problems of disadvantage, and the third was to recruit parents to attend group sessions that were organized in their local school.

MOTHERS' INVOLVEMENT IN THE SCHEME

At group meetings mothers were given an opportunity to discuss with the teacher and teacher-aide their child's behaviour and progress. In addition, themes common to all parents were raised and discussed. As a playgroup was simultaneously organized, mothers were able to observe their children at play.

  Because of the lack of sufficient project team staff to visit mothers the parent programme was severely restricted in achieving its objectives. However, all parents were visited at home at least once but only 40 per cent of mothers attended at least one of the three group meetings. Nevertheless, this attendance rate was higher than that usually reported in work with disadvantaged families (Chilman 1973).

We do not deny that fathers have an important role in nurturing children and, indeed, certain children's problems may stem in part from the absence of a father or father figure to whom they can relate. However, there were obvious practical difficulties in attempting to involve men as teacher-aides in experimental nurture work programmes, but in any future project the possibility needs to be borne in mind.

It needs to be noted that parental involvement in the group sessions was limited to mothers mainly because such groups were organized at times that were inconvenient to fathers. However, there was some contact with fathers during home visits.

Some practical problems

DIVIDED AUTHORITY AND DUAL LOYALTIES

Initially, all the project teachers expressed anxiety about having an additional person in their classroom. From our review of the literature we had anticipated this problem and have summarized the arguments earlier in the chapter. To recapitulate, Cowen and colleagues (Cowen and Zax 1969; Cowen *et al*. 1975a) encountered similar problems: their solution was to modify the approach and remove the teacher-aides from the classroom. They have reported neither the children nor adults were certain who was really in charge of the class. Further, some teachers felt that the teacher-aides often got to play the role of all-caring, all-giving, and affectionate mother while the teacher was forced to be the disciplinarian (Cowen and Zax 1969; Cowen *et al*. 1975a). Such potential problems were discussed with the Head-teachers, teachers, and teacher-aides before the programme started. The project team also stressed the importance of the teacher-aides' responses being consistent with those of the teachers in any particular situation.

COMMUNICATION PROBLEMS

In the Rochester work there were suggestions that inadequate communication between the project team, teachers, and teacher-aides led to both misunderstanding and frustration. In our study, the project team held regular fortnightly discussions with each teacher/teacher-aide pair. These lasted from thirty to forty minutes, and helped to keep such problems to a minimum. In keeping with our own impressions, the teachers and teacher-aides would have preferred more frequent meetings.

TEACHER VOLUNTEERS VERSUS TEACHER RECRUITS

It is worth re-emphasizing that the teachers involved were not volunteers. After an initial discussion about the programme, though, only one teacher felt that she could not teach happily with another adult in the classroom; for this reason her class was not assigned a teacher-aide.

DIFFERENCES IN EXPERIENCE, ATTITUDE, AND STYLE OF TEACHERS

Throughout, we worked with fifteen teachers who represented a cross-section of ages, teaching styles, and teaching experience found throughout the schools. For instance, in one class a teacher was a first-year probationer, while in another the schools' Deputy Head-teacher was involved. Motivation, enthusiasm about the approach, and sensitivity to the children's difficulties also varied between these teachers. After the initial seminars and subsequent meetings some variations were still apparent. One notable variation was the extent to which they used our guidelines of management – particularly in relation to contingent praise and ignoring inappropriate behaviour (Becker *et al.* 1967).

CONTINUITY OF CONTACT BETWEEN CHILD AND TEACHER-AIDE

As the project spanned five school terms there was the possibility that the children would be dispersed when changing class and would lose continuity of contact with the teacher-aide. This was prevented by negotiating with the school for the treated children to remain to-gether, and the teacher-aide with them. Thus, during the duration of the study each group of children had at least two teachers, but only one teacher-aide.

A problem associated with this negotiation was the difficulty for the second teacher to establish a rapport with her new class while the well-known figure of the teacher-aide was present. We decided, after discussion, that the best solution was to exclude the teacher-aide from the classroom, at the teacher's discretion, during the first two weeks of the new term in order to allow the new teacher to get to know her class.

RELATIONSHIP BETWEEN TEACHER AND TEACHER-AIDE

We believed that the development of a partnership between the teacher and teacher-aide had to evolve naturally. This generally occurred, with the pair creating their own distinct pattern of co-operation and work. On the few occasions that problems arose these were, for the most part, sorted out by the project team who ensured that they were always available for consultation. In the main, we avoided the demarcation disputes that beset the Rochester research by ensuring that the defined roles and functions of the teacher-aides, and any subsequent modifications of these, were acceptable to the teachers.

SPACE AND TIMETABLING PROBLEMS

As we were working in schools in deprived areas space was inevitably at a premium. This difficulty required the co-operation of all the teaching staff in the schools and teacher-aides in using any available space, such as corridors and medical rooms, for individual work with children. In practice, the completion of the scheme depended on the goodwill of the other teaching staff, whose co-operation had not originally been sought or envisaged. They were asked through the Headteacher if they would assist by 'standing in' for the nurture work teachers during discussion time and were, invariably, helpful in covering for the project teachers during the fortnightly discussions.

OTHER CHILDREN'S RESPONSES

The confines of the research design made it necessary, as far as was practicable, for the teacher-aide to concentrate on the target children in particular. Such restriction at first created considerable anxiety among certain teachers (which did not entirely disappear) that the treated children would be adversely 'labelled'. This is always likely to be a problem when additional help is provided only for some children. Nevertheless, a survey, at the end of the research, both of teachers and teacher-aides revealed that three-quarters of them considered that some of the other children in the classes appeared to feel 'left out' of an interesting experience. On the other hand, we know of no incident where overt resentment by untreated children gave rise to disruptive behaviour. Further, it was our impression that these children were spending more time with their teachers as a result of the teacher-aide's presence.

How to improve the programme

We believe that this sort of programme would be improved if the teachers were volunteers, if they were given longer training programmes (see *Table 6(1a–c)*) both at the beginning of, and during, the project (which implies the use of paid supernumeraries to 'stand in' for the teacher while he or she attends discussion), and if motivation could be maintained at a steady level by the award of some form of recognition by the education authorities. More specific training would allow systematic identification of pupils with difficulties. We would like to stress that none of these suggestions implies a radical organizational or administrative change, nor would the financial costs be excessive.

Above all, we believe that in colleges of education greater attention should be paid to the identification and handling of psychological problems of children in the classroom. *Table 6(1a–c)* provides support for this suggestion and it is discussed later in this chapter.

Future possibilities

Many people are still of the opinion that schools should not be involved in developing mental health projects – that mental health should be the domain of existing traditional agencies. However, we believe that a preventive approach in schools constitutes a unique opportunity to reach large numbers of children in difficulty. In addition, our experience with this teacher-aide project has convinced us that there are many people in the community (both lay and professional) who, in conjunction with school staff, can make an important contribution to the prevention of maladjustment. Such beliefs must be confirmed by careful evaluation.

An important question is whether or not our approach could be adopted and adapted for use by schools elsewhere. We consider that the only expense that need be incurred is the salary of the teacher-aides, as it is our impression that the appropriate professional expertise is already available in the health, social, and educational services of the different areas of the UK. The overlapping and unique contributions of the professionals in these services could be harnessed to organize and direct similar school-based schemes. Guidelines are now widely available from work in the USA (Cowen *et al.* 1975b), south-east England (Boxall 1973), and now north-east England.

Teacher and teacher-aide perceptions of the programme

TEACHER AND TEACHER-AIDE CHARACTERISTICS

The initial group of teachers taught in classes that had been randomly allocated to the teacher-aide regime; the second group took over these classes and their respective teacher-aides at the end of the first school year (Kolvin *et al.* 1976). From the information available to us we concluded they constituted a cross-section of teachers in junior schools. All were teacher-trained and specialized in arts, crafts, and science subjects; nearly half had taught in three or more schools and the same proportion had more than eleven years' teaching experience.

The teacher-aides were all married women with children of their own. Their age range was from thirty-six to fifty-five years and, as already described, they were a highly selected group (Hulbert, Wolstenholme, and Kolvin 1977).

METHODS OF ASSESSMENT

We were interested in teacher and teacher-aide responses to the four main components of the scheme, which comprised: (a) introductory seminars and review meetings; (b) consultation and discussion with the project team; (c) maternal involvement; and (d) working together in the classroom. Favourable attitudes towards the scheme suggested some measure of success for one or more of these components.

At the end of the project, a total of twenty-four teachers and teacher-aides who had been involved received a questionnaire from the Research Director. (For the purpose of this particular analysis we included the additional teacher/teacher-aide pair working in the 'pilot' school. This resulted, then, in the inclusion of sixteen teachers and eight teacher-aides in this exercise.) However, only twenty questionnaires were returned. The four non-responders were all teachers, three of whom had a good reason for not replying. This was insufficient exposure to the programme – for example, one teacher had moved to another school after being involved in the programme for only three months. However, even if the fourth teacher had responded, and done so negatively, this would not have greatly affected the overall results.

The replies of the teachers and teacher-aides are presented in *Table 6(1a–c)*. Their responses were compared – two of the three categories in each question were combined and the data were analysed using Fisher's exact probability test (a test specifically designed to assign significance in the case of studies of small sample size). It will be appreciated that, with such small numbers, differences would have to be considerable before proving to be statistically significant (see following section on results).

In addition, the teacher-aides were asked to complete a second questionnaire, relating to their work in the classroom and school as a whole.

RESULTS

There were no statistically significant differences between the responses of the eight teacher-aides and twelve teachers who completed the questionnaire: consequently, for analysis and discussion purposes, the teacher-aides and teachers were regarded as a single group of respondents.

QUESTIONNAIRE FOR TEACHERS AND TEACHER-AIDES

Table 6(1a) indicates favourable attitudes towards the scheme, with reports from the majority of the school personnel that they had derived moderate or marked benefit from the programme. It was not possible to determine which particular feature of the scheme gave rise to the favourable responses, but it seemed likely that the items in

Table 6(1)   *The responses of teachers and teacher-aides to the nurture work scheme*
            (a) In relation to consultation (n = 20)

item		nil	slightly	moderately + markedly
		%	%	%
1.	has enhanced my understanding of the children identified	0	15	85
2.	has increased my understanding of the children's families	15	30	55
3.	has improved my ability to handle the children's behaviour	0	35	65
4.	has led to an increase in my understanding of my own reactions to the children	10	30	60
5.	has enhanced my knowledge about the psychological techniques of handling children	15	40	45
6.	has enhanced my knowledge about emotional development in general	15	45	40
7.	*has provided me with useful information from psychological tests	16	37	47
8.	it helped me to have someone to talk to about the children's problems	0	5	95
9.	it helped me to think out the alternative ways of coping with disturbed behaviour	0	10	90

Note: percentages are rounded off to nearest whole number; * only 19 responses were available.

Table 6(1a) related primarily to the regular consultation meetings and to the seminars. Responses to items (1), (8), and (9) demonstrated substantial appreciation of the help provided in understanding or managing difficult behaviour in children, with at least four out of five endorsing these components of the scheme. Categories detailing increased understanding of the children's families (2), of their own reactions (4), and an improved ability to handle the children's behaviour (3) were also favourably viewed by the majority of staff. The scheme appeared least successful in increasing knowledge about

Table 6(1)   *The responses of teachers and teacher-aides to the nurture work scheme (b) In relation to consultation and wider aspects of child management*

item		not really	possibly	definitely
		%	%	%
10.	I would have liked more advice	25	65	10
11.	there were sufficient opportunities to discuss everything I wanted to discuss	25	35	40
12.	I would have liked to be told more about how to handle children	50	30	20
13.	I could usually see what the project team discussions were getting at	0	15	85
14.	It helped to foster links with the families of disturbed children	45	30	25
15.	It led to a sharing of responsibility for individual children	10	45	45
16.	I was told enough of what was found in interviews with parents	55	30	15
17.	I would have preferred it if the *very disturbed* children had been removed to special classes or schools than to help them to be maintained in our school with the help of this scheme	75	20	5
18.	I think the project team should have spent more time visiting the homes	40	45	15
19.	I would have preferred it if the project team had undertaken direct treatment of the children	65	25	10
20.	the project team should encourage unco-operative parents to come into (contact with) the school	0	60	40
21.	I would have preferred to contact the parents myself	60	30	10
22.	the project team should confine themselves to social problem families	79	21	0
23.	the project team should concern themselves with staff tensions that might arise in school	70	25	5
24.	the project team should be more informative about the psychological information they elicit about families	15	40	45

psychological technique of child management (5), emotional development in general (6), and in providing information from psychological tests (7).

In *Table 6(1b)* the pattern of responses was slightly different. This was in some ways related to the nature of the statements in that items (10) to (16) inclusive, and item (24), consisted of comments about the actual scheme as directly experienced by the school staff, while the remaining items were concerned with views about alternative ways in which the scheme could be run, or with potential tasks for the project team.

Referring to the items directly related to the scheme, the responses were less clear-cut with, in many cases, a fair percentage of respondents opting for the midpoint 'possibly' category. Three-quarters of the respondents would have liked more advice (10), but the desired nature of this advice was uncertain as only half wanted to be told more about handling children (12). Three-quarters of the group felt that there were sufficient opportunities for discussion (11), and, according to the participants, the implications of the discussions were invariably easy to grasp (13).

The teachers and teacher-aides did not perceive the scheme as making a major contribution to increasing links with families (14), sharing information about the families (16), nor to sharing responsibility for individual children (15). Hence, in their view, the main deficiency of the scheme was the lack of feedback of information.

On the other hand, they clearly thought that unco-operative parents should be encouraged to have links with the school (20), and that more time and effort on the part of the project team should have been devoted to the families (18), but not to direct treatment of the children (19), nor to involvement in teaching staff tensions (23). In addition, they were opposed to the scheme being restricted to social problem families (22). In relation to alternative approaches to pupil management, three-quarters of the staff did not want very disturbed children to be removed to special classes or schools (17) but, on the other hand, few were enthusiastic about taking on the task of personally contacting parents (21).

The items listed in *Table 6(1c)* were specifically related to the fourth component of the scheme, which concerned the practice of having a teacher and teacher-aide working together in the same classroom. This was endorsed as a useful technique by all the respondents (26), with little or no evidence of major problems having arisen from the presence of an extra adult in the classroom (28, 29). Furthermore, the teachers and teacher-aides appeared to appreciate the importance of good relationships between the adults in the classroom (36).

Table 6(1)   *The responses of teachers and teacher-aides to the nurture work scheme (c) In relation to the roles, functions, and interactions of teachers and teacher-aides in the classroom*

item		not really	possibly	definitely
		%	%	%
25.	it is easy for other children to feel left out of things if the teacher-aide concentrates on the target children	21	37	42
26.	having a teacher-aide working in the classroom is a very useful way of helping children	0	10	90
27.	the teacher-aide should have her own room in the school and children referred to her by teachers	75	20	5
	having two people working in the classroom leads to:			
28.	confusion for the children	85	10	5
29.	misunderstanding between the two adults	70	30	0
30.	teachers are able to run such a scheme without outside assistance	60	40	0
31.	the teacher-aide's role would be facilitated by some training in basic educational techniques	10	70	20
32.	teacher-aides should be full-time and not only part-time	40	40	20
33.	teacher-aides should also be involved in contacting parents	30	45	25
34.	there should be more meetings for both teachers and teacher-aides together with their counterparts in the other schools involved	20	55	25
35.	the individual teacher should meet with the teacher-aide before a programme starts	5	15	80
36.	the amount of success a teacher and teacher-aide have with children depends on how well the teacher and teacher-aide get on together	0	30	70

A number of items were concerned with methods of improving such teacher-aide schemes. Two obvious suggestions emerged: that there could be increased training for the teacher-aides in educational techniques (31), that the teacher and teacher-aide should be introduced before a programme is started (35). With regard to the potential duties of the teacher-aide there was little real support for the idea of their being involved in contacting parents (33), or being employed on a full-time basis (32).

No respondents felt that teachers could run such a scheme unassisted (30). Finally, there was concern that children not directly involved in the programme could feel left out (25).

THE TEACHER-AIDE QUESTIONNAIRE

The first item on the second questionnaire, completed only by the teacher-aides, related to the reaction of non-target children to the teacher-aides' presence, with the latter being unanimous in reporting that they met with a high level of acceptance from other children in the class.

Teacher-aide/school relations were also studied, with three instances of an 'excellent' relationship being recorded, three of a 'good' relationship, and only a single instance of a 'fair' relationship.

Overall, the seven teacher-aides working on the project assessed their relationships with fifteen teachers (six of the teacher-aides worked with two teachers and the seventh worked with three, as one of the teachers left the school and was replaced by another). Of the fifteen relationships, seven were rated as 'excellent', four as 'good', three as 'fair', and one as 'poor'. Similarly, teacher-aides were asked to give their impressions of the degree to which their skills were used by their teacher colleagues. Of the fifteen teacher/teacher-aide pairs, the teacher-aides considered that on seven occasions their skills had been employed 'considerably', on four 'fair' use was made of their skills, on three 'some' use, and in one instance 'minimal' use was recorded.

The seven teacher-aides were asked to estimate the nature of the relationship they achieved with individual treated children. This was measured on a five-point scale. For 87 per cent of pupils, the teacher-aides felt that an 'excellent' or 'good' relationship had been established, while for 13 per cent they felt the relationship was 'fair' or 'poor'. No one considered that only a 'minimum' relationship had been achieved.

Finally, in relation to social improvement (peer and adult relationships) the teacher-aides considered that 87 per cent of the children were 'slightly' or 'much' improved and 13 per cent were considered not to have changed, or to have deteriorated.

Although the reports were highly subjective they nevertheless provided a crude index of evaluation by those adults involved in the scheme.

DISCUSSION

The above data suggested that, for teachers and teacher-aides alike, while there had been an improvement in the self-reported ability to manage and understand children, there was far less improvement in terms of understanding of the children's families and increasing links with them (14). It may have been that this latter response was a reaction to the meetings that were arranged for mothers in the schools, which were relatively poorly attended. This response seemed a fair one, and reflected the considerable difficulties encountered in attempting to arrange co-operative ventures between teachers and parents; in this particular instance, it also related to the problem of encouraging mothers from disadvantaged backgrounds to attend group meetings on the school premises.

The very positive response to the notion that discussions with the mental health specialists were supportive to teachers and teacher-aides (8) suggested that junior school teachers, in particular, usually do not have sufficient opportunities within the school for discussing the problems involved in coping with difficult children. In a parallel study of teachers' responses to a social work scheme in schools the authors found that teachers in junior schools were much more likely than their counterparts in senior schools to report that discussions with mental health specialists were supportive (Wolstenholme and Kolvin 1980).

It also seems that the nurturing approach was seen by teachers and teacher-aides to be preferable to the removal of disturbed children from the class, and that it should be widely available for children with problems. A number of the respondents thought that there were insufficient opportunities for discussions between the teacher/ teacher-aide pairs and mental health workers and this is important because, in a similar American study, it was found that teacher satisfaction was significantly related to the amount of contact allowed with other professional staff (Dorr and Cowen 1972).

The positive reactions of the respondents to working in the same classroom stands in contrast to the American experience, where it proved necessary to remove the teacher-aides from the classroom as a result of teacher pressure (Zax et al. 1966). However, we must emphasize that from the start our teacher-aides spent time both inside and outside the classroom. The general success of the teacher/ teacher-aide pairs is likely to be determined by three factors: the careful collaborative selection of the teacher-aides, regular contact with the project team, and the accountability of the teacher-aides to the teachers. Only 40 per cent of the teachers felt that the teacher-aides should be employed on a full-time basis: it would therefore seem a more sensible use of resources to allow aides to work between several classes.

Perhaps the anxiety expressed about non-target children feeling left out reflected the positive view of the scheme held by the participants. We have evidence that the teacher-aides devoted at least some time to other children, and they unanimously agreed that these children responded very well.

Figure 6(1)   Overall severity: juniors: per cent outcome (good and poor categories only)

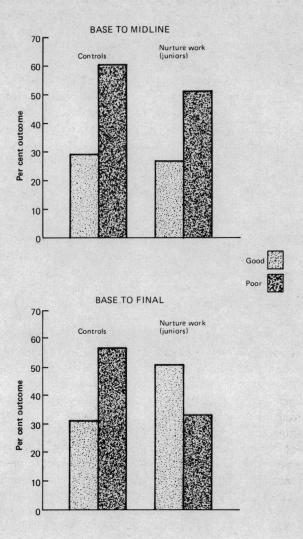

Figure 6(2)   Neurotic behaviour: Juniors: per cent outcome (good and poor categories only)

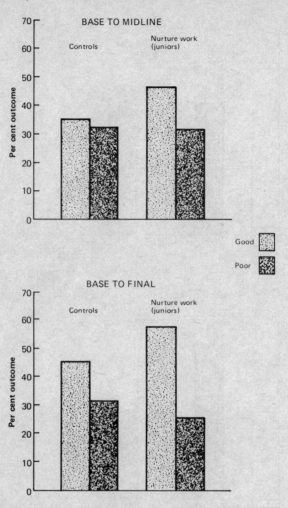

Figure 6(3)   Antisocial behaviour: juniors: per cent outcome (good and poor categories only)

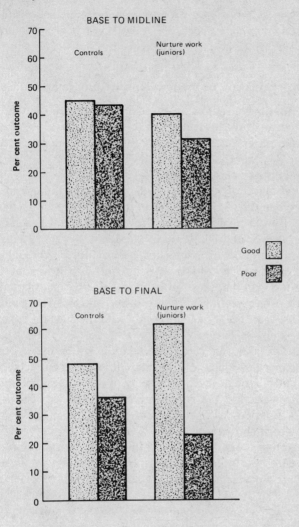

Overall, the very favourable responses were in keeping with those of other reports (Zax *et al.* 1966) and are one commendation for such programmes in schools. The programme seems to have influenced the teacher-aides and teachers: whether or not it influenced the children will be discussed in the next section.

Independent evaluation of the teacher-aide programme

The independent evaluation assessed both outcome and improvement; these terms have been defined in Chapter 3 and Appendix 2.

For the sake of simplicity, we have presented data on outcome in the categories of 'good' and 'poor' (but not 'moderate') for global, neurotic, and antisocial behaviour (*Figs 6 (1)–6(3)*, pp. 165–67). When comparing behavioural outcome, it will be seen that there were no differences between the at-risk controls and the nurture work children at the midline. By the final follow-up, however, there was a significant difference in favour of the latter work on overall severity (with half of them showing a good outcome but only a third showing a poor outcome), compared with the at-risk controls (in whom a third showed a good outcome and more than half a poor outcome). The same pattern occurred for both neurotic and antisocial behaviour, but the differences at the final follow-up did not achieve statistical significance.

More complex analyses were undertaken to study improvement, in which allowance was made for the initial differences between regimes in terms of child behaviour and a variety of other personal and social factors. In this section we report only on those aspects in which significant differences were found between the at-risk controls and the nurture work children.

We studied five types of data: (a) child behaviour and temperament based on parental interview; (b) a more general type of child behaviour based on teacher accounts (Rutter B2 scale); (c) classroom-related behaviour based on teacher accounts (Devereux scale); (d) social relationships based on peer reports; and (e) cognitive measures. There were no differences between the nurture work children and at-risk controls on measures (d) and (e). The significant differences that we did find are shown in *Table 6(2)*, and it is clear that the main differences occurred in relation to classroom-related behaviour. It should be emphasized that the ratings at the final follow-up were made long after the treatment was over and almost always by a different teacher to the one who participated in the project. Some of the improvements constituted short-term gains, others were maintained to the final follow-up and yet others emerged only at the final

Table 6(2)   *Significant differences between the nurture work group and the at-risk controls, with regard to improvement*

assessment point	data source		
	parent interview	*teacher general (Rutter B2)*	*teacher classroom-related behaviour (Devereux)*
base to midline	antisocial behaviour	nil	impatience inattentive/withdrawn blaming external circumstances increase in needing closeness
base to final	antisocial behaviour	neurotic behaviour	impatience blaming external circumstances quits easily comprehension aggregate behaviour score

follow-up. Consistent improvement occurred both in cases of reduction in antisocial behaviour, reported by the parents, and in certain items of classroom-related behaviour, reported by teachers. Finally, it was clear that there was only little overlap between the types of improvement that were recorded by means of the three different instruments (parental interview, the Rutter B2 scale, and the Devereux scale).

CONCLUSION

It is evident that the nurture work approach had an effect both on outcome and on improvement. The outcome scores showed that it produced good results with regard to global (overall) behaviour at the final follow-up; neurotic and antisocial behaviour showed encouraging trends. Improvement at the end of the treatment programme was apparent mainly for classroom-related behaviour, this being understandable as most of our efforts were directed at classroom-related behaviour. However, some of the gains were short-term, others more long-term, and yet more were 'latent', in the sense that they emerged only in the course of time. The detection of this latter point acts as an important warning, because had we relied only on the Rutter B2 child behaviour scale, we could easily have given up monitoring the cases at the midline point (by which time treatment had ended) because of lack of evidence of effectiveness of the programme.

It is also important to note that neither at the midpoint, which was at the end of treatment, nor at the final follow-up, which was eighteen months after the end of treatment, were there widespread differences of improvement between the at-risk controls and the nurture work children on the cognitive measures, in particular on reading. The only evidence that the nurture work children excelled the at-risk controls on cognitive measures was on verbal comprehension on the English picture vocabulary test at the midline follow-up, but this then washed out (see Appendix 3). Drawing from the literature on compensatory education and stimulation we would have expected more widespread immediate cognitive improvement on the part of the treated children, consisting of gains both in intelligence and in academic attainments. However, we can only speculate that this did not occur because our main endeavours were directed at behaviour rather than attainments and, therefore, the response was specific. For similar reasons, we would have expected a reported improvement from parents or peers on socialization, but, again, this did not occur to a significant extent. Other workers have reported immediate effects that did not last but, more recently, in the Head Start programme, there have been suggestions of better long-term effects. The latter seems to tie in with some of our findings.

Our most impressive results were on classroom-related behaviour so that we appeared to get a rather specific classroom effect such as improved comprehension at final follow-up, as reported by the teachers (which is not related to improved attainments or IQ on the basis of formal tests). In addition, we saw improvement in many of the other characteristics that are important to classroom functioning, such as decreased impatience, increased persistence in tasks, increased attentiveness, and, finally, improvement on the aggregate behaviour score on the Devereux scale at the final follow-up. Such progress was complemented by the general impressions of teachers, and teacher-aides about the usefulness and success of the venture, which are broadly in accord with the findings of the projects of Boxall and Cowen. Their projects and the Newcastle upon Tyne one, had different emphases and yet all three, using either descriptions and impressions and/or systematic assessments, have produced findings that endorse the nurture work approach.

The Cowen group (Cowen, Gesten, and Wilson 1979a; Cowen et al. 1979b) have recently published outcome results that, while addressing a different question, afford a comparison with our own. Cowen was looking at the effect on outcome of specific training of teacher-aides. He showed greater positive change on a wide variety of cognitive and school-based behaviour measures in a group who were exposed to trained teacher-aides in comparison to one with untrained teacher-aides. These results were encouraging and, of course, are generally in accord with our own, except that they reported more widespread cognitive results.

A number of factors made comparison between the Cowen research and our own difficult. For example, Cowen did not appear to have used systematic screening techniques or random allocation to treatment groups. His gains tended to disappear when he analyzed the treated children alone rather than the wider group of children who came into contact with the teacher-aides. Cowen did not have an untreated control group, so that there was no guarantee that the trained therapists were of more benefit to the children than no treatment at all.

In our study there was a significant lessening in antisocial behaviour, as reported by parents, both at the end of treatment (the midline point) and at the final follow-up, eighteen months later. General neurotic behaviour as reported by the teachers (Rutter B2 scale) was significantly improved only at the final follow-up. We do not quite understand this contrast between home and general school behaviour and can only speculate that the relief of pressure at school, as reflected by a lessening of classroom-related type of disturbance, gave rise to an immediate lessening of antisocial disturbance at home. It is possible that by the final follow-up the reduction of disturbance in the classroom had extended its effect to general neurotic behaviour in the school, as measured by the Rutter B2 scale. In comparison, in the Cowen work only immediate post-treatment gains appeared to have been made, which means that we can only speculate about the long-term impact of that project. Furthermore no parental data was reported.

7 Parent counselling-
teacher consultation

Summary

In this chapter we describe the introduction of six specially trained social workers into ordinary schools. Their task was to work, over one academic year, with teachers and parents with the aim of helping 147 identified children with adjustment problems. More specifically, the school social workers had a dual role – consulting with teachers about the management of identified pupils and in this way expanding and enhancing the pastoral role of the schoolteacher; and establishing short-term casework programmes with the parents of these children. Complementing the above were attempts to improve links between parents and teachers. Twelve schools were involved, each school social worker being allocated to one junior and one senior school for a period of one academic year.

Attention was focused, therefore, on the important adults with whom the children had daily contact – and not on the children themselves. This indirect approach distinguished the parent counselling–teacher consultation regime from the others described in this book, all of which involved some element of direct or face-to-face contact with pupils.

From the teachers' responses to questionnaires, we believe that their awareness and understanding of child behaviour expanded as a result of the programme, and that their repertoire of management techniques had moderately increased, too. This appeared true, also, in the case of parents. In addition, from the parents' point of view at least a greater understanding, if not a link, was forged between them and the school. Drawing on the subjective impressions of the therapists it appeared that the behaviour of the maladjusted children had also improved.

However, the results of more objective assessments suggested that, with the exception of school functioning in the juniors, there was little impact on the children's maladjustment. In relation to this finding it was perhaps not surprising that where there was significant improvement it was confined to measures that very specifically reflected school behaviour.

We discuss all the above issues in this chapter but begin by reviewing the literature on the topic.

A review of the literature

The idea of introducing specially trained social workers into ordinary schools and giving them a wider range of duties than those customarily held by Education Welfare Officers has, within the last twenty years, attracted a fair amount of support from educational and social work sources alike (Younghusband Report 1959; Plowden Report 1967; Seebohm Committee 1968; Braide Report 1969; Lyons 1973; Rose and Marshall 1974; DHSS 1977). Notwithstanding this support, few school social work schemes have been implemented in the UK. A primary problem has been the position of school social work at the interface of education and social work (Rose and Marshall 1974). Certainly there are considerable interorganizational and interprofessional barriers to overcome before any such projects can reach fruition (Davies 1976; Robinson 1978). Questions about accountability and appropriate professional tasks have also been posed (BASW 1974). In addition, there have been conflicting views about the role of the Education Welfare Service – while some have advocated a much expanded role for the Education Welfare Officer (Ralphs Report 1973; Fitzherbert 1977), others have identified the difficulties in such a proposal (Rose and Marshall 1974). While an examination of these issues is beyond the scope of the present review, it is nevertheless important to point out that the difficulties encountered in resolving such issues have probably done much to inhibit the expansion of school social work programmes to date.

In the UK the major documented accounts of school social work are restricted to the work of the Central Lancashire Family and Community Project (Rose and Marshall 1974), which remains one of the few studies to have provided empirical data in this field, an Educational Priority Area project that examined the work of an education social worker (Lyons 1973), and a number of small-scale local experiments (Watkins and Derrick 1977). This paucity of effectiveness studies of school social work practice is not restricted to the UK, the position being only slightly different in the USA (Radin 1979) despite the fact that school social work has been established there as a specialization for over fifty years (Costin 1969a). In contrast, descriptions of social work activities in schools (Costin 1969b; Anderson 1974; Watkins and Derrick 1977; Meares 1977), or accounts of potential tasks and functions for the school social worker, are relatively common (BASW 1974; Robinson 1978).

THE ROLE OF THE SCHOOL SOCIAL WORKER

Generally speaking, the work of the school social worker can be viewed as consisting of four broad areas of activity. The first area centres on consultative work with teachers. Second, there are those duties that fall into the category of direct services to pupils and/or parents. Third, there are activities directed to work in the community, for example, liaison with other agencies, and the fourth relates to the school social workers' contributions to the formulation of school policies, especially those affecting pupil welfare (Costin 1975).

The first two areas of activity have the most relevance to the Newcastle upon Tyne project. However, before we go on to discuss these in detail, it is worthwhile noting those recent studies that have looked at the part school factors play in the adjustment of pupils, since such findings have important implications for school social workers (Gath *et al.* 1977; Rutter *et al.* 1979). In the USA a view has emerged among some observers that school social workers have a shared responsibility with their colleagues in education in ensuring that the school provides an appropriate learning environment (Anderson 1974; Magill 1974; Gitterman 1977). Indeed, many have advocated that school social workers must play a major part in the formulation of those school policies that directly affect pupil welfare (Costin 1975; Meares 1977). Whether or not this type of duty is acceptable in British schools is another matter (Lyons 1973).

CONSULTATIVE WORK WITH TEACHERS

We mentioned earlier that a number of reports have outlined the need for a social work consultation service to schools, especially one that involves regular and direct contact with teachers (Robinson 1978). This was one of the main conclusions reached by Lyons in her work on three London primary schools (Lyons 1973). Support also comes from teachers themselves (Rose and Marshall 1974). What has not been nearly so clear, though, is which particular aspects of a collaborative service are of most value to teachers.

Consultation services to schools have differed according to the needs of the school (Morse 1967) and the skills, training background, and orientation of the consultant (Berlin 1967). Such services have proved a popular way for social workers and teachers to work together, and this has especially been the case in the USA (Berlin 1965, 1967, 1969; Costin 1969a, 1969b; Anderson, 1974; Fox 1974; Carter 1975; Radin 1979; Schild, Scott and Zimmerman 1976). On the other hand, examples of the application of these techniques in the UK are rare, making it difficult to assess the relative advantages of different aspects of the services.

Historically, the consultation models favoured by school social workers have been heavily influenced by the theories underlying Mental Health Consultation, and it is interesting to note that these theories were first devised for use with teachers (Caplan 1964, 1970). Mental Health Consultation lays great emphasis on the interpersonal qualities and skills of the consultant such as attentive listening and the ability to empathize. As these skills can be linked with an appreciation of the dynamics of the problem behaviour of youngsters and their parents it is not difficult to see why the approach has proved so popular with school social workers (Berlin 1969; Kadushin 1977). If consultation methods with teachers prove as effective as direct services with pupils and parents then the interest shown in them will have been justified, since consultation is less expensive and more efficient in the use of scarce manpower resources than are direct services, and it has considerable training and preventative possibilities. As yet, though, the impact of such schemes on clients is by no means clear.

By means of a consultation approach school social workers have aimed to increase the effectiveness of teachers in helping those pupils with emotional or behavioural problems. The social work contribution has taken a number of forms. First, it has involved encouraging teachers to collect and pool information on pupils. In this respect school social workers have contributed directly by providing details on the possible effects on a child of adverse family functioning. Second, the interpretive and diagnostic skills of school social workers, derived from their knowledge of child development and child psychopathology, have been of use in tracing the aetiology and the course of development of problems. Third, school social workers have made a direct contribution to decisions about pupil management, and fourth, as the stressful aspects of teachers' job have been recognized, the school social workers have provided teachers with support.

OUTCOME OF SCHOOL CONSULTATION PROGRAMMES

It is possible to consider three major areas of outcome of school social workers' consultation programmes with teachers (Mannino and Shore 1975). These are: (a) changes in the behaviour, knowledge, and skills of the consultee (teacher); (b) change in the client group (children) with which the consultee works; (c) change in the organization (school).

Traditionally social workers in schools have concentrated on the first area in attempting to increase both teacher awareness of the dynamics of pupil behaviour and also their repertoire of pupil management techniques. However, because the ultimate, though not the sole, test of effectiveness of a consultation programme is the impact it has on the client group, we are largely concerned with this (second) type of outcome.

In their review of the effects of a variety of consultation programmes, Mannino and Shore (1975) included a number of school-based studies that had objectives broadly similar to those of the present project. Eight of the school-based programmes used a consultation approach as the predominant method of intervention, and all of these were controlled studies. However, any direct comparison with the present study ends there because the theoretical models of the consultants varied as did the characteristics of the target groups, the duration of the schemes and, undoubtedly, the skills of the consultants. Six of the eight programmes revealed significant changes in some aspects of teacher attitudes, skills, or behaviour, but only three reported change in the pupil group.

In reviewing consultation programmes that used more traditional theoretical models, Mannino and Shore concluded that the impact of these programmes on clients was by no means clear, and the outcome for the selected group of school-based studies was consistent with this conclusion. They pointed to the problems inherent in conducting research on subjects who are not directly influenced by the experimental condition, and to the lack of understanding of the linkage between the consultant, consultee, and client, as possible factors leading to the uncertain state of affairs in this field.

PARENTAL INVOLVEMENT

Involving parents in the school system requires considerable adjustment on the part of the school staff and simultaneously exerts pressure on the relationships between teachers and school social workers (Davies 1976). However, there are three principal reasons for developing close links between parents and teachers: (a) to encourage parents to become involved in the educational process; (b) to involve the parents of pupils with behaviour problems in the co-operative management of the child; (c) to help school personnel to appreciate the social and parental influences in relation to particular children. In this section we comment on the first two issues only and consider the potential contribution of the counselling techniques of the school social worker in relation to them.

PARENTS AND THE EDUCATIONAL PROCESS

The influence of parental attitudes and behaviour on child cognitive performance has been well documented (Douglas 1964; Miller 1972; Marjoribanks 1979). Other reports have described how the school's interests can be taken up and supplemented by the parents (Newson and Newson 1977) (see also Chapter 5).

The importance of parental involvement is also borne out by reviews of compensatory education programmes in which home-based intervention appears to have led to impressive and enduring cognitive gains among pre-school children (see review by Bronfenbrenner 1974). It is not surprising, therefore, that major educational reports have emphasized the need for parental involvement in the educational process (Newsom Report 1963; Plowden Report 1967; Warnock Report 1978). The Plowden Report devoted a chapter to parental participation and recommended a 'minimum programme' that would involve increased opportunities for parents to see school staff, to learn more of what happens at school, and to find ways in which they could encourage their children to learn. Thus, as a first step towards this linking of home and school, the school social worker may serve a function in education similar to that of the social worker working with GPs, i.e. helping to secure the patients' co-operation (Cooper 1971). Likewise, the school social worker may help a pupil to derive greater benefit from the educational process 'by identifying and trying to help solve some of the *social* problems affecting him and his family' (Seebohm Committee 1968: 63). Thus, as far as educational issues are concerned, the school social worker's role can be seen as facilitating the links between the teachers and families – an apparently simple task, but one that does have difficulties (Harvey *et al.* 1977). In the next section we consider what may be required of the school social worker when problems stem from, or are related to, faulty family functioning.

PARENTS AND PUPIL MANAGEMENT

We have asked previously whether maternal involvement in a child's treatment is as necessary for the child's achievment of social and emotional adjustment as it is for his or her cognitive development (Wolstenholme, Hulbert, and Kolvin 1976). This may seem an unusual question in view of the tradition in child psychiatry for the treatment of the child to be allied to parental counselling. There have been surprisingly few studies examining this important question

(Bergin 1971), but the weight of clinical experience, and findings from studies based on a behavioural approach, have strongly suggested the importance of parental participation in the treatment of maladjustment (O'Leary and Drabman 1971; Johnson and Katz, 1973; Atkeson and Forehand 1978). Indeed, some clinical practices are based entirely on the involvement of all family members (Minuchin 1974; Haley 1977).

Contacting the parent(s) at an early stage may reduce the chances of problems escalating and the service becoming solely crisis-orientated (Anderson 1974). Invariably, such contact provides valuable information concerning the aetiology and the possible management of problems (Berlin 1967). Early involvement of parents is important not only for data-gathering and assessment purposes, but also in the promotion of mutual understanding between parents and teachers (Harvey *et al.* 1977), and the prevention of diametrically opposed views being developed between home and school. Such a polarization of views is often encountered in the case of non-attendance at school, and a meeting between teachers, parents, and pupil at an early stage is an effective way of re-establishing attendance (Johnson 1976).

A key aspect of parent counselling is that parents can, if necessary, be given help in dealing with a child's behaviour. For many pupils the achievement and maintenance of adequate functioning at school can be facilitated if their family is helped to recognize the problems involved, to realize the adjustments a child might have to make (Moore 1966). In many cases families may be able to do this only if they, too, receive external support. This is particularly the case with disorganized families and with those who are suspicious of the school with its different system of values to the home.

PROBLEMS OF ESTABLISHING LINKS BETWEEN TEACHERS AND PARENTS

The implementation of social work in schools depends heavily on the extent to which parents and teachers accept the need for such programmes. For example, one writer has observed that those parents with whom teachers could most profitably collaborate are those who are least likely to have contact with the school (Cave 1970) and it is in this area – with alienated or disadvantaged families – that the school social workers' potential contribution is greatest. This situation is in many respects reflected in the differences reported between the various occupational classes in the frequency of parent-school contact (Schools Council 1968). In the Schools Council's survey of school leavers, 38 per cent of parents in non-manual occupations, 46 per cent in skilled manual occupations, and 54 per cent in unskilled occupations, had not discussed their children with school staff. Similarly, in the Newson study the difference in 'concordance' (i.e. in how school interests are taken up and expanded at home) mirrored social class differences: the authors stressed that the least concordance occurred among boys of working-class families who were most seriously disadvantaged in this respect (Newson and Newson 1977). Again, among the 'socially disadvantaged' group of children described by Wedge and Prosser (1973) 60 per cent of parents had not visited the school as compared with 33 per cent of parents of the 'ordinary' group in that study.

At present, the burden of encouraging parental involvement has been left almost entirely to the teaching profession, though there is much debate as to whether this is sensible and practical. The Seebohm Report recommended that 'social work in schools should be the responsibility of the Social Services Department' (Seebohm Report 1968: 66). This was met with criticism by a number of educationalists who argued that it was unwise to pass the responsibility for links with parents to yet another agency (Clegg and Megson 1968; Plowden 1968). This line of argument seems to depart from the central issue, i.e. the application of relevant professional skills. So far there have been few attempts to assess the effectiveness of different methods of increasing contact between home and school (Sharrock 1970) and the Plowden Report's 'minimal programme' (see page 177) has been the exception rather than the rule.

There appear to be two important reasons for this lack of exploration. First, the extent, range, and evaluation of schemes are limited because of the additional time and effort needed to organize them, and because their implementation constitutes extra responsibilities for the hard-pressed teacher. While there are those teachers who manage to involve parents and provide a useful, informal counselling and supportive service, it is unlikely that the teaching profession unilaterally has sufficient resources to meet the social needs of pupils and parents (even though these are closely related to academic functioning) and, at the same time, to continue their classroom activities. The families of children with severe behaviour problems not only require a disproportionate *amount* of skilled help in addition to that which is provided in the school by pastoral staff, but they probably also need a different *type* of help.

The second reason is an attitudinal one and therefore more difficult to resolve. Not all teachers are enthusiastic about parental involvement and different surveys of teacher opinions have produced different answers on this topic. Ten years ago a large-scale survey found that a majority of teachers were in favour of encouraging home-school links, and over half of those who thought that someone should visit the home were of the opinion that such calls should be made by some kind of social worker (Schools Council 1968). However, a more recent survey, in relation to younger pupils, reported that few constructive statements were forthcoming on the subject of improving contacts with parents and that, on the whole, there existed 'little enthusiasm among urban schools for home visiting' (Chazan *et al.* 1976:284).

Again, this complex picture is difficult to decipher. Cave pointed out that while teachers may be too easily satisfied with their relationships with parents (based on information submitted to the Plowden Committee), there was 'little factual evidence of any real dissatisfaction about relationships between home and school on the part of many parents' (Cave 1970:21). It would seem that this statement is as applicable today as it was ten years ago.

To these views we must add those of social workers, who have tended to emphasize the importance of family, rather than school, influences on a child's development (Home Office Research Unit 1966). Whichever is the predominant view, it is clear that, in attempting to promote home-school links, social workers and other professionals should not under-estimate the resistance they may meet from those sections of the community they are most concerned to help.

The parent counselling–teacher consultation programme in action

INTRODUCTION OF THE SOCIAL WORKERS INTO THE SCHOOLS

The notion of seconding or placing social workers in schools was introduced into the schools in which we intended to work by officials of the local education authority who discussed the matter with the Headteachers at these schools. Following this, we felt that an essential step to undertake before the scheme started was for our social workers to visit the schools involved, to meet teachers, and generally to 'pave the way'. The involvement of teaching staff with positions of responsibility within the school was particularly important – lack of support from these key members of the school community could have had serious repercussions.

TRAINING OF THE SOCIAL WORKERS

The six professionally qualified social workers had not previously worked in schools. They were, therefore, given three months' preparatory training to introduce them to some of the issues they might face. Weekly seminars were arranged in the Newcastle upon Tyne University's Child Psychiatry Unit on casework and other psychotherapeutic topics, with particular attention being paid to school-based psychodynamic interventive techniques; attempts were made to anticipate problems likely to confront the school social worker. Additional seminars geared to school-based work were provided by psychologists, a Headteacher of a school for the maladjusted, and a school social worker. Each school social worker carried a small caseload and attended weekly seminars and consultations with a senior caseworker and psychiatrists, and attended sensitivity groups (see Chapter 8).

The transfer of social work skills to the school setting was considered through the examination of consultation theory, relationship development skills (Anderson 1974), and 'threat reduction techniques' (Klein 1959). It was recognized at this stage that basic skills in the art of diplomacy would be extremely important in the programme.

During the initial training period we also explored jointly some aspects of the school as a social institution with its own philosophy, organization, and management.

A PARTNERSHIP WITH TEACHERS

The consultation programme
The aims of consultation in this scheme were as follows:
(i)   to heighten teacher awareness of the psychodynamic aspects of pupil behaviour and to use this as the basis for managing the child;
(ii) to provide the teaching staff with relevant family and social information in order to assist them in formulating the management plan.

The programme, which lasted for one school year, consisted of two overlapping phases: a preliminary phase from May until September (apart from holidays) and an active phase from September to the end of the following April. Thereafter it was intended that the school social worker be called in by the teacher at times of crisis over the following three months but, in fact, this rarely occurred. As the school social workers were still visiting the schools while working on another part of the research programme their informal contact with teachers may have fulfilled this function sufficiently to obviate additional contact over this period.

The early stage was very much a settling-in period for the school social workers. During this time a maximum of two days per week was split between the two schools (one senior and one junior) covered by each school social worker. Discussions had to be arranged around both the additional duties of the school social worker (family visits, contact with other child-care agencies, and administrative duties) and the teachers' timetables, which meant that they were largely restricted to break and free periods.

At first, the notion that social workers could be useful in a school setting was met with some scepticism but, as trust was established, the teachers became able to discuss child behaviour and teacher-child interactions more freely. Other issues were teachers' fears about intrusion on their professional domain, and, conversely, their feeling that psychotherapeutic skills were being demanded from staff whose roles and functions were essentially educational. These anxieties had to be allayed early in the course of discussions, and only when a relationship based on some degree of trust had been established could the school social workers progress from giving support to teachers to introducing discussions about pupils' difficulties.

One factor that limited the programme in the senior schools was the number of teachers (up to fifteen) that a single child might have contact with in any one week. Moreover, this high number was found to accentuate children's sense of anonymity in the large secondary school, the caring for each child being split between many different people who tended to react to him or her in different ways. Seen from the teacher's viewpoint the problem was equally severe: each teacher had between 200 and 300 children a week to teach in large classes, and this was likely to preclude them from getting to know individual children well. Our solution to the difficulty was to concentrate on teachers who taught a child for more than three lessons per week. Occasionally, however, it proved useful to talk to a particular subject teacher who took only one or two lessons – notably art, music, or games. In practice this meant that in senior schools any one school social worker collaborated with, on average, sixteen teachers in order to discuss all the identified children in that school. In contrast, in the junior schools each school social worker worked, on average, with only four teachers.

The official pastoral staff proved to be key figures because other teachers usually referred the child to his or her house or year tutor if the child was emotionally upset or in trouble. Where possible, therefore, we tailored the programme for an individual child around the work of the pastoral staff, or at least encouraged such staff to be involved. Some of them proved enthusiastic about developing their pastoral skills, and the school social workers devoted much time to this aspect of the programme. Some teachers had a 'knack' of handling a particular child: this often became evident from talking to a selection of teachers about the child or from hearing from the parents about the child's regard for a particular teacher. Such teachers were encouraged to take a more active pastoral role with the child.

Analysis of the records kept by the school social workers for the period September–December showed that the majority (80 per cent) of contacts between teachers and school social workers were initiated by the latter. This trend continued into the final term and, therefore, was a consistent feature of teacher-school social worker interaction. It is noteworthy that the majority of teachers indicated that there were insufficient opportunities for contacting school social workers, probably because of the school social workers' part-time status.

A discussion lasting a minimum of ten minutes, during which there was a 'mutual exchange of information' about a pupil, was regarded as a reasonably detailed contact in relation to that pupil. While this may have been an arbitrary definition, it was useful for classifying the type of exchanges between teachers and school social workers. Two-thirds of all discussions in both senior and junior schools were of this variety: in senior schools an average of four such consultations took place each week, and in junior schools the average was two per week. It must be emphasized that these figures under-estimate the total time shared by teachers and school social workers. Half as many discussions (35 per cent) were classified as briefer contacts. Clearly, important exchanges of information could and did take place in a shorter period than ten minutes.

We expected more use to have been made of group consultation (one school social worker and more than one teacher) because this seemed an economical way of obtaining multiple views of the child and arranging collaborative action. However, it was used in only 21 per cent of all teacher contacts. We suspect that this was because it was difficult to bring teachers together at the same time, and also because the school social workers preferred individual work.

In complex organizations such as schools, opportunities for contact has to be fitted into the teachers' working day. We found that more than half (56 per cent) of the meetings were planned in advance. Such planned meetings were more common in the junior schools than in the senior ones: of the 159 contacts made in the autumn term of 1973, 62 per cent were planned, whereas in senior schools 50 per cent of 330 contacts during this same period were planned. This implies that the school social workers in the senior schools relied more on 'catching' teachers whenever they were available than did their counterparts in the junior schools. Certainly, teachers in junior schools had the least free time and, therefore, the advance planning of meetings was important. There were no other differences between senior and junior schools in the pattern of consultation: ratios of detailed to brief discussions, group to individual sessions, and teacher- to school social worker-initiated contacts were similar.

Although the average number of detailed contacts in senior schools was double that in junior schools, these were distributed between an average of sixteen, rather than four, teachers. Consequently, the teachers in junior schools were seen, overall, twice as often as their colleagues in the senior schools.

Frequency of consultations per child

Of the sixty-six pupils in junior schools exactly half were discussed in detail with at least one teacher, or more briefly with several teachers, on each weekly set of school visits. The corresponding figure in senior schools was 24 per cent of the total of eighty-one such pupils. In addition, 39 per cent of these junior and 52 per cent of these senior children were discussed in detail with one teacher, or more briefly with several teachers, approximately once every three weeks; 11 per cent of the junior and 24 per cent of the senior pupils were discussed less than once a month. Thus, the amount of detailed contact varied considerably.

The consultation method

To enable the teacher to use psychodynamic ideas and methods three consultation techniques were found useful. First, the school social worker could act as an emotional support. This arose naturally from the school social worker-teacher transaction and was well received. Second, the school social worker could act as a 'sounding board' to enable the teachers to formulate and crystallize their ideas about management of the children. Third, the school social worker could engage the teachers in discussion of child management. The aim of this was to help teachers to see beyond superficial explanations of seriously disturbed behaviour (Long, Morse, and Newman 1971) and thus to move towards a fuller appreciation of the inner feelings of the child. In this way, irrational, unpredictable, or irritable behaviour could be examined more carefully for what it might reveal about the child's mechanisms for coping with stress, his or her conflicts, and preoccupations. Guides to detailed techniques of helping children in class either individually (Redl 1959) or in groups (Kounin and Obradovic 1968) are available in literature. In practice, the introduction of a different view of classroom behaviour and discussion of methods of intervention proved to be one of the school social workers' main tasks, and tended to generate sympathy and a positive attitude to helping the child on the part of the teacher.

In providing the teacher with relevant factual information, the school social workers supplied details on the treated pupils drawn from psychological, educational, and social reports of the research programme. They also offered factual advice on child development issues, welfare facilities, and cultural problems.

Detailed plans for individual children

As well as developing a general approach to consultation with teachers we examined our data and knowledge of the individual children and considered, with the teacher, a treatment plan for each one. These plans were aimed at providing the school social workers with guidelines as to where the main emphasis in the teacher consultation programme should be placed. The treatment plans were made under six main headings.

(i) *Individualization of the curriculum.* Discussion on this topic was to ensure that, as far as possible, each child's individual requirement (emotional, social, academic) could be fulfilled within the school system. For example, we discussed how checks might be made on whether certain aspects of the curriculum were giving rise to stress in a particular child. Discussions concerning pupils' known 'sensitive' areas heightened the teachers' awareness so that they could offer reassurance. Arrangements for extra help for under-achievers or co-operative activities for isolated children were also discussed. It was agreed that it was important to make it possible to allow the child to succeed in some activity, for example, in a limited academic area, in art, in stories, in hobbies, or in games, so that he or she might gain self-confidence and proceed to identify with a group in the school. This was seen as being particularly important for the dull child or for one lacking in self-confidence.

(ii) *Adjustment of classroom activities and structures.* Schools and teachers vary widely in the degree to which they structure classroom activities, and it was discussed that approaches may have to be adjusted if they are to meet the needs of certain children or situations. For example, free and exploratory classroom activities might sometimes be allowed, projects could be chosen, or other activities interspersed with academic work. The school social worker could here again act as a catalyst to the teachers' ingenuity. It was suggested that re-structuring could be physical as well as curricular: for instance, an aggressive child may have to be seated near the teacher or distant from peers who provoke aggression.

Other children could be placed near the teachers for support or because they need shielding from distraction.

(iii) *Consistency of classroom management and rules.* The experienced teacher realizes that rules must be minimal and consistently applied in relation to each child. Although such rules must be defined in concrete terms, so that children are not tempted to test their limits, rigidity must be avoided as rules may occasionally have to be 'bent' for the benefit of certain children (Catterall 1970). We discussed how consistency of rules is difficult to achieve in those schools where children are exposed to a large number of teachers with varying classroom management styles and views about discipline, and how this can be a source of confusion and frustration for children. Consultation, particularly with groups of teachers, can increase consistency of management.

(iv) *Linking of home and school.* The teachers were encouraged to develop their awareness of the need for links between the home and the school, and supported in achieving this contact. Meetings between parents and teachers were encouraged, or the school social worker took work set by the teacher home to an absent child. Joint meetings between teacher, parents, and school social worker did occur, but on the whole these were rare. Some of the issues involved in linking home and school are discussed more fully later in this chapter.

(v) *Discussion of child's home environment.* Those aspects of the child's background that had relevance to his or her behaviour or performance were discussed – for example, the disciplinary pattern at home which might play a part in understanding a child's reaction to authority at school. The nature of intra-family relationships and wider, cultural problems were also brought to the attention of the teacher. Particular behaviour problems were considered, for example, school refusal, or whether parents seemed to be exerting too much or too little pressure on a child. Current family crises, together with any details of the child's home life that might help the teacher to decide what to do, were also discussed.

(vi) *Discussion of extra-curricular activities.* In some cases the child's functioning and adjustment outside academic activities merited attention. It was suggested that the child may be helped to relate better to peers or adults through hobbies or sporting activities, especially if these occurred in informal settings, and his or her ability to participate in such activities was explored.

PARENT COUNSELLING

The work undertaken with the families became known as the 'parent counselling' programme although in many respects the activities of the school social workers *vis à vis* the parents of the treated children were influenced mainly by short-term casework models (Reid and Shyne 1969; Reid and Epstein 1972, 1977) and traditional casework methods. The basic aim of the work with parents was to promote in them an awareness of the way family factors influence the child's performance. To do this it was necessary to try to keep the focus of discussion on the child, especially on the child in school. The tactics used by the school social workers to achieve this end were as follows: (a) they provided parents with detailed information about relevant aspects of the child's school performance; (b) they promoted parental support for the changes that were being worked on at school, for example, they were encouraged to ask about and praise the child when they heard of appropriate behaviour of achievements; (c) they provided direct social work help for the attendant family problems (which proved in fact to be numerous). In this particular aspect of their work with the families the approach varied according to the nature of the problem. Task-centred approaches were applicable in cases involving interpersonal conflict, or problems with formal organization as in the case of relations with the school (Reid and Epstein 1977). On the other hand, when difficulties involved either physical health or financial problems these were, in the main, dealt with by more traditional methods.

THE INITIAL STAGE

This stage involved the assessment and planning of casework with parents. All families involved in the research were seen by one of the members of the project team prior to the start of the parent counselling-teacher consultation programme. This contact took the form of an assessment interview the aim of which was to provide a baseline measure of child behaviour (Garside *et al.* 1975; Kolvin *et al.* 1975b). In addition, many other child and family details were obtained (see Chapter 4 and Nicol *et al.* 1981).

The purpose of the school social workers' initial contacts with families was to add to this baseline information and also to:
(i)   establish a rapport with the family;
(ii) explain the objectives of the school social work programme, and its limited duration;
(iii) gain some understanding of the interactive factors at work in the family;

(iv) begin discussing problems identified at school by the family and by the school social worker;

(v) begin discussing how family problems might impinge on the child and affect his or her school functioning.

After two introductory visits to the family the school social workers and their back-up teams of social work tutors and psychiatrists assessed the number of problem areas (illness reactions, social interaction, or other problems) and the severity of problems in each area. Treatment aims were also recorded and estimates were made of parental attitudes towards help being offered (motivation). There were commonly multiple problem areas in these families, the modal number being four to six problems per family, with a maximum of sixteen; these problems were also of great chronicity, nearly all of them having been of more than three years' duration. The various problem areas are listed in *Table 7(1)*.

The amount of disturbance in each problem area was assessed. Despite the fact that the difficulties in many families were multiple, they did seem to focus on certain areas, six of which contained over one-third of cases (*Table 7(1)*). These areas were physical illnesses, emotional problems, financial difficulties, marital problems, parent-child problems, and problems of schooling.

Having identified and described the main problems in each family,

Table 7(1)   *Type and frequency of family problems (junior and senior children combined n = 146)*

---

most common problems (present in over two-thirds of families)
personal:	emotional problems in member of family
interactional:	marital problems
	relationship problems between parent and child
other:	problems about schooling

moderately common problems (one-third to two-thirds of families)
personal:	physical illness in family
social:	financial difficulties

less common problems (less than one-third but more than one-tenth – in order of frequency)
personal:	parental dullness
	alcoholism and psychopathy
	mental illness in family
social:	unemployment
	housing difficulties
	material deprivation of child
	poor home management
	dependency on social services
interactional:	problems with relatives (apart from spouse or children)
	problems with neighbours
other:	communication with other agencies (medical, probation, housing, etc.)

---

the next step was to decide what to do about them. In a brief, focused approach to families with so many problems it would clearly not have been sensible to have tried to help with each difficulty: we had to be selective. Therefore, four areas of family life were chosen for further intervention in the majority of cases. These were emotional problems, marital problems, problems in the relationship between parent and child, and problems about schooling. In some cases help was also offered for many other types of problems but much less commonly so than in the case of these four areas.

At the end of the treatment programme the school social workers recorded the areas in which they had actually intervened. In practice, it was in these four areas that treatment had most often been given, particularly in the area of relationship problems between parent and child, where it appeared that aid had been administered more often than had been originally intended. Altogether, 147 families were seen, involving eighty-one senior school pupils and sixty-six junior school pupils.

THE MIDDLE STAGE

The middle stage of the parent counselling programme was the main treatment period. The programme in total consisted of up to ten visits per family (including the preliminary interviews) though the number of visits actually carried out varied, with most families receiving four to six calls in all (see *Table 7(2)*). In only a minority of visits were both parents seen together, although in 55 per cent of cases there was at least one joint interview.

A feature of the Newcastle upon Tyne approach that was particularly important to the school social workers during this stage was the 'back-up service', which offered regular supervision. Before each family meeting, the school social workers were expected to set out the particular objectives they were aiming for in that session. It was

Table 7(2)   *Frequency distribution of the number of school social workers' visits to parents (includes joint interviews)*

number of visits per family	n = 147
	%
3 or less	11
4–6	44
7–9	36
10 or more	9
total	100

hoped that this would reduce the likelihood of opening up new areas of discussion to the detriment of the specific goals already set. Recording methods ensured easy identification of the school social worker's activity: the purpose of the visit, any important interaction during the call, and the amount of attention given to particular objectives. Thus attempts were made to ensure that the specificity that characterized the initial stages was continued into this stage.

We will describe the middle stage of the programme more fully in two ways: by a series of typical case histories and by a work analysis.

The middle stage: case descriptions
  Physical illness
  Bob S.
     Initial severity: marked. Proposed help: maximal.
     Help given: maximal. Goal: partly achieved.
Bob S. was an eleven-year-old who had been showing markedly disturbed behaviour at school. He was from a family where there was very little supervision, and where there were few restrictions on aggressive behaviour. His father had been unemployed for many years and an older brother had recently left home after a family argument. During the course of the first interview the school social worker realized that Mrs S. was nearly blind and that this was creating many problems. Mrs S. had lost her spectacles three years earlier and had not replaced them. Despite some initial resistance, the school social worker arranged an ophthalmic appointment for Mrs S., transported her to it, and generally supported her in getting her new glasses. She seemed pleased with the result but there was some doubt about whether she would regularly wear her glasses.

  Parental loss
  Billy K.
     Initial severity: marked. Proposed help: maximal.
     Help given: maximal. Goal: mostly achieved.
On her first visit the school social worker was received with hostility when she tried to explain the school's concern about this seven-year-old boy's reading problem. In the presence of a neighbour, whom it was felt had been 'brought in' for support, the story emerged of the death of Billy's father after a heart attack six months earlier. Over a series of visits Billy's mother became more open and confiding. Billy, the youngest of four brothers, had been very attached to his father and, since the death, an overdependent relationship had grown up between mother and son. The school social worker was able to help Mrs K. to work through some of her feelings about the loss, and

about her current relation with Billy. By receiving help herself, it was hoped that Mrs K. might in turn help Billy with his own grief.

Emotional problems
Alan W.
   Initial severity: marked. Proposed help: moderate.
   Help given: moderate. Goal: minimally achieved.
The school social worker was aware at the time she made her home visit that she was likely to meet with a hostile reception from Alan's mother. The aim was to see whether there was any way of making an alliance with the family of the anxious and overprotected obese seven-year-old who was frequently absent from school. The mother's previous contact with school had been disastrous because of her behaviour when she went to complain about the school's handling of her son. It rapidly became clear that there were vast problems in the marriage in addition to Mrs W.'s aggressiveness and drinking problem. The child was smothered at home and his mother sided with him in a paranoid way over any minor dispute at school.

   In planning intervention it was realized that any radical pro-gramme would fail. The school social worker restricted her efforts to being accepting of Mrs. W., despite her abusive language and aggressiveness, and to tactfully finding ways that the boy could individuate, for example, by entering for a cycling proficiency course. These limited goals met with some success over eight visits.

Financial difficulties
Keith W.
   Initial severity: moderate. Proposed help: great.
   Help given: moderate. Goal: achieved.
An eleven-year-old was showing nervousness and getting into fights at school. He was being brought up by his mother, a European immigrant, alone. Difficulties were compounded because her quali-fications were not recognized in the UK and she had to do poorly paid work for long hours. This reflected on Keith who saw little of his mother and seemed to lack love and attention. Shortly after the intervention commenced a crisis was precipitated by the boy's poor behaviour at school. This allowed the school social worker to discuss with Keith's mother, in some emotionally charged interviews, her feelings about the boy. Subsequently, the school social worker was able to mediate between Mrs W. and the school and channel off a quantity of projected hostility on both sides. Shortly after this Mrs W. obtained a full-time, better paid job, where the regular hours allowed her more time with Keith, whose behaviour improved markedly.

Marital problems

Leslie T.

   Initial severity: severe. Proposed help: great

   Help given: great. Goal: nil achievement.

Leslie was a seven-year-old boy who was showing a behaviour disturbance at school. When the school social worker called, the family seemed quite prepared to discuss the ways in which the home might be contributing to the difficulties. Leslie's father was unemployed, which led to some financial problems as there were five children in the family; however, his attempts to find work seemed half-hearted and he tended to apply for jobs that he had little hope of getting. Mrs T. seemed chronically depressed and ineffective and, indeed, her husband seemed to have moved comfortably into the role of housekeeper. The marital problems were clearly great. There were difficulties in contraception that neither partner seemed motivated to sort out in any way and the family seemed to be hit by one crisis after another, which they seemed to meet with general immobility and lack of motivation. Despite quite extensive involvement over a year there was no appreciable change in the family situation.

Parent-child problems

Anthony R.

   Severity: moderate. Proposed help: great.

   Help given: great. Goal: minimally achieved.

Anthony, a seven-year-old boy, had a reading problem and antisocial behaviour at school. In addition, he was isolated and rejected by his peers. On early visits to his large family (he was sixth of the seven children) his mother seemed poorly motivated but did complain of the boy's restlessness and of difficulties in handling him. The family had a number of problems, which remained ill-defined. Mrs R. was unforthcoming and, despite repeated requests, Anthony's father did not make himself available. However, the school social worker did make a number of visits and was able to have useful discussions with Mrs R. centred on the handling of the boy and on the family being able to recognize his individual needs. The weight of her other problems, including two enuretic older siblings, probably prevented Mrs R. from using the help fully.

Kathy C.

   Initial severity: severe. Proposed help: great.

   Help given: great. Goal: moderately achieved.

The school social worker had heard before her first visit that there were great problems between mother and child. The mother was bringing up Kathy by herself and in early interviews it became clear that she was finding this a very lonely task and was unable to provide limits to the behaviour of her eleven-year-old daughter. It was felt that a simple directive counselling approach would be the most effective, and, indeed, over six interviews the mother's distress over her handling difficulties decreased markedly.

Problems with schooling
Donna T.

> Initial severity: severe. Proposed help: great.
> Help given: little. Goal: mostly achieved.

An eight-year-old girl showed the features of a moderate conduct disorder at school, including truancy as a leading symptom. The household turned out to be a large one where Mrs T. was bringing up five daughters alone. Donna was the youngest and in many ways one of the least disturbed, although by the same token, one of the most attention-needing. Much of the focus of treatment was to support Mrs T. in her anxieties about her adolescent daughters who had numerous problems; however, during the course of the programme, Donna's behaviour improved and she began to attend school regularly.

The middle stage: parent counselling: a work analysis
The intention throughout contacts with parents had been to retain a focus on the child. How far had this been possible? We were able to check by examining a sample of sixty case records relating to 350 interviews. The records included details about the purpose of the visit, the important interactions that took place, and the areas discussed. Certain features of the counselling approach became apparent. First, the stated intention of the visit had been adequately covered in only 40 per cent of the sample of interviews studied. We were aware that the families were experiencing many problems, and to a certain extent this was reflected in the work pattern of the school social workers in that attention was diverted to other problems that emerged during the course of the interviews. This served to make the approach, especially in the middle stage, more diffuse and represented a limitation of the scheme. Nevertheless, the analysis also revealed that the four most commonly discussed topics were the parent-child relationship, child management by parents, educational matters, and parent-school relations, and so some focusing had been possible.

Another feature which represented a departure from the stated intentions of the approach was the failure to involve fathers, shown by the low level of joint interviews. One factor contributing to this was that most of the visits were conducted during the day. Also, fathers may be less responsive than mothers to reports coming from the school. Whatever the reasons, failure to involve fathers was a serious deficiency, as other studies have pointed to the importance of paternal involvement in a child's education in both disorganized families (Tonge, James, and Hillam 1975) and general populations (Chazan *et al.* 1976).

THE FINAL STAGE

During the final stage of contact the planned visits came to an end, and the achievement value of the contacts was assessed. It was decided that the school social workers should provide a crisis service to families in the final term, but in actual fact this service was rarely requested.

Linking home and school

A most difficult task for the school social worker was to find ways of linking home and school. Attempts were made to lessen mutual distrust and prejudice and ways sought to increase parental interest in the child's education and progress or, more generally, in school activities. Initially, the work consisted of carrying the teachers' ideas to the parents. Occasionally, it was necessary to reassure teachers that parents were concerned and interested, and sometimes to repeat the process with the latter.

There was also the far more difficult operation of helping certain teachers to appreciate their personal impact on parents. This was perhaps the most sensitive area the school social workers had to deal with; when it constituted an important issue, it had to be broached with great diplomacy and caution.

Sometimes, before meeting, parents or teachers proposed angry confrontations with each other but, once together, their reactions usually proved quite different. Teachers were often anxious about meeting parents of difficult children, and sometimes did not know what to say. In general, both making contact with parents and linking home and school proved to be more difficult in the senior than the junior schools. This was probably due to a number of factors, including the relative extent of the senior schools catchment areas, the size and organization of the comprehensive schools (which parents and children often found daunting), and the projection over a long period of time of parents' own unhappy school experiences.

Sometimes the teacher thought the school social worker was siding with the parents, while the parents thought the opposite. Problems occurred when teachers thought that a child's classroom behaviour was unalterable in view of adverse features in his or her environment and, in such cases, it was important to focus attention on classroom activities once more.

In general, it is unusual for teachers not to have a rough idea of their pupils' home problems. An outline of these problems often acts as a catalyst to endeavours to help the child.

Interviews with parents provided some idea of the parents' child-rearing patterns, such as their disciplinary methods, the degree of stimulation, they offered, and the amount of attention and affection the child was given. The school social worker aimed to draw a picture of the total family and cultural milieu in which the child was being reared. As already mentioned, some of the families had multiple problems, but only a small proportion of them did not want to hear about the views of teachers and we found few occasions when a real lack of interest in the child's progress was evident, although ways of helping were often ill-understood.

The transfer of selected information from home to school was an important part of the school social worker's duties and this raised a potential problem concerning confidentiality. This subject has been regarded as a problem area within recent British school social work projects (Watkins and Derrick 1977) and has been discussed else-where in the context of school-home co-operation (Smethells 1977). If a parent revealed previously unknown information to the school social worker and it was relevant to the child's functioning, it was left to the school social worker to indicate that this sort of infor-mation might well help the teacher to understand the child's present predicament and to ask for permission to discuss this with the teacher. Our view is that teachers interested in expanding their pastoral roles and functions have high professional ethical standards similar to those of any other of the 'helping' or 'caring' disciplines and should not be denied relevant information. In our project there was no abuse of information. Nevertheless, we believe that such infor-mation should not be incorporated in permanent school records, but should be seen as related to transient or current 'here-and-now' problems that the school social worker or teacher is attempting to solve.

Perceptions of the programme by teachers, parents, and school social workers

The degree to which teachers and parents accept schemes that directly involve them will obviously affect the success of such schemes. In this section we consider teachers' and parents' perceptions of the school social work programme. This is followed by a description of the school social workers' views about their effectiveness.

SOCIAL WORKERS IN SCHOOLS – THE TEACHERS' RESPONSES

In the early stages of the project we found that teachers did not appear to be very sure of the precise roles, functions, and skills of the school social workers. For instance, they were perceived as having more authority in relation to the families and a more directive role than they had in reality. On the other hand, in no instance did a teacher expect the school social worker to undertake the role of a school messenger, nor such non-social work tasks as checking for lateness, as described by Fitzherbert (1973). Teachers were concerned about becoming too involved with complex psychosocial and family problems, and undertaking home visits and other treatment procedures. Such views filtered back to the project team during the first days of the programme, but as mere impressions they were of limited value. We therefore decided to send out a questionnaire to all those teachers who had taken part in the scheme.

There is a lack of objective information in this particular area of interdisciplinary co-operation, largely because so few schemes have been implemented. Even when material has been available, however, its usefulness has been limited, first, by a failure to collect information systematically, and, second, by a lack of distinction between the views of teachers who had worked with a school social worker and those who had not. In our investigation it was possible to ask the opinion of teachers who had first-hand experience of working with a school social worker, and accordingly to study their attitudes to a specific social work service. Our questionnaire was based partly on one used in other studies (e.g. Freeman 1973), but was modified and extended to meet the needs of our project. The questionnaire was piloted in the early stage of the research at which time it became apparent that completion would only be possible if there were guarantees of anonymity and also that we would have to dispense with the checking of questionnaire reliability.

There were five broad areas in which we considered feedback from teaching staff would be valuable. Some of the areas were entirely concerned with aspects of the consultation offered in this programme, the others with wider themes associated with alternative approaches to helping pupils with special needs:

(i) teachers' views about consultation and its impact on practice;
(ii) teachers' views on alternative approaches to management of pupils with behavioural problems;

(iii) teachers' reactions to the feedback they received from school social workers, and to the availability and appropriateness of school social work consultation;

(iv) the extent to which teachers were able to understand social work concepts;

(v) teachers' views on the actual and potential duties of social workers in schools.

A full account of the survey of teachers' views is presented elsewhere (Wolstenholme and Kolvin 1980). A shortened version of the procedure and the main findings of the survey are outlined below.

Method

Three months after the programme ended a self-rating questionnaire was used to ascertain the views of teachers who had been involved in the project. All those teachers with whom the school social workers had at least one detailed pupil-orientated discussion (as defined on page 183) were contacted by senior members of the project team who had not been personally involved in providing a social work service to the school. In all, 117 teachers were contacted and seventy-three completed questionnaires were returned – a response rate of 62 per cent. There appeared to be four main reasons for this rather moderate response: (a) staff mobility; (b) insufficient contact between teachers and school social workers hindering the completion of the questionnaire with any degree of confidence (some teachers had only one discussion with the school social worker and an analysis of the amount of time teachers spent in consultation with school social workers revealed that non-respondents were usually those who had spent the least time in consultation); (c) resistance to the completion of yet another questionnaire and (d) more rarely, resistance of some teachers to aspects of social work or to the programme in general. It should be emphasized that there have been similar difficulties in maintaining contact with teachers in other studies (Rose and Marshall 1974).

Teacher sample

The teachers who replied represented a fairly typical cross-section in terms of training and experience, although there was a slight over-representation of teachers in senior posts.

Findings

Teachers' responses to individual items are shown in *Table 7(3)*. These responses constituted a crude index of the usefulness of a social work programme designed to assist teachers both in coping with and helping pupils with psychological problems. Some of the items referred specifically to the impact on teacher practice of working with a school social worker – all the items in *Part A* of *Table 7(3)*, and items 14 and 15 in *Part B*, fell into this category. The remainder referred to overall aspects of the school social work scheme or were statements of a more general nature relating to the management of pupils.

(i)   *Views about what was achieved.* A primary task for the school social workers was to help teachers maximize their practical management skills in dealing with pupils with difficulties. While the responses of the teachers did not suggest the social workers made a major impact in this area, there was evidence that over 50 per cent of the teachers did consider consultation to be of at least *some* use in improving handling ability (3), in increasing their knowledge about psychological methods of handling children (5), and in thinking out alternative ways of coping with disturbed behaviour (9). The school social workers appeared to have made a greater impression when it came to providing support for the class teacher, with over three-quarters of the teachers reporting that collaboration helped, at least slightly (8). More than half of the teachers endorsed the notion that consultation led, at least to a small extent, to a sharing of responsibility (15). A number of items covered the topics of increased teacher awareness of child and family problems and home-school relations. It appeared that the school social workers had their greatest success in increasing teachers' understanding of child behaviour (1) and the child's family background (2). This was not accompanied by a similar improvement in teachers' understanding of emotional development in general (6), nor by a substantial increase in their awareness of their own reactions to pupils (4). Furthermore, two-fifths of the teachers indicated that consultation had not been successful in the areas of fostering links between parents and school (14).

(ii) *Views on alternative methods of management.* The teachers had the opportunity to indicate their preferences for other helpful techniques. A clear majority were against the idea of moving disturbed children into special classes or schools (17). In addition, there were few teachers who would definitely have preferred to see the school social worker undertake direct treatment of children (19), and even fewer who would definitely have preferred to contact parents themselves (21), although more than half indicated that this was a possibility.

(iii) *Reactions to (a) feedback and (b) content of consultation.* Despite an agreement among the research team that information would not be lightly withheld, one-third of teachers were generally dis-

Table 7(3) *Teacher questionnaire: the teachers' responses to consultation*

Part A		nil	slightly	moderately/ markedly
		%	%	%
1.	enhanced my understanding of the children identified	14	38	48
2.	increased my understanding of the children's families	13	30	57
3.	improved my ability to handle the children's behaviour	46	36	18
4.	led to an increase of my understanding of my own reactions to children	45	39	16
5.	enhanced my knowledge about the psychological techniques of handling children	49	44	7
6.	enhanced my knowledge about emotional development in general	62	28	10
7.	provided me with useful information from psychological tests	64	22	14
8.	it helped me to have someone to talk to about the children's problems	16	39	45
9.	it helped me to think out alternative ways of coping with disturbed behaviour	35	33	32

Part B		not really	possibly	definitely
		%	%	%
10.	I would have liked more advice	36	39	25
11.	there were sufficient opportunities for discussing everything I wanted to discuss	40	24	36
12.	I would have liked to have been told more about how to handle children	57	32	11
13.	I could usually see what the school social worker was getting at	4	29	67
14.	it helped to foster links with the families of disturbed children	43	37	20
15.	it led to a sharing of responsibility for individual children	42	45	13
16.	I was told enough of what was found out in interviews with parents	36	33	31
17.	I would have preferred it if the very disturbed children had been removed to special classes or schools than to help them to be maintained in our school with the help of a school social worker	58	17	25
18.	I think the school social workers should have spent more time visiting the homes	48	49	3
19.	I would have preferred it if the school social worker had undertaken direct treatment of the children	53	34	13
20.	school social workers should encourage unco-operative parents to come into (contact with) the school	4	16	80
21.	I would have preferred to contact the parents myself	42	54	4
22.	school social workers should confine themselves to social problem families	61	26	13
23.	school social workers should concern themselves with staff tensions that might arise in the school	74	23	3
24.	school social workers should be more informative about the psychological information they elicit from families	29	49	22

satisfied with the actual feedback of information about families
(16), and more than two-thirds considered there was poor transmission of information from the psychological testing of children
(7) and of psychological information elicited from the families (24).
As opportunities for discussion with teachers had to be fitted
around existing timetable demands, which proved a difficult task
in senior schools, it was not surprising to learn that two-fifths of
teachers clearly indicated that the opportunities for consultation
with school social workers were insufficient (11). Furthermore,
three-quarters of the teachers would have liked more advice (10)
but the nature of this advice is uncertain.

(iv) *Ability to understand social work concepts*. Technical jargon is often
reported as being a hindrance to interprofessional co-operation,
but the response to this item (13) suggested that it did not constitute a major problem. However, nearly a third of teachers had
sufficient reservations to mark the 'possibly' column, thus
emphasizing the need for greater clarity on the part of school
social workers in communication with other professionals.

(v) *Views of the actual and potential duties of social workers*. First, it was
clear that three-quarters of the teachers were unwilling to have
school social workers concern themselves with staff tensions (23).
Second, the notion that school social workers should confine
themselves to social problem families obtained a strong negative
endorsement from nearly two-thirds of the teachers, which suggested that other aspects of the school social workers' contributions were perceived as valuable (22). Finally, teachers felt
strongly that the school social worker should be the person to
contact unco-operative parents (20): indeed, the greatest agreement among teachers was reported in this area, with over three-
quarters 'definitely' seeing this as an important role for the
school social worker.

Two further aspects of the scheme were singled out for
comment. First, more than three-quarters of teachers endorsed
the notion of the school social worker having a base (i.e. an
office) inside, rather than away from, the school. Second,
teachers were asked how convenient they found the consultation
pattern (which involved organizing discussions to fit the
teachers' timetable). The majority (two-thirds) found it slightly
inconvenient.

Re-analysis of data by school and teacher characteristics
Teachers' responses to each of the twenty-four items in *Table 7(3)*
were re-analysed according to the type of school in which the teacher

worked (junior or senior) and four teacher characteristics: age, sex, training, and parental status. The results suggested that the responses were not influenced by the type of school nor by these personal characteristics. Alternative explanations are therefore necessary (Wolstenholme and Kolvin 1980).

The survey – implications for the future
The main conclusions drawn from this teacher survey were that, even with a limited amount of contact, school social workers can make a positive contribution in schools, and that this contribution is likely to be welcomed. Only a few teachers reported that they gained no help from consultation and, bearing in mind the limited school social worker-teacher contact, this was encouraging. Within this general pattern, school social workers were particularly appreciated for their emotional support and for the information about families that they could pass on to teaching staff. On the other hand, the teachers were less inclined to think that their pupil management skills had improved as a consequence of discussion with the school social workers and, at the same time, there was some dissatisfaction about the amount (and perhaps the nature) of some of the information teachers received.

In general, the findings also suggested that the teachers *did* want to play as full a part as possible in dealing with difficult and/or disturbed pupils. They also saw the need to involve parents, but did not wish to see school social workers become involved in staff tensions. All this could be considered to augur well for the future. Above all, the findings of this survey lend considerable support to the view that closer links between the educational and social services are attainable at a practical level.

SOCIAL WORKERS IN SCHOOLS – THE MOTHERS' RESPONSES
It seemed important to us that we should find out how a non-referred group of clients responded to the home visiting scheme. For example, did the scheme help mothers to cope with their children and, more specifically, the child in question? How were their attitudes towards school affected? What did they see as the advantages and disadvantages of the scheme?

Three to six months after the end of the project all the mothers who had been involved were asked to complete a questionnaire containing the items listed in *Table 7(4)*.

Method

The questionnaire was administered by research staff previously involved with the families. In all, 84 per cent (122) of the eligible mothers completed this questionnaire. The non-respondents comprised families who had moved away from the area, those we were unable to contact, and those who refused to continue in the research. The respondents and non-respondents were compared with regard to motivation levels (assessed by the school social workers nine months earlier) and to exposure (number of contacts). In neither of these characteristics did the non-respondents differ significantly from the respondents. The motivation measure was a composite score consisting of a series of five-point scales covering such items as family acceptance of problems, desire for help, willingness to work with (a) teachers and (b) school social workers, and previous attempts to seek help. These assessments were made by the school social workers involved, after two visits to the families.

Discussion of questionnaire findings (see Table 7(4))

About 70 per cent of mothers reported that following counselling they had an increased understanding of their children (Q). Success in self and family understanding, though, was less marked (D and I). For all items a majority of mothers reported some benefit, although the items concerned with the concept of understanding were characterized by a high percentage of responses in the mid-point of the scale. We suggest that this was the result of a difficulty in coping with as nebulous a concept as understanding.

With regard to home-school relations, it was clear that school social work involvement did not inconvenience mothers (O). Furthermore, maternal understanding of school and schooling improved (M).

Two-thirds of the mothers were unequivocal in their response that it had helped to have someone with whom to talk over their problems, while one-fifth did not find this to be the case (G).

It seemed that a model of brief intervention received support, in that almost two-thirds of mothers considered that there were sufficient visits in which to discuss their problems, and only a quarter felt that more visits were merited. Because the frequency of visits did not appear to be crucial, it was likely that other factors, such as the needs of the client and the nature of the casework, were more important in determining satisfaction than the number of visits.

There are allegations that casework consists of too much talk and too many questions. The responses of these mothers strongly contradicted this view (H). In a similar fashion, any suggestion that the sessions might have distressed or unsettled mothers was also rejected

Table 7(4)   *Mothers' responses to counselling* (n = 122)

statement		no	possibly	yes
		%	%	%
A.	I would have liked more advice	64	19	17
B.	it was just talk and not really helpful	57	18	25
C.	it helped me think out problems	25	25	50
D.	it helped me understand myself more than before	40	34	26
E.	it made me think of different ways to cope	47	21	32
F.	there were not enough visits to discuss all the things I wanted to discuss	62	10	28
G.	it helped to have someone to talk to	20	12	68
H.	too many questions were asked	78	8	14
I.	it helped me to understand my child/ren more	31	30	39
J.	it was very easy to talk to the school social worker	3	5	92
K.	it was difficult to see the point of some of the things brought up	57	17	26
L.	it helped me to understand things about the whole family	36	28	36
M.	I understand what happens at school more clearly now	29	20	51
N.	discussions are just a waste of time	77	9	14
O.	I found it inconvenient to have someone to visit from school	83	9	8
P.	it would have been much better if other family members had joined the discussions more than they did	60	21	19
Q.	it helped me to understand . . . . (child)	30	23	47
R.	I sometimes felt upset after the discussions	92	3	5
S.	I would have liked to have been told more about handling my child/ren	73	15	12
T.	I worried over what was discussed	87	8	5

(R and T). This was particularly important in view of the fact that these were families who had not personally requested social work help.

Finally, most mothers appeared to be satisfied with an individual approach and with the level of advice they received (P and A).

The mothers' motivation levels (assessed during the initial stages of contact) appeared to affect their responses, with those considered by the school social worker to be the most motivated proving the most positive to social work intervention in their responses to the questionnaire. However, it is possible that the school social workers' own responses to a family were affected by their initial perceptions; some of the mothers may, consequently, have received a different service to the majority.

In conclusion, there was much in these findings to support the notion that school social workers can make a useful contribution both in helping parents to understand more about school and in providing more direct help with the management of children.

SOCIAL WORKERS' IMPRESSIONS OF THEIR EFFECTIVENESS

With teachers
Table 7(5) reveals the intention of the school social workers to concentrate mainly on the four topics of classroom management,
individualizing the curriculum, linking home and school, and the
child's home environment. With the exception of the first of these
themes, all were viewed as particularly important in the case of two-
thirds to three-quarters of the treated pupils, i.e. moderate or major
objectives had been set. It may be that the two areas of linking home
and school and discussing the child's home environment were more
accessible to enquiry simply because these were areas in which the
technical expertise of the school social worker was recognized by the
teacher.

Table 7(5)   *Themes of consultation, objectives, and achievement: the school social*
workers' views

consultation theme	objectives			achievement
	no aims	*slight*	*moderate/ major*	*moderate/marked success*
	%	%	%	%
individualizing the curriculum	22	8	70	61
classroom structure	55	22	23	40
classroom management	33	12	55	46
linking home and school	12	20	68	49
discussion of child's home environment	8	26	66	87
discussion of extra-curricular activities	75	10	15	20

The right-hand column of *Table 7(5)* shows the extent to which
the school social workers rated their success. Proportionately, they
thought they achieved the greatest success in the areas where they
had the greatest aims. It is interesting to note that the areas of linking
home and school, child's home environment, and individualizing the
curriculum, required a high level of information transfer from school
social worker to teacher, as distinct from discussions of pupil
management procedures. Therefore, the strengths of the consultation

component as viewed by the school social workers coincided on the whole with those identified by the teachers.

It was something of a surprise to see the extent to which discussions also centred on classroom practices. This helps to refute the idea that teachers would not tolerate 'intruders' in their classrooms.

With families

The school social workers were asked to rate whether or not they thought the families had been helped by their intervention, and *Table 7(6)* shows that, in a large majority of cases, they felt that they had been of assistance.

Table 7(6)   *School social workers' rating of their helpfulness to families*

achievement	juniors	seniors	total numbers
considerable help	14	22	36
moderate help	31	29	60
little if any help	11	20	31
no positive effect	10	10	20
total numbers	66	81	147

A pilot study questionnaire on parental motivation, completed by social workers, discriminated between a sample of parents selected from our hospital clinic and a school-based parent sample. The parents in the clinic sample showed a greater desire for help, greater understanding that the child had an emotional problem, and greater willingness to increase teacher contact than did their school-based counterparts. They had also made more attempts in the past to seek help than had the school-based families. If we accept the premise that the clinic families were likely to have been better motivated towards intervention, as they had sought help rather than been approached by a school-based social worker, it would seem that increase in the motivation level of the parents in this treatment programme along these dimensions would demonstrate that the school social worker's intervention had been useful even if no tangible direct benefit had ensued.

In relation to the main study *Table 7(7)* demonstrates that the school social workers thought there were highly satisfactory changes in potential attitudes to the child's problem and to social work contact. No changes were noted in other attitudes and they are therefore not reported in detail.

Table 7(7)   *School social workers' assessments of attitude changes in parents'*
motivation

	frequencies	
aspect of motivation	rating before intervention	rating after intervention
desire for further help:		
sincere request for further sessions	20	34
agrees to suggestions of further sessions	81	76
agrees to further sessions with resignation	35	20
further sessions under protest or refused	11	12
total numbers =	147	142
Recognition of child's problem:		
clear understanding that child has an emotional problem	23	41
prepared to discuss possibility that child has an emotional problem	63	62
grudgingly accepts that problem may be emotional	41	23
refuses to accept that problem may be emotional	20	16
total numbers =	147	142

Note: five fewer parents were rated after intervention than before.

It will be realized, of course, that the results reported here were
based on school social workers' assessments of their own work and
hence may have been unduly optimistic. Nevertheless, we note that
the school social workers were not indiscriminately optimistic in making their ratings and that they were highly specific in picking out
those areas in which they felt that they had been of real help to the
families.

Independent evaluation of the parent counselling-teacher consultation programme

We compared the two sets of pupils who were involved in the parent
counselling-teacher consultation programme with their age-appropriate at-risk and maladjusted controls.

RESULTS OF PARENT COUNSELLING-TEACHER CONSULTATION IN JUNIOR SCHOOLS

Outcome (see Figs 7(1), 7(2), and 7(3))
Outcome was based on clinical assessment of psychiatric status. On
the antisocial dimension outcome at the midline assessment revealed a

Figure 7(1)   Antisocial behaviour: juniors: per cent outcome (good and poor categories only)

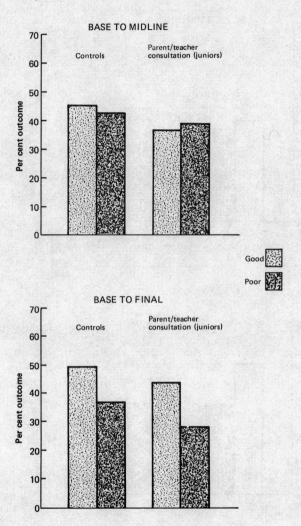

Figure 7(2)   Neurotic behaviour: juniors: per cent outcome (good and poor categories only)

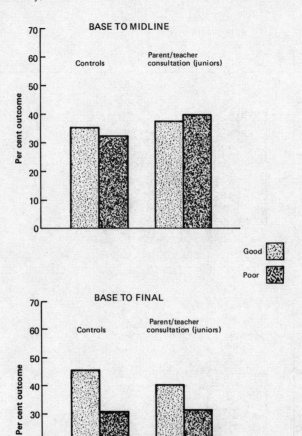

Figure 7(3)   Overall severity: juniors: per cent outcome (good and poor categories only)

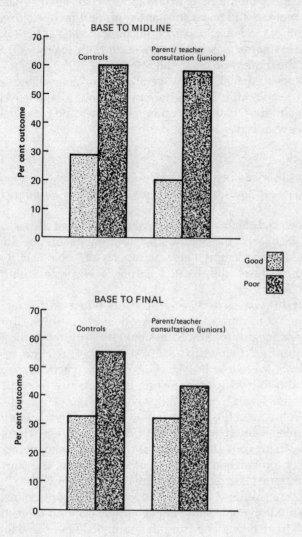

similar picture for both the parent counselling-teacher consultation and at-risk control children. This was repeated at the final follow-up where both regimes still had a substantial proportion of children with a poor outcome. On neurotic behaviour the outcome at both midline and final assessments was again similar for both regimes. This was true also for the dimension of overall severity.

Thus, it appeared that, taken overall, parent counselling-teacher consultation made little impression in relation to the psychiatric status of the children. However, other techniques and measures gave more positive results (see below).

Improvement
This section describes results of the various measures completed by children, parents, and teachers. Only significant differences are reported.

There were no differences between the treated and at-risk control children at either of the follow-up assessments on measures of academic performance and parental reports of behaviour. On the base-to-final analysis the treated pupils were significantly less isolated ($p < .05$).

Significant differences were more apparent when teacher reports of behaviour were considered. On the neurotic sub-score of the Rutter B2 scale, the treated group showed a significant gain over the at-risk controls at the final follow-up. The most numerous gains over the at-risk controls were on the Devereux scale. There was, at the eighteen-month follow-up, a reduction in impatience ($p < .05$); improved comprehension ($p < .05$); improved attention levels ($p < .05$); an increase in the need for closeness ($p < .01$); a reduction in the time taken to complete work ($p < .05$); and, finally, an increase in the sum of the Devereux items ($p < .05$). All but three of these short-term gains (improved comprehension, reduced impatience, and the sum of all the Devereux items) had disappeared by the final follow-up.

From this brief outline it would appear that parent counselling-teacher consultation made some impact on the classroom functioning of the junior treated pupils during the immediate period of the programme, although not all of these gains lasted. The home picture was quite different, and there were no significant findings.

RESULTS OF PARENT COUNSELLING–TEACHER CONSULTATION IN SENIOR SCHOOLS

Outcome (See Figs 7(4), 7(5), and 7(6))
The outcome in terms of neurotic behaviour proved similar for the treated children and maladjusted controls at both the midline and the

Figure 7(4)   Antisocial behaviour: seniors: per cent outcome (good and poor categories)

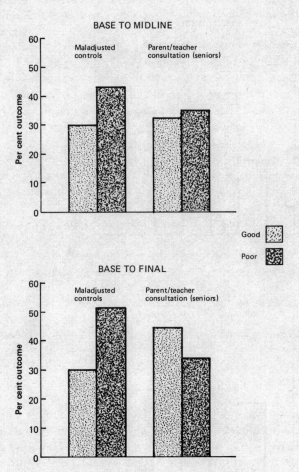

Figure 7(5)   Neurotic behaviour: seniors: per cent outcome (good and poor categories)

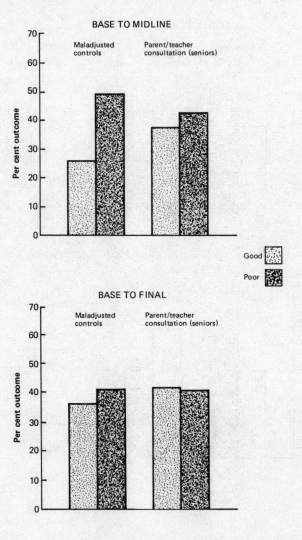

Figure 7(6) Overall severity: seniors: per cent outcome (good and poor categories)

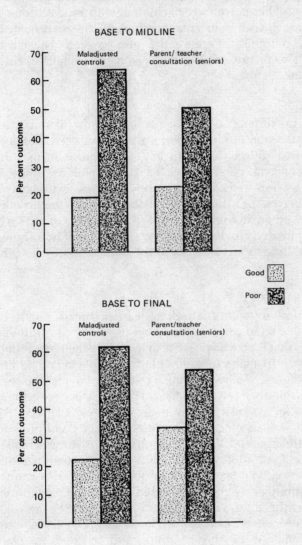

final follow-ups. However, on the antisocial scale the treatment regime had a higher percentage of children with good outcome and a lower percentage with poor outcome than did the maladjusted control regime, but this difference did not prove to be statistically significant. The picture on the dimensions of overall severity was similar for both regimes.

Improvement
There were no differences between the treated children and maladjusted controls on academic performance and peer relationships, and only three differences from all other sources. First, on the base-to-final analysis parents reported that the children in the parent counselling-teacher consultation group were less withdrawn than previously. Second, on the base-to-midline analysis the maladjusted controls showed greater improvement ($p < .05$) in neuroticism (JEPI) than did the treated children. Third, the treated children showed an improved attitude to school work at the midline assessment (Barker Lunn scale).

DISCUSSION

Our exploration of parent counselling-teacher consultation in British schools enabled us to consider a number of points, the most obvious of which was that it proved possible to introduce the programme on a systematic basis in a largely representative sample of both junior and secondary schools. To recap, having set up the programme in a systematic fashion we looked at the sort of work pattern adopted by the school social workers. This was, of course, pre-planned to some extent, but it was also moulded by the constraints and pressures of the school situation and the sorts of problems that the school social workers were confronted with. As far as the work with parents was concerned, the school social workers found themselves confronted with many family problems, but worked mainly on those concerning the marriage, the child, and the school. In relation to the teachers, they mainly promoted links between home and school, discussed the home environment of the children, and assisted in plans to individualize the curriculum in the light of their knowledge of a child's circumstances. It seems safe to conclude that the main area that presented itself as ripe for school social worker intervention was in the borderland between the home and the school, although our original intention had been for a broader approach to the child's problems in these two important environments.

We carried out various forms of evaluation by collecting the views of the teachers, mothers, and the school social workers themselves.

As far as the teachers were concerned, a clear picture emerged of their view of the school social worker's potential. Again, this seemed to point to the school social worker being most useful in the border-land between home and school, and also in giving support to teachers. It was equally clear that their possible role as mediators in staff difficulties was less acceptable. A complementary picture emerged from the mothers' viewpoint: they also found the chance to talk to the school social worker helpful, but this was mostly in relation to helping them understand their child and the school, rather than being of assistance with any other problems they may have had.

From the social workers' impressions, it seemed as if they felt they had achieved some useful changes in parental attitude to children's problems and enhanced parents' and teachers' understanding of children's group functioning. It is particularly interesting to note that they felt they had achieved the greatest success in areas where they had the greatest aims and we believe this again underlines the importance of focusing on particular tasks in casework.

Such views have to be balanced by independent evaluation con-sisting of monitoring of symptomatology and various types of severity of disturbance over the period of the study. As indicated earlier, the parent counselling-teaching consultation programme seems to have made little differential impact in relation to this type of data. A number of possible explanations for the lack of statistically significant differences between these types of measures need to be considered. Elsewhere (Chapters 2 and 10) it is pointed out that a single assess-ment social interview, even though directed towards diagnosis rather than treatment, may be sufficient to bring about change. We have no way of knowing what impact our assessment interviews had – they may in fact have had a therapeutic effect and so reduced the differences between the at-risk and maladjusted controls and the treated children. As the regime relied entirely on indirect intervention, it seems possible that its results were more submerged by the effects of the assessment interviews than those of regimes that dealt directly with the child.

An important point, which we have frequently referred to, was that children in the parent counselling-teacher consultation regime did not come to the attention of the therapists because of concern on the part of their parents but rather because they were picked up by a screening programme. For this reason the parental motivation towards interven-tion may not necessarily have been high. A related matter was that families were approached about children's behaviour that was termed 'deviant' in school, though the parents did not necessarily see it as problematic.

Also of great consequence was the fact that the families nearly all had a wide range of longstanding difficulties. It seems quite possible, therefore, that the impact of the intervention on the child was dissipated in the welter of other difficulties that the school social worker was confronted with in the family. It may have been that the short-term approach, shared as it was between home and school, was not intensive enough to counteract the severity of the family difficulties. It is interesting that the impact on the senior pupils, who manifested the most clear-cut maladjustment, was less impressive than in the case of the juniors, who had lesser degrees of disorder.

Another point of importance was the focusing of treatment. In casework with families one can either range widely, according to the needs of the family, or concentrate more specifically on the child's problem. While our programme, as illustrated above, paid particular attention to focusing, it may not have been sufficiently concentrated to allow changes in the children's behaviour to emerge. The greatest degree of focusing occurred in teacher consultation in the junior schools as the children in these schools were only exposed to a small number of teachers. It is interesting to note that the junior schools showed the most positive gains in relation to the more specific help accessible via this programme.

8 Group therapy for children

Summary

In this chapter we discuss the rationale for group therapy methods. Psychotherapy attempts to ease human problems by psychological methods. Group, as opposed to individual, therapy can be useful in various ways and, for young children, play therapy may also be helpful.

We describe the numerous previous studies of group therapy of various types, but conclude that they were on too small a scale to have properly assessed the problem, which requires a wide spread of measures, an adequate size of sample with comparable control groups, full descriptions of the treatments, and long-term follow-ups.

We discuss the development of our programme, in which six trained social workers held discussion sessions for seventeen groups of four to five same-sex senior children, and play-group sessions for seventeen groups of four to five mixed-sex juniors, within the ordinary school setting. There were ten sessions for each group, over a three-month period. This group therapy gave good results and the outcome was significantly better for all categories of children, with the exception of antisocial and overall behaviour at mid-point for juniors. As far as the main improvement measures were concerned, accounts of favourable changes occurred mostly in teacher and parent reports of behaviour and, for the senior children, in the self-report ratings. The only inconsistency was that the significant improvements found in academic performance of the seniors at the first (eighteen-month) follow-up had disappeared by the final (three-year) follow-up.

Fundamental ideas and assumptions underlying group therapy methods

Every activity in school takes place in the context of human groups. This is true of formal classroom work and also of all other areas of school life. A child's successful adjustment in school will be largely dependent on how well he or she adapts and relates to groups of peers and to the authority structure that is necessary for the education of a large number of children. Indeed, this realization is a theme that runs throughout our book.

In this chapter we focus on one particular aspect of groups: their use as a therapeutic medium. Group treatment has an obvious application in situations where professional time is limited, and there is an analogy here to education, where classroom teaching is more economical than individual tutoring. Also, as every teacher knows, there are ways in which groups, in themselves, can influence the behaviour of children. While clinicians have for many years discussed and explored the therapeutic potential of groups, social psychologists have looked at their qualities in experimental studies. The results of such studies shed light on some preliminary questions.

WHAT IS A GROUP?

There is general agreement that a human group is more than a mere collection of individuals. Freud (1922) believed that of central importance to any group was the existence of a leader, who was a father figure for the group members. Having shared their leader, the group members then recognized their common identification and dependency and the feeling of group identity developed.

Recently, academic social psychologists have attempted a tight and operational definition of the group. For example, Sherif and Sherif defined a group as a 'social unit consisting of a number of individuals who stand in role and status relationships to one another, stabilized in some degree at the time, and who possess a set of values or norms of their own regulating their behaviour, at least in matters of conse-quence to the group' (Sherif and Sherif 1969:131). Many features of groups are contained in this brief definition and Freud's idea of the leader is broadened to include any role and status relationships. The idea of a sense of group identity is implied in the concept of a social unit, which delineates that some people are inside and some are outside the group. It is this that, on a subjective level, gives a feeling of 'we-ness' to the group. The formation of a group is dependent on the same set of people being involved with one another over a long period. This is sharply different from many role and status relationships, such as doctor-patient, officer-men, which may be transient ones with no continuing interaction over time between individual people.

The above qualities of groups in general can be turned to good effect in therapeutic groups. The therapy group becomes a microcosm of other social group situations and is thus a vehicle for the full range of potential in social relationships, including those maladaptive mechanisms that may have a bearing on the patients' problems. Many theorists have attempted to develop a model of group function-ing that would have relevance to the therapeutic process. One sensitive example was that of Whitaker and Lieberman (1965). These authors considered that the behaviour of patients in therapy groups is governed by a balance of emotional forces. On the one hand there are those individual needs and concerns that, in their expression, carry the danger of disrupting group function – the 'disturbing motives'. Examples of disturbing motives might be a wish to have the therapist for oneself or angry feelings about other group members. The intro-duction of a disturbing motive generates destructive forces and anxiety in the group and this in turn influences the behaviour of members, encouraging them to cope and compensate – the 'reactive motives'. The balance of disturbing and reactive motives leads to a group solution to the problem. The solution may be helpful to the therapeutic effort – an 'enabling solution' – or one that stunts development – a 'restrictive solution'. The therapist's task is to understand this interplay of forces, which is in constant flux through the life of the group. We found this set of ideas useful in under-standing adolescent groups.

One of the most sensitive writers on groups (Yalom 1975) outlined eleven ways in which they may be therapeutic. It is worth reviewing these in terms of their application in group therapy with children.

(i)   *Instillation of hope.* This is a most important principle which applies to all forms of therapy, not just groups. It is very important in the case of children to give a feeling of hope and optimism, not only to the child but also to the key figures in his or her environment, such as the parents and teachers. A par-ticular advantage of group treatment is that the children are able to see their peers at various stages of improvement in their dif-ficulties.

(ii) *Universality.* Children have a great need to 'belong'; it is par-ticularly helpful if, through group treatment, they can observe that their peers have problems they thought they alone had to suffer.

(iii) *Imparting of information.* Education traditionally concentrates on the cognitive aspects of child development. There is movement, reflected in the American literature (Jones 1972; Catterall and Gadza 1977; Gadza 1978), towards including a component of understanding of self and feelings in school work.

(iv) *Altruism*. It is often forgotten that human beings like to give as much as to take and this may emerge in the group situation. For example, a very disruptive and disturbed seven-year-old came to one of our playgroups one day, very upset because his father had just been sent to prison. One of the girls in the group spent the rest of the day with him and was able to give considerable comfort. This was a mutually beneficial experience.

(v) *Recapitulation of the primary family group*. Experience with families soon teaches us that children's techniques, often maladaptive, of coping with strong effects are moulded by patterns learnt in their own family. The group experience provides an opportunity to examine and correct these maladaptive patterns.

(vi) *Development of socializing techniques*. Group treatment allows opportunities for children to learn social skills, such as turn-taking, delaying gratification, persuasion, and so on. This may be particularly true of play and activity groups.

(vii) *Imitation*. In group treatment children have a chance to observe and model themselves on their peers. Some studies have capitalized on this by setting up groups where modelling is systematically encouraged (e.g. Hansen, Niland, and Zani 1969).

(viii) *Interpersonal learning.* This is a most important aspect of all group therapy, in which the therapist uses the interpersonal encounters of the children to deepen their understanding of their own feelings and their relationship to others. This is likely to be the main aim of any dynamic group technique.

(ix) *Group cohesiveness*. This is a very central concept in social psychology; it simply means the mutual attraction of members of a group for each other. Research on small group functioning has uncovered many ways in which individuals in small groups are affected by the level of cohesiveness of the group. These were summarized by Goldstein and Simonson (1971) and included eleven items of the greatest relevance to psychotherapists: for example, members of cohesive groups are more open to influences from other group members, they place greater value on group goals and are more accepting of other members' hostility than are members of less cohesive groups. Ginott (1961) claimed that group cohesiveness was of little importance with young children. However, as we show later in this chapter, it may be of much more importance in adolescent groups.

(x) *Catharsis*. This is an important principle, particularly in play-groups where children are permitted to discharge affect within overall limits. Sometimes aggressive impulses have to be channelled, as when a child's attack on a peer is diverted to a punch ball or drum.

(xi) *Existential factors*. Under this heading Yalom listed a number of issues that confront us all, adults and children alike. Some of these are particularly relevant to children; these are: (a) recognizing that life is at times unfair and unjust; (b) recognizing that there is ultimately no escape from some of life's pain; and (c) learning that people must ultimately take responsibility for the way they live their own lives, no matter how much guidance and support they get from others.

This last issue is, *par excellence*, the problem of adolescence – the stage when responsibility for one's own life becomes a key issue (Erikson 1950).

A group discussion may help members to become aware of these problems of living.

WHAT ARE PSYCHOTHERAPY AND COUNSELLING?

In a survey of the literature on this topic Nicol (1979) concluded that psychotherapy can be characterized by two main features. First, it involves a special confidential relationship deliberately and freely entered into by therapist and client, or clients, with the aim of helping with a problem. The nature of the problem and the approach should be agreed between them in advance, if only in a general way. The second feature is that the proceedings of psychotherapy should be guided by some form of psychological theory. The main ones that have been used are psychoanalytic and related theories, behaviourist theories, derivatives of existentialist ideas, and, finally, didactic-rationale theories (Patterson 1973).

The therapist's and client's understanding and agreement about the nature of therapy is commonly called the treatment alliance (Sandler, Holder, and Dare 1970). This concept may not hold true for children and young adolescents because in such cases the patient has usually been brought to treatment by someone else. Nevertheless, those responsible for the child should have an understanding of the nature of the treatment and, except in the case of the very young, the child itself should have some age-appropriate comprehension that treatment is taking place. In the area of educationally based therapy the nature of the treatment alliance needs careful thought, as we shall see later in this chapter.

WHAT IS PLAY?

Play is not a necessary component of child psychotherapy but, like groups, it incorporates phenomena that have often been turned to therapeutic account. Many authors baulk at defining the seemingly heterogeneous group of activities that are usually considered as play, and some, such as Berlyne (1969), think that the term should be dropped from scientific discourse. Garvey (1977), though, has suggested some criteria by which play can be differentiated from children's other activities. For example, play is intrinsically pleasurable, is undertaken spontaneously and voluntarily by the child, and demands his or her entire engagement. It has no intrinsic goals and constitutes an enjoyment of means rather than effort devoted to some particular end. Again, play has certain systematic relations to what is not play. These defining features, while not providing a watertight definition, do suggest ways in which play may be used for psychotherapy, for example, by channelling the arousal of interest and involvement and, perhaps most important, by determining its relation to non-play. This last point merits particularly close examination and we must now attempt to put play into the context of the developing child.

Piaget (1951), in a major work on the subject, attempted a classification of different types of play. He dismissed mere content as being an unsatisfactory basis on which to classify play – for example, both a one-year-old child and a seven-year-old may play with marbles: the former is likely to be exploring the properties of the balls and the effect he or she may have on them by moving them about, whereas the older child is likely to be involved in social, rule-bound games with the marbles. It is the contrast between the more immature sensori-motor behaviour and the rule-bound game that Piaget saw as the important differentiating feature. He recognized three major stages in the development of play, each with a number of finer gradations. The most important of these from our point of view was the second stage: symbolic and representational play. Except at its simplest level, this type of play is unique to humans. It consists of 'make-believe', 'fantasy', and 'sociodramatic' play. It first becomes manifest in the second year of life and is of the greatest importance with regard to the therapeutic potential of play.

How can we use play in psychotherapy? Basically in two separate ways: first, for its potential in facilitating communication between the patient and the therapist and, second, as a means of bringing about beneficial behaviour change.

We will first talk about the potential of play for facilitating communication as in our short-term treatment regime this was its most important function. In young children the observation of play may reveal the feelings they are struggling with and give clues as to how they are coping with them. There are different opinions in the various schools of psychotherapy as to the use of play in the therapy process (Bentovim 1977). One group of techniques, including activity group therapy (Slavson and Schiffer 1975) and client-centred approaches (Axline 1947a), considers that play or activities in themselves have an important function and that the task of the therapist is to provide conditions within which the child can use the play materials to promote self-discovery and learn to cope with strong and potentially dangerous feelings. This technique is well illustrated by the examples of Conn (1939).

At the opposite extreme the psychoanalytic school of Klein (1928) considers play to be of use purely as a means of access to the child's unconscious thoughts and feelings. Winnicott (1971) also saw play as closely linked with the child's inner reality. The theme of psycho-therapy as, basically, an act of communication, whether with self, with therapist, or between both, is an important one, and one of the main ways in which 'dynamic' forms of psychotherapy can be dis-tinguished from those therapies aimed directly at changes in behaviour or attitudes. Rycroft (1966) considered psychoanalysis to be a communicative activity. He argued that this view resolved all the difficulties about the status of psychoanalysis: the means of com-munication are through such channels as dreams, mistakes, actions, free association, non-verbal material, and play. Anyone who has observed or participated in psychotherapy must have sympathy with this viewpoint. In our regime the function of play as a means of communication was particularly important.

There are many ways in which play may have an important developmental function. A brief review of these will show ways in which play may come to the aid of psychotherapy. One theory is that play allows the child to rehearse bits of behaviour and perfect these without damaging consequences. For example, a little girl can make a 'pretend' cup of tea and pour it into the cups without the danger of pouring scalding water over her hands. Reynolds (1972), from his studies of rhesus monkeys, has suggested that play can be considered in this way. He pointed out that few behaviour patterns occur only in play and also that few occur in 'real life' that are not reflected in some way in play: the difference is that the play sequences are divorced from their consequences (e.g. damage to another in aggressive play or impregnation in sexual play).

Play is a very sociable phenomenon – maybe this is because human beings are in all ways a very sociable species. Even isolated play often includes an imaginary companion (Newson and Newson 1976) or revolves around social themes. A considerable amount of work has appeared recently concerning play and social behaviour in young children. Social play has traditionally been described along one dimension, ranging from unoccupied behaviour through solitary play, onlooker behaviour, parallel play, and associative play to co-operative play. This sequence of behaviour is supposedly related to increasing maturation (Parten 1933; Smith and Connelly, 1972); how-ever, more recent evidence (Roper and Hinde 1978) has suggested that solitary play may be a sign of maturity as well as immaturity. The suggestion was that individual differences in social play are con-sistent over quite long periods (Rose, Blank, and Spalter 1975; Roper and Hinde 1978), although there is less consensus about whether the behaviour of individuals is consistent from one situation to another (Kohn and Rossman 1972; Rose, Blank, and Spalter 1975; Roper and Hinde 1978). These findings illustrated the complexity of social play, and suggested ways in which the analysis of social relationships in the small group play setting could help the therapist to understand the idiosyncracies and needs of the individual child.

Another important function of play is as a component of learning: this is certainly relevant to the learning of instrumental tasks, as Kohler (1925) showed many years ago, and also probably to learning how to cope with feelings and relationships.

Sylva (1977) carried out experiments with young children which illustrated the function of play in the learning of instrumental tasks. Children of various ages sat at a table and were given sticks and clamps. They had to use these to retrieve a small prize from a box. There were three experimental groups: in the first, the children were allowed to play with the implements; in the second, they watched a demonstration by the adult; and, in the third, they had little prior acquaintance with the problem. The results of the experiment sug-gested that the children who had been allowed the play period approached the problem on a far more flexible and exploratory way and were less liable to 'opt out' than were the children in the other groups. These experiments illustrated well the way in which play may influence children's subsequent problem solving behaviour.

The part of play in the emotional organization and development of the child has received a great deal of attention in clinical studies by psychoanalysts and other psychotherapists. The original Freudian notion was that play and fantasy originate in the context of depriv-ation of immediate gratification (Freud 1911). Under these conditions, the infant 'hallucinates' the object of his or her instinctual need. This forms the basis of thought, play, and, subsequently, ego development. Anna Freud (1936), who was one of the pioneers of child psychoanalysis, was very sensitive to the special difficulties of applying psychoanalytic techniques with young children. The main problem is that children cannot easily be induced to lie on a couch and give free rein to their fantasies, so that the mainstay of analysis with adults is not available. Anna Freud pointed out that unconscious conflicts can be understood not only by uncovering them, but by understanding the ways in which their painful effects are kept out of consciousness. These constitute the 'ego defence mechanisms'. The importance of play and make-believe is that by observing and understanding it, we can see how the child attempts to cope with painful conflicts.

Freud's original notion of fantasy and play as responses to deprivation was at most a partial explanation. Their functions are, as indicated in Sylva's experiments on problem solving, far more important. Erikson (1950) gave play a central place in his theorizing. He saw the development of the ego identity as a synthesis of the personal experience of the developing child, cultural pressures, and training. Play becomes an essential mediator in this process in that it enables the child to rehearse and experiment with his or her responses in the relatively safe world of make-believe. The importance that this may have was illustrated in a study by Biblow (1973). This author submitted groups of high and low 'fantasy prone' children to a frustration task and then measured their aggressive behaviour and mood changes in a play situation. The low fantasy children showed higher overt aggression and aggressive mood than did high fantasy children or control groups. If fantasy and aspects of imaginative play are parts of the same phenomenon then further research on play and the regulation of behaviour and affect could be extremely fruitful.

The importance of play in developing problem solving and social skills has become an article of faith among many child-centred educationalists. This has led to a number of experiments that have sought to enhance imaginative play by different training methods (Marshall and Hahn 1967; Smilansky 1968; Freyberg 1973). While showing that under the right circumstances training is effective in increasing children's predisposition to imaginative play, none of the studies has looked at whether or not this has an enduring effect on skill development.

To summarize this discussion of some of the important ideas and assumptions underlying group therapy methods, group, as opposed to individual, therapy can further psychotherapy in a variety of ways, and play, particularly its communicative function, may also do so where young children are concerned, in either a group or an individual setting. In the present study we had to keep these principles in mind in designing our treatment regime.

Previous studies that evaluated outcome

In this section we report and analyse a group of previous research studies (see list at end of chapter) designed to evaluate the helpfulness of psychotherapy techniques with school problems. We found sixty studies that seemed broadly relevant and fulfilled the minimal requirement of comparing a treatment sample with a control sample. All the studies reviewed were concerned with children's problems as manifested at school, and all the subjects reported were of normal or borderline subnormal intelligence. We excluded those that evaluated the effectiveness of group therapy on essentially normal populations of children in reference to such universal problems as improved studying techniques or career choice. The majority of the studies come from the USA.

The reports varied widely in their presentation and in some cases were available only in summary form or in a review (Abramowitz 1976; Henry and Kilmann 1979). The samples of children within the studies were in most cases within a year or two of the same age, but a wide age range (seven to eighteen years of age) was covered in the various studies overall. We included a small number of studies of individual therapy where these focused centrally on school problems or employed a non-directive technique (Dorfman 1958; Winn 1962; Lawrence 1973). Some of the studies incorporated behaviour modification principles within a group context (Clement and Milne 1967; Hansen, Niland, and Zani 1969; Hinds and Roehike 1970; Hubbert 1970; Warner and Hansen 1970; Kelly and Mathews 1971; Abraham 1972; Randolph and Hardage 1973). Unfortunately, many of the studies were based on such small numbers as to be dubious on this ground alone.

In most of the studies the subjects were allocated to treatment and control samples either at random or by a matching process. In three the various comparison groups were in different schools (a between-schools design) and in one the more severe cases tended to be allocated to the treatment rather than the control group. These designs were unsatisfactory. In particular, the between-school situation did not allow for the fact that it was well known that children's development is quite markedly influenced by factors in the environment of the school they attend, independent of any specific treatment they may receive.

The studies can be fairly clearly classified according to the aspect of functioning that they sought to modify. The largest group of studies (twenty-five) was aimed mainly at improvement in academic performance. The rationale of this was that the retarded reader is in such constant difficulties in class that he or she feels 'labelled' and loses enthusiasm for work. Clearly, more and more attempts at remedial reading are likely to be self-defeating in this situation; this is why investigators have turned to less direct approaches, such as group therapy.

Children for these studies were selected in various ways. In some the criterion was attendance at a special remedial reading class, while in others teachers were simply asked to refer those children they felt needed special help. More objective screening methods, such as simple reading tests or more complex assessments such as 'under-achievement' were also sometimes used. The rationale underlying 'under-achievement' is that children of high ability should also show high attainment. Unfortunately, the authors of the various studies did not seem aware of the theoretical and statistical problems associated with the concept of 'under-achievement' (Thorndike 1963).

In view of these potential faults in design, and the generally gloomy prognostications about the effectiveness of psychotherapy (detailed with destructive panache by Levitt 1971 and Shepherd, Oppenheim, and Mitchell 1971), it is interesting that sixteen of the twenty-five studies that tackled educational problems gave a positive result. Overall, the group of twenty-five studies varied in many ways. The average size of treatment samples was twenty-seven subjects; however, the range was from six subjects in the two smallest studies to ninety in the largest one. Some of the studies reported results on incredibly small samples, for example Fisher (1953) reported positive gains in reading with six children, whereas the study with the largest sample, comprising many small groups of children (Ewing and Gilbert 1967), came to negative conclusions.

The most commonly reported positive result in the attainment studies was a gain in 'grade point average'. This is a composite continuous assessment score that is part of normal school routine. While this type of measure may have advantages, it is necessary to have some estimate of its reliability and to be sure that the assessment was not contaminated by knowledge of the fact that the child was taking part in a special treatment project. As this was not commented on in any of the studies, the results must remain in doubt. In only seven of the studies was there a significant change in more formal measures of attainment, such as a reading test (Fisher 1953; Shouksmith and Taylor 1964; Deskin 1968; Vriend 1969; Moulin 1970; Barcai et al. 1973;

Lawrence 1973). In some studies there was no formal attainment testing; it was therefore impossible to tell whether the results were positive or negative.

The studies also varied in the type of therapy that was offered. Description of the therapy process is one of the most difficult aspects of psychotherapy research: for example, Lieberman, Yalom, and Miles (1973) found little relationship between the professed type of therapy, in encounter groups, and the results of objective observations. Many of the studies gave scant details of the therapy process beyond a label such as 'non-directive' or 'didactic'. Summarizing from within these severe limitations, there seems to have been a slight tendency for the more successful treatments to have been focused on solving academic issues, thus emphasizing the more 'didactic' aspect of group therapy described earlier in this chapter.

Twelve studies were aimed primarily at improving the children's peer relationships. In all but one of these, the children were selected for study by a sociometry instrument. Each child chosen by this means was selected because he or she had few friends rather than because they were unpopular with other children. Five of the twelve studies reviewed showed an improvement in sociometry scores (Kranzler *et al.* 1966; Schiffer 1966; Hansen, Niland, and Zani 1969; Bevins 1970; Thombs and Muro 1973). Another study in this group showed changes on a self-concept test (House 1971), although the children were selected by low scores on sociometry.

As with the studies based on improving academic performance, the peer relationship studies varied enormously among themselves. The size of the treatment groups ranged from eight to forty-five subjects; some of the smallest-scale studies gave positive results. One ingenious study (Hansen, Niland, and Zani 1969) used a structured modelling approach where underchosen children (i.e. children least selected by others as close friends) were mixed in groups with very popular children (so-called sociometric stars). This was one of the studies that yielded a clear, positive result; there were others that reported success using more conventional, non-directive approaches.

In the next group, of eight studies, the main problem was teacher reports of bad behaviour. Some of these studies were, as one might expect, based on behaviour modification principles, but not all of these were successful in generalizing better behaviour to the classroom. (The successful behaviour modification studies were those of Hinds and Roehike (1970) and Randolph and Hardage (1973).) Other studies were successful using group therapy (Barcai and Robinson 1969; Hubbert 1970) and indirect consultation approaches (Taylor and Hoedt 1974). Again, there were major variations in the sizes of subject samples.

Six studies centred on other aspects of adjustment. All but one of these showed some positive result, although the sample sizes were in all cases very small indeed, the largest treatment group being a mere twelve subjects. The presence of positive results may be due to the fact that in this group of studies more outcome measures were made than in the other groups so far discussed.

The final homogeneous group of six studies focused on improving children's self-concepts. This seems to be a useful area for group methods with four of the six studies yielding positive results (Dorfman 1958; Hume 1967; Mann, Barber, and Jacobson 1969; Hugo 1970). There were also four positive results from other studies: three of the studies of academic performance showed some changes in personal adjustment or self concept (Baymur and Patterson 1960; Broedel et al. 1960; Winn 1962) and, as mentioned above, one of the studies of peer relationships gave a positive result (House 1971).

Finally, four studies do not fit easily into the above classification. The first was a study by Persons (1966) of group and individual therapy among delinquents. This was successful in lowering the conviction rate among institutionalized delinquents. Irwin, Levy, and Shapiro (1972) compared children treated with psychodrama and activity therapy with a control group. The treatment groups were very small, only five subjects in each, but the authors claimed positive results. Tolor (1970) carried out a wide-ranging study based on clinic referrals, comparing combinations of individual and group therapy approaches applied to different ages of children. The results showed mixed changes of self-concept and teacher reports. The final study, by Crow (1971), was available only in a secondary report (Abramowitz 1976); it is reputed to have shown gains in self-report and sociometry in a sample given group therapy.

Having briefly surveyed the individual studies we can make some general comments on their standards and methodologies.

The first striking point was that although most of the studies took place in school there was, with one exception (Barcai et al. 1973), no mention of the general climate or staff relationships in the schools concerned, nor, for that matter, of whether or not the therapists had any contact with the staff at all. We have discussed the special characteristics of school psychotherapy elsewhere (Nicol 1979).

A second, very serious problem with many of the studies was that they were based on numbers too small to make group comparisons reasonable.

The types of statistical analyses used in the studies also require some comment. While in most there was some form of group comparison by analysis of variance, there was no consensus on the correct way to proceed. Some studies, for example, compared change scores between measures taken before and after therapy. Others relied on comparison of levels at follow-up, having checked that there were no significant differences at baseline. None of the studies made adequate allowance for the effect of initial level on rate of change. As explained in Chapter 3, this is necessary because statistical consider-ations dictate that change is greater if the initial level is more extreme.

Finally, only two of the studies (Mezzano 1968; Warner 1971) had any kind of follow-up measures, apart from the immediate post-treat-ment ones. As we show in the present study, long-term follow-up measures are essential in order to study the effects of psychotherapy adequately. It is interesting that both the above studies showed gains at follow-up.

To sum up, there have been many previous studies of group therapy of various types. The drawback is that they are on far too small a scale to do justice to the problem, which requires a wide spread of measures, an adequate size of sample with comparable control groups, adequate descriptions of the treatments, and long-term follow-ups (Wright, Moelis, and Pollack 1976). Despite this criticism, in view of the limited nature of such studies and, in many cases, the encouraging results, the gloomy commentaries of Levitt (1971) and Shepherd, Oppenheim, and Mitchell (1971) seem unwarranted.

The development of the Newcastle upon Tyne playgroup and group therapy programmes

Our programmes for both junior and senior children were based on the same philosophy, that developed by Carl Rogers (Rogers 1959; Hall and Lindzey 1970), but both differed considerably in detail. We have fully described the setting-up of the groups in previous publications (Nicol and Bell 1975; Nicol and Parker 1981; Parker and Nicol 1981). The therapists were the same six social workers who took part in the parent counselling-teacher consultation programme (see Chapter 7).

THE JUNIOR PLAYGROUPS

In adapting the group therapy technique to younger children we were greatly influenced by the excellent account of Virginia Axline (1947a). It is not possible to summarize Axline's book here, but we should point out that one of its strengths is its provision of a clear set of eight principles that can be followed in practical play therapy. These are: that the therapist must develop a warm, friendly relationship with the child, must accept the child exactly as he or she is, must develop a feeling of permissiveness in the relationship, must be alert to the expression of feelings in the child, must maintain a deep respect for the child's ability to solve his or her own problems, must not attempt to direct the child's actions or conversation in any manner, must not hurry the therapy along, and must establish only those limitations that are necessary to anchor the therapy in the real world.

The technique allows the play to speak for itself, and the children to work on their problems unhurried by therapist interventions. At the same time, while the children may be sensitive to all their feelings and may express them verbally, they are not necessarily allowed to act as they please. In this connection we found both Axline's (1947a) and Ginott's (1961) accounts of limit-setting to be very important. The setting of a minimal number of necessary limits both allowed the groups to function in the difficult environment of the school and also seemed important in strengthening the ego controls of the more impulsive children.

Ginott emphasized that group cohesiveness and, hence, many of the phenomena that are so important in adult groups do not occur in those of young children. However, Axline's principles were complicated by the presence of other children. The therapist must be careful to establish contact with all the children in the group.

Every session ran for one lesson period (forty minutes to one hour), and each group consisted of four to five boys and girls. Each group had ten sessions within a single school term. There was a total of seventeen groups in the six junior schools in the study, so that two or three groups were running in each of the schools during the same term.

THE SENIOR GROUP THERAPY

There were seventeen discussion groups, consisting of four or five children of the same sex. Ten sessions for each group ran for one lesson period each (thirty to sixty minutes) over one school term. The focus of discussion was always on the 'here-and-now' interaction in the group and the therapist did not direct the discussion in any way. This was in keeping with the method of Rogers (1952), where the therapist's task is to discover how the world looks through the client's eyes. The emphasis on the group *as* a group was reflected in the physical arrangement of chairs in a circle. The somewhat greater maturity of the children meant that there was more opportunity for cohesiveness to develop in the senior groups than in the junior ones.

Other methods of group work were considered in developing the programme but in the event they were rejected. One that was considered particularly carefully was activity group therapy (Forward

1965; Jeffrey 1973; Slavson and Schiffer 1975; MacLennan 1977). We decided not to use this therapy because it did not suit the skills of the social workers, and required specialized accommodation and equipment. In addition, it is commonly considered to be a longer-term treatment, incorporating a large educational-cum-developmental component that, we hoped, could be provided in the ordinary classroom.

The more traditional approaches to activity therapy advocate great freedom and lack of limits, but this tends to lead to great difficulties in school, as some of the accounts have suggested (Schiffer 1971; MacLennan 1977).

THE TRAINING PROGRAMME

A key issue in any type of intervention is not only its quantity and type but, perhaps most important, its quality. The techniques employed in the present programme, while not as highly specialized as some psychoanalytical types of psychotherapy, required considerable levels of sophistication, maturity, and experience on the part of the therapists. Group work with well-motivated adults involves special problems, such as the complicated phenomena of group dynamics, that are not present in individual therapy. To this must be added the particular requirements of child management, the fact that the clients were poorly motivated, indeed, in some cases had no subjective distress at all, and the fact that the project was located in school, an institution which had different goals and methods than those envisaged for the groups.

As described in Chapter 7, the therapists were well-trained and, in most cases, experienced social workers, which meant that they had a grounding in the client-centred approach (Rogers 1952). Some had even previously run adolescent groups in different settings. The problem was to train the therapists to a uniform technique of reasonable standard, with, needless to say, limited resources. To this end each therapist started by taking clinic children for individual treatment. They had experience with two to five children in this way for a period of up to one year. In addition, as a pilot group experience, for ten sessions each therapist took both a playgroup and a senior therapy group in schools separate from those involved in the main treatment programme. During this period, training sessions were arranged with a psychotherapist who had experience of child psychotherapy. The psychotherapist also attended sensitivity groups. These consisted of groups of trainee therapists in the role of group members. Their purpose was to provide an opportunity for the trainees to gain insight into their own feelings and responses, the effect they have on others, and the functioning of groups through a personal experience. This self-knowledge is essential if a psychotherapist is going to do his or her job properly. There were also opportunities to consult the child psychiatrist who was supervizing the project.

During the treatment programme itself, each therapist was allotted a half- to one-hour personal supervision session per week with the child psychiatrist and there was an opportunity each week to take special problems to the psychotherapist. During the latter part of the programme the therapists ceased to feel the need for such close supervision, but regular weekly sessions for individuals or in small groups continued.

This training should not be considered to have constituted a thorough grounding in psychotherapy. On the other hand, if such workers prove helpful to children, it does mean that there is a realistic basis for the introduction of such trained personnel on a wider basis. The point that needs greatest emphasis is that the therapists had continued supervision and access to skilled back-up resources. We could not envisage such work being undertaken by isolated workers in the school.

COMPOSITION OF THE GROUPS

The different circumstances of the children in the two age groups led to rather diverse criteria being adopted in constituting the groups. First, there was a general consensus in the literature that sexual anxieties among twelve-year-olds are likely to severely inhibit interaction if their groups are of mixed sex. The groups at this age level were, therefore, constituted on a single-sex basis. Among the seven- to eight-year-olds the groups were all mixed-sex. The literature also, in general, advocated a mixture of problems in any one group. The complexities of school timetables made it impossible to achieve this criterion among the senior groups and they had to be taken on a class-by-class basis. Among the junior groups, problems were mixed so that they comprised, as far as possible, a selection of conduct, neurotic, and educational problems. It should be stressed that the children were allocated to groups by the programme organizer, so that the therapists remained ignorant of the 'objective' assessments of the children's problems.

JUNIOR GROUPS – THE SELECTION OF TOYS

As Ginott (1961) pointed out, there is little consensus on the correct equipment of a therapeutic playroom, although many therapists have dogmatic opinions. In looking for general principles to guide us, we were impressed by Schiffer's (1971) concept of *valence* as the potential of a toy for facilitating communication. Thus, a family of doll figures is likely to have high valence and a game of draughts low valence (the latter being likely to allow a child to conceal his or her thoughts or feelings rather than to express them).

We were aware that our programme was brief and that we should therefore concentrate on the psychotherapeutic aspects of play (i.e. its potential to build relationships, its diagnostic function, its potential to promote interaction and communication and to facilitate insight and change, and the opportunity it creates for experimentation with social roles) rather than on its more general developmental function, such as the promotion of creativity and the attainment of skills.

It was important to have a range of equipment that allowed the children to function at different developmental levels (Jeffrey 1973). With this in mind we used the following materials (Schiffer's classification (1971) modified):

A.   Objects representing significant persons and animals
     miniature dolls' family and furniture
     simple, dressable baby doll
     glove puppets
B.   Objects identifiable with significant persons
     old clothes for dressing up
C.   Plastic media with variable valence
     plasticine
     paper and crayons
D.   Materials to enhance social play
     toy soldiers
     toy cars
     toy telephone

This classification was necessarily a loose one: each of these materials could be used – and misused – in a multitude of ways. We would emphasize that no materials designed primarily to enhance craft or manipulative skills were provided, and there were no competitive games.

Accommodation
Schiffer (1971) described the ideal playroom for therapeutic purposes as being soundproof, breakproof, free from interruption, and situated at a distance from the ordinary classroom. The range of accommodation in the present study fell far short of this and was as follows:
(i)   a cloakroom, with the inevitable interruption of children passing through on their way to the lavatories;
(ii) an empty classroom with desks, other children's work, and the classroom atmosphere;

(iii) a hall in which were housed percussion and other musical instruments that the children were forbidden to touch;

(iv) a school secretary's office, complete with typewriter, books, and out-of-bounds medical scales;

(v) the large hall of a nearby comprehensive school – a difficult environment, as limits had to be set on the children moving out of a marked-off corner of the room, where it was found necessary to invoke prohibition frequently and where little provision was made for the relaxed and permissive atmosphere that the treatment aimed to achieve;

(vi) a room in the Maternal and Child Welfare Clinic across the road.

Each of these environments had disadvantages and increased therapeutic difficulties. The school staff were, in every case, most helpful and offered the best accommodation available. There was no reason to think that better accommodation would be available, on average, in other schools in the UK.

The accommodation in the senior groups posed less of a problem than that in the junior schools. Two of the leaders had to take groups in large, empty classrooms, with the accompanying temptations for the children to run about and draw on the blackboards; however, the other groups were accommodated in appropriately sized rooms.

PREPARATION OF CHILDREN FOR THE GROUPS

A series of studies in adults has shown that preparation may have an effect on the subsequent process and, possibly, outcome of therapy. Some studies found effects on the frequency and type of statements made in therapy (Yalom and Rand 1967; Heitler 1973). Two have focused on outcome of therapy as well as process; thus, Hoehn-Saric *et al.* (1964) showed differences between prepared patients and controls, not only in a number of process measures, including rate of attendance at the group, but also in therapist and self-ratings outcomes. Sloane *et al.* (1970) attempted to disentangle the effects of information about therapy from expectation of success of therapy. They found that the information group showed a reduction of target symptoms. However, this study is difficult to assess because, for example, 50 per cent of the patients had received previous treatment. Holmes and Urie (1975) carried out a study in which eighty-eight children were randomly allocated to a preparation interview or a control group before therapy. It was found that the prepared group showed a better understanding of therapy, and also that there was better attendance among them in comparison with the controls; however, there was no difference in outcome between the two groups. The results of preparation, although rather inconsistent, have suggested that this is an aspect of therapy that deserves our attention.

The present study posed different problems from that of Holmes and Urie and whereas those authors focused on target symptoms in their role-induction interview, we followed the logic of Rogers's method. This meant that our therapists did not know any details of the children's problems, as such knowledge might have prevented them from participating in the authentic person-to-person encounter so essential to Rogers' approach. The fact that the project was located in the school also meant that care had to be taken not to put the children in a situation in which they would appear 'sick' or special in any way.

The social workers who undertook the project were already familiar with the schools where they were to work. Some months before the programme was due to start they began to talk to the teachers about the work that was to come. This was aimed at allowing the teachers, particularly those with pastoral responsibilities, to talk to the children about the groups. Teachers took different lines with the two age ranges. With the seniors, it was stated that there would be discussion groups in which the children would have a chance to say whatever they wanted. With the juniors, it was stated that there would be a special lesson where the children would be free to play with some toys. In two instances the social workers felt that a more definite introduction was necessary for the children and in these cases, the project leader visited the school and addressed the children as a group, repeating the teachers' message. In the event, there was no evidence that this extra input was particularly helpful.

Confidentiality and relationships with school staff
The problem of confidentiality was one that concerned us in pre-liminary discussions, particularly in the senior groups. Most of the groups at some time raised the topic and the following example illustrates its importance to the children:

> As part of the programme of assessment the parents of each child were visited by a research interviewer who obtained information about the child's social background. On one occasion such a visit to a boy's home took place after the group meetings had started. The group had already met for two sessions and the therapist had reported that the boys seemed glad to discuss their problems openly without fear of 'comeback'. However, the boy concerned was very upset by the visit and took it to mean that the therapist had talked about what went on in the group. He continued to attend the group but remained distrustful and for the next three sessions contributed little to the group. After this he began to relax again.

With this sort of problem in mind, it was decided that all the groups should be strictly confidential and that the therapists should not see themselves as providing a bridge between children and teachers, but more as a sounding board for the children, as outlined by Rogerian principles. On the other hand, it was clearly nonsense to have no contact with staff and it was therefore decided that the therapists would make appointments to meet them, to talk about the children's problems. At the beginning of contact with staff, it was pointed out that because it was necessary to group members' security (and to the senior children's in particular), confidentiality would be observed and nothing would be passed on without the permission of the child. Therapist-teacher discussion therefore centred rather on the child and his or her problems than on the content of the group. It was hoped that each discussion would allay any anxieties or antagonisms that might occur, increase insight, and offer suggestions as to the handling and management of the children.

In the senior groups there were large numbers of staff teaching any one child. It was therefore felt that each therapist should make the decision about which staff to work with and that the decision should be made according to the organization of the school. Pastoral staff were most often involved, and, occasionally, other staff members who were particularly interested joined in discussions.

In the junior groups the problems of therapist-teacher relationships were simpler, as there was only one teacher to contact for each class. However, there was the problem of noise in the groups, and the difficulty in explaining to teachers that the therapists' permissiveness was a valuable part of therapy, not just a 'free-for-all'. Again, each therapist was left to organize contact in their own school and this varied according to the therapist and willingness of staff, but normally consisted of a weekly meeting.

A further problem of which we were aware was the possibility of attempts by the children to get the therapist to side with them against staff and school rules. Children in the senior groups *did* attempt this on occasions, for example by attempting to smoke during sessions. The form of the therapy, though, with its prescribed and clear limits, meant that this behaviour did not in fact present a problem but provided a further opportunity to encourage the children to understand their feelings and motivations.

The setting of limits

An important aspect of planning was to reach agreement on what constituted acceptable behaviour in the group, so that the six therapists were able to set limits on certain types of conduct. The actual situations encountered in therapy were so varied and unique that detailed planning of limits in advance would have been of little value. However, there was general agreement on guidelines for forbidden behaviour, as follows:

(i)   any infringement of the general school rules, such as smoking, climbing out of windows, damaging school property, and so forth;
(ii)   any behaviour that seriously disrupted group interaction, such as wandering about or leaving the room;
(iii) any overt physical aggression shown either to other children or to the therapist.

The limits were not outlined to the children in advance, as this would have led to a negative atmosphere and suggested to them that the therapist was expecting trouble. Instead, they were made clear to the children as the situation demanded.

THE PROCESS OF THERAPY – JUNIORS

The therapist coded the child's behaviour (see Parker and Nicol 1981); a child was rated positive on any of the scales of behaviour if he or she demonstrated this behaviour during the playgroup session. The proportions (expressed as a percentage) of the children demonstrating the behaviour in any session, over all seventeen groups, were examined. The following comments on these results and reports on the types of behaviour, as set down in the therapists' descriptive accounts.

Absenteeism

The small increase in the number of absentees, as in the senior groups, was probably attributable to the fact that the sessions took place in the summer term. Towards the end of this term it is usual for children to be away on school trips or on family holidays.

Aggression

Aggression tended to increase during the course of the playgroups. Examination of the written accounts suggested that it covered a number of situations. In some groups one particular child seemed to need to retain control of the group in an omnipotent and domineering way and would challenge all comers – sometimes including the therapist – who threatened this. In other cases aggression was no more than enjoyable horse-play, but in others horse-play rapidly escalated into group excitement and frayed tempers. In some cases the behaviour labelled 'aggressive' came at the end of a chain of interactions that was more subtly enticing or provocative. Boy-girl conflict was a feature of some groups. In some cases more disturbed children seemed only to bring their inner turmoil and rage to the group. In the last sessions the therapists thought that for some children frustration at the ending of the sessions was an important factor in relation to their aggression. The ending of the groups is an important topic and is dealt with on page 245.

Isolation

Isolation and its obverse, co-operative play, showed little in the way of overall change, although there were fluctuations from group to group. It is noteworthy that isolated play was relatively infrequent. Only 55–65 per cent of the children on average demonstrated this behaviour in any session over the seventeen groups.

Isolation in the early sessions was often seen as a manifestation of shyness and of the child's witnessing the situation as strange. The isolated children preferred to play alone, although this was often parallel play which later became co-operative play. Later on, timidity during a rowdy game was quite common. The isolated children often seemed to want to join in but could not bring themselves to do so, even if encouraged by the other children. Very occasionally a depressed child would be sitting at the edge of the group waiting for the session to end, or sulking after having lost a game, but by far the most usual pattern was for an isolated child to be playing contentedly alone, or drawing. Two other types of partial isolation were communication indirectly, via the toy telephone, and passive watching of activity while ostensibly playing alone.

Attention-seeking behaviour

This declared itself in many ways, the important feature being the therapist's feeling that the child was putting him- or herself in a dependent role or seeking to monopolize the therapist's attention. Some common types of behaviour described were asking numerous questions, general complaints, and complaints by girls that only the boys were receiving attention. Showing pictures, wanting to give pictures and presents, eye contact in shy children, and telling tales about other children were also common.

THE PROCESS OF THERAPY – SENIOR GROUPS

Attendance

Among a disturbed population of children, especially if unselected by a referral mechanism, truancy from school is likely to be a problem, and, if too great, will severely handicap any school-based treatment efforts.

The total mean attendance rate in the senior groups fell slightly during the programme, starting at a mean of 87.2 per cent and ending with a mean of 71.4 per cent. As the programme took place in the summer term, a fall-off in attendance might be expected as a general trend towards the end of term. We were able to confirm, by examining attendance registers, that the children were absent from school as a whole, not just from the groups.

Content of sessions

In recording the senior sessions the therapists were asked to make a rating of the amount of group time spent discussing subjects in four broad categories – school problems, home problems, leisure, and here-and-now interaction (see Nicol and Bell 1975). *Fig. 8(1)* shows that there was a marked shift in the content of the sessions as time progressed. (A pilot study on twelve groups had shown that the inter-rater reliabilities of the content ratings were: school problems 75 per cent agreement; family problems 100 per cent; leisure 83 per cent; and here-and-now 92 per cent).

Figure 8(1) Number of groups out of 17 where more than 10 per cent of group time was spent on a given topic: senior groups

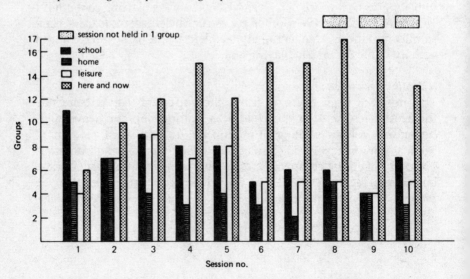

In the first session discussion was heavily centred on school, likes and dislikes of teachers, peers, school rules, and discipline. In many cases it was possible to recognize disguised communication of anxiety about the purpose of the groups and the school at large. The therapists attempted to label the feelings brought to the group, as well as to provide explanations.

School as a focus of discussion became less prominent after the first session and the children began to focus on home problems, although there was great variation between the groups in the extent to which home issues were brought up for discussion. In one very silent boys' group home life was never mentioned, whereas in one girls' group home problems were focused on at all sessions – following the lead of a talkative girl who used the first session to discuss her new step-father. In later sessions similar confidences were shared by the other girls.

In addition, in these early sessions, leisure activities assumed a prominent place, particularly in the third session. Many different topics were discussed under this general heading and some, such as boys' boasts about their own, their brothers', or their friends' violence and delinquency, clearly represented rivalry within the group, or a bid for the therapist's attention.

Attention-seeking behaviour was not always expressed noisily or even verbally. Quiet and inhibited children would often engage the therapist in eye contact or position themselves next to the therapist in successive group sessions. To the practitioner of adult psychotherapy these overtures often show an engaging simplicity and straightforwardness.

After the first three or four sessions the trend of discussions began to be directed away from topics outside the group and towards interaction between members of the group. Various aspects of non-verbal group interaction were recorded, using operational definitions of the various behaviours.

Fig. 8(1) shows how the focus shifted to here-and-now interaction, and *Fig. 8(2)* shows that this was accompanied by an increase in the expression of negative affect, both verbal and non-verbal, and a reduction in the frequency of prolonged silences by group members (defined as any member remaining silent for more than five minutes). All these changes were statistically significant. *Fig. 8(3)* shows that there were changes in the rates of other behaviours as well, such as a marked reduction in giggling, some reduction in lateness, and an increase in leaving the room (often a corollary of major disruption). There was a marked increase in the amount to which limits had to be imposed.

Figure 8(2)   Here-and-now group interaction I: senior groups

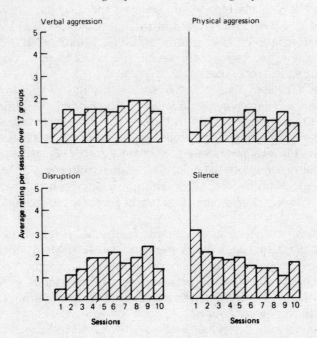

Another feature of the groups was the fact that the last group session was often quite different from the others and on average represented a return to the situation of the first group. Unlike the overall changes, these trends achieved significance only in the case of silence, but certainly merit further research.

These findings raised the question of the stages through which a therapeutic group has to pass in order to achieve maturity. MacLennan and Felsenfeld (1968), in talking of adolescent groups, mentioned an initial stage of orientation after which testing operations and defences came into play. This seems to be very much what happened in our groups. Yalom (1975) spoke of three stages, the first two of which corresponded with those found in our study, although he was writing about adult groups. His stages were:

(i)   the initial orientation stage with hesitant participation and a search for meaning;

(ii) the second stage of conflict, dominance, and rebellion;

(iii) the third stage of increasing cohesiveness and working through.

We have referred to the concept of group cohesiveness, the attraction of a group for its members, earlier in the chapter: it is a central concept in small group research, with many implications of

Figure 8(3)   Here-and-now group interaction II: senior groups: mean number of children exhibiting behaviour per session across 17 groups

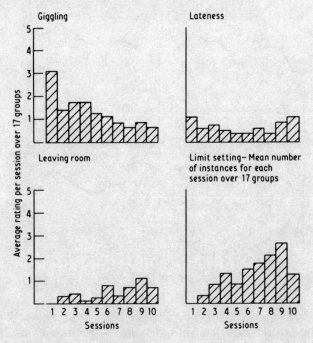

therapeutic importance. For example, a cohesive group has more ability to modify the attitudes of its members than a non-cohesive group.

Fig. 8(4) shows the therapists' estimates of the cohesiveness of their groups in three dimensions. These ratings had a moderately high level of agreement with ratings made by an outside observer who sat in on one group session of each group. Correlations ranged from 0.53 to 0.76. It can be seen that the seeds of Yalom's third stage seem to have been sown in the groups, as the mean cohesiveness rose significantly over the course of the programme.

Dynamic group themes
Dynamic group themes have been described by MacLennan and Felsenfeld (1968), and were readily identifiable in our senior groups, as the following examples show. It is important for the therapist to recognize these themes as they may block the groups' progress towards higher functioning.

(i) *Monopolization of the group by one member.* This, with the tacit agreement of the other group members, was commonly demon-

Figure 8(4)   Mean ratings for 17 groups of aspects of group cohesiveness over 10
sessions: senior groups

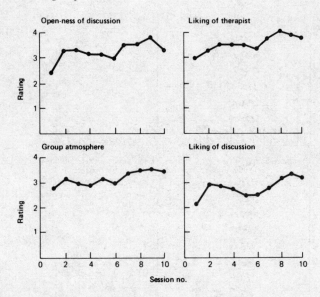

strated. In the first session, a simple, guileless, and rather dis-
inhibited girl launched into details of her home life. Other
members at first welcomed her constant talking, but in later
sessions brought pressure to bear by grumbling that they
couldn't get a word in edgeways. She continued, despite this, to
be the most active group member.

(ii)   *Taking the therapist role.* A small and deprived boy obviously
shared the group discomfort in the first session, but dealt with
this by a flood of chatter about his hobbies and activities – all of
which he did very well! In later sessions he became the 'question
master' of the group and, in particular, took it upon himself to
speak up for another very silent member.

(iii)   *Conflict about self-disclosure.* One group was very silent in the first
session, but the ice was broken in the second by one girl who
launched into a description of her family. Although this was only
a superficial description she seemed to feel herself out on a limb
and put pressure on other girls to talk more, as well as blaming
herself for being a chatterbox.

(iv)   *Splitting the group to avoid anxiety.* An active member positioned
her chair away from the therapist and began a private conversation with two other girls. The therapist brought the group's
attention to this manoeuvre.

(v) *Scapegoating*. A boy's group showed terrific aggression that consistently spilled over into fights from the second session
onwards. On some occasions the boys seemed unable to cope
with the situation they had created, and left the room before the
session had ended. The therapist persisted in her effort to help
the boys to understand and channel their feelings, but they
focused their aggression on one boy who took up a stance of
cowering in the corner. In later sessions the boy was coaxed out
of his corner and the situation became considerably calmer.

The problems of limit setting

This problem could well rank as another 'dynamic group theme', but
is dealt with separately, as it created some of the most difficult problems encountered in the groups. One of the most effective ways that
children could avoid personal anxiety or conflict was to engineer a
limit-testing confrontation with the therapist, making it extremely
difficult for the inexperienced therapists to avoid a head-on clash
(which the child was likely to win). The correct and effective
manoeuvre in this situation, but one requiring considerable intuitive
skill, was to point out the limit but, at the same time, to show an
understanding of the feelings that had led to the situation. With
experience, the therapists were largely to master this technique.

The termination of the groups

The children were warned at an early stage that the groups would run
for ten sessions. In later sessions the subject was reintroduced. In
some groups the members dealt with their feelings in a very direct
way: they wanted to know what the therapist would be doing,
whether sessions would be continuing the following term, and
whether the therapist would continue to work in the school. Some
children showed great sadness that the groups were ending. At the
close of the final group session, the children were given a short questionnaire concerning their feelings about the groups. Many expressed
great resentment at this, as if it symbolized the therapists' rejection of
them as merely parts of a research project and, as such, could be
abandoned at the end of treatment.

The uniqueness of the last session was reflected in the objective
data collected by the therapists, as shown in *Figs 8(2)* and *8(3)*.

The therapists' assessment of the children's progress

At the completion of the treatment period the therapists were asked
how much they thought the children in their groups had progressed.

Table 8(1)   *Therapists' assessment of progress*
            (a) *Senior groups: frequency of children in various categories of progress*

degree	sympton improvement		positive dynamic change	
	n	%	n	%
marked	1	1	3	4
moderate	10	13	26	33
slight	35	45	33	42
unchanged	31	40	15	19
worse	1	1	1	1

(b) *Junior groups: frequency of children's progress in various problem areas*

degree	aggressive, impatient		stands up to others		co-operative play		less isolated		attention-seeking		observes limits	
	n	%	n	%	n	%	n	%	n	%	n	%
definite improvement	3	4	12	18	12	18	10	15	0	0	2	3
somewhat improved	18	27	26	39	32	48	19	28	15	22	18	27
unchanged	17	25	6	9	7	10	8	12	25	37	17	25
never a problem	29	43	23	34	16	24	30	45	27	40	30	45

For the senior groups the therapists made simple ratings of symptom change and of underlying psychodynamic change, whereas for the junior groups ratings were made of the children's progress in various problem areas. The results are set out in *Table 8(1)*. It can be seen that in the senior groups, at the point of termination, the therapists were somewhat more optimistic in their assessment of dynamic change than they were in actual behavioural change. In the junior groups the therapists seemed to have seen the main progress to comprise the children being more able to stand up for themselves, having more capacity for co-operative play, and being less isolated, whereas there was relatively less progress in the control of aggressive behaviour, attention-seeking, and ability to observe limits without therapist intervention. The therapists based all these ratings on the behaviour observed in their groups, but also on reports and discussions with the teachers of the children's behaviour in class.

Outcome and improvement on objective measures

Throughout this book outcome is defined as change score derived from clinical ratings whereas improvement is defined as change derived from statistical analysis of behavioural dimensions. The main findings of this chapter can be presented in various ways, the most important of which are answers to the main hypotheses presented in Chapter 3. These hypotheses consist of a comparison of all the regimes, at each age level, and look for differences between them in changes in the various measures used.

In the present section we focus on comparisons between the group therapy regimes and the controls at both the seven-year-old (at-risk) and eleven-year-old age (maladjusted) levels. This perspective will be of use to those who are committed to group techniques and who want guidance as to which problems might be helped by them. Two follow-up assessments were made at the junior level. These were at eighteen months and three years after the baseline. The same two follow-ups were undertaken at the senior level, but in addition some measures were repeated immediately after the end of treatment.

THE PSYCHIATRIST'S ASSESSMENTS OF DISTURBANCE
(OUTCOME MEASURES) FOR JUNIORS

As has been described above, and by Wrate, Nicol, and Kolvin (1981), all the information from the study was gathered together and an overall judgement was made of the diagnosis, the overall severity, and the severity of neurotic and antisocial aspects of disturbance. The judgements were made independently at each level of follow-up, three separate judgements being made thus: at baseline, first, and second follow-ups. Outcome scores were then computed according to Sainsbury's formula (see Appendix 2). The results for the junior group are set out in *Figs 8(5), 8(6),* and *8(7).* For clarity only good and poor outcomes are shown in the diagram. It can be seen that for neurotic behaviour, the playgroups showed a considerably better (and statistically significant) outcome compared with the at-risk controls, both at first and at final follow-ups. For antisocial behaviour, there was little change at first follow-up, but at final follow-up there was a trend favourable to the playgroups, although this did not reach statistical significance.

Taking all aspects of behaviour into consideration, a rating of outcome in overall severity showed playgroups making significant progress compared to the at-risk controls at final follow-up.

Figure 8(5)   Neurotic behaviour: juniors: per cent outcome (good and poor categories)

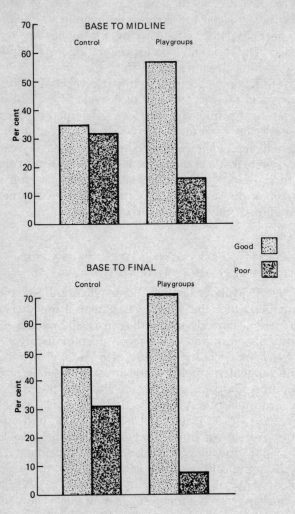

Figure 8(6)   Antisocial behaviour: juniors: per cent outcome (good and poor categories only)

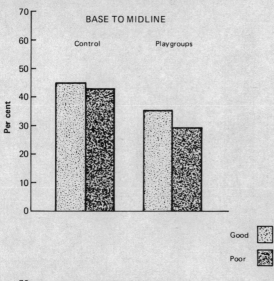

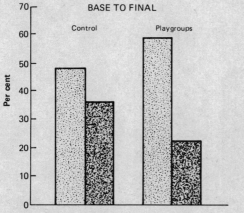

Figure 8(7)   Overall severity: juniors: per cent outcome (good and poor categories)

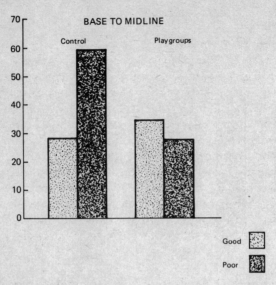

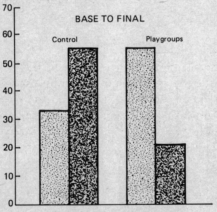

IMPROVEMENT MEASURES IN THE JUNIOR PLAYGROUPS

These are set out in *Table 8(2)* overleaf.

Academic performance
The teachers' report of comprehension on the Devereux scale, showed significantly greater improvement for the playgroup children than for the at-risk controls at both follow-ups. The individual questions of this scale were: 'gets the point of what reads or hears in class'; 'able to apply what has learned to a new situation'; and 'likely to know the material when called on to recite in class'. Two further items showed significant improvement for the treated children: these were 'quits easily' and 'slow to complete work'. These items, of course, concerned behaviour as much as academic performance.

The ability and attainment tests showed some improvements for the treated children at the eighteen-month follow-up, but, for technical reasons, these were difficult to interpret (see Appendix 3).

Peer relationships
The playgroup children showed no significant improvement compared with the at-risk controls on sociometric measures.

Teachers' reports of behaviour
Here there were a number of significant results. At the eighteen-month follow-up the Rutter B2 scale showed significant improvements for the playgroups when compared with the at-risk controls. This was true also of the antisocial sub-scale. The Devereux scale also showed significant improvement for the playgroup children on the classroom disturbance sub-scale. The aggregate score on the Devereux scale also showed their significant improvement (this was a sum of all the Devereux items).

At the final three-year follow-up the playgroup children's improvements as measured by the Rutter B2 scale were even more pronounced, as were the changes on the aggregate score on the Devereux scale. The 'impatience' sub-score in particular showed their significant improvement, as did the category 'unable to change' and the classroom disturbance sub-scale.

Parental reports of behaviour
At the three-year follow-up playgroup children's improvement was seen in antisocial behaviour, psychosomatic disturbance, and the aggregate of behaviour interview.

Table 8(2)   *Significant differences between at-risk controls and playgroup children (for detailed results see Appendix 3)*

---

1. *Eighteen-month follow-up*

   academic performance

   Devereux lack of comprehension**
   Devereux quits easily*
   Devereux slow work*

   teacher reports

   Rutter B2 total**
   Rutter B2 antisocial**
   Devereux classroom disturbance**
   Devereux aggregate*

---

2. *Three-year follow-up*

   academic performance

   Devereux lack of comprehension**

   teacher reports

   Rutter B2 total**
   Rutter B2 neurotic**
   Rutter B2 antisocial**

   Devereux impatience**
   Devereux unable to change*
   Devereux classroom disturbance*
   Devereux aggregate**

   parental reports

   behaviour interview: antisocial**
   behaviour interview: psychosomatic*
   behaviour interview: aggregate of neurotic, antisocial, and psychosomatic**

   global reports

   global behaviour**
   global neurotic*
   global antisocial**

Note: *significantly greater change than at-risk controls at 5% level; **significantly greater change than at-risk controls at 1% level.

Global scores
It can be seen from the above results that there were widespread changes in the playgroup children's behaviour. Such change was also reflected in the global composite score (see Chapter 9), in which there was significant improvement in the total global behaviour scale and, particularly, in the antisocial, though also in the neurotic, global scales.

THE PSYCHIATRIST'S ASSESSMENT OF DISTURBANCE (OUTCOME MEASURES) FOR SENIORS

The overall assessments of disturbance for seniors were carried out in the same way as for the junior groups (see *Figs 8(8)*, *8(9)*, and *8(10)*). For neurotic behaviour, children undergoing group therapy showed significantly better outcome than did the maladjusted controls, both at first and at final follow-ups. The same was true for antisocial behaviour: the group therapy children showed significantly better outcome over the maladjusted controls both at the midline and at final follow-up, and on overall severity they did so again, also at both follow-ups.

IMPROVEMENT MEASURES IN SENIOR GROUP THERAPY

These are set out in *Table 8(3)*, on p. 257.

Academic performance
There were significant improvements on the National Child Development Study test (NCDS) at the eighteen-month follow-up for the group therapy children. This was both on the total score and on the verbal and non-verbal sub-scores. By the three-year follow-up, however, the maladjusted control children had caught up with them.

School attitudes
Results of the Barker Lunn self-report questionnaire showed significant improvements for the group therapy children on the 'liking for school' sub-scale at the immediate six-month follow-up. At eighteen months there were improvements among the sub-scales reflecting school anxiety and good peer relationships. At the final three-year follow-up these improvements had washed out.

Self-report
At the eighteen-month follow-up there was improvement on the JEPI 'N' scale. In other words, at eighteen months the group therapy children showed less neuroticism than did the maladjusted controls: however, at three years the difference seemed to have washed out.

Figure 8(8)   Neurotic behaviour: seniors: per cent outcome (good and poor categories)

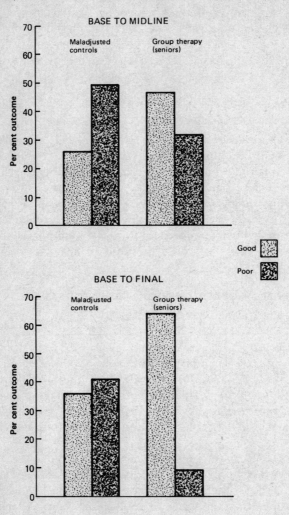

Figure 8(9) Antisocial behaviour: seniors: per cent outcome (good and poor categories)

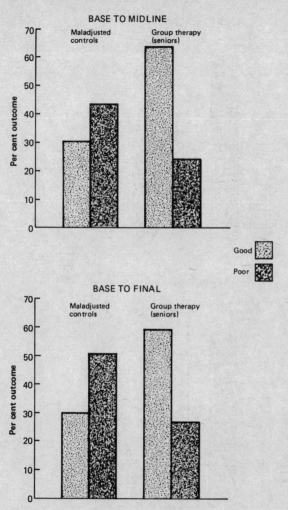

Figure 8(10)   Overall severity: seniors: per cent outcome (good and poor categories only)

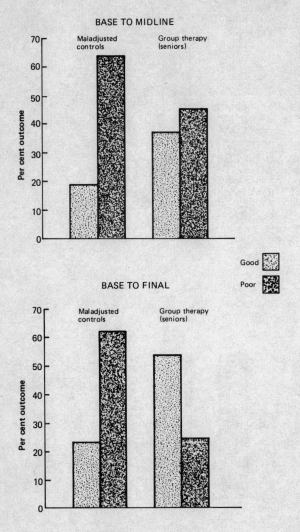

Table 8(3)   *Significant differences between maladjusted controls and senior group therapy regime (for detailed results see Appendix 3)*

1. *Immediate post-treatment follow-up*

    Devereux needs more closeness**
    Barker Lunn liking of school*

2. *Eighteen-month follow-up*

    academic performance

    verbal ability test (NCDS)**
    non-verbal ability test (NCDS)*
    total ability score (NCDS)**

    school attitudes

    Barker Lunn social adjustment*
    Barker Lunn neurotic anxiety about school*

    self-report

    JEPI neuroticism*

    parental reports

    behaviour interview: psychosomatic*
    behaviour interview: aggregate of neurotic, antisocial, and psychosomatic*

    global reports

    global maladjustment*
    global antisocial*

3. *Three-year follow-up*

    teacher reports
    Rutter B2 total**
    Rutter B2 neurotic*
    Rutter B2 antisocial*

    peer relationships

    isolation*

    parental reports

    behaviour interview: antisocial*
    behaviour interview: aggregate of neurotic, antisocial, and psychosomatic*

    global reports

    global maladjustment*
    global neurotic*

Note: *significantly greater change than maladjusted controls at 5% level; **significantly greater change than maladjusted controls at 1% level.

Peer relationships
There was a significant improvement in the group therapy children's level of isolation at the three-year follow-up.

Teacher reports
Apart from the one Devereux measure 'needs more closeness', which showed changes at six months, differences emerged only at the final three-year follow-up, where the group therapy children's behaviour, as measured on the Rutter teacher scale total, neurotic, and antisocial sub-scales, showed significant improvement.

Parental reports
At eighteen months the behaviour interview aggregate of neurotic, antisocial, and psychosomatic behaviour showed significant changes for the group therapy children, while at three years both the aggregate dimensions emerged as significant.

Global measures
A global measure of maladjustment, made up of fourteen measures, showed improvement for the group therapy children at eighteen months and three years, and antisocial behaviour, made up of five measures, showed improvement at eighteen months. This washed out, but there was significant improvement in neurotic behaviour.

How accurate were the therapists' assessments of the children's progress?

As clinicians, we assess most of our day-to-day clinical work in much the same way as the therapists did in the study: simply from the way the children seemed to progress during the therapy sessions. We can see from *Table 8(1)* that the therapists were, in fact, quite guarded in their optimism about progress. How realistic were they? To check this we correlated the therapists' ratings with the clinical measure of outcome in terms of overall severity at follow-up (*Table 8(4)*). As can be seen, fourteen out of the sixteen correlations were high. It seems safe to conclude that the therapists were well aware of the relative progress of the children during treatment.

Did the atmosphere of the groups influence outcome?

We have described the measures of cohesiveness and openness of discussion that were made during the course of the senior groups, and have shown how these seemed to change as the groups pro-

Table 8(4)   *Correlation of therapists' assessment of progress during treatment with overall clinical measure of outcome at follow-ups eighteen months and three years later*

junior groups (n = 60)

		therapists' assessment	
clinical rating of outcome	*improvement in aggression impatience*	*improvement in standing up for self*	*improvement in co-operative play*
	r =	r =	r =
base to midline	0.81***	0.49***	0.81***
base to final	0.82***	0.00 ns	0.48***

		therapists' assessment	
clinical rating of outcome	*less isolated*	*less attention-seeking*	*responds to limits*
	r =	r =	r =
base to midline	0.83***	0.35**	0.72***
base to final	0.45***	0.34**	0.57***

senior groups (n = 60)

	therapists' assessment	
clinical rating of outcome	*symptom improvement*	*positive dynamic change*
	r =	r =
base to midline change	0.01 ns	0.33**
base to final change	0.70***	0.32*

Note: * p < 5%; **p < 1%; ***p < 0.1%.

gressed. Earlier in the chapter we explained that group cohesiveness is a very important phenomenon, with likely implications for therapy. What effect did it have with our groups? To test this we correlated the two indices of cohesiveness and openness of discussion with the outcome measures. The results showed no correlation between the levels of cohesiveness and openness of discussion in the groups and outcome. Thus, the importance of group atmosphere was not confirmed in this study.

We should mention that questionnaires designed to tap therapists' and children's liking of the groups failed to predict outcome (for details of the questionnaires see Nicol *et al.* (1977)).

Summing up

The results of the group therapy regime present a surprisingly consistent picture. In both the junior and senior groups there was better outcome and improvement in comparison with the at-risk and maladjusted controls. Only in the case of antisocial behaviour at the junior level did the outcome changes not reach significance. On looking at the individual measures the favourable changes seemed to occur mostly in teacher and, to a lesser extent, parental reports of behaviour and, in the senior groups, in self-report ratings and, minimally, in sociometry. In the senior eighteen-month follow-up, there were significant improvements in academic performance. However, these improvements failed to persist at the final (three-year) follow-up.

How can we explain the less-than-exciting results of other studies reviewed earlier in this chapter? We can do so quite simply by saying that these other investigators seemed to have looked for the wrong things at the wrong time in studies that had often been on far too small a scale. Most of them looked for academic gains, yet this area seems the least likely to have yielded positive results (despite this, a substantial minority of the studies *did* show improvement). The second most commonly used measurement in these other studies was sociometry. Again, our study suggested that sociometric 'isolation' indicates only very modest changes as a result of group therapy: nevertheless, some previous studies reported positive results. It is very surprising to find that such meagre resources have been devoted to evaluating the effectiveness of group therapy, considering that it is a technique so widely practiced. The most encouraging results from previous studies were in the outcome areas of teacher-reported behaviour and of self-ratings, the same areas that showed good outcome in the present study. None of the previous studies, though, included parental reports of behaviour as outcome measures. This was unfortunate on methodological grounds alone, as they provide a relatively independent measure, less likely than school-based ones to be influenced by knowledge of the type of treatment the children received. Over and above this, it does seem that behaviour as reported by parents is a sensitive measure of treatment effectiveness.

The other clear lesson that emerged from a comparison of the present with previous studies concerned the importance of long-term follow-ups. Changes may occur over quite a long period after therapy is complete: a clear indication of this was provided by the immediate follow-up in the senior groups, which showed a meagre change on two measures only. Possibly, if other studies had instituted systematic longer-term follow-ups they, too, would have yielded more positive results.

A further set of findings that merit comment were the agreements between the objective outcome measures and the therapists' judgements that had been made nearly three years earlier. The fact that the therapists seemed to some extent to be aware of which children they were helping gives added weight to the assertion that the changes that were observed were the specific results of the therapy process rather than some relatively extraneous events.

We were not successful in discovering aspects of the process of therapy that correlated with outcome; however, we return to the theme of therapeutic qualities in Chapters 9 and 10 and Appendix 4.

The outcome studies reviewed were:

(i) *Directed mainly to educational problems*: Altmann, Conklin, and Hughes (1972); Barcai *et al.* (1973); Baymur and Patterson (1960); Broedel *et al.* (1960); Cheatham (1968); Coles (1977); Creanage (1971); Deskin (1968); Dickenson and Truax (1966); Ewing and Gilbert (1967); Finney and Van Dalsem (1969); Fisher (1953); Gilbreath (1967); Lawrence (1973); Light and Alexakos (1970); Mezzano (1968); Moulin (1970); Myrick and Haight (1972); Shaw (1962); Shouksmith and Taylor (1964); Speilberger, Weitz, and Denny (1962); Vriend (1969); Winkler, Teigland, and Munger (1965); Winn (1962).

(ii) *Directed mainly at peer relationships*: Bevins (1970); Biasco (1966); Briggs (1968); Hansen, Niland, and Zani (1969); House (1971); Kranzler *et al.* (1966); Lewis and Lewis (1977); McBrien and Nelson (1972); Meyer, Strowig, and Hosford (1970); Schiffer (1971); Thombs and Muro (1973).

(iii) *Motivated by teacher report of bad behaviour*: Abraham (1972); Barcai and Robinson (1969); Hinds and Roehike (1970); Hubbert (1970); Kelly and Mathews (1971); Randolph and Hardage (1973); Seeman, Barry, and Ellinwood (1964); Taylor and Hoedt (1974).

(iv) *On children reported as poorly adjusted*: Clement and Milne (1967); Elliot and Pumphrey (1972); Hargrave and Hargrave (1979); Lisle (1968); Pelham (1972).

(v) *Focused on children's self concepts*: Clements (1963); Dorfman (1958); Hugo (1970); Hume (1967); Mann, Barber, and Jacobson (1969); Warner and Hansen (1970).

(vi) *On child guidance referrals, delinquents and others*: Crow (1971); Irwin, Levy, and Shapiro (1972); Persons (1966); Tolor (1970).

Part Four
Results and conclusions

9 Final analysis:
junior and senior schools*

Summary

This chapter presents the results of our evaluations of treatment effectiveness in two forms: in terms of *outcome* and *improvement*.

Considering *outcome for junior children*, no significant differences emerged between the groups for antisocial behaviour, at either midline or final follow-up. On neurotic behaviour, the playgroup children did significantly better than the at-risk controls and parent counselling-teacher consultation group at midline, and better than all three other groups at final follow-up. No differences were apparent on overall severity at midline but, at the final follow-up, nurture work and playgroup children did significantly better than the at-risk controls, and playgroup children also did better than the parent counselling-teacher consultation group.

Broadly similar results were apparent for *improvement*. Considering measures of neurotic and antisocial behaviour, plus general maladjustment derived by factor analysis, no significant differences were apparent at the midline comparison. By the final follow-up, the playgroup children did significantly better than the at-risk controls on all three measures, and also did better than the parent counselling-teacher consultation group on general maladjustment. On the aggregate score on the Devereux Classroom Behaviour Scale both playgroup children and the parent counselling-teacher consultation group did significantly better than the at-risk controls at the midline comparison, and all treatments did better than the at-risk controls at the final follow-up. We discuss each treatment separately in terms of its performance in relation to the at-risk controls, the pattern of change over time (across follow-ups), and whether or not changes occurred in home as well as school settings.

* All Tables and Figures are grouped at the end of the chapter; see p. 281.

Considering *outcome for senior children*, both behaviour modification and group therapy children did significantly better than the maladjusted controls on neurotic behaviour at the midline, and better than both maladjusted controls and parent counselling-teacher consultation children at the final follow-up. On antisocial behaviour, group therapy children were superior to all other groups at midline, but at the final follow-up all treatments were significantly better than the maladjusted controls. On overall severity, group therapy children did better than the maladjusted controls at midline, and both group therapy children and the behaviour modification group did better than the maladjusted controls and the parent counselling-teacher consultation group at the final follow-up.

With regard to *improvement*, group therapy children and the behaviour modification group generally did best, and the maladjusted controls or parent counselling-teacher consultation group did worst. This pattern was also evident when summary maladjustment scores were derived from multiple data sources. Much of behaviour modification's impact was demonstrated in school-based measures, whereas with group therapy this was not quite so marked. The pattern of change over time and performance in relation to the maladjusted controls is also considered for these two treatments.

There was some evidence, taking senior and junior data together, that girls showed better outcome than boys, and that children with neurotic disorder showed better outcome more often than did those with conduct disorder. Improvement data showed similar patterns.

None of the treatments conducted with junior children produced significant improvements in relation to at-risk controls on cognitive or achievement measures. With the seniors, behaviour modification and group therapy children were the most successful on ability measures but only at the midline comparison. Where differences existed on these measures between children with neurotic and children with conduct disorders these were always in favour of the former.

No interaction effects were observed between the four regimes (i.e. three treatment and a no-treatment regimes) and type of disorder, nor between treatment and sex. However, with junior children interaction effects were found between treatment and patterns of behaviour, with playgroups and nurture work regimes having been more effective with antisocial than with neurotic behaviour. The pattern of effectiveness observed amongst the junior treatment regimes was not affected when children were separated into those with mild and those with severe disturbance.

Of the therapeutic qualities studied in relation to group therapy and parent counselling-teacher consultation, therapists' assertiveness, extroversion and openness had some positive associations with out-come and improvement.

Introduction

OUTCOME EVALUATIONS

As previously described, two types of evaluation were used: the first was outcome and the second was improvement. The outcome scores were based on severity of disturbance as rated clinically at three points in time – the beginning of research (baseline), the eighteen-month (midline) follow-up, and three-year (final) follow-up. A for-mula was applied to pairs of ratings (i.e. base to midline and base to final) and the scores obtained from the use of the formula allowed us to derive three categories of outcome – good, moderate, and poor (Sainsbury 1975; see also Chapter 3 and Appendix 2). We were, there-fore, able to calculate the percentage of cases falling into each of the above three categories. This was a crude way of comparing progress but had the advantage of presenting data in percentage form and, furthermore, gave added reassurance that the changes had clinical as well as statistical significance. The progress of the children was rated in three ways: in terms of disturbance of emotion (neurotic be-haviour), disturbance of conduct (antisocial behaviour), and general disturbance (overall severity). It should be noted that all the children were scored on each of these three ratings of disturbance. To put it another way, we examined three measures or dimensions of be-haviour: neurotic behaviour, antisocial behaviour and overall severity. Within these three dimensions we looked at severity of dis-turbance.

IMPROVEMENT EVALUATIONS

Improvement was a more rigorous method of evaluation in which statistical allowance was made for the initial differences between the groups in terms of social and family background and the children's behaviour.

Both outcome and improvement were studied at two points in time irrespective of the length of treatment – eighteen months and at three years from the start of the research. Moreover, in the case of the senior school children improvement was also assessed at the end of treatment.

Using the above forms of evaluation, two primary hypotheses were tested: (a) that the four regimes (i.e. the three treatments and the controls) differ in effectiveness from each other; and (b) that one or more of the treatment regimes is better than the no-treatment regime (the controls). Five other hypotheses are listed, in Chapter 3, which relate to comparisons of mutually exclusive categories (i.e. male or female; conduct disorder or neurotic disorder) and the varying effectiveness of regimes on different patterns of behaviour (i.e. in reducing neurotic or antisocial behaviour).

Outcome – junior level

Our findings are presented, in percentage form, as good or poor outcome in *Figs 9(1a)* and *9(1b)* and more fully in Appendix 3. In addition, simple comparisons have been undertaken of each regime with every other regime, using a X^2 technique (*Table 9(1)*).

NEUROTIC BEHAVIOUR

At the midline the beginning of a pattern emerged with children in all the regimes showing a general tendency to improve, the highest percentage of cases with a good outcome being the playgroup children followed by the nurture work ones (*Fig. 9(1a)* and Appendix 3). At the final follow-up this pattern was more pronounced: the nurture work cases had a higher percentage with good outcome and a lower percentage with poor outcome than earlier, but the most notable change occurred in the case of playgroup children where more than 70 per cent had a good outcome and only 7 per cent a poor outcome (*Fig. 9(1b)*). On this occasion the playgroup children did significantly better than *each* of the other three groups (*Table 9(1)*).

ANTISOCIAL BEHAVIOUR

At the midline (*Fig. 9(1a)*) there were no major differences between the groups in terms of good outcome. However, at the final follow-up (*Fig. 9(1b)*) we saw what could have been a repeat of the pattern with neurotic behaviour, with very little change being recognizable in the at-risk controls and the parent counselling-teacher consultation children, but some change having occurred in the nurture work children (where 61 per cent presented a good outcome and only 23 per cent a poor outcome) and in the playgroup children (where the picture was almost identical to this). None of the differences in outcome between the four regimes was significant with regard to antisocial behaviour, but we will return to this category in the section on improvement.

OVERALL SEVERITY

Overall severity was a measure based on clinical judgement, taking all information into consideration. From base to final assessment (*Fig. 9(1b)*) both the playgroup and the nurture work children did significantly better than the at-risk controls (*Table 9(1)*). It should be noted that there was a trend towards better outcome by the nurture work children on the other outcome measures. In addition, the children in the playgroups did significantly better than those in the parent counselling-teacher consultation regime.

As far as juniors were concerned therefore, it seems that there were some differences between the four regimes with regard to outcome, particularly at the second follow-up.

Improvement – junior level

In Chapter 3 and Appendix 2 the theory underlying making allowances for the initial differences of behaviour of the children and differences in social and family environment is discussed. Although these techniques constituted a far more sophisticated analysis of the data than that carried out in the case of outcome the findings were broadly similar to the outcome results. *Table 9(2)* summarizes the significant differences between the regimes and shows the source of the data upon which these findings were based. The differences in improvement on the various measures between pairs of regimes were also tested, using a technique that makes allowance for the fact that when comparing any two of a number of *pairs* of groups there is an increase in the likelihood of differences occurring by chance (*Table 9(3)*). Details of these techniques and results are provided in Appendices 2 and 3.

A statistical technique that allowed us to isolate the important components in a large number of measures of behaviour was employed. The technique is called factor analysis. Three such components were obtained from the ten measures studied. These were as follows:

(i)   A *neurotic behaviour* score (*Fig. 9(2a)*) was derived by adding the standardized score (this was simply a means of giving equal weight to the relevant measures) of the following five measures: parents' reports of children's emotional and psychosomatic disturbance; isolation as perceived by peers; and of neurotic behaviour derived from parent checklists (Rutter A scale) and from teacher checklists (Rutter B2 scale). It was found that by the final follow-up all the treatment regimes appeared to do better than the at-risk controls on this measure, but this was significant for playgroups only.

(ii)   An *antisocial behaviour* score (*Fig. 9(2a)*) was derived by adding
the standardized scores of the following five measures: parents'
reports of the children's antisocial behaviour; antisocial behaviour scores from the parent and teacher checklists (Rutter A
and B2 scales respectively); rejection by peers; and, finally,
moodiness as reported by parents. Here a different picture
emerged. While the children in the playgroups eventually
showed a significantly greater improvement than those in any of
the other three regimes, there was no evidence that improvement after parent counselling-teacher consultation was any different from that shown by the at-risk controls. In addition, it will
be seen from *Fig. 9(2a)* that the spread of mean improvement
scores in antisocial behaviour was greater at both the midline
stage and the final follow-up than occurred in the case of
neurotic behaviour. We tested these differences and found them
to be significant. This implied that the differing effects of treatment was more marked in the case of antisocial than neurotic
behaviour.

(iii) *General maladjustment* (*Fig. 9(2b)*) was represented by the summation of the standardized scores on the above ten measures. At
the mid-point of the research there was a non-significant trend
suggesting that any of the treatments led to a better improvement than no treatment at all, but it was interesting to note the
direction in which the different regimes appeared to be moving
(*Fig. 9(2b)*). By the final follow-up, which was eighteen months
later, it was evident that the trend continued and became significant in the case of the playgroup children. Thus, gains continued
to occur after the end of treatment. The playgroup children did
significantly better than the parent counselling-teacher consultation children. Further, the nurture work children improved
more than the at-risk controls, but the difference was not significant.

Devereux (aggregate score). We have not yet described progress
measured globally in different situations, using measures specific to
those situations. An example of such a situation is the school, and an
important scale in this respect is the Devereux, which reflects classroom-related behaviour. A factor analysis demonstrated that a
general component of maladjustment could be derived by adding the
separate item scores of the Devereux. For technical reasons, we
summed the standard scores of thirteen Devereux items so as to
produce an aggregate Devereux score of general maladjustment (see
Appendix 3). On this aggregate score, at first follow-up, the parent
counselling-teacher consultation and playgroup children did signifi-

cantly better than the at-risk controls, but by the second follow-up all children in all three treatment regimes had improved significantly more than the at-risk controls (*Fig. 9(2b)*).

RE-ANALYSIS OF THE DATA

An analysis of progress, measure by measure, such as outlined above, constitutes one way of looking at the improvements that occurred on the multiple sources of data and multiple instruments used in the study. *We have described our measures according to the following system: (a) aggregate or sum measures, derived by adding together two or more main measures or scales; (b) main measures that provide a substantial description of behaviour: those derived from such scales as the Rutter ones, for example, conduct and neurotic scores; and (c) individual measures, for example, individual scales on the Barker Lunn and Devereux.* Another way of analysing the data is in relation to the following five questions:

(i)   on how many measures did children in the treatment regimes do significantly worse than the controls?
(ii) on which measures was there improvement that revealed itself at the mid-point and was maintained right until the end of the study?
(iii) on which measures was there improvement that revealed itself at the mid-point but then washed out or was lost?
(iv) on which measures was there latent improvement, namely improvement occurring for the first time at the end-point of the study (i.e. the final follow-up)?
(v)   on which measures was there spread or extension of improvement from the school to the home?

In this type of analysis we confined ourselves to those dimensions on which there were significant differences.

The playgroup children did not do significantly worse (i) than the at-risk controls on any measure. Initial improvement at mid-point was maintained right until the final follow-up (ii) on the following measures: the total and also antisocial sub-scale of the Rutter B2 scale, the sum score of the Devereux scale, and two items on this scale. Initial improvement only (iii) occurred on two Devereux items. However, latent improvement (iv) was very common, being found on the total, antisocial, and psychosomatic scores derived from parent interview; on the temperament measure of mood; on the neurotic score of the Rutter B2 scale; on all three global scores, i.e. total, neurotic, and antisocial; and on two Devereux items. Finally, there was an extension of improvement from the school to the home on scales based on the parent interviews, i.e. antisocial, psychosomatic, and total scores.

Again, the nurture work children did not do significantly worse (i) than the at-risk controls on any measure. Maintained initial improvement (ii) occurred only on the antisocial sub-scale of the parent interview and two items of the Devereux. Initial improvement that was lost (iii) occurred only in the case of two Devereux items. Latent improvement (iv) sometimes occurred, for example, on the neurotic sub-scale of the Rutter B2 scale, on two Devereux items, and, finally, the sum score of the Devereux. Again, there was a spread of improvement to the home (v) on behaviour scales based on parental interviews, but it was confined to antisocial behaviour.

On no measure did parent counselling-teacher consultation children do significantly worse than the at-risk controls (i). Only on the Devereux scale was there initial improvement that is maintained (ii), on measures of 'impatience', 'comprehension', and the sum score. As found with the playgroup and nurture work children, improvement that washed out (iii) occurred only on the Devereux (on items relating to 'inattentiveness', 'needs closeness', and 'slow at work'). On no measure was there latent improvement (iv) and there was no spread of improvement to the home (v).

Yet another way of looking at the data is by studying the source of the measures on which improvement occurred. By and large it seemed that on the aggregate measures the playgroup children were most effective no matter what the source of the data (home or school) and this is well illustrated by *Figs 9(3a)* and *9(3b)*. However, when the main measures from the parents were studied the playgroup children did better than the nurture work children, and both were more successful than the parent counselling-teacher consultation children and the at-risk controls. However, most of the significant differences were achieved by the playgroup children when the source was the school (excluding the Devereux scale). On the individual measures of the Devereux the children in the three intervention regimes showed significant differences from the at-risk controls in an equal number of instances (four) from base to midline; from base to final follow-up the picture changed slightly, with playgroup children showing greater improvement on four measures, nurture work children on four, and parent counselling-teacher consultation children on two measures.

Outcome – senior level

Figs 9(4a) and *9(4b)* show, in percentage form, the outcome of treatment for senior children with different types of disorder. *Table 9(4)* compares the significant differences in outcome of the various regimes.

NEUROTIC BEHAVIOUR

On neurotic behaviour, from base to midline (*Fig. 9(4a)*), group therapy and behaviour modification children did significantly better than the maladjusted controls. From base to final (*Fig. 9(4b)*), each did better than both the maladjusted controls and the parent counselling-teacher consultation children, with performances that were particularly impressive by this stage.

ANTISOCIAL BEHAVIOUR

On antisocial behaviour, from base to midline, there were no significant differences between the maladjusted controls, parent counselling-teacher consultation children, and behaviour modification children. However, the group therapy children had much better results than all three (*Fig. 9(4a)*). Nevertheless, from base to final assessment (*Fig 9(4b)*), the children in each of the three treatment regimes did significantly better than the maladjusted controls, and this was particularly true for those who had undergone group therapy.

OVERALL SEVERITY

On overall severity, from base to midline, the group therapy children did better than the maladjusted controls (*Fig. 9(4a)*), and, from base to final, both they and the behaviour modification children did significantly better than the maladjusted controls and the parent counselling-teacher consultation children (*Fig. 9(4b)*).

Improvement – senior level

As previously explained, improvement scores were based on a more sophisticated analysis of data than that used in the case of outcome, but, again, the findings using both methods were broadly similar. *Table 9(5)* indicates on which measures the children in the four regimes differed in relation to improvement at the two main follow-ups. *Table 9(6)* shows significant differences between pairs of regimes, including comparisons with the maladjusted controls.

BASE TO END OF TREATMENT

As treatments were of different duration it may well be more fair to consider progress from the beginning to the end of treatment (*Table 9(6)*) rather than to the two other follow-ups. This is particularly relevant in the case of behaviour modification where it has often been found in other studies that changes tended not to be maintained beyond the treatment phase. For this analysis we used all the cases on

whom data had been gathered at baseline and at the end of treatment. This meant that we had rather more cases than had we used
only those on whom we had complete data at the other follow-up
points. The measures on which data were available at this point in
time were the JEPI (personality), sociometry, Rutter A scale, the
Devereux (Classroom Behaviour), the Barker Lunn scale (Children's
School Attitude Scale), and cognitive data.

Tables 9(6) and A3(13 and 14) (p. 370) show that, when looking at improvement at the end of treatment, the behaviour modification and
group therapy children only did well on some measures in relation to
the maladjusted controls or the parent counselling-teacher consultation
children (behaviour modification on six measures and group therapy
on two measures), but no clear-cut pattern emerged. With regard to
behaviour modification there was an increase in the treated children's
popularity, and on this measure they did better than all the other
regimes. On the classroom-related measures there was an expansion
of creative initiative and an increase in the behaviour modification
children's 'needing to be closer to the teacher', which reflected the
extent to which the teacher was positively valued by the child and
which, we believe, constituted improvement. However, this need of
closeness washed out, and there was no transfer of this improvement
to the home situation; on the contrary, the parents reported increased
disturbance. Where group therapy children were concerned there
was improvement on one classroom-related measure (the children
needing to be closer to the teacher) but this, similarly, washed out.
Also, on a parental questionnaire method (Rutter A scale) the behaviour of group therapy children improved significantly in comparison with that of behaviour modification cases.

BASE TO MIDLINE AND FINAL FOLLOW-UP

Here, data were available on the full range of measures (details of
significant results are provided in Appendix 3) and hence there were
many more opportunities for differences to emerge than in the
previous analysis. First, the improvement scores of the four regimes
were compared to see whether or not there were significant differences (Table 9(5) and Appendix 3). These are listed both for base to
midline and base to final. It was found that there were significant
differences from base to midline on 37 per cent of the main measures
and on 42 per cent when comparing base to final assessments.

Table 9(6) provides some important supplementary information
because it indicates where there were significant differences between
pairs of regimes. Two patterns were evident: the group therapy
children, closely followed by those in the behaviour modification

group, usually did best, and the maladjusted controls or the parent counselling-teacher consultation children did worst.

Another way of studying the data in an attempt to identify patterns is by producing a summary table of the aggregate or main measures on the different instruments on which treated children showed significantly greater improvement than the maladjusted controls. For these purposes we have concentrated on the behaviour modification and group therapy regimes. *Table 9(7a)* reveals that while there was an almost equal number of main measures on which change occurred in children in both these treatment regimes, it was apparent that behaviour modification's impact was particularly demonstrated in school-based measures, while with group therapy this pattern was not quite so marked.

Figs 9(5a-b), *9(6)*, and *9(7a-b)* present the findings for improvement in the senior children as a series of graphs. On the scale using behavioural information derived from parental interviews (behaviour A + B + C shown in *Fig. 9(5a)* and Appendices 2 and 3) it will be seen that, from base to midline, the group therapy children improved most and, while this improvement was maintained, the behaviour modification children appeared to catch up by the final follow-up. A study of the temperamental dimension of activity showed that, again, behaviour modification and group therapy children did well at both midline and final follow-up. However, when we moved to withdrawal, it was apparent that this was one of the few occasions when parent counselling-teacher consultation seemed to be most effective (*Fig. 9(5b)*). Turning to school data when the source was the teacher (Rutter B2), we saw that group therapy children did best at both follow-ups, but when the source was the child (JEPI – 'N') the behaviour modification children did best (*Fig. 9(6)*).

We thought it essential to try to get an overall view of these findings from multiple sources (see *Fig. 9(7a-b)*). For this purpose we derived a maladjustment score based on fourteen of the above-mentioned items. *Fig. 9(7a)* shows that the pattern was broadly similar to that already found, with behaviour modification and group therapy children doing roughly the same by the final follow-up. This was true, too, for the antisocial behaviour measure, based on five items (*Fig. 9(7b)*). In the latter case, it was seen that the group therapy children initially did extremely well, but were subsequently caught up with by those in the behaviour modification regime and that, at the final follow-up, there were no significant differences between them.

RE-ANALYSIS OF THE DATA

Again, it is worthwhile attempting to answer the five crucial questions posed previously in relation to improvement in the junior regimes:

(i)   on how many measures did children in the treatment regimes do significantly worse than the controls?

(ii) on which measures was there improvement that revealed itself at the mid-point and was maintained right until the end of the study?

(iii) on which measures was there improvement that revealed itself at the mid-point but then washed out or was lost?

(iv) on which measures was there latent improvement?

(v)   on which measures was there spread or extension of improvement from the school to the home?

Starting with group therapy it was evident that on no measure did the maladjusted controls do better than the group therapy children (i). On the two measures constituting aggregate behaviour scores, A + B + C based on interviewing the parents and the aggregate maladjustment score, there was improvement for the treated children at the midline follow-up that was maintained at the final follow-up (ii). On six measures these children showed improvement at the midline that was subsequently lost (iii): the first centred on the parents' reports of children's psychosomatic symptoms; the second was shown on the aggregate antisocial behaviour scale; the third on the scale of JEPI measuring neuroticism; the fourth in terms of neurotic anxiety about school work on the Barker Lunn scale; and, finally, it occurred in relation to both verbal and non-verbal ability. However, on a number of measures there were latent improvements by the group therapy children (iv) and these consisted of all three Rutter teacher scores (total, neurotic, and antisocial sub-scores); the isolation score based on sociometry; and the global neurotic score based on the summation of nine items. Finally, it was noted that in reports based on parental interviews the improvement described in many areas of functioning appeared to have transferred to the home (v) on two measures.

On two occasions the behaviour modification children did worse than the maladjusted controls (i). Clearly there was no short-term maintenance in the treated children's improvement, i.e. between end of treatment and the midline. Further, on no measure did they show improvement at the end of treatment that was maintained to the final follow-up, nor, indeed, improvement at the midline that was maintained to the final follow-up (ii). However, on four measures the treated children showed improvement at the midline that was subsequently lost (iii): the first consisted of improvement on the neuroticism sub-scale of the JEPI; the second on anxiety about school work on the Barker Lunn scale; and, third and fourth, in verbal and non-verbal ability. They also showed latent improvement (iv) on five measures: first, in terms of antisocial behaviour as described by parents; second, on the total and neurotic sub-scales of the Rutter B2 scale; and, finally, both in terms of total behaviour based on the summation of fourteen items and neurotic behaviour based on the summation of nine items. Finally, there was a transfer of improvement to the home (v) on one measure, namely, antisocial behaviour as reported by the parents.

Effects of sex of child and type of disorder on outcome (juniors and seniors)

One of the questions we sought to answer was whether or not girls and boys respond differently to treatment. The only patterns that emerged, based on data derived from both senior and junior analyses, showed girls did significantly better than boys twice as often as boys did better than girls. In addition, it appeared that when boys excelled girls it was always on neurotic behaviour; and when girls did better than boys it was always on antisocial behaviour. These findings suggest neurotic behaviour is less deeply ingrained or intractable in boys than in girls and antisocial behaviour less deeply rooted in girls than in boys.

The data were also analysed to ascertain whether children in the conduct disorder categories showed different patterns of outcome to those in the neurotic disorder categories. As would be expected from previous research, children with neurotic disorders showed better outcome than those with conduct disorders on thirteen occasions, while the reverse occurred only on three occasions. Furthermore, when children with neurotic disorders showed better outcome than those with conduct disorders it was, with one exception, on the associated dimension of antisocial behaviour; and when conduct-disordered children showed greater improvement than neurotic-disordered ones, it was only on the associated dimension of neurotic behaviour. From this we inferred that neurotic behaviour in children with conduct disorders was less deeply ingrained than in those with neurotic disorders, and that the same was true for antisocial behaviour in children with neurotic disorders.

Effects of sex of child and type of disorder on improvement (juniors and seniors)

The Devereux Classroom Behaviour Scale revealed some interesting findings. In the junior programme (see *Fig. 9(8)*) there was a clear picture of girls showing greater improvement than boys, but this became significant only at the final follow-up. In addition, children with neurotic disorders did better than those with conduct disorders, but, again, this was significant only at the final follow-up (*Fig. 9(8)*). While the pattern was similar at the senior level, the only significant finding was that children with neurotic disorders had improved more than conduct-disordered children at the final follow-up.

With regard to other data the findings on juniors were similar to those described in the previous section on outcome: boys did significantly better than girls on neurotic behaviour (Rutter B2 scale – base to final; Rutter A scale – base to midline) and girls did significantly better than boys on the antisocial behaviour scale (Rutter B2 scale – base to midline). In addition, children with conduct disorders excelled children with neurotic disorders on scales or dimensions reflecting neurotic behaviour (Rutter B2 scale – base to midline) and also on neurotic behaviour as measured by parent interview (base to final). The group of children with neurotic disorders did better than those with conduct disorders on a number of scales depicting antisocial behaviour (parent interview – base to midline; Rutter B2 scale – base to final; a scale representing global antisocial behaviour – base to midline; and, finally, the temperament scale of activity – base to midline). In addition, children with neurotic disorders showed greater improvement in reading than did children with conduct disorders (base to final).

In the senior programme boys again did better than girls on measures of neurotic and psychosomatic behaviour (Rutter B2 scale – base to midline; JEPI neuroticism scale – both base to midline and base to final; parent interview – base to midline and base to final) and while girls excelled boys on measures of antisocial behaviour this only reached statistical significance on the temperament measure of 'activity' (parent final interview). Children with conduct disorders did better than children with neurotic disorders on measures reflecting neurotic and psychosomatic behaviour and this proved significant on a number of occasions (Rutter A scale – base to midline; parent interview – both base to midline and final follow-up). Finally, the neurotic-disordered children did best on a wide range of cognitive measures, namely verbal and non-verbal ability and reading comprehension (see *Table A3(22)* in Appendix 3).

The interpretations of these findings were similar to those advanced in the case of the outcome measures described above.

Cognitive and educational findings – improvement

In the junior programme there were no significant differences in improvement, on any of the cognitive measures used, between the at-risk controls and the treated children. This was most unexpected and will be commented on in the next chapter. However, as was to be expected, we found that children with neurotic disorders showed greater improvement in reading ability at the midline than those with conduct disorders.

With regard to the seniors there were many differences between the treated children and the maladjusted controls at the mid-point of the study, but all of these had washed out by the end of the programme. Both the behaviour modification and group therapy children did significantly better than the maladjusted controls and parent counselling-teacher consultation children on the measures of general ability, verbal ability, and non-verbal ability. Nevertheless, at the final follow-up only behaviour modification children had done significantly better than those in parent counselling-teacher consultation group on improvement on reading comprehension (see Appendix 3).

Finally, we compared cognitive changes for both junior and senior boys and girls, but found no significant differences. We also compared changes in children with conduct and children with neurotic disorders and found that the latter group always did better than the former. This was significant in the cases of non-verbal ability at the midline, and *all* cognitive measures employed at the final follow-up.

Interaction

We wanted to know whether some regimes (for example, behaviour modification) were most effective for certain types of children (for example those with neurotic disorder) and other regimes (for example playgroups) for other types of children (for example those with conduct disorders). We were also interested to find out if some regimes were most effective for boys and others for girls. These investigations are of great practical importance and are usually described as interaction between regime and diagnostic category, or between regime and sex. We tested the former on all measures and found that interaction occurred only fortuitously both in the junior and senior programmes. We also studied the interaction between regime and sex of the child and, again, the findings were essentially negative.

As there was no interaction between regimes and diagnostic category or sex the results we have presented deal with the differences between the regimes, between diagnostic categories, and between the sexes quite separately. Further details of the principles of this analysis are described in Appendix 2.

The interaction considered above was between regime and type of child (whether in relation to diagnostic category or sex), but there is another kind of interaction – between regime and pattern of be-haviour – whereby some regimes are shown to be more effective in reducing the neurotic component in a child's behaviour and other regimes in reducing the antisocial component in the same child's behaviour (hypothesis 5). We found that in the case of the juniors there was a significant interaction in this respect in that playgroups and nurture work regimes were comparatively more effective in reducing antisocial components of behaviour than neurotic com-ponents, particularly at final follow-up. There was no evidence, though, of such interaction in the case of the senior pupils.

Outcome of severely and mildly disturbed children

A further analysis was made comparing outcome in the junior chil-dren with established disorders to that of children whom, though displaying only mild disorders, we still regarded as being 'at risk'. This showed that the direction of the results was the same for both the established and the dubious disorders – the playgroup and nurture work regimes were associated with better outcome as far as overall severity was concerned. However, none of the differences between outcome scores for severely and mildly disturbed children was statistically significant.

Therapeutic qualities of therapists

With regard to the therapists involved in the senior group therapy regime a range of therapeutic qualities was studied by observation of individual therapists' sessions and from the ratings made by the supervising staff. The only three qualities that appeared to have a positive association with outcome and improvement were therapeutic assertiveness, extroversion and openness. These had a persistent, but not necessarily highly significant correlation with change in relation to both parent counselling-teacher consultation and group therapy regimes. Therapeutic assertiveness had a significant correlation with outcome in antisocial behaviour in our senior group therapy pro-gramme, both at the midline follow-up and at the end of treatment. The association was less powerful for neurotic behaviour at the mid-line follow-up and at the end of treatment. In the playgroup pro-gramme there was a reasonably high correlation, at the end of treat-ment, for assertiveness (0.73), but extroversion was not so well correlated. Concerning parent counselling-teacher consultation in junior schools the correlations for therapist assertiveness were low, and not significant. In senior schools there were, again, moderate but interesting correlations in relation to assertiveness, and lower but also interesting correlations *vis-à-vis* extroversion.

Finally, a large number of different clinical measures were made during the course of the various treatment regimes. These measures related to the treatment processes, to motivation, and to the thera-pists' subjective estimates of severity of disorder and of change. A summary of these measures would have little meaning outside the context of the individual therapies and we therefore refer the reader to the appropriate chapters for further study.

Figure 9(1a)   Juniors: per cent outcome: base to midline (good and poor categories only)

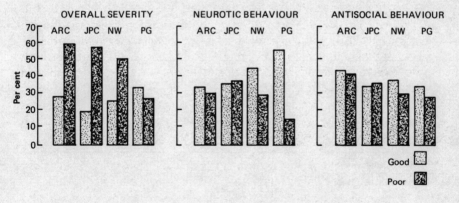

Figure 9(1b) Juniors: per cent outcome: base to final (good and poor categories only)

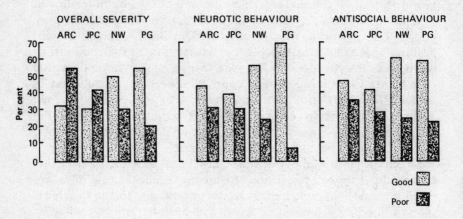

Table 9(1)   *Juniors: outcome*

base to midline			
neurotic behaviour	PG > ARC		p < .05
	PG > JPC		p < .01
antisocial behaviour		ns	
overall severity		ns	
base to final follow-up			
neurotic behaviour	PG > NW		p < .05
	PG > ARC		p < .01
	PG > JPC		p < .01
antisocial behaviour		ns	
overall severity	NW > ARC		p < .05
	PG > ARC		p < .01
	PG > JPC		p < .01

Note: ARC = at-risk controls; JPC = junior parent counselling-teacher consultation; NW = nurture work; PG = playgroups; ns = not significant; > means 'better than' in this table.

Figure 9(2a)   Mean improvement scores: juniors: aggregate – neurotic and antisocial behaviour

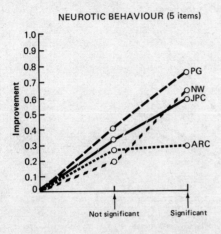

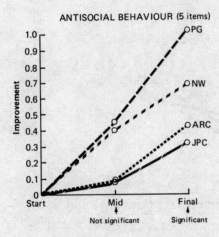

Figure 9(2b)   Mean improvement scores: juniors: aggregate behaviour

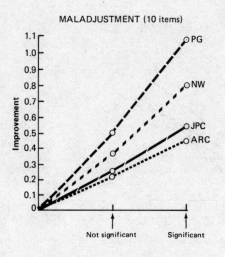

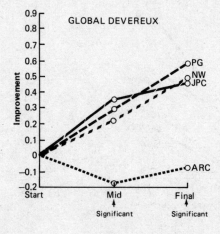

Figure 9(3a)   Mean improvement scores: juniors: parent interview

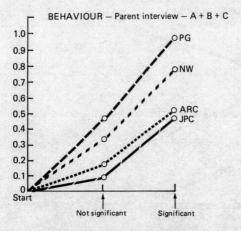

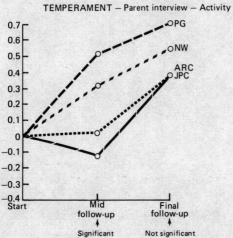

Figure 9(3b)   Mean improvement scores: juniors: teacher questionnaire

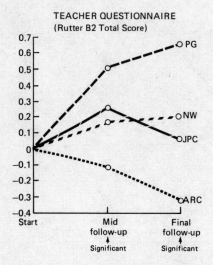

Table 9(2)   *Junior programme: comparison of the four regimes*

measure	statistical significance of the differences between the four regimes	
	base to midline	base to final
home data		
behaviour A = neurotic	ns	ns
B = antisocial	ns	highly significant
C = psychosomatic	almost	ns
A + B + C	ns	highly significant
temperament activity	significant	ns
mood	ns	significant
Rutter A total behaviour	ns	ns
neurotic behaviour	ns	ns
antisocial behaviour	ns	ns
school data		
Rutter B2 total behaviour	significant	highly significant
neurotic behaviour	significant	highly significant
antisocial behaviour	almost	highly significant
sociometry isolation	ns	ns
reading	ns	ns
aggregate data		
maladjustment (sum score of 10 items)	ns	highly significant
neurotic behaviour (sum score of 5 items)	ns	significant
antisocial behaviour (sum score of 5 items)	almost	highly significant
global behaviour (Devereux scale) (sum score of 13 items)	significant	highly significant

Note: this table includes main measures only; other details are available in the Appendices; ns = not significant; 'significant' indicates a difference at 5 per cent level; 'highly significant' indicates a difference at 1 per cent level.

Table 9(3)   *Junior programme: comparison of pairs of regimes (significant results only)*

measure	base to midline	base to final
behaviour B = antisocial	NW* > ARC	PG + NW > ARC
		PG + NW > JPC
C = psychosomatic	PG > JP	PG > ARC
A + B + C	ns	PG > ARC + JPC
temperament activity	almost PG > ARC	
mood	ns	PG + NW > JPC
Rutter B2 total behaviour		
at school	PG > ARC	PG > ARC + JPC
neurotic behaviour		
at school	ns	PG + JPC + NW > ARC
antisocial behaviour		
at school	PG > ARC	PG > ARC + JPC + NW
sociometry isolation	ns	JPC > ARC
maladjustment (sum of 10 items)	ns	PG > ARC + JPC
neurotic behaviour (sum of 5 items)	ns	PG > ARC
antisocial behaviour (sum of 5 items)	ns	PG > ARC + NW + JPC
Devereux scale		
classroom disturbance	PG > ARC	PG > ARC
impatience	JPC + NW > ARC	JPC + NW + PG > ARC
external blame	NW > ARC + JPC	NW > ARC
comprehension	JPC + PG > ARC	PG + JPC + NW > ARC
inattentive withdrawn	JPC + NW > ARC	ns
needs closeness	JPC + NW > ARC	ns
unable to change	ns	PG > ARC
quits early	PG > NW + ARC	NW > ARC
slow at work	PG + JPC > ARC	ns
	JPC > NW	
aggregate (sum score of 13 items)	JPC + PG > ARC	JPC + NW + PG > ARC

Note: * for details of abbreviations see p. 282; > means 'better than' in this table.

Figure 9(4a)   Seniors: per cent outcome: base to midline (good and poor categories only)

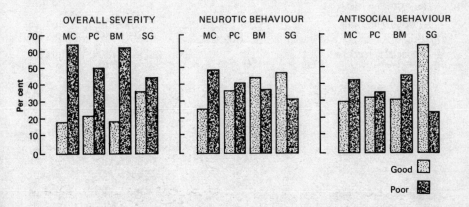

Figure 9(4b)   Seniors: per cent outcome: base to final (good and poor categories only)

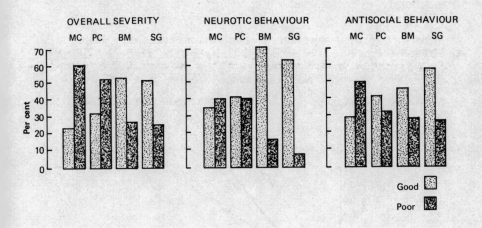

Table 9(4) *Seniors: outcome*

---

base to midline follow-up

neurotic behaviour	BM > MC	p < .05
	SG > MC	p < .05
antisocial behaviour	SG > MC	p < .01
	SG > PC	p < .01
	SG > BM	p < .01
overall severity	SG > MC	p < .05

base to final follow-up

neurotic behaviour	SG > MC	p < .01
	SG > PC	p < .01
	BM > MC	p < .01
	BM > PC	p < .01
antisocial behaviour	BM > MC	p < .05
	PC > MC	p < .05
	SG > MC	p < .01
overall severity	BM > MC	p < .01
	BM > PC	p < .01
	SG > MC	p < .01
	SG > PC	p < .01

Note: MC = maladjusted controls; PC = parent counselling-teacher consultation; BM = behaviour modification; SG = group therapy; > means 'better than' in this table.

Figure 9(5a) Mean improvement scores: seniors: parent interview, aggregate behaviour

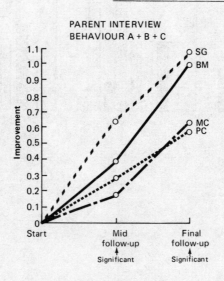

Figure 9(5b)   Mean improvement scores: seniors: parent interview, temperament

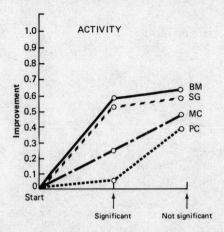

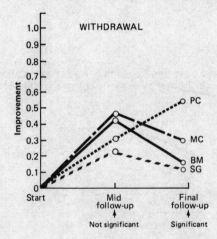

Figure 9(6)   Mean improvement scores: seniors: teacher questionnaire and JEPI neuroticism

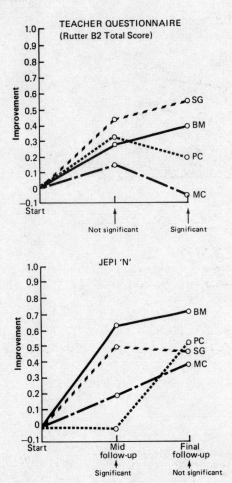

Figure 9(7a)   Mean improvement scores, aggregate behaviour (14 items): seniors: at start, midline, and final follow-up

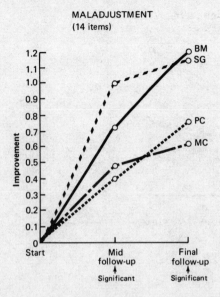

Figure 9(7b) Mean improvement scores, aggregate neurotic and antisocial behaviour: seniors: at start, midline, and final follow-up

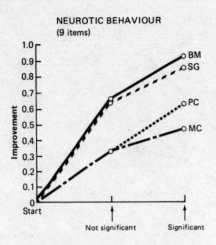

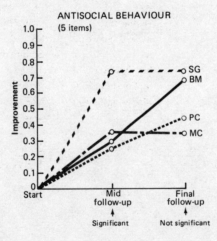

Table 9(5)   *Senior programme: comparison of the four regimes*

measure	statistical significance of the differences between the four regimes	
	base to midline	base to final
home data		
behaviour A = neurotic	ns	ns
B = antisocial	ns	significant
C = psychosomatic	ns	ns
A + B + C	significant	significant
withdrawal	ns	highly significant
activity	highly significant	ns
mood	ns	highly significant
Rutter A total behaviour	significant	ns
neurotic behaviour	ns	ns
antisocial behaviour	significant	ns
school data		
Rutter B2 total behaviour	ns	highly significant
neurotic behaviour	ns	significant
antisocial behaviour	ns	significant
sociometry isolation	significant	significant
JEPI neuroticism	highly significant	ns
JEPI introversion	ns	significant
verbal ability (NCDS)	highly significant	ns
non-verbal ability (NCDS)	highly significant	ns
total ability (NCDS)	highly significant	ns
reading	ns	significant
aggregate data		
maladjustment (sum score of 14 items)	significant	highly significant
neurotic behaviour (sum score of 9 items)	ns	highly significant
antisocial behaviour (sum score of 5 items)	significant	ns
global behaviour (Devereux scale) (sum score of 14 items)	ns	ns
Barker Lunn scale anxiety about school (sum score of 3 items)	highly significant	ns
attitude to school (sum score of 7 items)	ns	ns

Note: this table includes main measures only; other details are available in the Appendices; ns = not significant; 'significant' indicates a difference at 5 per cent level; 'highly significant' indicates a difference at 1 per cent level; NCDS = National Child Development Study test.

Table 9(6)   *Senior programme: comparison of pairs of regimes (significant results on main measures only)*

measure	base to end of treatment	base to midline	base to final
behaviour B = antisocial	no data	ns	BM > MC
C = psychosomatic	no data	SG > MC	ns
A + B + C	no data	SG > MC + PC	SG > MC
temperament activity	no data	BM + SG > PC	ns
Rutter A total behaviour at home	SG > BM MC> BM	SG + MC > BM	ns
antisocial behaviour at home	ns	SG + MC > BM	ns
Rutter B2 total behaviour at school	no data	ns	SG + BM > MC
neurotic behaviour at school	no data	ns	SG + BM > MC
antisocial behaviour at school	no data	ns	SG > MC
sociometry isolation	BM > PC + MC + SG	BM > SG	SG > PC + MC
JEPI neuroticism	BM > PC	BM + SG + MC > PC BM + SG > MC	ns
verbal ability (NCDS)	ns	BM + SG > PC + MC	ns
non-verbal ability (NCDS)	ns	BM + SG > MC + PC	ns
total ability (NCDS)	ns	BM + SG > MC + PC	ns
reading	ns	ns	BM > PC
maladjustment (sum of 14 items)	no data	SG > MC + PC	SG + BM > MC
neurotic behaviour (sum of 9 items)	no data	ns	SG + BM > MC
antisocial behaviour (sum of 5 items)	no data	SG > MC + BM + PC	ns
Barker Lunn scale anxiety about school	BM > PC	SG + BM > MC BM + SG > PC	ns
withdrawal	no data	ns	PC > BM + SG + MC
mood	no data	ns	SG > PC

Note: > means 'better than' in this table; single item data from the Devereux Classroom Behaviour Scale and the Barker Lunn School Attitude Scale have been excluded; NCDS = National Child Development Study test.

Table 9(7a)   *Senior programme: number of different main measures on which change was obtained**

	behaviour modification regime	group therapy (seniors) regime
end of treatment	4	2
midline	6	9
final	4	5
total	14	16
total school-based	13	13
total home-based	1	3

Note: *significant improvement compared with the controls.

Table 9(7b)   *Senior programme: source of measures*

	ability		self		peer		teacher		parent	
	BM	SG	BM	SG	BM	SG	BM	SG	BM	SG
end of treatment	0	0	1	1	1	0	2	1	0	0
midline	3	3	3	4	0	0	0	0	0	2
final	0	0	1	0	0	1	2	3	1	1
total	3	3	5	5	1	1	4	4	1	3

298   Help Starts Here

Figure 9(8) Mean improvement scores: juniors: according to diagnosis and sex, aggregate Devereux measure at start, midline, and final follow-up

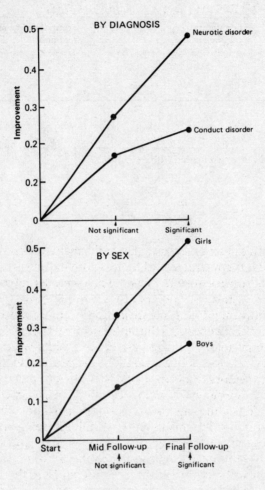

10   Summary and conclusions

Summary

In the first part of this chapter we summarize the main findings of our research and discuss them with regard to the seven hypotheses stated in Chapter 3. The positive results of our work were as follows: (a) some regimes were better than others; (b) every one of the regimes showed some improvement on some measures but there were major differences in the effectiveness of the different treatments. Broadly speaking, at the final follow-up the best junior results were in the playgroup regime and, to a lesser extent, in the nurture work programme, while the seniors responded best to behaviour modification and group therapy; (c) there was evidence that some regimes were more effective in relieving the neurotic symptoms and others in relieving the antisocial symptoms in any one child; it was found that for the junior children the nurture work and playgroup regimes, were the most successful in reducing antisocial symptoms; (d) irrespective of regime, children with conduct disorders differed from those with neurotic disorders in outcome and improvement, with neurotic-disordered children improving more than conduct-disordered children on certain measures; (e) irrespective of regime, boys differed from girls, in that girls improved more on some measures.

Other important findings were that effectiveness of treatment on behavioural measures seemed to increase with time; some treatments showed situation-specific improvements in children (for example, improvements were limited to classroom-related behaviour) whereas others had more widespread effects; associated antisocial behaviour in neurotic children seemed to be less deeply ingrained than in antisocial children, and the same seemed true of neurotic behaviour in antisocial children; senior children with neurotic disorders did better than seniors with antisocial disorders on cognitive measures; and neurotic behaviour responded better to treatment in boys than in girls, the reverse being the case with conduct behaviour.

Turning to the theoretical implications of these findings, we discuss the nature of the at-risk and maladjusted control groups and the rate of spontaneous remission, and emphasize that, because it was far from certain that these control groups did not receive any form of help, the differences reported in our research were likely to have underestimated the true effect of the intervention.

We consider four main components of psychotherapy in relation to our findings. For example, with regard to time it was particularly interesting to find that outcome and improvement continued to gain ground in effective therapies even when treatment had finished. Concerning the therapist and his or her techniques, we have suggested that direct therapy may be more effective than indirect. Also, the shorter-term treatments (group therapy, playgroups, and behaviour modification) were seen to have had the best outcome: *our results suggested that it is type rather than amount of treatment that is a critical factor in intervention*.

We discuss various aspects of the design of our programme to see whether or not they influenced our results, and we also comment on the ethical issues involved in our research.

Finally, we discuss the practical implications of our findings, and consider how they may be useful to educationalists, mental health professionals, and planners. In particular, we analyse the cost effectiveness of the various regimes, and show that *those therapies* (group therapy, playgroups, and behaviour modification) *that have given the most promising results have done so in the shortest possible time, at the least expense*.

Introduction

In this chapter we bring together the main conclusions of our research project and offer some interpretations which will set them in the context of the wider theoretical issues discussed in the opening chapters. Most important, we need to discuss the practical aspects of our findings which have implications for educational and mental health planning. Our interpretations of the data and their implications will, we hope, be seen as the first rather than the last words on the subject. We feel that our findings were important enough to warrant widespread debate and analysis, and have, therefore, provided extended technical and statistical appendices at the end of this book so that other workers can examine the data and draw their own conclusions.

The findings

The object of our research was to explore ways of helping maladjusted children in the setting of ordinary schools. This included the development and evaluation of treatment models reaching beyond the traditional child guidance approach. Early in Chapter 3 we listed seven linked hypotheses on which our research was based. In brief, these postulated that there would be differences in the amelioration of maladjustment between four comparable groups of children who had received different types of treatment or no treatment at all. In addition, the outcome would be different for two diagnostic groups and for boys and girls.

The study was carried out with two different age groups – seven- and eleven-year-olds. Initial screening was undertaken for approximately 4300 children in six senior and six junior schools (Kolvin *et al.* 1977; Macmillan *et al.* 1980). Additional information was obtained on 574 children selected for study: this was gathered from parental interviews, parent and teacher completions of behaviour checklists, individual and group tests of children, and observation of children in certain programmes. All data were reviewed by a psychiatrist who produced a global clinical assessment of the type and severity of disorder.

The children selected were randomly allocated by school class to various treatment regimes or to at-risk (junior level) and maladjusted (senior level) control regimes. In order to overcome difficulties arising from differences between schools we ensured that all regimes were undertaken in each school. The number of subjects in each group ranged from sixty to ninety. We studied three types of treatment in both junior and senior schools: in the juniors these were parent counselling-teacher consultation, nurture work, and playgroups; in the seniors they were parent counselling-teacher consultation, behaviour modification, and group therapy. Detailed accounts of these treatments can be found in Chapters 5 to 8. The major follow-ups were undertaken at eighteen and three years after the baseline assessments. We looked at patterns of change in two ways, both of which allowed for variations in initial severity of disturbance. First, an outcome measure was derived, based on clinical ratings at three points in time – baseline, midline follow-up, and final follow-up. These ratings were made by clinicians who did not know to which regime the children belonged (see Appendix 2). Second, improvement on individual measures was evaluated by comparing baseline and follow-up data.

WERE THE HYPOTHESES CONFIRMED?

The first hypothesis was that the four regimes (which included the control regime) differ in effectiveness in reducing maladjustment; in other words, some regimes are better than others. This hypothesis was confirmed by our research, and we can say with confidence that certain of our treatment efforts had tapped some important forces for change. Furthermore, there were substantial differences in effectiveness of the different treatments.

Narrowing the focus, hypothesis 2 stated that one or more of the three treatment regimes would prove more effective in reducing maladjustment than the no-treatment regime (the controls), that is, any treatment is better than no treatment at all. Some complex and interesting results emerged. The overall picture was that relative to controls, every one of the regimes showed *some* improvement on *some* measures. *In the remainder of this chapter improvement should be taken to mean significant improvement of treated children in comparison with their respective controls. Similarly, outcome means significantly better outcome for treated children than for the comparable controls.*

At the junior level (seven- to eight-year-olds) the playgroups were effective over the widest range of measures and most successful on the aggregate measures, both clinical and statistical. At the senior level (eleven- to twelve-year-olds) the group therapy and behaviour modification regimes were both effective over a wide range of measures, but with different combinations of measures. They were also both effective on aggregate measures.

Looking at the results in more detail, a very complex picture emerged. First, various time patterns became apparent: in some treatments, and on certain measures, improvement appeared to be immediate, but then washed out; on other treatments and measures improvement occurred slowly but surely, so that the gap between treated children and their respective controls increased over time; with yet other treatments and measures there appeared to be a latent effect, with improvement appearing only after a delay.

To examine the results in terms of hypotheses 1 and 2 still more closely and specifically it is best to present the major positive results of each regime separately, bearing in mind throughout whether the data came from the child, his or her peers, parents, or teachers.

Parent counselling-teacher consultation programme in junior schools
On outcome measures there were no significant differences between
the at-risk controls and the treated children. On improvement there
were significant differences but these were on classroom-related
behaviour measures only, both at the eighteen-month follow-up and
three-year follow-up (about eighteen months after the end of treatment).

Parent counselling-teacher consultation programme in senior schools
There was positive change compared with the maladjusted controls
on one outcome measure – antisocial behaviour at the three-year
follow-up (that is, again, eighteen months after the end of treatment).
At the same point in time the treated children made two positive
changes on improvement measures.

The nurturing approach (a junior school programme)
In this regime, while treated children seemed to have had better
results than the at-risk controls on all three outcome measures, it was
only on overall severity at the final follow-up that changes were
significant. In relation to improvement, there were several
classroom-related changes at both midline and final follow-ups, and,
in addition, there were improvements on home-based measures of
behaviour (i.e. antisocial behaviour) at both follow-ups.

Group therapy in senior and junior schools
To some extent the junior and senior group therapy programmes can
be considered together as they were based upon the same Rogerian
principles (Axline 1947a; Rogers 1952). However, they differed in
detail in that the junior programmes were playgroups and the senior
programmes discussion groups.
    When studying data based on clinical assessment it was evident
that group therapy gave rise to good outcome at both the junior and
senior levels. At the junior level there was encouraging outcome in
relation to neurotic behaviour at the midline and at the final follow-
up; at the senior level there was good outcome in terms of all three
measures (neurotic, antisocial, and global severity).
    The various main measures that were employed provided a view of
precisely where improvement occurred. In the case of the junior
playgroups there was improved classroom functioning and general
behaviour (as viewed by teachers at the midline follow-up) and also
improvement on a wider variety of measures at the final follow-up.
This was true, too, on a large number of measures as viewed by
parents. As far as the seniors were concerned there was again

improvement on a wide range of measures derived from different sources. At the midline, there was improvement both in achievement and adjustment. At the final follow-up there was again widespread improvement in adjustment, both in the home and the school. The improvement in achievement did not seem to have been maintained.

Behaviour modification (a senior school programme)
There was significantly better outcome on all three measures at the final follow-up, and on neurotic behaviour at the midline. In terms of improvement, at the end of treatment the children had become less isolated and had also showed improvement on some aspects of school behaviour (Devereux) and attitude to school (Barker-Lunn), but these washed out. On the other hand, at the end of treatment and at the midline follow-up, parents' reports of the treated children's behaviour at home (based on the Rutter parent scale A) revealed an increase in disturbance – fortunately this did not persist. At the midline follow-up there was improvement in terms of both verbal and non-verbal intelligence and also a decline in neuroticism.

At the final follow-up there was improvement in behaviour in the classroom as viewed by the teachers, (particularly of neurotic behaviour – Rutter teacher scale B2), and there was a reduction in the amount of antisocial behaviour as viewed by the parents.

We have examined these results in detail in Chapters 5–8, and the numerous differences between treatments are reported in Chapter 9. We will now consider the remaining five hypotheses.

Hypothesis 3 stated that some regimes are more effective in helping children with neurotic disorders than those with conduct disorders, and vice versa. Our results showed little evidence that this was the case. Similarly, hypothesis 4 postulated that some regimes are more effective in helping boys and some in helping girls, but, again, we found little evidence that this was true.

Whereas hypotheses 3 and 4 related to categories of children, hypothesis 5 referred to dimensions of behaviour, that is, different aspects of behaviour occurring in any one child. It stated that some regimes are more effective in reducing the neurotic component of a child's behaviour and others in reducing the antisocial component of his or her behaviour. Here there was some evidence that playgroup and nurture work regimes (junior children) were more effective in relieving antisocial than neurotic behaviour. In the senior programme there was little or no evidence of any such differences.

The final hypotheses were that, irrespective of regime, children with conduct disorders differ from those with neurotic disorders in outcome and improvement and that, again irrespective of regime, boys differ from girls. Both these hypotheses were confirmed, particularly in the junior programmes. On certain measures, neurotic-disordered children showed more improvement than conduct-disordered children, and girls fared better than boys.

Further important findings

Most striking, and quite unexpected, was the evidence that treatment effectiveness seemed to increase with time (see *Tables A3(2)* and *A3(3)*): the follow-up at three years from baseline showed, overall, more and greater positive results than did the intermediate eighteen-month follow-up.

A second point was that some treatments seemed to show situation-specific improvements (for example in the junior parent counselling-teacher consultation regime improvement was confined to classroom-related behaviour) whereas others seemed to result in more widespread improvement.

Third, when the diagnostic and sex groups were analysed in more detail, some further important findings emerged. For example, children with neurotic disorders tended to lose associated antisocial behaviour and those with antisocial disorders soon lost any associated neurotic behaviour. This suggested that associated antisocial behaviour in neurotic children is less deeply ingrained than in antisocial children and that the same is true of neurotic behaviour in antisocial children as compared with neurotic children.

Fourth, senior children with neurotic disorders did better than those with antisocial disorders on measures of cognitive development.

Fifth, further analysis of sex differences suggested that neurotic behaviour was more easily modified in boys than in girls, whereas antisocial behaviour responded better to treatment in girls than in boys.

Some further findings merit a brief mention. The first concerned the measures of educational progress. At the junior level there was evidence of some improvement on some measures in nurture work and playgroup regimes at the eighteen-month follow-up. At the senior level, at the midline assessment, there was improvement on cognitive measures generally in the group therapy and behaviour modification regimes, though these were not maintained at the final follow-up.

Finally, there were some interesting findings concerning the effective qualities of the therapist and these are reported in Chapter 9 and Appendix 4. Surprisingly, good outcome was associated with therapeutic assertiveness, extroversion, and openness.

In the remainder of this chapter we discuss the theoretical and practical implications of the findings summarized above.

Some theoretical issues

IS TREATMENT EFFECTIVE?

In Chapter 2 we briefly reviewed the debate that has been taking place since the early 1950s. The most crucial question to be asked by Eysenck (1952) for adult and by Levitt (1957) for child psychotherapy was 'Is psychotherapy effective?'. Having established that the answer to this question is 'Yes, it is', we can examine the nature of the control groups, discuss rates of outcome and patterns of improvement, and use new techniques to compare the effectiveness of different forms of treatment.

NATURE OF THE CONTROL GROUPS – CONTAMINATION

In our programme there were obviously opportunities for the controls (i.e. at-risk and maladjusted) to be exposed to some treatment. A handful received treatment from other sources anyway, but of far greater consequence was the possible influence of the ethos of the school: as receptivity to new and more humane approaches grew the opportunities for controls to receive help were likely to have also increased. In other words, contamination was unavoidable. In such circumstances the results of some of the treatment programmes are even more impressive than earlier outlined, for they reveal differences, not between true, control groups and treated children, but between the latter and control groups that may, in fact, have received help. In these circumstances the differences between the parent counselling-teacher consultation programme and the controls may have been minimized, and our results may not have constituted a true index of the effectiveness of this programme. Furthermore, it will be remembered that our control families were subject to interviews and specific testing – Lambert (1976) has pointed to evidence that indicated that a testing session or even one interview may have a therapeutic effect on the patient, with particular weight being given to the initial interview. Unfortunately, we have no idea of how much help may have been obtained, nor of the extent to which the behaviour of the controls may have been influenced by any such help. We cannot even hazard a guess as to what would have resulted were there really no contamination. In the next section we discuss the issue of spontaneous improvement in more detail, and in relation to other studies.

Related to the issue of control groups is the considerable controversy
about rates of spontaneous remission, i.e. the rates of improvement
in neurotic disorders in the absence of systematic treatment. These
rates are important because they are viewed as 'baseline figures' in
untreated neurotic patients. Eysenck (1952), after reviewing the literature, concluded that two-thirds of such patients showed a spontaneous remission. Bergin (1971) re-examined the evidence and cited
a median remission rate of 30 per cent: he, in turn, was criticized by
Rachman (1973), who supported Eysenck's original figures. Lambert
(1976) and Bergin and Lambert (1978) again reviewed the evidence
and reported a median spontaneous remission rate of 43 per cent,
adding the warning that 'this is an average figure which obscures
considerable variation' (Bergin and Lambert 1978:147). Hence, it is
essential to draw comparison groups from the total population under
study.

The controversy about the extent of spontaneous remission and
base rates in adult patients was taken up by Levitt (1957) in relation to
child patients. He used the study by Lehrman *et al.* (1949) which
included 110 untreated controls, to provide a base rate. Lehrman's
study showed a success rate of 32 per cent and a partial success rate of
38 per cent, i.e. a base rate of about 70 per cent. This has been
considered by some (Barrett, Hampe, and Miller 1978) an excellent
study for the provision of such a base rate: however, as it was undertaken in the 1940s, it is not possible to say what kinds of other help
were available at the time, to judge the impact of the evaluation and
diagnostic interviews, nor are details of the ratings available. Unfortunately, Levitt's base rate was dependent on Lehrman's and one
other study, which is also questionable by modern standards. In our
senior and junior programmes we had 144 controls, and calculated a
base rate of good plus moderate outcome, after three years, of only 41
per cent, which is closer to the Bergin and Lambert (1978) base rate
with adults than to those of Eysenck (1952) and Rachman (1973).

Despite the shortcomings of Levitt's review, written in 1957, of
outcome in child guidance cases receiving treatment, his conclusion
that one-third improved, one-third partly improved and one-third
did not improve has become the hallmark against which other
therapies are compared. His rate consisted of 67 per cent improved at
the end of treatment and 78 per cent (40.5 per cent greatly and 37.6
per cent partly) improved at follow-up. However, it needs to be noted
that Levitt included a number of 'slightly improved' cases in his
'improved' category. Levitt has not been alone in this. A more

stringent test is, therefore, to see what percentage of cases fall into the 'much improved' category. Our examination of Levitt's later data (Levitt 1963) indicated a further problem. This was that these early studies were overloaded with cases with known high rates of spontaneous improvement: these patients were classified as having 'special symptoms' which, in addition to 'school phobia', included enuresis and tics. In this category, the 'much improved' rate was 54 per cent, whereas in neurosis (similar to adult neurosis) it was 15 per cent, in the mixed disorders 20 per cent, and in acting-out (antisocial disorders) it was 31 per cent. If allowance is made for these rapidly improving disorders then the 'much improved' rate falls to 25–26 per cent, i.e. one in four cases.

In evaluating outcome, our position was different and very much stronger than Levitt's. We had untreated control regimes drawn from the same populations as the treated children with random allocation. Moreover, we provided information on rates of improvement in all these groups. As *Table 10(1)* shows, the controls had a 'much improved' rate of 19 and 29 per cent for the seniors and juniors respectively at the midline follow-up, and 24 and 33 per cent respectively at the final follow-up. Our treatment regimes usually did better than this.

As already indicated, these findings probably constituted a conservative estimate of the effect of our treatment programmes, because of the unavoidable 'contamination' of the controls. Further, our data appeared to support the suggestion by Bergin and Lambert (1978) that spontaneous recovery rates may be far lower than has been assumed, not only because of the possible contamination described

Table 10(1)   *Percentage of children classed as having a good outcome in the Newcastle upon Tyne study*

age group and treatment regime	midpoint (18-month follow-up)	final follow-up (3-year follow-up)
juniors	%	%
controls (ARC)	29	33
parent counselling-teacher consultation (JPC)	20	32
nurture work (NW)	27	52
playgroups (PG)	35	56
seniors		
controls (MC)	19	24
parent counselling-teacher consultation (PC)	23	33
behaviour modification (BM)	18	54
group therapy (SG)	37	53

above but also because a handful of controls may have been provided with help elsewhere, and certain diagnostic groups with high
spontaneous remission rates, such as developmental disorders, may
have been included. Thus, some may argue that even our control
groups were not true control groups in the experimental sense: while
this may be true, it simply serves to emphasize that the differences
reported in our research are likely to *underestimate* the true effect of
the intervention. On the other hand, controls based in a different set
of schools in which we had not undertaken intervention would have
been less subject to contamination. Had we used this technique,
though, there would have been no guarantee that some controls
would not have sought treatment elsewhere: furthermore, studying
controls in a different set of schools would have been inappropriate
because there are such considerable differences between schools
(Rutter *et al*. 1979).

In some respects our findings were not what we expected (cf. Levitt
1957, 1963). It is therefore essential to now examine the results of
more recent studies. The one most comparable to ours in terms of
techniques used was that of Miller *et al*. (1972) who evaluated the
treatment of phobic children. The salient features of that study are
mentioned in Chapter 2. The treatments examined were psychotherapy and systematic desensitization. At a two-year follow-up the
rates of improvement were more impressive for younger than older
children but, overall, at the final follow-up, 73 per cent of the treated
groups were successful as opposed to only 34 per cent of the
untreated groups. When, in our study, we combined good and
moderate outcome, we obtained a rather similar picture (*Table 10(2)*).
Hence, our findings suggested a base rate for untreated cases, and
outcome rates for treated cases, more consistent with those suggested
by Miller *et al*. (1972) and Bergin and Lambert (1978) than with those
proposed by Eysenck (1952) and Levitt (1957, 1963). It must be
emphasized that the outcome rates on overall severity were less

Table 10(2) *Percentage of children with good and moderate outcome in the*
Newcastle upon Tyne study

juniors				seniors			
ARC	JPC	NW	PG	MC	PC	BM	SG
44	53	67	78	39	52	73	75

Note: ARC = at-risk controls; JPC = parent counselling-teacher consultation in the
junior schools; NW = nurture work; PG = playgroups; MC = maladjusted controls; PC
= parent counselling-teacher consultation in the senior schools; BM = behaviour
modification; SG = group therapy.

impressive than the rates on the more discrete dimensions of neurotic and antisocial behaviour. The difference, though, probably just reflected the greater specificity of these latter dimensions.

COMPARING EFFECTIVENESS OF DIFFERENT FORMS OF TREATMENT – NEW RESEARCH TECHNIQUES

Newer research has indicated that the previous suggestion that psychotherapy has no demonstrable effect was based on inadequate surveys or techniques, or both. For instance, Glass and Smith (1976) and Smith and Glass (1977) developed a method of comparing the results of different therapy regimes by standard scores. In their survey of 375 controlled studies they calculated outcome measures by dividing the mean difference on outcome measures between the control and treatment regimes by the standard deviation. While their work was statistically complex, their conclusions were simple – they demonstrated that the 'average study' showed a two-thirds standard deviation superiority of the treated group over the control group. Thus, the average client receiving therapy 'was better off than seventy-five per cent of the untreated controls' (Glass and Smith 1976:10). Though there has been some criticism of their procedures, it has been pointed out that their method was a considerable advance over merely counting positive and negative studies. Similarly, in our study we calculated the superiority in standard deviations of each of our treatment regimes over the control regime (*Table 10(3)*). These

Table 10(3)   *Comparisons of the effectiveness of the different treatment regimes in the Newcastle upon Tyne study*

treatment	standardized outcome scores at follow-up		average treated child better off than the untreated controls	
	sum neurotic and conduct	*total severity*	*sum neurotic and conduct*	*total severity*
juniors			%	%
junior parent counselling-teacher consultation (JPC)	0.21	0.14	58	56
nurture work (NW)	0.57	0.46	72	68
playgroups (PG)	0.70	0.74	76	77
seniors				
parent counselling-teacher consultation (PC)	0.26	0.20	60	58
behaviour modification (BM)	0.81	0.75	79	77
group therapy (SG)	0.91	0.76	82	78

standard outcome scores were based on psychiatric ratings of overall severity, irrespective of the type of disorder the child showed, with a consequent loss of degree of sensitivity on these measures. We recalculated the measures separately for children with conduct and neurotic disorders and then summated the standard scores; the relevant differences are given in *Table 10(3)*. These averaged standard outcomes were usually marginally better than when using only a single measure of outcome.

It is of considerable interest that the standard outcome score of behaviour modification was 0.81 while the average standard amelioration of behaviour therapies as reported by Glass and Smith was 0.80; in addition, the average of our group therapies was 0.80, while an average standard amelioration of 0.63 for client-centred studies was reported by Glass and Smith. As our group programmes were based on client-centred principles this was an interesting contrast. We believe that the difference was due to the greater uniformity in technique, measures, and therapists employed in our study than the composite and uneven group of studies analysed by Glass and Smith.

The crucial ingredients of psychotherapy

Having examined our two basic questions 'Is psychotherapy effective?' and 'Are some treatment approaches more effective than others?', we can now turn to a more fine-grain analysis.

In Chapter 2 we described the three main components of psychotherapy identified by Kiesler (1971). These were (a) the patient and his or her problems; (b) the therapist, his or her personality, style, and techniques; and (c) the dimension of time. To Kiesler's triad we added a fourth ingredient – the psychosocial context in which psychotherapy occurs (in our case the school). We now discuss these key ingredients in the light of our research.

THE PATIENT AND HIS OR HER PROBLEMS

The characteristics of the children and their problems have largely been described already. We discovered that sex and diagnostic categories, while important predictors of improvement in themselves, had little bearing on the children's differential response to treatment. This finding was contrary to a strong tide of opinion in psychotherapy that stated treatment needs to be tailored to the specific patient and his or her problems (Goldstein and Stein 1976). However, in one of the best studies of child psychotherapy to date (Miller *et al.* 1972) it was reported that neither sex, intelligence, socioeconomic status, nor chronicity, influenced the effectiveness of treatment. Our findings therefore supported other well-controlled studies.

THE THERAPISTS AND THEIR TECHNIQUES

In the introduction to this book we presented our rationale for selecting the therapy techniques. We aimed to choose a variety of treatments that would reflect fundamental differences in approach. Thus we compared direct with indirect therapies and psychodynamic with behavioural approaches. We now examine whether or not these contrasts have any relevance to the patterns of outcome and improvement. We will also comment on the two other closely allied topics, therapeutic skill and the intensity of therapeutic contact, to see whether our study can throw any light on the importance of these.

Direct versus indirect therapy

First we considered direct versus indirect therapy. Many services provided for children are indirect, such as education, prevention, and consultation services, i.e., they are not with children but rather with adults who, in turn, have direct contact with children (Adams 1975). Thus, children are what Adams calls 'parapeople', who are usually reached indirectly through 'paraprofessionals', such as parents and teachers.

Our service cannot easily be classified as either direct or indirect in this way, as it covered a spectrum of therapies. The most highly direct was group therapy, but even this contained a degree of indirectness because the group therapists were supervised and directed by another set of professionals. Behaviour modification was moderately direct in that it was applied by teachers who were given some initial training, then continuous support and supervision. Nurturing could be seen as being fairly direct, involving the least professional of the therapists, who were supervised and supported by a professional team. The parent counselling-teacher consultation programme was the least direct in terms of the above definition, because there was guidance but no specific training for teachers. It is tempting to suggest that the greater the directness of contact of trained professionals with disturbed children the better the outcome. Admittedly, this is a rather crude analysis as there are many factors that need to be disentangled.

Psychodynamic versus behavioural therapy

The second dichotomy we considered is psychodynamic versus behavioural types of therapy. The best method of comparison was to contrast the group therapy (psychodynamic) with the behaviour modification (behavioural) treatment at the senior level. These were strikingly similar in that both brought to bear a high degree of skill, stuck rigorously to the treatment model they were designed to represent, and took place over the same brief time span. The overall results were compared by using standard scores (see *Table 10(3)* and Chapters 5 and 8), and it can be seen that at the final follow-up they were almost identical for the two treatments: in the group therapy regime the average treated child had a better outcome than 78 per cent of the controls, whereas the comparable figure for behaviour modification was 77 per cent.

We might have expected that although the overall outcome was the same for the two treatments, the mechanisms by which they operated would have been different. Some light was thrown on this by examining the pattern of improvement scores for differences between the two treatments. There were, in fact, quite a number of differences in their scores, both at the end of treatment (the point at which we were first able to get an early look at the process) and at the eighteen-month and three-year follow-ups. At the end of treatment the two measures that favoured behaviour modification were socio-metric isolation and a classroom measure, creative initiative, where behaviour modification had a marked but early gain, the advantage with isolation being sustained at the eighteen-month follow-up. With regard to maladjustment as seen by parents (Rutter A scale and anti-social behaviour) the group therapy children showed significantly greater improvement than the children in the behaviour modification regime at the end of treatment and at the eighteen-month follow-up. By the final follow-up all the significant differences in results be-tween these two treatments had disappeared. In general, behaviour modification seemed to result in a number of early changes in children that then washed out, but there were positive changes at the midline follow-up and a larger number of changes oñ important measures at the final follow-up.

These differences were the total reverse of what was expected. Group therapies have commonly been thought to be particularly appropriate for isolated children – so much so that, as we saw in Chapter 8, isolation has been a common outcome measure in such studies. In a similar way, behaviour modification has been seen as the most suitable treatment for antisocial behaviour, and as showing effects specific to the period of treatment. The only finding that was in line with expectations was that therapy directly focused on changes in demonstrable behaviour gave rise to immediate change.

Therapeutic qualities and techniques

The third dichotomy we are able to comment on is between therapeutic qualities and techniques. There is a division of opinion in the literature, one school of thought claiming psychotherapy can usefully be viewed as a set of technologies that can be applied to psychological problems, the alternative stating that it is the meeting and communication between people that is important, with therapeutic technique playing a relatively small part in determining the outcome. When we looked for the evidence to resolve this controversy, we found that, so far, it has not been possible to show one approach to be clearly superior to another under reasonably controlled conditions, in research either with adult patients (Luborsky, Singer, and Luborsky 1975; Sloane *et al.* 1975) or with child patients (Miller *et al.* 1972).

This is not to deny, however, that certain qualities of the therapist may be of major importance. Like patients, therapists differ on a wide variety of factors, such as age, sex, cultural background, professional experience, sophistication, empathy, etc. Many of these factors may have a significant bearing on the therapist's theoretical orientation, techniques, and influence (Strupp 1978). The most radical view, advanced by Franks (1973), claimed that psychotherapeutic change is a result of therapist factors common to all therapeutic techniques and based on the relationship between the patient and the healer. On the other hand, Rogers (1952) and Truax and Carkhuff (1967) described a more discrete set of factors (accurate empathy, genuineness, and unconditional positive regard) as necessary and sufficient conditions for beneficial therapeutic change. Both of these authorities demote the effectiveness on the therapeutic techniques and promote the relationship factor to a position of importance.

One important practical implication of these findings is that non-professionals may be just as effective as highly trained professionals (Cowen *et al.* 1975b). Our non-professionals (nurture workers) had only moderate success when compared with professionals working as group therapists, but had greater success than the same set of professionals working as social workers in schools. This set of findings led us to conclude that the critical factor in treatment is the technique used.

Our findings concerning therapeutic qualities were really quite dramatically different from those of Truax and other workers, who found empathy and non-possessive warmth to be the therapist characteristics that correlated with outcome. Indeed, we found that extroversion, therapeutic assertiveness, and openness in the therapist seemed to correlate with good results. One possibility for this is that extroversion and assertiveness are characteristics particularly appropriate to the ordinary school situation, where effectiveness may depend on negotiating with large numbers of people and making an impact in a large institution as well as with the individual children. This may be an easier task for a more outgoing and assertive personality than for a quieter person. In relation to this conclusion, it is interesting to note that Strupp (1978) considered the therapist should take a much more active stance, take greater responsibility for becoming a moving force in the therapeutic encounter, actively plan the intervention, and actively resist the temptation to broaden the therapeutic objectives once limited goals have been achieved.

Duration and intensity of therapy

There are practical aspects of the therapist's technique, such as duration and intensity of the therapeutic contact, where our results can perhaps give some guidance.

In terms of patients' expectations and motivations, educational or health service resources, and many other practical considerations, it is essential to identify psychotherapies that give rise to a successful outcome in the shortest possible time with the least expense (Strupp 1978). We have been able to demonstrate that *the shorter-term treatments* (group therapy and behaviour modification) *had the best outcome.* While in no sense could parent counselling-teacher consultation and nurture work programmes be considered long-term, they were substantially longer in duration than group therapy and behaviour modification. Thus, although we did not specifically study length of treatment it was noted that our two shorter-term treatments had the best outcome and, like Luborsky and Spence (1978), we concluded that certain time-limited psychotherapies are effective.

Another important point is whether or not frequent contact with the therapist is more effective than less frequent contact over the same period. We indicated in Chapter 2 that some recent work suggested that the more intensive or the more frequent contact in psychoanalytic-type therapy the more impressive the results.

In nurture work, contact was daily over many months; in teacher consultation and behaviour modification we could only speculate that contact was reasonably frequent; in group therapy, contact was probably the least frequent. Our results therefore suggested that is is *type rather than intensity of treatment that is a critical factor in intervention.*

THE DIMENSION OF TIME IN TREATMENT PROGRAMMES

We found that, overall, however brief, treatment effects seemed somehow to remain active for eighteen months or more. This was extraordinary considering the many experiences the children must have had in their normal lives during this time, which one would think were as, or more, important than the therapy. Why, then, did outcome and improvement continue to gain ground in effective therapies, even when treatment had finished?

First, we should note that this finding has a bearing on the question of whether psychotherapy merely brings forward improvement rather than produces change that would not have occurred without therapy. If the former was true we would have expected the controls to catch up but, as they did not, it is clear that by intervening we produced change that would not have occurred otherwise.

The next point to make is that this was not a unique finding. We mentioned in Chapter 8 that in those two studies of group therapy which had long-term follow-ups there appeared to be a similar trend towards further improvement after active therapy had finished. Levitt (1971), in the light of uncontrolled studies, concluded that further improvement at follow-up was merely an expression of 'spontaneous improvement'. However, Wright, Moelis, and Pollack (1976) analysed six reasonably well-controlled studies of child psychotherapy, with particular reference to continued improvement after active therapy had finished. At the end of treatment only one of the six studies showed significant gains compared with the control group. At follow-up four of the studies showed significant improvement and only one showed a deterioration compared with the control group.

To summarize, there seems quite good evidence, which our study heavily reinforced, that improvement continues and may, indeed, become demonstrable for the first time long after active therapy has finished. The mechanism behind this process is not known but several explanations could be examined in further studies. The first possibility is that the early changes that must occur are of too subtle a nature to be detected by our current, rather crude, techniques of measurement and analysis. In particular, our criterion of 'statistical significance' must be examined because between-group variation may be quite irrelevant to subtle within-subject changes.

Wright, Moelis, and Pollack (1976) suggested that their findings supported the view that psychotherapy affects underlying central or structural aspects of personality functioning rather than overt behaviour. This is certainly another possibility, but subtle shifts in behaviour and social functioning during therapy could, equally, be undetected and could lead to adjustments in the individual's interactions with others: these alterations, through subsequent positive feedback mechanisms, could eventually result in demonstrable changes.

THE PSYCHOSOCIAL CONTEXT OF THERAPY

This is the final component of psychotherapy that we have delineated. Taking treatment techniques into the school, rather than taking the child out of school to a clinic setting, has enormous advantages in that it allows study of the effect of therapy in its social context. It also has the advantage of avoiding labelling the child as a psychiatric patient. It was clear from the results reported earlier in this chapter that the characteristics of the schools had a major impact on the children's progress. At a more detailed level, it was difficult to disentangle the effects on progress of the type of therapy, the therapeutic qualities, and the school social context; some further results on school differences are reported elsewhere (Mullin 1979).

SPECIFICITY OF TREATMENT

One of the crucial questions in psychotherapy research is whether or not different kinds of treatment are effective with children with particular types of disorders. We found no consistent evidence of such specificity, neither in the junior nor senior school programmes. Such attractive concepts of specificity, which are important in adult disorders, do not seem to have held up over the range of treatments we used in relation to the types of children we studied. It seems logical that there may be good reasons for the use of different treatments in the school setting, but until these can be demonstrated we have to accept that the case for specific treatment for neurotic and conduct disorders has not been proved. We have mentioned this important matter in relation to the children's problems in Chapter 2.

Some comments on our research design

We believe that our findings pointed strongly to the effectiveness of our interventions, particularly in the cases of the group therapy and behaviour modification regimes. However, we need to report some of the ways in which we ensured that artefacts had not crept into and influenced our research.

The first issue concerns the possibility of biased reporting at follow-up. This problem really needs to be examined at two levels of data collection: the initial point at which questionnaires or interview schedules were completed and the subsequent points where assessments and analyses were made on this data base.

Although we were not dealing with a 'double-blind' situation, it seemed unlikely that there were biases in data collection. First, parent counselling-teacher consultation, the regime that had the greatest contact with parents and teachers and hence may have been expected to be the one most influenced by report bias, proved to be the least effective treatment.

Second, apart from in the parent counselling-teacher consultation regime, the reported improvements were spread across several of the different reporters simultaneously, some of whom would have had minimal knowledge of the treatment. For example, while parents were fully informed of the group therapy they were minimally involved in it, yet there were significant improvements on the parent measures. A third point was that the interviewers and testers were also quite ignorant of the main hypotheses of the research and of the groups from which the children came. For these reasons bias at the point of data collection seemed very unlikely.

The subsequent assessments were, as we explained in Chapters 3 and 9, carried out in two ways: clinical ratings were made on the basis of examination of all the data and, independently, change was measured on mathematically derived main measures and aggregate measures. The clinical ratings were made by psychiatrists who were completely unaware of the regime from which the cases came. These clinically derived ratings were, in addition, largely supportive of the mathematical ratings, which were handled entirely by machine from data collection onwards and hence could not have been subject to bias at this stage.

A second design consideration that merits discussion is that the research took place over two years, with the group therapy, behaviour modification, and nurture work regimes taking place in the second year, and showing better results than the first year parent counselling-teacher consultation regime. There are various ways in which the better results of these three therapies might have been due to the fact that they all occurred in the second year. Two possible explanations are fluctuations in the levels of disturbance in the schools and the sensitization of the teachers, as a result of the first-year experience, leading to biased reporting. Fluctuations could have been due either to treatment in the previous year or to other extraneous factors.

Looking more closely at our data it appeared that comparison of initial levels of disturbance for the two years might throw light on whether either of these artefacts was operating. If the initial levels were markedly different then perhaps either fluctuation of levels of disturbance between the years was important or exposure to the first year had seriously biased teacher reports (or both). In fact, on examination, the initial levels were much the same for both years: it seemed unlikely, therefore, that either of these processes was operating. In addition, it seemed unlikely that reporter bias could have affected parents' or children's reports. The consistency of behaviour over time within schools was in line with other research results (Rutter *et al.* 1979).

An allied argument might be that as a result of the first-year programme the schools became generally more 'therapeutic' environments, so that the second-year children had added non-specific help that was unrelated to the particular regimes in which they took part. It seemed to us that there were two reasons why it was unlikely that this process contributed to the results. First, there was continuing greater positive change in outcome and improvement in the second-year children over the three-year follow-up period than there was in the first-year children. Over this time the school environment would have been acting on all the treatment and control regimes, first- and second-year, to the same extent, so that one might expect, if non-specific therapeutic factors were at work, that positive change would be equal in both year cohorts.

A second point is that the first-year treatment was the least impressive when applied directly to the families. Again, therefore, it seemed unlikely that its indirect effect on subsequent years was of very major importance. One additional point should be mentioned: both first- and second-year cohorts were relatively new to their schools at the start of treatments, so that they could not have been much exposed to 'treatment' indirectly before the specific programmes started.

A further point also merits comment at this stage. The most successful regime at the junior level was the only one where children were withdrawn from the class (i.e. playgroups). We cannot therefore rule out the possibility that withdrawal from class was important in itself. Maybe the psychological effect of the special treatment under such conspicuous circumstances is therapeutic in itself. This goes against sociological ideas about 'labelling' being important in the perpetuation of behavioural deviance.

Finally, we must discuss why there were apparent discrepancies between outcome measures (based on clinical judgement) and improvement measures (based on mathematical analyses). In actual fact, the overall trends for these very different types of analyses were remarkably similar. Perhaps the biggest discrepancy was between the results at final follow-up in the junior regimes. Here the outcome measures showed rather modest (in fact statistically non-significant) changes on the antisocial behaviour measure whereas on the improvement measures there were quite impressive changes on the aggregate antisocial score.

It is important to realize that there were quite fundamental dif-

ferences in approach between the two types of measure. First, the
clinical outcome measures were most heavily influenced by data
collected at home. This was because we considered parents to be the
most sensitive source of information about children. A second, and
equally important, difference is that the clinician can judge and give
clinical meaning to the symptoms shown and his or her judgment is
not simply summation of results. It seemed likely that it was this
second difference that gave rise mainly to the above-mentioned discrepancies in the findings in the junior programme. Finally, of
course, outcome is not simply a measure of change but takes into
account both change and final state (see Appendix 2).

Ethical issues in research and practice

The research worker always has to ask him- or herself 'Is what I am
doing ethical?' We were confronted with two ethical questions: first,
was it ethical not to treat those children who were maladjusted and
who were allocated to the control groups? When we started our
research, our evaluation programme would have been morally, socially, and psychologically indefensible had two conditions been met:
(a) if we had known that treatment worked (we did not); and, (b) if
there had been enough treatment for all (there was not). As neither
condition existed, our strategy allowed a moral and permissible
allocation of varieties of psychotherapeutic help in order to enable us
to learn the true value of the intervention we provided. However, we
were careful never to stand in the way of any referral that a family or
school felt appropriate.

The second ethical question that arose was whether we were
justified in offering to help people who had not specifically asked for
it. This was an extremely delicate question – no less so in those of our
interventions that proved to be most effective. It was absolutely
essential in the application of these techniques that clients maintained
the right of refusal and that they were not subjected to coercion that
might serve a social system or be administratively convenient. A
particularly difficult ethical issue arises when interventions have a
partly educational component, because education is compulsory up
to the age of sixteen years. The crucial distinction seemed to us to be
that therapeutic interventions involved an element of the child's
private life. For this reason, we felt that children and their families
should be fully informed of all investigations and treatment carried
out and that they should have the right to refuse to participate. We
pursued this policy and the number of refusals was negligible.

Practical issues: practical guidance for educationalists, mental health professionals, and planners

The whole thrust of our research project was a practical one. We are sure that our findings have implications in the academic debate, but consider that our most important audience comprises practical planners and workers in the field. What lessons does our research have for them? Again, we can discuss the issues under a variety of headings.

THE FEASIBILITY OF INTRODUCING SPECIAL HELP

We suspect that most efforts to introduce new services get no further than this preliminary question of feasibility. For us it was just a starting point though, nevertheless, it raised important issues.

All the treatments that we introduced into the schools were carried through to their conclusion. We must point out, however, the hard work that was undertaken by the project team and the sympathy and understanding that was forthcoming from the education authorities and schools, all of which contributed greatly to the project's success. First of all, it was necessary for us to convince hard-headed administrators of the local authority that the project was worthwhile. The positive results of our study should help further projects a great deal in this respect; nevertheless, funding for mental health projects in schools still has to compete with other major priorities in local authority or health service budgets. One view is that mental health projects would be more favourably received if the results of research were more widely disseminated. It would then be for local education authorities, working with health authorities either *ad hoc* or through established consultative machinery, to decide which measures, if any, to introduce in their respective areas. Such new services do not need official sanction.

The next set of problems we faced was in convincing an equally hard-headed and often sceptical group of Headteachers and staffs that, among the new and 'trendy' ideas in education, our proposals were worth taking seriously. The crucial ingredient in our being able to do this was that we were able to offer special help to some of the children about whom they were most worried, and with whom they felt they needed assistance. We found universally that both the Headteachers and their staff were acutely aware of the emotional and social problems of their pupils and that the schools had potential far beyond that of learning in the narrow sense. In some cases the teachers had moved quite consciously into a strongly pastoral role and we came to realize that our more specialized efforts were extending and enlarging on work that was already being done, rather than adding a whole new facet to the curriculum.

TREATMENTS THAT APPEARED INEFFECTIVE

When a treatment does not work, the investigator naturally looks for explanations for its failure. We have already discussed one possible explanation for the rather limited success of the parent counselling-teacher consultation regime, which was that it coincided with the introduction of something new into the school.

There are potentially a multitude of other explanations for the apparent failure: perhaps more personnel were needed, with smaller case loads; perhaps we looked at the wrong factors in our evaluation; perhaps the evaluation was too crude. We could presumably explain away failure in any one of these ways. However, there are three explanations in particular that merit further scrutiny and that should be taken into account by anyone who attempts to replicate or extend our research.

The first of these centres on the fact that, as we have seen in Chapter 7, in the parent counselling-teacher consultation groups the families had severe and widespread problems. It may be that these were so deeply ingrained in the fabric of the family behaviour patterns that they were not modifiable. In other words, the social workers' efforts could possibly have been dissipated in a welter of family difficulties, so that the impact of their work on the children was hopelessly attenuated. If this was the mechanism in operation, it can be taken as a clear indication for jettisoning the indirect approaches of the project and concentrating resources on the more direct professional interventions of behaviour modification and group therapy.

The second possibility, and one with quite different implications, hinges on the fact that the social workers were 'uninvited guests' of their clients. This had a far-reaching impact on the type of work they undertook in that they had to keep a rather low profile and act mainly as a support and helper to the family, being only secondarily an active agent of change in family functioning. It may be that this type of intervention is less appropriate for the school and more appropriate for the clinic.

A third possibility is that work with parents and teachers was a potent but insufficient intervention. In normal practice such work would often be accompanied by time spent with the child and it may be that work on all three fronts together, and perhaps over a more limited time span, could have more success than the sum of any partial interventions.

Whether or not any of these explanations and suggestions are valid, we feel it would be premature to condemn indirect work on the basis of our findings alone.

COST EFFECTIVENESS (*Tables 10(4) and 10(5)*)

The costs of the different treatment programmes can be only roughly estimated. They can be divided into overt costs and hidden costs.

The group therapy programme would seem to be the least expensive as it consisted of thirty-four groups of ten sessions each, undertaken by a total of six social workers over a period of three months (one school term). However, the hidden costs in training and supervising the social workers were extensive and had to cover some months spent gaining prior experience of working part-time in schools; a period of sensitivity training (see Chapter 8) (provided by two trained therapists); training and experience in group therapy (provided by a consultant psychiatrist and psychotherapist, and covering about three months); and continuous supervisory discussions with other trainee group therapists and the consultant. As all six social workers were already fully trained when they joined the project we conclude that in costing terms, we were using three full-time trained workers who needed a year's further training before they could be employed as group therapists.

The behaviour modification programme's hidden costs consisted of providing a generalized practical and theoretical training to improve the psychologists' skills in relation to behaviour modification. We estimated that this would normally require training for about six to

Table 10(4)   *Comparative staff costs of treating 60–70 children by various methods, in the initial and subsequent programmes*

treatment	programme(s)	number of workers and time required	
		fieldworkers (full-time equiv.)	back-up
GT*	initial	3 for 15 months	at least 1 for 15 months
	subsequent	3 for 3 months	½ for three months
BM	initial	1¼ for 12–15 months	possibly 1 for 6 months
	subsequent	1 for 6 months (includes further courses for teachers)	nil
JPC/PC	initial	3 for 15 months	1½ for 15 months
	subsequent	3 for 12 months	nil
NW	initial	3½ for 18 months	at least 1 for 18 months
	subsequent	3½ for 18 months	at least ½ for 18 months

Note: * for details of abbreviations see p. 309.

Table 10(5)   *Months of professional time to treat 60–70 cases*

programme	treatment			
	BM	GT	JPC/PC	NW
initial	25	60	72	45*
subsequent	6	10	36	36*

Note: the figures for nurture work have been adjusted to reflect the cost of professional time; * minimum.

nine months on a part-time basis. We followed this with the training of thirty-nine teachers over a period of three weeks prior to the start of the programme itself and supervised them over a twenty-week period. We estimated the cost of this programme to be at least half the cost of the group therapy approach.

Parent counselling-teacher consultation utilized the equivalent of six part-time social workers over an academic year (three school terms). The hidden costs were incurred by their additional training by the back-up university team and by supervisory sessions. It was therefore at least 100 per cent more expensive than the behaviour modification programme, but similar to that of group therapy. However, subsequently, group therapy would be substantially less expensive.

Finally, the nurture work programme was based on the use of seven part-time teacher-aides (three full-time equivalents) over five school terms. However, there were hidden costs of back-up support consisting of, at least, a social worker and a psychologist. While neither of these needed to be full-time, we estimated that they would have to be employed for at least eighteen months. Teacher-aides earned about half the salary of a trained professional and therefore the cost of the programme was about half that of the parent counselling-teacher consultation approach.

A *crude* comparison of staff costs for treating between sixty and seventy children is shown in *Table 10(4)*, while *Table 10(5)* shows the costs in terms of months of professional time and allowances needed to be made for the cost of such time. Thus, initially group therapy and parent counselling-teacher consultation were 100 per cent, and nurture work 200 per cent more expensive than behaviour modification. Subsequently, the amount of professional time needed for group therapy and behaviour modification was dramatically reduced, but that for parent counselling-teacher consultation was reduced by only 50 per cent, and that for nurture work not at all. We have already shown that, of the four treatments used, behaviour modification and group therapy were of the shortest duration: it is therefore evident that *those therapies that gave rise to the most promising results did so in the shortest possible time with the least expense.* As group therapy and behaviour modification were not only relatively inexpensive to mount, but also gave rise to a successful outcome, they would appear to be treatments that should be looked on favourably by administrators. Both, of course, require a high degree of expertise and training.

PARENTAL INVOLVEMENT

One very topical theme is the relative importance of home and school factors in the perpetuation of psychological problems and poor academic progress. A number of influential reports have contributed to the notion that schools do not have an important influence. For instance, Coleman (1966) in the USA suggested that educational achievement was largely independent of the type of schooling the child received and Jensen (1969) concluded that compensatory education had failed in relation to attainment and ability. The pre-eminence of family factors and social class factors over ability in the case of educational achievement (Douglas 1964; Plowden Report 1967) led us to speculate about how far positive school influences can counter-act the adverse effects of negative home influences. Wall (1973) argued for the primacy of the home over the school in determining academic success and adjustment, but concluded that schooling may serve to accentuate difficulties. Schools are presented either with the problem of trying to get children to adjust to their standards, thus possibly creating out-of-school difficulties for them, or with the problem of trying to get the teacher to tolerate different behavioural norms. More recent work has begun to indicate that when home factors are controlled some schools have a higher incidence of anti-social behaviour (Power *et al.* 1967; Power, Benn, and Morris 1972) and of poor educational progress (Rutter *et al.* 1979) than others. Many reviewers have been impressed by research evidence of effects of teachers' attitudes and expectations on children's behaviour. Perhaps attention should be focused on determining what part the home can contribute towards (Douglas 1964) and the school co-operate in (Plowden Report 1967) meeting the child's needs. This leads us on to the subject of parental contribution.

Clinical tradition, going back to the roots of child psychiatry, dictates that parental involvement is an important ingredient in the relief of symptoms (Freud 1911). This claim has received some empirical support in the case of maladjusted children (Love and Kaswan 1974) and, in the case of deprived children, Bronfenbrenner (1974) has argued that parental participation is essential. While aware of the importance of the involvement of the mother and, indeed, of the father as well (Love and Kaswan 1974), for the practical reason that we had insufficient funds we were unable to involve parents to the extent we desired. Nevertheless, it was evident that some of the treatments were singularly effective despite complete lack of contact with parents. This led us to suggest that the *child's experiences in school are critical for psychological adaptation* and second only to their home experience. Often, treatment has been denied to children because of what are considered to be intransigent social and personal family problems and also poor motivation or lack of organization on the part of the family in getting to the clinic. The *consistency of our findings emphasizes the importance of treatment of the children themselves*, with parental contact taking a secondary but probably important place.

BEHAVIOURAL ADJUSTMENT AND ACADEMIC PROGRESS

Educators and mental health specialists are likely to see school adjustment from different perspectives (Cowen 1971a). The former are likely to emphasize academic progress and the latter, behavioural adjustment. It is usually argued that the two areas are not unrelated and that poor functioning in one may give rise to problems in the other. The fact that the two are interrelated was confirmed by our screen measures, where there was a positive correlation between educational and behavioural measures. There are, of course, many ways in which the two may be linked. Lack of encouragement and supervision at home may lead both to poor achievement (Douglas 1964) and poor adjustment (Craig and Glick 1963).

What is far less well-substantiated is whether improvement in one area can generalize to improvement in others (for example, can psychotherapy, via behavioural adjustment, lead to educational improvement?) We have not been able to demonstrate consistent academic improvement – despite considerable behavioural changes. Our efforts were, of course, mainly directed towards behaviour and the main changes witnessed were specific to this area, though, as in other studies (see Chapter 8) we did find some short-term educational gains in the group therapy cases. In this part of the study we have not concerned ourselves with the reverse aspect, i.e., whether specific help with educational problems gives rise to a secondary improvement of behaviour.

The Warnock Committee asserted that 'Educational failure is now recognized as a significant factor in maladjustment and the contribution of successful learning to adjustment is more widely recognized. . . . Areas of conflict between therapeutic and educational objectives are still evident, especially where the latter are characterized as formal and academic' (Warnock Report 1978:222). The Committee went on to express the opinion that special education for maladjusted pupils 'is not complete unless it affords educational opportunities of quality' (Warnock Report 1978:222). Our findings led us to support strongly the view that direct treatment of maladjustment is unlikely to lead to substantial and permanent educational gains and needs to be complemented by the adaptation or development of special curricula to meet individual needs, applied, wherever possible, by teachers from the child's own school. The evidence for this conclusion was shown particularly clearly among the junior schoolchildren, who showed minimal educational improvement despite the fact that many were identified and included in the treatment groups on grounds of educational failure.

EDUCATING MALADJUSTED CHILDREN IN AN ORDINARY CLASSROOM

The concept of educating children with psychological problems in the ordinary classroom reverses the move towards labelling children as abnormal and then recommending special schools or classrooms for them. It makes psychological sense because the child will not perceive him- or herself as different nor be perceived as such by others; it makes educational sense because the child is kept in the ordinary stream of education where there are many more opportunities to take advantage of the full curriculum and to mix with a wide range of children; and it makes financial sense in that special educational facilities are rapidly becoming prohibitively costly. However, all this cannot be achieved unless there is special intervention either at home or at school, and unless teachers are provided with the skills and the back-up support to enable them to cope effectively with likely problems.

One of the main worries voiced by teachers and parents is the impact of maladjusted children on non-disturbed children. Saunders (1971) has studied the subject and his work seems to suggest that no disruptive influences were found, particularly if classroom management was effective.

CLINIC AND SCHOOL APPROACHES TO TREATMENT

Over the past two decades there have been some cogent criticisms of traditional forms of child psychotherapy, particularly of the child guidance approach. We have discussed these in Chapter 1. In addition, reviews have pointed out that there is little evidence to suggest that long-term psychotherapy is helpful – naïve counselling is often considered as useful as other forms of therapy: however, there is better evidence in favour of the effectiveness of shorter-term psychotherapies (Tizard 1973). There is also the theoretical possibility that different forms of treatment may be more effective if correctly employed for the right type of patient – such a specific programme of psychotherapy, for phobic disorders in children, was mounted by Miller and colleagues (1972). Tizard concluded that, with certain important exceptions:

'individual treatment of maladjusted children is a pessimistic one. Psychotherapy, play therapy and other forms of individual therapy based on dynamic beliefs have not proved successful in practice. Changes in children's behaviour are consequences either of growth (as every wise GP and teacher knows) or, more immediately, they occur as a response on the part of the child to changes in his environment. Where there is no growth and no environmental changes occur, the counsellor is unable to cure.'

(Tizard 1973:31)

He suggested that what the counsellor *could* do was undertake the very important support of listening and giving advice. He further stressed that there is only slight evidence that prompt remedial treatment in infancy or early childhood will prevent later psychiatric breakdown. It is only when there is a marked change of environmental circumstances that children tend to respond (Clark, Lachowicz, and Wolf 1968). Similarly, when these circumstances deteriorate, behavioural development also suffers. Tizard's solution was to look for ways of helping a large number of children, possibly at classroom level, rather than to seek an individual therapeutic solution.

While we thought that these were unduly pessimistic views, we noted that they were advanced at a time when apparently impressive research programmes, such as that of Shepherd, Oppenheim, and Mitchell (1971), were producing negative conclusions about traditional therapeutic approaches in child psychiatry. Such conclusions were unlikely to be fully supported by more recent research, but they were, nevertheless, views that strongly influenced us, especially as they seemed to have much in common with the newer, attractive, community approaches to identification, prevention, and treatment of psychiatric disorder advocated in the USA (Caplan 1964; Bower 1969; Cowen *et al.* 1971a). Our basic objective, therefore, became to explore the suggestion that schools could play a vital role in ameliorating psychiatric disorders in children, through their recognition, prevention, and treatment.

Our programme of redeploying mental health personnel within the schools was, in certain ways, more successful than we had ever anticipated: we have therefore had to consider what part such programmes should play in the range of services available for helping with children's problems. It is unlikely that new services would totally replace existing ones: rather, they would constitute one part of a network of services that would continue to incorporate psychiatric and psychological outpatient facilities and, of course, a small number of special settings, such as hospital or hostel units and special schools.

The question that now faces health service personnel is 'How much time should be devoted to conventional psychiatric work, and how much to developing the type of work explored in this project?' Our research findings, tempered by clinical experience with more serious forms of psychiatric disorder, have continued to lead us to advocate caution. While we can see how a child and adolescent psychiatrist, psychologist, or psychiatric social worker can effectively function in the community as a consultant to other professionals, we think that he or she still needs to accept full responsibility for the treatment of severely disturbed children and adolescents, and apply techniques that have clinical components. Another point is that recipients of consultation need to have a high degree of background skill and be given defined tasks. Whatever the different models of service eventually established, it is essential that these should provide a network of services, incorporating both the community and the health service, that will cater for a wide variety of acute and chronic disorders.

BACK-UP TEAMS

While there will certainly need to be modifications to the traditional child guidance approach, the concept of a core team of mental health professionals who work regularly together and who can deliver a high level of expertise in community settings is one that must be preserved if the findings of our study are to be applied effectively. The reason for this is that personnel in schools will need back-up teams both for training and for continued professional and emotional support.

The training needs of school mental health programmes are likely to be continuous, particularly for the more indirect approaches. This is because the background training of the teacher-aides in nurture work and the teachers in behaviour modification was less extensive than that in, for example, group therapy. The social workers had all undergone a thorough background training, so that in the case of the two social work programmes we cannot point to a deficiency of skills, but we could suggest, rather, that these skills should be applied in a different way. There is a pressing need for further research into the components of effective casework.

In all programmes there will inevitably be some turnover of staff due to promotion and other changes. The issue of adequate professional and emotional support is, in our opinion, a far more important one than changes in staff. The school is a powerful social system with a very necessary well-defined structure, specified roles for staff, and often strongly underlined norms of behaviour. The responsibility for operating successfully as a therapist in this system must be firmly that of the mental health specialist, who will need special skills in managing the strong emotional forces that are generated, particularly in conflict situations. The mental health worker must, as it were, join the system, yet be able to operate also from a base outside the system and keep a somewhat separate identity. This may be particularly difficult for paraprofessionals, such as nurture workers, who have lower status in the school and are less equipped by training to manage the situation than are specialists. We found that they needed continuous close supervision from a trained professional. We also found that the teachers in behaviour modification needed constant reinforcement and stimulation if they were to maintain interest and apply the technique systematically. Treating a number of children involves the co-operation of many teachers and this is unlikely to be achieved without the help of a skilled supervisor – either a teacher counsellor or a psychologist.

The group therapists were, of course, far better equipped by training than the therapists in the above-mentioned two groups. The technique is, however, a particularly stressful one for the therapist, who has to cope not only with the school social system, the cultural basis of which may be very different from that of the therapy group, but also with the powerful interplay of emotional forces in the groups themselves. It may be that, with experienced therapists, support can be offered from a peer group.

It seems to us that the community mental health services (which may equally be staffed from child guidance clinics or hospital-based clinics) have a major role in the future in supporting school-based programmes, even though the work that might take place may be rather different from that done in the past. We should emphasize that there will, in addition, always be a need for a clinic service for the more seriously disturbed child.

CONTRIBUTION OF RESEARCH TO EDUCATIONAL POLICY

From a practical point of view the value of our research can be measured in terms of its contribution to decisions about educational policy. Such decisions may concern ways of using the budget, either by employing staff, developing facilities, or supporting one type of development rather than another. Carefully controlled studies should point to the 'best buy' in terms of developing services. The evidence that the administrator examines will include the cost and effectiveness of the programme, its ease of implementation, and the reaction of parents. The likely response of ratepayers, who will be looking for both helpfulness and cost-effectiveness will, of course, also be under consideration. We recognize, at the same time, that decisions concerning the allocation of resources are political ones and will, therefore, be influenced by the wider political and economic climate. This apart, we feel that our work has been in a field that is largely free of entrenched traditions and vested interests, one where innovation is accepted.

With these points in mind, we would recommend that mental health programmes in schools be extended, with a particular emphasis on psychodynamically based group therapy and behaviour modification. It is particularly important to maintain a high level of expertise and adequate training among professionals doing this work. This is not likely to be an easy task because the skills required for such training are not widely available, in the UK at any rate, at present. Of critical importance, also, will be the quality of back-up aid that can be offered from existing child psychiatry and child guidance settings: these will play a major role as centres of training and support for such new developments, as well as continuing their established role with more severely disturbed children and their families.

With regard to the other regimes, we advocate caution over dismissing them entirely. Nurture work may have a very valuable contribution to make in two situations: first, where only lower levels of expertise are available (although in the long run it may be more expensive and less effective than playgroup therapy); second, in the treatment of deprivation rather than psychiatric disturbance (the effects of deprivation were not specifically assessed and monitored in this study). A large question mark must remain over parent counselling-teacher consultation. In the form in which it was applied in our study it seemed to have had minimal effect; however, as we discussed above, it may be that in combination with direct contact with the child, or with some other change of procedure, this technique could become much more effective.

This study has shown that group therapy (both play and discussion groups) and behaviour modification, applied with a high degree of expertise, are clearly effective. They should be additionally attractive to health and education administrators because of their short-term natures and relatively low costs.

Part Five
Technical appendices

Appendix 1: Evaluative measures used

This appendix contains brief details of those main evaluative measures that have not been fully described in Chapter 3, on method. For the sake of completeness we list all the main measures.

Screen measures

Multiple criterion screen techniques were used to identify children with all degrees and types of maladjustment, including those who were 'at risk'. The nature of our screens reflected our concept of maladjustment, and the fact that we were particularly interested in its behavioural and social aspects. Our screen techniques gave rise to a wider spectrum of maladjustment than occurs with a screen based on a single scale and was therefore representative of psychiatric disturbance usually found in clinical practice in a wide range of settings. A full account of our screen techniques is provided elsewhere (Kolvin *et al.* 1977; Macmillan *et al.* 1980; Nicol *et al.* 1981).

RUTTER TEACHER SCALE B2 (JUNIORS AND SENIORS)

Test-re-test reliability for total scores over a three-month interval was reported as 0.89. Inter-rater reliability of 0.72 was reported, but this was over a two- to three-month period (Rutter 1967).

With regard to validity it was reported that total scores on a sample of normal nine- to thirteen-year-old children were significantly lower than scores of a group of children attending a psychiatric clinic.

The B2 scale is a slight revision of the B scale, differing in the wording of a few items. Our use of the former is discussed further in Chapter 3.

SOCIOMETRY
See Chapter 3.

YOUNG GROUP READING TEST (JUNIORS)
See Chapter 3.

JUNIOR EYSENCK PERSONALITY INVENTORY (JEPI) NEUROTICISM
(SENIORS)

A detailed account of this measure has been provided in the evaluation of the results (Chapter 9) as one of its scales (extroversion/introversion) was used as an additional measure.

The JEPI was constructed by Eysenck (1965). It consists of sixty items which generate two dimensions of personality: neuroticism and introversion/extroversion. There is also a lie scale. There is no psychoticism dimension as in the Eysenck personality questionnaire (Eysenck and Eysenck 1975).

We used the inventory for the senior group who were eleven to twelve years of age. At this age the split-half reliability co-efficient of the neuroticism scale is 0.86, of the introversion/extroversion scale it is 0.75, and of the lie scale it is 0.72.

Principal component analyses were carried out for children of different ages and Eysenck concluded from the results that neuroticism can be measured adequately at all the ages covered by the inventory, i.e. seven to sixteen years, but that introversion/extroversion does not clearly emerge as a dimension of personality measurable by questionnaire until the age of nine or ten. Our senior group, on which this inventory was used, were all older than this.

THE RUTTER A SCALE QUESTIONNAIRE (JUNIORS AND SENIORS)

This questionnaire was developed for completion by parents as an instrument to identify psychiatric disorder on a population basis (Rutter, Tizard, and Whitmore 1970). The test-re-test reliability was reported as 0.74. Rutter reported that the scale discriminated well between normal and clinic populations, 67 to 71 per cent of a clinic population achieving a score above cut-off as opposed to 8 to 15 per cent of a normal population sample. The questionnaire yields conduct and neurotic sub-scales composed of items that have been found to discriminate significantly between the two groups of disorders. For the purposes of the present study the conduct and neurotic sub-scales were lengthened. This was done by our including all those items that discriminated each sub-group from the control in the Isle of Wight results (Rutter, Tizard, and Whitmore 1970). The reason for lengthening the scale was to increase its stability. The lengthened scales consisted of items 12, 16, 27, 28, 37, 41, and 42 for the antisocial scale and items 8, 9, 13, 20, 23, 30, and 39 for the neurotic scale.

DEVEREUX ELEMENTARY SCHOOL BEHAVIOUR RATING SCALE (DESB) (JUNIORS AND SENIORS)

Spivack and Swift (1967) designed the DESB to measure overt behaviours that reflect a child's overall adaptation to the demands of the classroom setting and that may affect his or her achievement in that setting. Since their intention was to measure behaviours of specific relevance to the classroom, and not behaviours relating to disturbance in a psychiatric context, the initial pool of 111 items for study was derived from a series of discussions with seventy-two normal- and special-class teachers.

The DESB consists of forty-four items, defining eleven behavioural factors, the items being selected on the basis of factor loadings, similar patterns of correlation with other variables (such as IQ and sex), and significant correlation with academic achievement. There are three additional items that do not contribute to the eleven factors.

Norms are based on ratings by thirty-two kindergarten to sixth-grade teachers of the behaviour of 809 children in the USA. Test-re-test reliabilities over a one-week period range from 0.85 to 0.91 for the factors and from 0.71 to 0.80 for the three additional items. Inter-rater reliability, based on forty pairs of ratings in a normal classroom, ranges from 0.62 to 0.77, with a mean of 0.70. Schaefer, Baker, and Zawel (1975) also reported data indicating satisfactory consistency both between raters and over time.

As regards validity, Spivack and Swift (1973) reported that each of the eleven factors had been shown to correlate significantly with teacher grades, after the influence of IQ had been partialled out, both with normal American and French children and with groups of emotionally disturbed children.

It is to be noted that we used both the eleven factors and the three additional items and referred to all fourteen as items. An account is provided in Appendix 2 of the factor analysis undertaken in this study.

BARKER LUNN CHILDREN'S ATTITUDE SCALES – S7 (SENIORS)

These attitude scales were developed in the context of a study by the National Foundation for Educational Research (NFER) into the effects of streaming and non-streaming in junior schools (Barker Lunn 1967 and 1969).

The questionnaire contains ten attitude scales: attitude to school; interest in school work; importance of doing well; attitude to class;

'other' image of class; conforming versus non-conforming pupil; relationship with teacher; anxiety about school work; social adjustment; and self-image. Each scale is made up of six to ten statements made by children during group discussions and selected by factor analysis and scalogram analysis.

Some 2300 third- and fourth-year junior schoolchildren in twenty-eight schools completed the final form of the questionnaire. Inter-correlation of the scales showed two clusters: one dealing with attitudes towards school and school work and the other with social relationships and the personality of the pupil. The internal consistency of the scales was determined by Cronbach's Alpha-co-efficient, yielding a range of 0.69 to 0.90 with a mean of 0.81. A large number of correlations are reported with other measures, such as teacher and parent ratings of ability, sociometric data, achievement scores, and interest scores.

The expectation of a relationship between school performance and attitude was borne out. All the scales correlated significantly with test scores in English, problem arithmetic (all except conforming/non-conforming), essays, verbal reasoning, and non-verbal reasoning. A similar pattern was evident for teacher ratings and also (with the exception of conforming/non-conforming) with parent ratings. The social adjustment scale correlated 0.21 with sociometric status. Interest scores correlated most highly with 'attitude to school' and 'interest in school work'.

An account is provided in Appendix 2 of the factor analysis undertaken in the current study.

The Devereux and Barker Lunn results have been presented separately because we considered them to be measures of general functioning and attitudes highly relevant to the classroom setting.

Child behaviour and temperament: based on parental reports (juniors and seniors)

BEHAVIOUR

An inventory, administered as a semi-structured, open-ended interview with mothers, was used to quantify behaviour (Kolvin *et al.* 1975b). It consists of twenty-nine questions with appropriate probes which relate to three of the four scales originally developed – neurotic behaviour (scale A), antisocial behaviour (scale B), and psycho-somatic behaviour (scale C). The inter-rater reliability of the original scales were all above 0.90. For the purposes of the study we adopted the above three scales but modified and extended the content so that it was more clinically relevant and more appropriate to an older population of children. The scores on the above three scales were summed to provide an aggregate behaviour score (scale A + B + C). In addition, we added a narrower dimension of purely somatic disturbance which reflects abdominal pain, headaches, and vomiting.

TEMPERAMENT

An inventory, again administered as a semi-structured, open-ended interview with mothers, was used to measure temperament (Garside *et al.* 1975). This, too, was slightly modified to meet the purposes of the current study. There are twenty-nine questions with appropriate probes which relate to the four dimensions of withdrawal, activity, mood, and irregularity. The inter-rater reliabilities of these dimensions were all above 0.90.

Additional information – cognitive

When deciding which cognitive and achievement measures to employ, in addition to technical considerations, we found that ease of application of tests and, where possible, group application, were important, since such large numbers of children were involved and disruption of schools' normal working routines had to be minimized. Another limiting factor in the selection of measures was the need for a test to span the age range encountered in the three-year period in which assessments were conducted. We included the English Picture Vocabulary Test and Holborn Reading Scale in our battery with the junior children since data from these tests were available to us from the local education authority's routine assessments in the schools.

ENGLISH PICTURE VOCABULARY TEST (EPVT) (JUNIORS)

The English Picture Vocabulary Test (Brimer and Dunn 1962) is described as measuring 'listening vocabulary' or, more generally, verbal comprehension, and is regarded as being functionally and administratively independent of reading skill.

Form 2 of the test was employed in this study. It covers the age range of seven years to eleven years and eleven months, and can be used as either an individual or group test. The test comprises forty items arranged in order of increasing difficulty. A page of pictures together with a spoken word constitutes a test item and the child is required to identify the picture to which the word refers.

The EPVT was derived from the Peabody Picture Vocabulary Test (Dunn 1959), developed in the USA. English standardization of the EPVT (2) was conducted in Wiltshire schools, being administered to over 5000 children. Kuder Richardson reliabilities are presented for each year group, and the mean reliability is 0.92.

As a means of measuring concurrent validity, the EPVT (2) was administered to 223 primary schoolchildren aged between eight years and eleven years eleven months, along with the Schonell Comprehension Test (Schonell and Schonell 1963), and an experimental test of 'expressed' vocabulary involving 'written sentence completion within an orally presented sentence context' (Brimer and Dunn 1962:35). A random sample of seventy-eight of these children was also administered the Wechsler Intelligence Scale for Children (WISC) Vocabulary and the Schonell Graded Word Reading Test (GWR). The product-moment correlations with Schonell Comprehension and Expressed Vocabulary were 0.61 and 0.73 respectively, and with WISC Vocabulary and Schonell GWR, 0.76 and 0.80 respectively. It was suggested that these results, especially the correlations with tests purporting to measure vocabulary, provide evidence that EPVT (2) measures a function common to other tests of vocabulary.

The correlation of 0.76 with WISC Vocabulary supported Brimer and Dunn's claims that the EPVT (2) yields a measure indicative of verbal ability. In addition, a correlation of 0.79 with the verbal ability test in the eleven-plus examination was reported for 271 of the standardized sample. Further evidence of the relationship with verbal ability came from a study by Phillips, cited in the test manual, where a correlation of 0.81 with Stanford-Binet Vocabulary was found with a sample of 124 ten- to eleven-year-olds. This sample was reported to have departed from national representativeness in sex distribution.

MORAY HOUSE PICTURE INTELLIGENCE TEST (MELLONE 1948) (JUNIORS)

This is a well established test and, according to the manual, has a reliability of about 0.95. It has been reviewed by Banks and Pringle (in Buros, *The Fifth Mental Measurements Yearbook* (1959)). We used it to test the non-verbal intelligence of junior children at the initial testing. By the time of the midline assessment the age ceiling of the Moray House had been reached and at this assessment, and at the final one, the Cattell Intelligence Test Scale 1 was employed.

CATTELL INTELLIGENCE TEST SCALE 1 (JUNIORS)

This is an established, well standardized, non-verbal test of intelligence, although there is no information regarding its reliability or validity. It has been well reviewed by MacFarlane Smith (in Buros, *The Fifth Mental Measurements Yearbook* (1959)). We used it in the follow-ups of the junior children. The IQs on this test were rescaled to make them comparable with those of the Moray House Test.

HOLBORN READING SCALE (WATTS 1948) (JUNIORS)

This is an individual test of reading and comprehension and was used by us to test the reading of the junior children. There is no information regarding its reliability, but according to Nisbet (in Buros, *The Fifth Mental Measurements Yearbook*, (1959)) it is 'quite obviously a sound test' (Buros 1959:635).

GENERAL ABILITY TEST (USED BY THE NATIONAL CHILD
DEVELOPMENT STUDY (NCDS)) – PREVIOUSLY DEVELOPED BY
THE NFER (SENIORS)

This test comprises alternate verbal (forty items) and non-verbal (forty items) with eight practice items. It yields a verbal score, a non-verbal score, and a total score. The task for each verbal item is to discover the principle or concept underlying the grouping of four words and then to supply the missing word – on a multi-choice basis – for a second group of three words, according to the same principle. The task is the same for non-verbal items but here the groupings involve shapes. It is designed for group administration.

At age eleven, test-re-test reliability of 0.94 was reported by Douglas (1964). Douglas found a correlation of 0.93 with the NFER verbal test 8A (eleven-plus selection test) (n = 74) and, in addition, reported from his survey data with an eleven-year-old sample correlations of 0.69 with both a mechanical reading test and a vocabulary test, and 0.75 with an arithmetic test.

READING COMPREHENSION TEST (DEVELOPED BY NFER)
(SENIORS)

This is a thirty-five-item test of reading comprehension, constructed as a parallel test to the Watts-Vernon (Start and Wells 1972), so that for each item in the Watts-Vernon there is an item of comparable facility value in the parallel test. The child is required to choose the correct word from a selection of five given, in order to complete a sentence meaningfully. It is designed for group administration.

A test-re-test correlation of 0.90 was reported by Douglas (1964) for a sample of 124 eight-year-olds, as well as correlations of 0.87 with the mechanical reading test and 0.68 with the vocabulary test employed with this sample.

Appendix 2: Method

Two methods, measurement of outcome and improvement, were used to compare the effects of the four different regimes, both for junior and senior children. This appendix gives details of these two methods, as briefly outlined in Chapter 3.

Clinical measures of outcome

Sainsbury argued that:

> 'Four distinct post-treatment (or care) categories can now be recognized: (1) *clinical status*, or how well the patient is after treatment; (2) *improvement* (difference), or how much better the patient is after treatment; (3) *base-free* improvement (ratio or covariance), or how much better the patient is by comparison with others who started at the same level; (4) *outcome*, or how well the patient is before and after treatment.'
>
> (Sainsbury 1975:143)

Outcome was measured by the procedure given by Sainsbury (1975). As he pointed out, the problem associated with outcome 'stems from the situation, often crucial in clinical studies, in which patients at the top (or bottom) of the scale have no room to improve (or worsen)' (Sainsbury 1975:143). He suggested the following formula to solve this problem:

$$0 = M_1 + M_2 + 2(M_2 - M_1)$$

where 0 = outcome; M_1 = initial score; M_2 = final score

Sainsbury did not indicate how this formula was derived, but it simplifies to the following:

$$0 = 3M_2 - M_1$$

Thus, in measuring outcome by Sainsbury's method, the initial score is not merely subtracted from the final score, but a differential weighting of three to one is introduced. Therefore, using this measure of outcome is much the same as carrying out an analysis of covariance when the regression co-efficient of final upon initial scores is one-third. The correlation between initial and final scores, using reliable measures (as we have done), is not usually below two-thirds and therefore, assuming standard deviation of initial and final scores to be equal, the regression co-efficient of final upon initial scores will usually be about two-thirds or more. Thus, Sainsbury's outcome method places about twice as much relative weight upon the final score as does analysis of covariance. This means that outcome is not merely a measure of change (adjusted for initial score difference): it depends both upon change and upon final state. It is, therefore, a realistic measure of clinical outcome which should take actual clinical states after treatment into account, in addition to any change which may have been brought about.

In using this method, the children's behaviour was rated by a child psychiatrist on three occasions: at base, at midline assessment (about eighteen months later) and at final follow-up (eighteen months after the midline follow-up). On each occasion the rating psychiatrist used all the available information gathered about the child. This information did not always include a complete set of data and, therefore, the numbers of children about whom outcome was available (see *Tables A3(2)* and *A3(3)* in Appendix 3) was a little greater than the numbers who had a complete set of improvement data.

The psychiatrists did not attempt to assess improvement, but rated the children on three distinct occasions. Their ratings were therefore more reliable than if they had rated improvement, which is a more difficult task. Each child was rated on a four-point scale at the midline and final follow-ups: (a) no disturbance; (b) slightly disturbed; (c) moderately disturbed; (d) markedly disturbed. The same scale was used at base, except that the 'no disturbance' rating was, of course, rarely used, and then only for junior children who were 'at risk'. The range of outcome at each follow-up therefore was minus 1 to 11. This range was then divided into three categories, corresponding to good outcome (minus 1 to 3), moderate outcome (4 and 5), and poor outcome (6 to 11). Percentages of children corresponding to these three levels of outcome were then calculated; it is these percentages that are reported in *Tables A3(2)* and *A3(3)* in Appendix 3. In the Figures in the book itself the percentages of the moderate group have been omitted, in order to give a clearer picture.

Statistical measures of improvement – covariance analysis

To compare regimes in relation to improvement we used analysis of covariance in preference to analysis of variance. Covariance analysis takes into account differences between the regimes that may affect improvement. For example, initial level of maladjustment (i.e. before treatment) is inevitably correlated with improvement and, therefore, if regimes differ initially, this should be taken into account when comparing the mean improvement of regimes. Analysis of covariance allows this to be done. In fact, the initial levels of some measures differed significantly between regimes (see Appendix 3); the use of covariance analysis was therefore justified.

As well as taking initial levels into account, we allowed for initial differences between the regimes in relation to general severity of maladjustment, non-verbal IQ, an index of social functioning within the family, and, for the junior children only, an index of family history of psychiatric illness. We did not allow for this last variable in the case of the senior children because of lack of scatter in some regimes. These particular 'covariates' were taken into account because we found that they were relatively important.

Provided that children are randomly allocated to regimes (as was the case in the present study), both analyses of covariance and variance are valid methods of testing the statistical significance of differences between regimes. However, analysis of covariance is the more sensitive procedure and, more important, it provides a greater degree of accuracy in the assessment of comparative improvement means than does analysis of variance.

Errors of measurement, as is well known, reduce the corrections to the adjusted means. Our covariates, though, were reliable, and thus under-correction was slight.

ASSUMPTIONS UNDERLYING COVARIANCE ANALYSIS

The assumptions underlying the analysis of variance – that variances are homogeneous and that distributions are normal – also apply to analysis of covariance. However, evidence from analysis of variance indicates that the analysis of covariance is robust with respect to the violation of these two assumptions. Thus, only one variable was excluded from analysis because of violation of either of these assumptions; this was the sociometric measure of rejection, which had a J-shaped distribution of scores.

Analysis of covariance also involves the further assumption that within-group regressions are homogeneous, that is, that the regression co-efficients of the variate (improvement in the present case) upon the covariates (for example, initial score) are the same for each regime. Although there is evidence that analysis of covariance is robust with respect to this assumption (Winer 1971:772) it was thought prudent to examine this, and a test of homogeneity of regression was carried out for each variable across regimes. As a result of this a few measures were dropped from the analysis of covariance (see Appendix 3). On the remaining measures (the great majority) analysis of covariance was carried out using improvement (initial minus final score of maladjustment) as the variate, with five covariates for the junior children and four for the senior children. In general, it was found that the initial score was the most important covariate in our analyses.

INTERACTION EFFECTS

Had the differences between regimes in relation to improvement been affected by the diagnostic category of the children or by their sex, that is, had there been interaction between regime and diagnostic categories, or between regime and sex, it would have been desirable to carry out comparisons between regimes for the two diagnostic categories and for boys and girls separately. Therefore, to check this possibility, two two-way analyses of covariance (using unweighted means) were carried out first, one with regime against diagnosis and the other with regime against sex, for both senior and junior groups.

In the case of seniors only in five out of ninety-two measures (including both comparisons at midline and final follow-up) was interaction with diagnosis found to be significant. Only four interactions with sex were found to be significant. Thus, for both diagnosis and sex, significant interactions with regime occurred no more than might be expected by chance.

For juniors in only one out of sixty-six measures was there an interaction between sex and regime, and in two measures an interaction between regime and diagnosis. Thus, for juniors also there was no evidence of interaction of regime with either sex or diagnosis.

Therefore, for both seniors and juniors, our hypotheses 3 and 4 (that regimes interact with diagnostic category and with sex) were not confirmed and, moreover, it was legitimate to compare regimes (hypotheses 1 and 2) without regard to diagnosis or sex. It was also possible to compare diagnostic categories, and boys with girls, independently of regime (hypotheses 6 and 7).

Did the regimes differ from each other?

Those measures for which analysis of covariance indicated that regimes differed significantly (hypothesis 1) were investigated further to ascertain which regimes differed from which; that is, pairs of regimes (including the controls), were compared by analysis of covariance. However, when there are four regimes and their change means are arranged in order, the probability that the largest and smallest means will differ is exaggerated. This had to be taken into account when comparing pairs of means. Thus, in making pair-wise comparisons in relation to our first hypothesis that the four regimes differ, we used the Newman-Keuls technique. This is fully described in the literature (for example, Winer 1971:191 *et seq.*). The technique allows for the fact that, where more than two means are arranged in order of magnitude, the probability of two means differing is altered by putting them in order. In using this technique, we had, of course, to amend the appropriate published tables of significance levels to take into account the fact that our results were in terms of the F ratio.

Which regimes were more effective than the controls?

Hypothesis 2, which postulated that one or more of the three treatment regimes is more effective than no treatment at all, raised quite a different point from hypothesis 1, and had to be dealt with separately. We wished to compare *three* treatments with a control regime, and, accordingly, used the procedure outlined by Dunnett (1955, 1964), which takes into account the fact that the number of treatment regimes is greater than one; it is more likely that one treatment in a group of three treatments would be significantly different from a control regime, than a single treatment only. Even though hypothesis 2 was written as one-tailed (Chapter 3), we have always used a two-tailed ($p < .05$) level of significance as this is a more stringent procedure.

   If the improvement mean of any treatment regime was statistically significantly better than the corresponding control mean using either the Newman-Keuls test (hypothesis 1) or Dunnett's procedure (hypothesis 2), then we regarded that treatment as superior to no treatment (in relation to the measure in question) and have reported it as such in the text.

Grouping of measures to make up aggregate measure

Principal component factor analyses were carried out to ascertain which measures should be summated. For both juniors and seniors an important general component was found underlying the fourteen Devereux items. For the juniors this accounted for 41 per cent of the variance, and for the seniors 48 per cent, having reversed items 7 and 10, i.e. comprehension and creative initiative, which are clearly both positive attributes. Thus, for both juniors and seniors it was decided to add the standardized items (reversing 7 and 10) to obtain an aggregate global Devereux score.

A further principal component analysis was carried out on the ten remaining junior measures and, again, a general component was obtained, accounting for 26 per cent of the variance, plus a bipolar component, accounting for 16 per cent of the variance. This bipolar component clearly contrasted the five neurotic measures (neurotic and psychosomatic behaviour derived from parent interview; isolation score derived from sociometry; and neurotic behaviour from the Rutter parent and teacher scales) with the five antisocial items (antisocial behaviour; activity and mood derived from parent interview; and antisocial behaviour derived from the Rutter parent and teacher scales). It was therefore decided to add the five neurotic items, the five antisocial items, and then all ten items together to generate three aggregate measures – neurotic behaviour, antisocial behaviour, and global behaviour. All items were standardized before being added.

The Barker Lunn Attitude Scale, which was used for the seniors, was next examined. It was found that although the first component was a general one, the second component (which accounted for 16 per cent of the variance) clearly distinguished the first seven items from the last three. (This agreed with Barker Lunn's (1969) own analysis.) Because of this differentiation it was decided to sum the first seven items to form an aggregate measure of attitude to school, and also to add the last three items, which measured what we have described as neurotic anxiety in relation to school and schooling.

A principal component analysis was then carried out on the remaining fourteen scores of the senior children. This excluded both the Devereux and Barker Lunn scales, which had already been analysed. Again, a general component was obtained (24 per cent of variance) and a bipolar component (15 per cent of variance). The latter contrasted nine neurotic measures (neurotic behaviour, psychosomatic behaviour, somatic disturbance, and withdrawal from the parental interview; neurotic behaviour from the Rutter parent and teacher scales; neuroticism and introversion from the JEPI; and the isolation score from sociometry) with five antisocial measures (antisocial behaviour, activity, and mood, from the parent interview, and antisocial behaviour from both the Rutter scales). Thus, it was decided to add the standardized scores of the neurotic measures, the scores of the antisocial measures, and the scores of all fourteen measures to generate three aggregate scales: neurotic behaviour (nine measures), antisocial behaviour (five measures), and global behaviour (fourteen measures). The data relating to this principal component factor analysis are shown in *Table A2(1)*.

Patterns of behaviour and change

Hypothesis 5 stated that regimes differ in effectiveness according to patterns of behaviour, that is, that some regimes are more effective in improving neurotic behaviour, and others more effective in reducing antisocial behaviour. This hypothesis was tested by seeing whether there was any interaction between two different measures of maladjustment (i.e. the aggregate measures of neurotic behaviour and antisocial behaviour) and the four regimes. We did this using the procedure outlined by Greenhouse and Geisser (1959). However, we wanted to carry out analyses of covariance, and not merely analyses

Table A2(1)   *Principal component analysis: seniors*

measure	factor loadings	
	general	bipolar
parent interview data		
neurotic behaviour	0.59	− 0.54
antisocial behaviour	0.70	0.48
psychosomatic behaviour	0.71	− 0.09
somatic disturbance	0.60	− 0.31
withdrawal	0.32	− 0.47
activity	0.65	0.39
mood	0.61	0.09
neurotic behaviour at home (Rutter A)	0.51	− 0.37
antisocial behaviour at home (Rutter A)	0.62	0.49
neurotic behaviour at school (Rutter B2)	0.11	− 0.02
antisocial behaviour at school (Rutter B2)	0.07	0.69
isolation (sociometry)	0.29	− 0.03
neuroticism (JEPI)	0.02	− 0.41
introversion (JEPI)	0.18	− 0.31
percentage of variance	24	15

Note: JEPI = Junior Eysenck Personality Inventory.

of variance as considered by Greenhouse and Geisser. Thus, we used a repeated-measures analysis of covariance method as described by Winer (1971: section 10.6). We were not, of course, using repeated measures – our measures were merely correlated. This necessitated standardizing our two measures so that the question of interaction was meaningful (see Greenhouse and Geisser 1959).

In view of the fact that the numbers in the four regimes were not the same (which does not invalidate the procedure), one of us (Ian Muir Leitch) had to write a special computer programme. The standard programmes available to us all assumed that the numbers in the groups were equal. Because of the complexity of the situation, we used only one covariant, i.e. the appropriate initial score for each measure. For both junior and senior groups we considered two measures, namely the neurotic and antisocial behaviour aggregate measures just described.

Appendix 3: Results*

Initial Levels

A wide range of measures was studied at the time of the initial assessment. For both junior and senior children, initial levels between the four regimes on these measures differed rather more than was to be expected by chance. Thirty-six per cent of the F ratios were significant for the juniors and 25 per cent for the seniors. The significant results are given in *Table A3(1)*. It will be seen from this table that, while there were differences between regime means for the measures listed in the table, there was no evidence that the regimes introduced last into the schools, namely nurture work, playgroup therapy for the juniors, and behaviour modification and group therapy for the seniors, generally started off with an initial advantage over the regimes that were introduced first. Thus, the fact that the regimes introduced last seemed to be more successful in reducing maladjustment than those introduced first would not have been due to the cumulative effect of general intervention in the schools; in fact, there did not seem to be any general improvement due to the mere presence of the research in the schools.

Outcome

The outcome results for juniors – in terms of percentages of children having had good, moderate, or poor outcome – are given in *Table A3(2)*. The outcome results of the senior children are given in *Table A3(3)*.

Improvement

Analyses of covariance were carried out to test hypotheses 1–7 regarding improvement. As indicated in Appendix 2, such analyses

* All Tables and Figures are grouped at the end of the chapter; see p. 357.

involved the assumption of homogeneity of regression and, thus, this matter was investigated first.

HOMOGENEITY OF REGRESSION WITH INITIAL SCORE

The initial score was much the most important covariate: that is, it had most effect upon improvement. The homogeneity of regression with this covariate was accordingly investigated first in order to ascertain which measures could be validly analysed using analysis of covariance.

In the junior regimes, six regressions out of a total of sixty-eight (including both follow-ups) were found to be significantly heterogeneous. These were for the following measures: withdrawal, irregularity, rejection, EPVT, non-verbal IQ, and Devereux item 3 ('disrespect'). None of these measures, except Devereux item 3, produced significantly different results between regimes at the final follow-up on analysis either of variance or of covariance. Regimes differed significantly on Devereux item 3 at the final follow-up using covariance, but not variance, analysis. Devereux item 3 was included in the factor analysis but not as part of the Devereux aggregate measure; on this aggregate measure of thirteen items, regressions were homogeneous at both follow-ups. It is worth noting that at the midline follow-up, on both analyses of variance and covariance, children in the nurture work regime did best on withdrawal, both nurture work and playgroup children on EPVT and the playgroup children on non-verbal IQ (see Chapters 6 and 8) but these differences washed out at the final follow-up.

In the senior regimes, eighteen out of 102 regressions with initial score (including both the midline and the final follow-ups) showed heterogeneity of regression. These heterogeneous results involved fifteen measures, which will now be considered: Five measures were discarded at the outset. One, motor activity, had a skewed distribution and, accordingly, was excluded from further analysis. For the four other measures – appetite, bowel and sleep disorders, and irregularity – no significant differences were found between regimes and, therefore, there was no point in considering them further.

The Rutter B2 total measure had heterogeneous regressions at both the midline and the final follow-ups. However, at the midline the regimes did not differ significantly by either analysis of variance (F = 1.84, p > .1) or covariance (F = 1.04, p > .1). At the final follow-up the results obtained by covariance were more conservative than those by variance analysis (*Table A3(4)*), and therefore we adopted the covariance results.

The Rutter B2 antisocial measures showed heterogeneous regressions at the midline follow-up *only* and there the regimes did not differ significantly on covariance (F = 1.82, p > .1) or variance analysis (F = 1.94, p > .1). At the final follow-up the regimes differed significantly. Thus, there was no conflict between the variance and covariance analyses and the latter was accordingly adopted.

The JEPI neuroticism measure had heterogeneous regressions at the midline and the final follow-ups and at the end of treatment. At the midline and the end of treatment similar significant results on analyses of covariance and variance were obtained, as shown in *Table A3(4)*. At the final follow-up, no significant differences were found, neither by analysis of variance (F = 1.87, p > .1) nor covariance (F = 1.64, p > .1). The covariance results were accordingly accepted.

The parental rating of neurotic behaviour (measure A) was heterogeneous at the midline follow-up and significantly distinguished between regimes by analysis of variance, but not by analysis of covariance (*Table A3(4)*). The latter, non-significant result was adopted as being more conservative.

Psychosomatic behaviour (measure C) was heterogeneous at both the midline and the final follow-ups. At neither follow-up did this measure significantly distinguish between regimes by analysis of variance or covariance. At the midline follow-up the respective results were F = 1.38 (p > .1) and F = 2.50 (p > .05). At the final follow-up the figures were F = 1.61 (p > .1) and F = 2.00 (p > .1). Thus, there was no conflict between the results introduced by heterogeneity of regression; no significant results were obtained by either analysis and this measure was not considered further.

The aggregate parental measure (A + B + C) was heterogeneous at the midline follow-up. The relevant comparative results are given in *Table A3(4)*. In view of their similarity, the covariance analysis figures were accepted.

The regressions on the mood measure were heterogeneous at the midline follow-up only. On neither analysis of variance nor covariance did the regimes differ in relation to this measure (F = 1.68 (p < .1) and F = 1.49 (p < .1) respectively) at the midline follow-up. At the final follow-up the regimes differed significantly and regressions were homogeneous. Covariance was therefore adopted.

The three NCDS measures – verbal, non-verbal, and total ability – all showed heterogeneity of regression with initial score at the midline follow-up. However, at this follow-up (*Table A3(4)*) all three F ratios were less by analysis of covariance than by analysis of variance. The more conservative results of analysis of covariance were therefore adopted and these three measures were retained in the analysis.

The sociometric measure of rejection had homogeneous regression upon initial score but was rejected from covariance analysis because of its J-shaped distribution.

HOMOGENEITY OF REMAINING REGRESSIONS

The heterogeneity of regression in the sex and diagnosis comparisons was distributed, as might have been expected, by chance and, thus, no additional measures were rejected on this account, for either the junior or the senior children.

As far as the other covariates were concerned – general severity, non-verbal IQ, social functioning within the family, and (for the junior children only) index of family history of psychiatric illness – the number of significant heterogeneous regressions were under one in twenty, which was less than that expected by chance; no more measures were discarded because of heterogeneity of regression upon these covariates.

DIFFERENCES BETWEEN THE FOUR REGIMES

These differences relate to the first hypothesis that the four regimes differ in effectiveness. Only those measures for which the probability of the F ratio was equal to less than 0.05 (i.e., for which differences between the improvement means of the four regimes were unlikely to have occurred by chance) at one or more of the follow-ups are reported here. Results are reported at all follow-ups if they were significant at any one follow-up.

The change means were all adjusted by taking into account the appropriate covariates – five for the juniors and four for the seniors. It was realized, of course, that these adjustments did not take into account errors of measurement in the covariates (see Snedecor and Cochran 1967:430), but our covariates were reliable and, furthermore, as is illustrated in *Table A3(4)*, the adjustments were, in general, small. Thus, the effect of not taking errors of measurement into account was relatively unimportant.

The change means were all standardized, in the sense that they were based upon change scores having a standard deviation of unity at the final follow-up. For initial to midline and end of-treatment follow-ups, change means were adjusted to make them comparable with those at the final follow-up.

Although the adjusted change means reported in the tables were based upon change scores having unit standard deviation at final follow-up, these change scores did not have a mean of zero. The grand change mean (including children in all four regimes) was expressed in terms of unit standard deviation. This does not imply that the grand change mean was zero. On the contrary, as one might expect, we found that there were overall changes as time went on.

For the junior children, the adjusted means and F ratios of the Devereux items are given in *Table A3(5)*. Their non-Devereux results are given in *Table A3(6)*. Sixty-four F ratios were calculated and twenty-four of these were significant at the 5 per cent level or less, i.e. 37 per cent. This was clearly more than would be expected by chance.

For those measures where probabilities in either *Table A3(5)* or *A3(6)* were equal to, or less than, 0.05 paired comparisons were carried out in the regimes using analyses of covariance. The significance of these results was tested by using the Newman-Keuls technique (see Appendix 2) in relation to the first hypothesis. The results are given in *Tables A3(7)* and *A3(8)*.

In comparing the three treatment regimes individually with the control regime (hypothesis 2) all measures were taken into account, whether they showed significance in *Tables A3(5)* and *A3(6)* or not; significance levels were adopted using Dunnett's (1964) tables. Significant differences by either the Newman-Keuls' or Dunnett's methods are given in *Tables A3(7)* and *A3(8)*. Those comparisons with the controls that were significant using the Dunnett method are labelled 'D'.

This same procedure was used in relation to the senior children. Their Devereux results are given in *Table A3(9)*, Barker Lunn results in *Table A3(10)*, and the remaining data collected at school are given in *Table A3(11)*. The parental data results, together with three of the aggregate measures of global maladjustment, neurotic behaviour, and antisocial behaviour, are given in *Table A3(12)*. End-of-treatment data were incomplete. Devereux, Barker Lunn, JEPI, sociometric, cognitive, and Rutter A data were collected at this follow-up.

From the senior group, 141 between-regime F ratios were calculated and, of these, thirty-six were significant, i.e. 26 per cent. This, again, was clearly more than one would expect by chance.

For those measures having a significant F ratio ($p < .05$) in *Tables A3(9)* to *A3(12)*, paired comparisons were carried out on the four regimes using analysis of covariance. Significant levels were derived using the Newman-Keuls technique (see Appendix 2). Results are given in *Tables A3(13)* to *A3(16)*.

In comparing the three treatments with the controls (hypothesis 2) all measures were considered, whether significantly differentiating between regimes or not. In making these comparisons with the control regime, Dunnett's tables (1964) were used (see Appendix 2). Significant differences (with controls) using either the Newman-Keuls or the Dunnett method are given in *Tables A3(13)* to *A3(16)*.

Those results that were significant only when using Dunnett's method are labelled 'D' in these tables.

INTERACTIONS BETWEEN REGIMES AND DIAGNOSTIC CATEGORIES AND BETWEEN REGIMES AND SEX (HYPOTHESES 3 AND 4)

Hypothesis 3 was concerned with the interaction between the effects of regimes and of diagnostic category, that is, it stated that regimes differ in effectiveness according to the diagnostic category (neurotic or conduct disorder) into which the child falls. This was tested by the appropriate statistical analysis (two-way analysis of covariance). As stated in Appendix 2, there was no evidence of such an interaction in either the senior or junior groups.

Hypothesis 4 stated that regimes differ in effectiveness according to the sex of the child. There was no evidence (see Appendix 2) of any such interaction for either junior or senior groups.

INTERACTION BETWEEN REGIMES AND PATTERNS OF BEHAVIOUR (HYPOTHESIS 5)

Hypothesis 5 stated that regimes differ in effectiveness according to patterns of behaviour, that is, some regimes are most effective in reducing neurotic behaviour, others in reducing antisocial behaviour.

For the junior group a significant interaction was found both at base to midline follow-up and at base to final follow-up. *Table A3(17)* and *Fig. A3(1)* give the relevant results (for the latter see p. 357). It will be seen that at both follow-ups there was a significant interaction, the nurture work and playgroup regimes both showing a comparatively greater reduction in children's antisocial behaviour than in their neurotic behaviour.

The results of the senior group interactions were not significant. At base to midline follow-up F = 2.07 with 3 and 235 degrees of freedom, p > .1. At final follow-up F = 1.39, p > .1. There was, therefore, no evidence that regimes and patterns of behaviour interacted in the case of the senior children.

IMPROVEMENT AND DIAGNOSTIC CATEGORY (HYPOTHESIS 6)

Hypothesis 6 (that improvement is related to diagnostic category) was investigated by analysis of covariance. Results for the junior group of the Devereux are given in *Table A3(18)*. Their non-Devereux results are shown in *Table A3(19)*. There were more significant junior results (23 per cent) than expected by chance; improvement was therefore related to diagnostic category, as indicated in *Tables A3(18)* and *A3(19)*.

The senior Devereux results are given in *Table A3(20)*, their Barker Lunn results in *Table A3(21)*, and the remaining results in *Tables*

A3(22) and *A3(23)*. Twenty per cent of the F ratios of the senior group were significant; thus, diagnostic category affected improvement in the senior group, as shown in *Tables A3(20)* to *A3(23)*.

For both junior and senior groups it appeared that neurotic children did better than conduct-disordered children in relation to the reduction of associated antisocial symptoms (for example, on classroom disturbance: *Table A3(18)*). Conversely, conduct-disordered children seemed to improve on measures of neurotic behaviour (for example, anxiety about school work: *Table A3(21)*) more than neurotic children. This implied that there was an interaction between diagnosis and pattern of behaviour in relation to improvement. We therefore carried out tests of significance of this interaction for junior and senior children at both midline and final follow-ups. For these tests we used the global neurotic scores (sum of five measures for the juniors and nine measures for the seniors) and the global antisocial scores (sum of five measures for both juniors and seniors). We found that at the midline follow-up this interaction was significant for both junior and senior children ($F = 4.62$, degrees of freedom = 1 and 83, and $p < .05$ for juniors; $F = 4.84$, degrees of freedom = 1 and 233, and $p < .05$ for seniors). However, at the final follow-up the interaction between diagnosis and pattern of behaviour was not significant for either junior or senior children; thus this interaction, which was present at the midline follow-up, may not have been maintained.

IMPROVEMENT AND SEX (HYPOTHESIS 7)

Results regarding hypothesis 7 (that improvement is related to sex) are given in *Tables A3(24)* and *A3(25)* for the junior group. Twenty-two per cent of the F ratios were significant. The results of the senior group are given in *Tables A3(26)* to *A3(29)*. Twenty-four per cent of these results were significant. Thus, improvement was related to sex, for both juniors and seniors. Girls seemed to improve more than boys on antisocial measures (for example, classroom disturbance: *Table A3(24)*), boys more than girls on the neurotic measures (for example, anxiety about school work: *Table A3(27)*). We tested this implied interaction between pattern of behaviour and sex using the same method as just described for diagnosis. We found that at the midline follow-up there was a significant interaction for both junior and senior children ($F = 5.02$, degrees of freedom = 1 and 198, and $p < .05$; $F = 4.84$, degrees of freedom = 1 and 237, and $p < .05$ respectively). At the final follow-up the interaction between sex and pattern of behaviour was significant for senior children only ($F = 12.75$, degrees of freedom = 1 and 237, and $p < .01$). These results indicate that, at least for senior children, there was a definite and continuing tendency for girls to improve more than boys on antisocial measures and, conversely, for boys to do better than girls on neurotic measures.

The concept of 'at risk'

The question has been raised of whether it is appropriate to treat children who are 'at risk'. A distinction has to be made between those who are 'at risk' and clearly disturbed, and those who are merely 'at risk'. There are no questions about the former category. In the case of the latter we found that almost 90 per cent of this group who were not given treatment subsequently had a poor outcome (i.e. three years after treatment had ended). However, of those treated, only 33 per cent had a poor outcome, and this difference was highly significant (p < .001). Of the three treatments playgroups once again proved the most effective.

Figure A3(1) Juniors: interaction of regime with pattern of behaviour

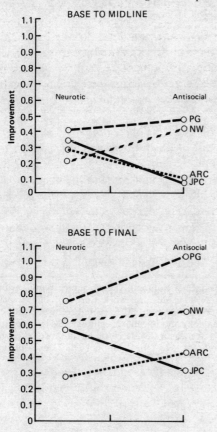

Table A3(1)   *Initial levels: significant differences*

measure	juniors (n = 265)				F ratio	p <
	means					
	ARC	JPC	NW	PG		
parent interview						
neurotic behaviour (A)	13.04	12.59	14.16	12.20	3.74	.05
antisocial behaviour (B)	15.30	15.95	17.41	16.85	2.78	.05
withdrawal	14.60	14.45	17.17	13.90	3.41	.05
activity	14.21	13.80	16.34	17.23	8.33	.01
Devereux						
item 2 (impatience)	12.09	15.52	11.37	11.71	8.07	.01
item 4 (external blame)	7.58	9.03	7.04	7.38	2.76	.05
item 6 (poor comprehension)	18.73	21.98	17.08	18.38	5.85	.01
item 8 (inattentive/withdrawm)	12.11	15.58	12.96	11.68	7.09	.01
item 12 (unable to change)	3.48	4.26	3.20	3.26	4.06	.01
item 13 (quits easily)	4.14	5.03	3.73	4.02	5.80	.01
item 14 (slow work)	3.92	5.01	3.73	3.92	4.76	.01
grand means of all behaviour						
measures	13.1	14.2	13.1	13.1		
RQ	85.9	82.7	91.1	88.0	3.67	.05

measure	seniors (n = 309)					
	means					
	MC	PC	BM	SG		
parent interview						
neurotic behaviour (A)	13.02	12.90	14.42	13.56	2.65	.05
somatic disturbance	3.48	3.73	4.80	4.29	7.95	.01
activity	13.93	14.69	16.94	15.46	5.46	.01
neurotic behaviour at home						
(Rutter B2)	2.94	3.67	4.83	4.34	4.87	.01
Devereux						
item 5 (achievement anxiety)	9.72	10.49	11.69	9.26	3.98	.01
item 6 (poor comprehension)	16.89	18.95	19.72	16.01	5.36	.01
grand means of all behaviour						
measures	12.00	12.5	13.2	12.3		
verbal ability (NCDS)	14.62	15.53	11.53	12.67	4.56	.01
non-verbal ability (NCDS)	15.20	16.01	11.64	13.32	7.13	.01
total ability (NCDS)	29.79	31.58	23.16	26.00	6.49	.01
reading comprehension	13.24	13.19	10.65	12.44	3.67	.05

Note: regimes: ARC = at-risk controls (juniors); JPC = junior parent counselling-teacher consultation (juniors); NW = nurture work (juniors); PG = playgroups (juniors); MC = maladjusted controls (seniors); PC = parent counselling-teacher consultation (seniors); BM = behaviour modification (seniors); SG = group therapy (seniors). *Miscellaneous:* F ratio = a measure of statistical significance; p = probability indicating level of statistical significance; NCDS = National Child Development Study.

Table A3(2)   *Outcome: juniors*

	ARC* n = 61	JPC n = 60	NW n = 52	PG n = 60	significance
	%	%	%	%	
antisocial behaviour: base to midline follow-up					
good	45	36	40	35	
moderate	12	26	29	35	ns
poor	43	38	31	29	
antisocial behaviour: base to final follow-up					
good	48	43	61	59	
moderate	16	29	16	19	ns
poor	36	28	23	22	
neurotic behaviour: base to midline follow-up					
good	35	38	46	57	PG > ARC (p < .05)
moderate	32	23	23	27	PG > JPC (p < .01)
poor	32	39	31	16	
neurotic behaviour: base to final follow-up					PG > NW (p < .05)
good	45	40	57	72	PG > ARC (p < .01)
moderate	23	29	18	21	PG > JPC (p < .01)
poor	31	31	25	7	
overall severity: base to midline follow-up					
good	29	20	27	35	
moderate	11	23	22	37	ns
poor	60	58	51	28	
overall severity: base to final follow-up					NW > ARC (p < .05)
good	33	32	52	56	PG > ARC (p < .01)
					PG > JPC (p < .01)
moderate	12	25	16	24	
poor	55	43	32	21	

Note: * for details of abbreviations see p. 358; > means 'better than' in this table.

Table A3(3)   *Outcome: seniors*

| | n = 289 | | | | |
	MC n = 83	PC n = 79	BM n = 67	SG n = 60	significance
	%	%	%	%	
antisocial behaviour: base to midline follow-up					
good	30	32	31	63	
moderate	27	33	24	13	SG > MC & PC & BM (p < .01)
poor	43	35	45	24	
antisocial behaviour: base to final follow-up					
good	30	44	48	59	
					BM > MC (p < .05)
moderate	19	22	22	14	PC > MC (p < .05)
					SG > MC (p < .01)
poor	51	34	29	27	
neurotic behaviour: base to midline follow-up					
good	26	37	45	47	
moderate	26	21	17	21	BM > MC (p < .05)
					SG > MC (p < .05)
poor	49	42	38	32	
neurotic behaviour: base to final follow-up					
good	36	42	73	64	
moderate	24	18	10	25	SG > MC & PC (p < .01)
					BM > MC & PC (p < .01)
poor	41	40	17	11	
overall severity: base to midline follow-up					
good	19	23	18	37	
moderate	17	27	20	18	SG > MC (p < .05)
poor	64	50	62	45	
overall severity: base to final follow-up					
good	24	33	54	53	
moderate	14	14	19	22	BM > MC & PC (p < .01)
					SG > MC & PC (p < .01)
poor	62	53	27	25	

Note: > means 'better than' in this table.

Table A3(4)   *Comparison of analyses of variance and covariance on measures showing heterogeneity of regression*

measure	type of analysis	regime change means				F ratio	p <
		MC	PC	BM	SG		
	n	72	72	62	51		
total behaviour score (Rutter teacher scale B2) final follow-up	covariance	−0.07	0.20	0.42	0.60	4.54	.01
	variance	−0.14	0.29	0.38	0.63	4.72	.01
	n	72	72	62	51		
neuroticism (JEPI) midline follow-up	covariance	0.23	−0.04	0.80	0.66	11.00	.001
	variance	0.22	0.00	0.83	0.59	8.14	.001
	n	81	80	68	61		
neuroticism (JEPI) end of treatment follow-up	covariance	0.23	−0.03	0.49	0.22	4.22	.01
	variance	0.23	0.00	0.51	0.17	3.23	.05
	n	75	64	51	50		
parent interview neurotic behaviour (scale A) midline follow-up	covariance	0.21	0.17	0.49	0.48	2.12	.1
	variance	0.20	0.09	0.55	0.51	3.13	.05
	n	75	64	51	50		
parent interview re child behaviour aggregate behaviour (scale A + B + C) midline follow-up	covariance	0.12	0.23	0.35	0.59	2.82	.05
	variance	0.09	0.23	0.44	0.56	2.50	.05
	n	72	72	62	51		
total ability (NCDS) midline follow-up	covariance	−0.04	0.02	0.41	0.45	7.89	.001
	variance	−0.07	−0.04	0.47	0.49	12.05	.001
	n	72	72	62	51		
verbal ability (NCDS) midline follow-up	covariance	−0.02	0.05	0.47	0.47	9.21	.001
	variance	−0.02	0.02	0.48	0.47	10.10	.001
	n	72	72	62	51		
non-verbal ability (NCDS) midline follow-up	covariance	−0.08	−0.01	0.31	0.37	4.79	.01
	variance	−0.15	−0.10	0.43	0.45	9.18	.001

Table A3(5)   *Improvement (adjusted change means) Devereux scale items: juniors*

item	grand change mean	regimes adjusted change means				F ratio	p
		ARC	JPC	NW	PG		
(a) base to midline follow-up							
1 classroom disturbance	0.11	−0.31	0.18	0.12	0.46	5.14	< .01
2 impatience	0.10	−0.14	0.28	0.28	0.03	2.38	.07
4 external blame	0.11	−0.07	−0.02	0.43	0.17	2.79	< .05
7 lack of comprehension	0.17	−0.15	0.37	0.11	0.33	3.60	< .05
8 inattentive/withdrawn	0.25	−0.11	0.49	0.42	0.23	2.96	< .05
11 needs closeness	−0.10	0.23	−0.35	−0.25	−0.05	4.23	< .01
12 unable to change	0.18	−0.16	0.27	0.20	0.45	1.96	.12
13 quits easily	0.06	−0.12	0.18	0.11	0.27	3.88	< .05
14 slow work	0.14	−0.01	0.27	−0.11	0.18	4.34	< .01
aggregate (sum of 13 items)	0.18	−0.18	0.36	0.23	0.31	2.90	< .05
(b) base to midline follow-up							
1 classroom disturbance	0.38	0.16	0.36	0.41	0.63	2.20	.09
2 impatience	0.18	−0.27	0.40	0.32	0.32	5.49	< .01
4 external blame	0.13	−0.17	0.20	0.33	0.20	2.39	.07
7 lack of comprehension	0.15	−0.26	0.29	0.26	0.35	4.46	< .01
8 inattentive/withdrawn	0.38	0.13	0.56	0.51	0.35	2.00	.12
11 needs closeness	0.07	−0.08	0.03	0.14	0.22	0.93	.43
12 unable to change	0.32	−0.02	0.40	0.33	0.57	3.29	< .05
13 quits easily	0.39	0.09	0.52	0.55	0.42	2.47	.06
14 slow work	0.23	0.08	0.36	0.20	0.26	0.80	.49
aggregate (sum of 13 items)	0.35	−0.08	0.46	0.49	0.59	5.29	< .01
n =	216	58	59	45	54		

Note: grand change mean is the mean change of all the 216 children; item 3 has been omitted from the aggregate score (see p. 351).

Table A3(6)   *Improvement (adjusted change means) non-Devereux scale measures: juniors*

measure	grand change mean	regimes adjusted change means				F ratio	p
		ARC	JPC	NW	PG		
		(a) base to midline follow-up					
parent interview							
antisocial behaviour (B)	0.16	0.05	0.04	0.41	0.16	1.68	.17
psychosomatic behaviour (C)	0.19	0.18	0.02	0.12	0.42	2.61	.05
aggregate behaviour (A + B + C)	0.29	0.18	0.09	0.35	0.49	1.95	.12
activity	0.15	−0.01	−0.15	0.29	0.49	3.79	< .05
mood	0.18	0.08	0.01	0.23	0.39	1.40	.25
total behaviour score (Rutter B2)	0.15	−0.14	0.21	0.13	0.44	3.10	< .05
neurotic behaviour at school (Rutter B2)	0.06	−0.15	0.25	−0.07	0.22	2.96	< .05
antisocial behaviour at school (Rutter B2)	0.11	−0.08	0.13	0.00	0.39	2.62	.05
global maladjustment (10 measures – sum score)	0.32	0.21	0.24	0.36	0.49	1.03	.38
neurotic behaviour (5 measures – sum score)	0.29	0.26	0.33	0.19	0.39	0.53	.67
antisocial behaviour (5 measures – sum score)	0.25	0.08	0.07	0.40	0.45	2.59	.05
		(b) base to final follow-up					
parent interview							
antisocial behaviour (B)	0.36	0.21	0.05	0.50	0.72	7.61	< .01
psychosomatic behaviour (C)	0.57	0.43	0.52	0.60	0.75	1.91	.13
aggregate behaviour (A + B + C)	0.72	0.54	0.49	0.82	1.05	4.90	< .01
activity	0.51	0.38	0.38	0.56	0.71	2.18	.09
mood	0.56	0.45	0.37	0.73	0.70	3.56	< .05
total behaviour score (Rutter B2)	0.10	−0.33	0.02	0.16	0.58	6.62	< .01
neurotic behaviour at school (Rutter B2)	−0.09	−0.59	0.00	0.06	0.20	5.83	< .01
antisocial behaviour at school (Rutter B2)	0.15	−0.06	0.04	0.05	0.59	5.26	< .01
global maladjustment (10 measures – sum score)	0.71	0.44	0.54	0.80	1.09	5.73	< .01
neurotic behaviour (5 measures – sum score)	0.55	0.28	0.57	0.63	0.75	3.03	< .05
antisocial behaviour (5 measures – sum score)	0.61	0.43	0.32	0.69	1.04	6.80	< .01
n =	201	52	52	48	49		

Table A3(7)   *Significant differences (paired comparisons) Devereux scale items: juniors*

item	treatments better than controls			between treatments		
	treatment	F ratio	p <	treatment	F ratio	p <
(a) midline follow-up						
1 classroom disturbance	PG	14.98	.01			
2 impatience	JPC (D)	5.67	.05			
	NW (D)	5.74	.05			
4 external blame	NW	9.53	.05	NW > JPC	6.11	.05
7 lack of comprehension	JPC	7.44	.05			
	PG	8.29	.05			
8 inattentive/withdrawn	JPC (D)	6.77	.05			
	NW (D)	6.45	.05			
11 needs closeness*	JPC	11.54	.01			
	NW	7.31	.05			
13 quits easily	PG	10.68	.01	PG > NW	6.56	.05
14 slow work	JPC	9.31	.05	JPC > NW	6.73	.05
	PG	5.77	.05			
aggregate (sum of 13 items)	JPC (D)	5.96	.05			
	PG (D)	6.38	.05			
(b) final follow-up						
1 classroom disturbance	PG (D)	5.67	.05			
2 impatience	JPC	12.31	.01			
	NW	10.97	.01			
	PG	8.28	.01			
4 external blame	NW (D)	6.69	.05			
7 lack of comprehension	JPC	6.79	.05			
	NW	7.09	.05			
	PG	10.39	.01			
12 unable to change	PG	8.62	.05			
13 quits easily	NW	6.64	.05			
aggregate (sum of 13 items)	JPC	7.77	.05			
	NW	8.29	.05			
	PG	12.36	.01			

Note: > means 'better than' in this table; 'D' indicates that the F ratio is significant by Dunnett's method (see pp. 346 and 354); * JPC and NW children needed more closeness than controls.

Table A3(8)   *Significant differences (paired comparisons) non-Devereux scale measures: juniors*

measure	treatments better than controls			between treatments		
	treatment	F ratio	p <	treatment	F ratio	p <
(a) midline follow-up						
parent interview						
antisocial behaviour (scale A)	NW (D)	6.04	.05			
psychosomatic behaviour (scale C)				PG > JPC	7.91	.05
total behaviour score (Rutter B2)	PG	8.88	.05			
antisocial behaviour at school (Rutter B2)	PG	8.30	.05			
(b) final follow-up						
parent interview						
antisocial behaviour	PG	13.61	.01	PG > JPC	19.63	.01
(scale B)	NW	4.82	.05	NW > JPC	8.68	.01
psychosomatic behaviour (scale C)	PG (D)	5.85	.05			
aggregate behaviour (scale A + B + C)	PG	10.42	.01	PG > JPC	13.84	.01
mood				PG > JPC	7.28	.05
				NW > JPC	6.32	.05
total behaviour score (Rutter B2)	PG	24.24	.01	PG> JPC	9.88	.01
neurotic behaviour	JPC	8.54	.05			
at school	NW	7.07	.05			
(Rutter B2)	PG	11.81	.01			
antisocial behaviour at	PG	19.09	.01	PG > JPC	10.70	.01
school (Rutter B2)				PG > NW	7.78	.05
isolation	JPC (D)	6.49	.05			
global maladjustment (10 measures – sum score)	PG	19.56	.01	PG > JPC	14.57	.01
neurotic behaviour (5 measures – sum score)	PG	8.33	.05			
antisocial behaviour (5 measures – sum score)	PG	18.87	.01	PG > JPC	21.07	.01
				PG > NW	3.90	.05

Note: > means 'better than' in this table; 'D' indicates that the F ratio is significant by Dunnett's method (see pp. 346 and 354).

Table A3(9)   *Improvement (adjusted change means) Devereux scale items: seniors*

item		grand change mean	adjusted change means				F ratio	p
			MC	PC	BM	SG		
			(a) base to end of treatment					
10 lack of creative initiative		0.03	−0.03	−0.28	−0.38	0.08	8.19	< .05
11 needs closeness		0.09	0.32	0.36	−0.24	−0.15	12.67	< .05
	n =	286	75	78	70	63		
			(b) base to midline follow-up					
10 lack of creative initiative		−0.07	−0.05	−0.28	−0.06	0.12	2.34	.07
11 needs closeness		0.29	0.35	0.32	0.40	0.04	2.09	.10
	n =	257	72	69	62	54		
			(c) base to final follow-up					
10 lack of creative initiative		0.18	0.04	0.15	0.29	0.27	0.87	.46
11 needs closeness		0.30	0.47	0.29	0.31	0.08	2.11	.10
	n =	257	72	69	62	54		

Note: there was a significantly greater need for closeness immediately after end of treatment in the case of behaviour modification and group therapy. This subsequently washed out.

Table A3(10)   *Improvement (adjusted change means) Barker Lunn scale items: seniors*

item	grand change mean	adjusted change means				F ratio	p
		MC	PC	BM	SG		
		(a) base to end of treatment					
1 poor attitude to school	−0.21	−0.44	−0.33	0.01	0.01	4.71	< .01
2 lack of interest in school work	−0.27	−0.38	−0.45	−0.03	−0.15	3.31	< .05
6 non-conforming	−0.11	−0.04	−0.28	0.02	−0.16	1.92	.13
7 poor relationship with teacher	−0.19	−0.28	−0.28	−0.04	−0.20	2.10	.10
8 anxiety about school work	0.07	−0.05	0.02	0.23	0.13	1.24	.30
9 poor social adjustment	0.01	−0.08	−0.10	0.09	0.17	1.45	.23
aggregate of items 8–10 neurotic anxiety about school	0.06	−0.03	−0.10	0.32	0.09	3.18	< .05
n =	287	82	77	68	60		
		(b) base to midline follow-up					
1 poor attitude to school	−0.29	−0.43	−0.39	−0.21	−0.12	1.69	.17
2 lack of interest in school work	−0.35	−0.34	−0.45	−0.31	−0.28	0.42	.74
6 non-conforming	−0.11	−0.03	−0.21	0.12	−0.08	0.64	.59
7 poor relationship with teacher	−0.22	−0.29	−0.29	−0.17	−0.11	0.56	.64
8 anxiety about school work	0.15	−0.06	0.04	0.37	0.32	3.83	< .05
9 poor social adjustment	0.09	−0.05	−0.11	0.26	0.32	3.67	< .05
aggregate of items 8–10 neurotic anxiety about school	0.16	−0.01	−0.02	0.39	0.36	5.78	< .01
n =	274	79	73	65	57		
		(c) base to final follow-up					
1 poor attitude to school	−0.24	−0.37	−0.35	−0.14	−0.03	2.03	.11
2 lack of interest in school work	−0.16	−0.22	−0.10	−0.09	−0.22	0.54	.78
6 non-conforming	−0.15	−0.08	−0.39	0.00	−0.12	3.22	< .05
7 poor relationship with teacher	−0.23	−0.42	−0.31	−0.10	−0.01	2.85	< .05
8 anxiety about school work	0.41	0.36	0.30	0.67	0.33	1.89	.13
9 poor social adjustment	0.29	0.30	0.23	0.37	0.28	0.30	.83
aggregate of items 8–10 neurotic anxiety about school	0.39	0.34	0.31	0.60	0.33	1.97	.12
n =	274	79	73	65	57		

Table A3(11)   *Improvement (adjusted change means) school measures (excluding Devereux and Barker Lunn scales): seniors*

measure	grand change mean	adjusted change means				F ratio	p
		MC	PC	BM	SG		
(a) base to end of treatment							
isolation (sociometry)	0.02	−0.06	−0.18	0.39	−0.04	5.47	< .01
neuroticism (JEPI)	0.22	0.23	−0.03	0.49	0.22	4.22	< .01
introversion (JEPI)	0.27	0.31	0.32	0.15	0.30	0.59	.63
verbal ability (NCDS)	0.05	−0.01	0.04	0.10	0.09	0.67	.57
non-verbal ability (NCDS)	−0.02	−0.05	0.01	−0.05	0.04	0.28	.84
total ability (NCDS)	0.02	−0.02	0.02	0.03	0.08	0.37	.78
reading comprehension	0.29	0.29	0.21	0.39	0.30	0.78	.51
n =	290	81	80	68	61		
(b) base to midline follow-up							
total behaviour score (Rutter B2)	0.31	0.16	0.35	0.30	0.47	1.04	.38
neurotic behaviour at school (Rutter B2)	0.25	0.21	0.22	0.25	0.35	0.21	.89
antisocial behaviour at school (Rutter B2)	0.26	0.12	0.33	0.20	0.43	1.82	.14
isolation (sociometry)	−0.07	−0.04	−0.12	0.15	−0.31	2.93	< .05
neuroticism (JEPI)	0.38	0.23	−0.04	0.80	0.66	11.00	< .01
introversion (JEPI)	0.37	0.37	0.39	0.26	0.48	0.54	.66
verbal ability (NCDS)	0.21	−0.02	0.05	0.47	0.47	9.21	< .01
non-verbal ability (NCDS)	0.12	−0.08	−0.01	0.31	0.37	4.79	< .01
total ability (NCDS)	0.18	−0.04	0.02	0.41	0.45	7.89	< .01
reading comprehension	0.33	0.30	0.25	0.40	0.39	0.52	.67
n =	257	72	72	62	51		
(c) base to final follow-up							
total behaviour score (Rutter B2)	0.26	−0.07	0.20	0.42	0.60	4.54	< .01
neurotic behaviour at school (Rutter B2)	0.15	−0.01	−0.04	0.37	0.33	3.82	< .05
antisocial behaviour at school (Rutter B2)	0.19	−0.02	0.22	0.17	0.46	3.12	< .05
isolation (sociometry)	−0.09	−0.21	−0.29	0.05	0.19	3.62	< .05
neuroticism (JEPI)	0.67	0.51	0.69	0.89	0.62	1.64	.18
introversion (JEPI)	0.28	0.03	0.21	0.55	0.44	2.90	< .05
verbal ability (NCDS)	0.67	0.64	0.56	0.68	0.86	0.80	.50
non-verbal ability (NCDS)	0.62	0.56	0.56	0.60	0.80	0.79	.50
total ability (NCDS)	0.67	0.60	0.57	0.69	0.91	1.60	.19
reading comprehension	0.74	0.74	0.53	1.02	0.72	3.05	< .05
n =	257	72	72	62	51		

Table A3(12)   *Improvement (adjusted change means) parental and aggregate measures: seniors*

measure	grand change mean	adjusted change means				F ratio	p
		MC	PC	BM	SG		
(a) base to end of treatment							
total score (Rutter A)	0.18	0.26	0.24	−0.10	0.23	2.89	< .05
antisocial scale (Rutter A)	0.05	0.08	0.16	−0.11	0.03	1.64	.18
n =	290	81	80	68	61		
(b) base to midline follow-up							
parent interview							
antisocial behaviour (B)	0.21	0.11	0.13	0.23	0.44	1.27	.29
psychosomatic behaviour (C)	0.14	−0.01	0.19	0.06	0.38	2.50	.06
aggregate behaviour (A + B + C)	0.30	0.12	0.23	0.35	0.59	2.82	< .05
withdrawal	0.42	0.51	0.37	0.49	0.27	1.19	.32
activity	0.35	0.26	0.02	0.65	0.59	4.78	< .01
mood	0.31	0.42	0.15	0.21	0.45	1.49	.22
total score (Rutter A)	0.24	0.33	0.18	−0.02	0.46	2.80	< .05
antisocial scale (Rutter A)	0.16	0.25	0.13	0.10	0.34	2.94	< .05
global maladjustment (14 measures – sum score)	0.59	0.47	0.42	0.66	0.90	2.92	< .05
neurotic behaviour (9 measures – sum score)	0.50	0.36	0.36	0.70	0.67	2.52	.06
antisocial behaviour (5 measures – sum score)	0.45	0.41	0.30	0.34	0.82	3.17	< .05
n =	240	75	64	51	50		
(c) base to final follow-up							
parent interview							
antisocial behaviour (B)	0.29	0.07	0.18	0.59	0.46	3.44	< .05
psychosomatic behaviour (C)	0.68	0.68	0.55	0.71	0.83	2.00	.11
aggregate behaviour (A + B + C)	0.74	0.59	0.57	0.94	0.98	3.22	< .05
withdrawal	0.32	0.30	0.60	0.18	0.14	5.03	< .01
activity	0.53	0.48	0.36	0.69	0.66	1.76	.16
mood	0.56	0.62	0.23	0.69	0.75	4.82	< .01
total score (Rutter A)	0.36	0.33	0.16	0.45	0.56	2.42	.07
antisocial scale (Rutter A)	0.25	0.27	0.11	0.31	0.34	0.88	.45
global maladjustment (14 measures – sum score)	0.82	0.58	0.73	1.08	1.06	4.63	< .01
neurotic behaviour (9 measures – sum score)	0.75	0.53	0.67	1.00	0.94	4.52	< .01
antisocial behaviour (5 measures – sum score)	0.61	0.42	0.52	0.77	0.83	2.49	.06
n =	240	75	64	51	50		

Table A3(13) *Significant differences (paired comparisons) Devereux scale items: seniors (base to end of treatment)*

item	treatments and controls			between treatments		
	treatment	F ratio	p <	treatment	F ratio	p <
10 lack of creative initiative	BM > MC	11.35	.01	BM > PC	19.38	.01
				BM > SG	6.13	.05
				SG > PC	4.95	.05
11 needs closeness	BM > MC	21.80	.01	BM > PC	22.26	.01
	SG > MC	15.26	.01	SG > PC	17.23	.01

Note: there were no significant differences at base to midline follow-up or at base to final follow-up; > means 'better than' in this table; for an explanation of changes in the item 'needs closeness' see Chapter 9.

Table A3(14) *Significant differences (paired comparisons) Barker Lunn scale items: seniors*

item	treatments better than controls			between treatments		
	treatment	F ratio	p <	treatment	F ratio	p <
	(a) base to end of treatment					
1 poor attitude to school	BM	7.44	.05			
	SG	7.54	.05			
2 lack of interest in school work				BM > PC	7.53	.05
aggregate of items 8–10 neurotic anxiety about school				BM > PC	8.77	.05
	(b) base to midline follow-up					
3 unimportance of doing well	PC (D)	5.83	.05			
8 anxiety about school work	BM	8.27	.05			
	SG	7.45	.05			
9 poor social adjustment	SG	5.77	.05	BM > PC	7.34	.05
				SG > PC	8.54	.05
aggregate of items 8–10 neurotic anxiety about school	BM	7.08	.05	BM > PC	8.29	.05
	SG	7.63	.05	SG > PC	9.32	.05
	(c) base to final follow-up					
6 non-conforming				BM > PC	9.67	.05

Note: > means 'better than' in this table; 'D' indicates that the F ratio is significant by Dunnett's method (see pp. 346 and 354).

Table A3(15) *Significant differences (paired comparisons) non-Devereux and non-Barker Lunn school measures: seniors*

measure	treatments and controls			between treatments		
	treatment	F ratio	p <	treatment	F ratio	p <
(a) base to end of treatment						
isolation (sociometry)	BM > MC	7.47	.05	BM > PC	12.11	.01
				BM > SG	7.40	.05
neuroticism (JEPI)				BM > PC	10.75	.01
(b) base to midline follow-up						
isolation (sociometry)				BM > SG	8.69	.05
neuroticism (JEPI)	MC > PC	3.92	.05	BM > PC	32.67	.01
	BM > MC	12.30	.01	SG > PC	15.95	.01
	SG > MC	4.77	.05			
verbal ability (NCDS)	BM > MC	14.74	.01	BM > PC	18.71	.01
	SG > MC	10.60	.01	SG > PC	16.30	.01
non-verbal ability (NCDS)	BM > MC	5.86	.05	BM > PC	6.90	.05
	SG > MC	8.21	.05	SG > PC	11.33	.01
total ability (NCDS)	BM > MC	11.45	.01	BM > PC	14.73	.01
	SG > MC	10.77	.01	SG > PC	17.55	.01
(c) base to final follow-up						
total score (Rutter B2)	BM > MC	6.25	.05			
	SG > MC	14.61	.01			
neurotic score (Rutter B2)	BM > MC	6.47	.05			
	SG > MC	7.06	.05			
antisocial score (Rutter B2)	SG > MC	9.85	.05			
isolation (sociometry)	SG > MC	5.82	.05	SG > PC	7.15	.05
introversion (JEPI)	BM > MC	7.60	.05			
reading comprehension				BM > PC	10.47	.01

Note: > means 'better than' in this table.

Table A3(16)   *Significant differences (paired comparisons) parental and aggregate measures: seniors*

measure	treatments and controls			between treatments		
	treatment	F ratio	p <	treatment	F ratio	p <
(a) base to end of treatment						
total score (Rutter A)	MC > BM	9.27	.05	SG > BM	6.11	.05
(b) base to midline follow-up						
parent interview psychosomatic behaviour (C)	SG > MC (D)	6.87	.05			
aggregate behaviour (A + B + C)	SG > MC	8.62	.05	SG > PC	5.67	.05
activity				BM > PC SG > PC	10.46 11.28	.01 .01
total score (Rutter A)	MC > BM	7.82	.05	SG > BM	8.77	.05
antisocial score (Rutter A)	MC > BM	7.30	.05	SG > BM	7.37	.05
global maladjustment (14 measures – sum score)	SG > MC	7.31	.05	SG > PC	10.99	.01
antisocial behaviour (5 measures – sum score)	SG > MC	6.79	.05	SG > PC SG > BM	13.15 6.52	.01 .05
(c) base to final follow-up						
parent interview antisocial behaviour (C)	BM > MC	8.19	.05			
aggregate behaviour (A + B + C)	SG > MC (D)	5.80	.05			
withdrawal	PC > MC	7.25	.05	PC > BM PC > SG	12.31 15.02	.01 .01
mood				SG > PC	9.24	05
global maladjustment (14 measures – sum score)	BM > MC SG > MC	9.93 9.82	.05 .05			
neurotic behaviour (9 measures – sum score)	BM > MC SG > MC	10.40 8.15	.01 .05			

Note: > means 'better than' in this table; 'D' indicates that the F ratio is significant by Dunnett's method (see pp. 346 and 354).

Table A3(17)   *Interaction of regimes with pattern of behaviour (neurotic and antisocial): juniors*

treatment regime	improvement (adjusted change means)			
	base to midline follow-up		base to final follow-up	
	neurotic behaviour	antisocial behaviour	neurotic behaviour	antisocial behaviour
at-risk controls	0.26	0.08	0.28	0.43
junior parent counselling–teacher consultation	0.33	0.07	0.57	0.32
nurture work	0.19	0.40	0.63	0.69
playgroups	0.39	0.45	0.75	1.04
F ratio (interaction regime × behaviour)	2.72		3.11	
degrees of freedom	3 and 196		3 and 196	
p	< .05		< .05	

Table A3(18)   *Diagnostic categories and improvement: Devereux scale items: juniors*

item	grand change mean	adjusted change means		F ratio	p
		conduct-disordered children	neurotic children		
		(a) base to midline follow-up			
1 classroom disturbance	0.10	−0.12	0.27	8.84	< .01
4 external blame	0.15	0.06	0.23	1.78	.18
5 achievement anxiety	−0.01	0.17	−0.15	6.31	< .05
9 irrelevant responses	0.04	−0.11	0.16	5.02	< .05
13 quits easily	0.07	0.13	0.02	0.72	.40
aggregate (sum of 13 items)	0.18	0.15	0.20	0.33	.56
		(b) base to final follow-up			
1 classroom disturbance	0.35	0.19	0.47	5.29	< .05
4 external blame	0.19	−0.02	0.37	9.96	< .01
5 achievement anxiety	−0.04	0.00	−0.07	0.28	.60
9 irrelevant responses	0.10	−0.11	0.27	9.50	< .01
13 quits easily	0.43	0.17	0.64	14.78	< .01
aggregate (sum of 13 items)	0.35	0.23	0.45	5.54	< .05
n =	201	91	110		

Note: item 3 has been omitted from the aggregate score (see p. 351).

Table A3(19) *Diagnostic categories and improvement: non-Devereux scale measures: juniors*

measure	grand change mean	adjusted change means		F ratio	p
		conduct-disordered children	neurotic children		
		(a) base to midline follow-up			
parent interview					
neurotic behaviour	0.30	0.40	0.21	1.64	.20
antisocial behaviour	0.16	−0.06	0.35	8.57	< .01
activity	0.15	−0.09	0.35	8.68	< .01
neurotic scale (Rutter B2)	0.09	0.26	−0.05	6.10	< .05
antisocial scale (Rutter B2)	0.15	0.06	0.22	1.17	.28
antisocial behaviour					
(5 measures – sum score)	0.25	0.10	0.38	4.17	< .05
		(b) base to final follow-up			
parent interview					
neurotic behaviour	0.61	0.86	0.39	9.17	< .01
antisocial behaviour	0.36	0.35	0.37	0.03	.87
activity	0.53	0.54	0.52	0.02	.88
neurotic scale (Rutter B2)	−0.02	−0.01	−0.05	1.58	.21
antisocial scale (Rutter B2)	0.18	−0.02	0.32	4.03	< .05
antisocial behaviour					
(5 measures – sum score)	0.61	0.60	0.62	0.03	.87
n =	186	86	100		

Table A3(20) *Diagnostic categories and improvement: Devereux scale items: seniors*

item	grand change mean	adjusted change means		F ratio	p
		conduct-disordered children	neurotic children		
		(a) base to midline follow-up			
4 external blame	0.12	0.09	0.14	0.38	.54
8 inattentive/withdrawn	0.24	0.16	0.31	2.01	.16
9 irrelevant responses	0.07	−0.09	0.19	6.57	< .05
12 unable to change	0.19	0.22	0.16	0.31	.58
13 quits easily	0.09	0.08	0.09	0.01	.90
aggregate (sum of 14 items)	0.19	0.18	0.20	0.03	.87
		(b) base to final follow-up			
4 external blame	−0.10	−0.25	0.02	4.58	< .05
8 inattentive/withdrawn	0.23	0.05	0.38	8.72	< .01
9 irrelevant responses	−0.03	−0.23	0.13	6.97	< .01
12 unable to change	0.20	0.07	0.30	4.86	< .05
13 quits easily	0.02	−0.16	0.16	7.49	< .01
aggregate (sum of 14 items)	0.14	0.01	0.24	4.77	< .05
n =	254	111	143		

Table A3(21)   *Diagnostic categories and improvement: Barker Lunn scale items: seniors*

item	grand change mean	adjusted change means		F ratio	p
		conduct-disordered children	neurotic children		
		(a) base to midline follow-up			
8 anxiety about school work	0.14	0.30	0.01	6.33	< .05
aggregate of items 8–10 neurotic anxiety about school	0.15	0.28	0.05	5.36	< .05
		(b) base to final follow-up			
8 anxiety about school work	0.41	0.53	0.30	3.49	.06
aggregate of items 8–10 neurotic anxiety about school	0.39	0.42	0.37	0.23	.63
n =	270	119	151		

Table A3(22)   *Diagnostic categories and improvement: ability and achievement: seniors*

school measure	grand change mean	adjusted change means		F ratio	p
		conduct-disordered children	neurotic children		
		(a) base to midline follow-up			
verbal ability (NCDS)	0.23	0.17	0.27	1.07	.30
non-verbal ability (NCDS)	0.12	0.00	0.21	3.99	< .05
reading comprehension	0.33	0.23	0.40	3.58	.06
		(b) base to final follow-up			
verbal ability (NCDS)	0.67	0.52	0.79	4.88	< .05
non-verbal ability (NCDS)	0.62	0.48	0.72	4.35	< .05
reading comprehension	0.74	0.56	0.89	7.84	< .01
n =	253	111	142		

Note: none of the other school analyses (excluding Devereux and Barker Lunn scales) was significant.

Table A3(23)   *Diagnostic categories and improvement: parental and aggregate measures of behaviour: seniors*

measure	grand change mean	adjusted change means		F ratio	p
		conduct-disordered children	neurotic children		
		(a) base to midline follow-up			
parent interview					
somatic disturbance	−0.03	0.15	−0.17	8.13	< .01
activity	0.35	0.18	0.49	5.30	< .05
mood	0.32	0.19	0.43	4.49	< .05
neurotic scale (Rutter A)	0.10	0.23	0.00	4.78	< .05
antisocial scale (Rutter A)	0.17	0.01	0.29	7.55	< .01
antisocial behaviour					
(5 measures – sum score)	0.45	0.30	0.57	4.02	< .05
		(b) base to final follow-up			
parent interview					
somatic disturbance	0.25	0.31	0.19	1.83	.18
activity	0.54	0.31	0.73	13.35	< .01
mood	0.57	0.53	0.60	0.43	.51
neurotic scale (Rutter A)	0.22	0.20	0.25	0.23	.63
antisocial scale (Rutter A)	0.25	0.18	0.32	1.55	.22
antisocial behaviour					
(5 measures – sum score)	0.61	0.43	0.76	5.81	< .05
n =	236	106	130		

Note: aggregate measures include information from parents, school, and child.

Table A3(24)   *Sex and improvement: Devereux scale items: juniors*

item	grand change mean	adjusted change means		F ratio	p
		male	female		
		(a) base to midline follow-up			
1 classroom disturbance	0.11	−0.09	0.39	17.99	< .01
2 impatience	0.10	0.03	0.19	2.21	.14
4 external blame	0.11	0.17	0.04	1.22	.27
7 lack of comprehension	0.17	0.08	0.29	4.98	< .05
9 irrelevant responses	0.03	−0.09	0.20	6.74	< .05
13 quits easily	0.06	0.02	0.11	0.45	.50
aggregate (sum of 13 items)	0.18	0.14	0.23	1.13	.29
		(b) base to final follow-up			
1 classroom disturbance	0.38	0.19	0.63	17.71	< .01
2 impatience	0.18	0.02	0.39	11.45	< .01
4 external blame	0.13	0.00	0.31	6.66	< .05
7 lack of comprehension	0.15	0.12	0.19	0.45	.51
9 irrelevant responses	0.10	−0.04	0.29	8.34	< .01
13 quits easily	0.39	0.27	0.56	6.09	< .05
aggregate (sum of 13 items)	0.35	0.26	0.47	4.89	< .05
n =	216	125	91		

Note: item 3 has been omitted from the aggregate score (see p. 351).

Table A3(25)   *Sex and improvement: non-Devereux scale measures: juniors*

measure	grand change mean	adjusted change means		F ratio	p
		male	female		
		(a) base to midline follow-up			
parent interview					
mood	0.18	0.24	0.07	1.36	.25
neurotic scale (Rutter A)	0.17	0.26	0.03	4.40	< .05
neurotic scale (Rutter B2)	0.06	0.15	−0.07	3.30	.07
antisocial scale (Rutter B2)	0.11	−0.02	0.31	6.01	< .05
		(b) base to final follow-up			
parent interview					
mood	0.56	0.64	0.43	4.63	< .05
neurotic scale (Rutter A)	0.25	0.29	0.20	0.50	.48
neurotic scale (Rutter B2)	−0.09	0.05	−0.30	5.24	< .05
antisocial scale (Rutter B2)	0.15	0.08	0.26	1.87	.17
n =	201	120	81		

Table A3(26)   *Sex and improvement: Devereux scale items: seniors*

item	grand change mean	adjusted change means		F ratio	p
		male	female		
		(a) base to midline follow-up			
1 classroom disturbance	0.07	0.00	0.16	2.20	.14
2 impatience	0.09	−0.07	0.29	12.21	< .01
4 external reliance	0.25	0.14	0.38	5.56	< .05
8 inattentive/withdrawn	0.24	0.09	0.43	10.69	< .01
		(b) base to final follow-up			
1 classroom disturbance	0.06	−0.07	0.21	5.91	< .05
2 impatience	0.10	−0.06	0.30	9.90	< .01
4 external reliance	0.17	0.17	0.16	0.00	.96
8 inattentive/withdrawn	0.24	0.13	0.36	3.82	.05
n =	257	142	115		

Table A3(27)   *Sex and improvement: Barker Lunn scale items: seniors*

item	grand change mean	adjusted change means		F ratio	p
		male	female		
		(a) base to midline follow-up			
4 attitude to class	−0.04	−0.16	0.11	4.93	< .05
8 anxiety about school work	0.15	0.32	−0.08	12.95	< .01
10 academic self-image	0.10	0.20	0.04	4.97	< .05
aggregate of items 8–10 neurotic anxiety about school	0.16	0.31	−0.04	14.05	< .01
		(b) base to final follow-up			
4 attitude to class	0.13	0.16	0.10	0.33	.56
8 anxiety about school work	0.41	0.55	0.23	6.82	< .01
10 academic self-image	0.14	0.28	−0.04	6.63	< .05
aggregate of items 8–10 neurotic anxiety about school	0.39	0.51	0.23	8.54	< .01
n =	274	155	119		

Table A3(28)   *Sex and improvement: non-Devereux and non-Barker Lunn school measures: seniors*

measure	grand change mean	adjusted change means		F ratio	p
		male	female		
		(a) base to midline follow-up			
neurotic scale (Rutter B2)	0.25	0.40	0.07	7.81	< .01
neuroticism (JEPI)	0.38	0.51	0.22	5.52	< .05
		(b) base to final follow-up			
neurotic scale (Rutter B2)	0.15	0.17	0.12	0.13	.72
neuroticism (JEPI)	0.67	1.00	0.29	32.84	< .01
n =	257	140	117		

Table A3(29)   *Sex and improvement: parental and aggregate measures: seniors*

measure	grand change mean	adjusted change means		F ratio	p
		male	female		
		(a) base to midline follow-up			
parent interview					
psychosomatic behaviour					
(C)	0.14	0.24	0.01	5.16	< .05
somatic disturbance	−0.02	0.10	−0.16	5.41	< .05
activity	0.35	0.30	0.41	0.72	.40
total score (Rutter A)	0.24	0.15	0.36	4.45	< .05
neurotic behaviour					
(9 measures – sum score)	0.50	0.61	0.36	5.24	< .05
		(b) base to final follow-up			
parent interview					
psychosomatic behaviour					
(C)	0.68	0.70	0.66	0.30	.58
somatic disturbance	0.25	0.33	0.15	4.20	< .05
activity	0.53	0.38	0.72	8.64	< .01
total score (Rutter A)	0.36	0.33	0.39	0.35	.56
neurotic behaviour					
(9 measures – sum score)	0.75	0.89	0.69	7.33	< .01
n =	240	133	107		

Appendix 4: School and therapist effects on outcome

Introduction

Throughout the research we have tried to isolate components of therapy that may be helpful as opposed to those that may be redundant. We outlined in Chapter 1 the differences between direct and indirect therapies, behaviourist and dynamic approaches, and the possible effects of differences among the children, such as diagnosis and sex. However, there are other possible differences that we have not yet examined and two of these merit very special examination.

The first is the effect of school characteristics on the educational progress and behaviour of the child. It is now well established that schools vary greatly in their levels of truancy, delinquency, behaviour problems, and poor attainment and there is evidence that, in addition to a child's background characteristics the school itself has a very important impact on a child's development. As we have mentioned in Chapter 1, Rutter and his colleagues (1979) measured the characteristics of groups of children before they entered various secondary schools and were then able to chart the changes that occurred through a follow-up in the schools. In subsequent studies Rutter's group was able to identify characteristics of the school that were associated with good progress.

The most successful schools were those where the teachers set good standards of behaviour and where good work was acknowledged and praised in a variety of ways. It seemed more important that lessons were well prepared and conducted than that there was a good system of pastoral care.

In the present study there were similar differences in the progress of the children in different schools. Measures were made of school characteristics (Mullin 1979) and these will be reported elsewhere. For the present, we need to be aware that the school itself was likely to have had an important effect on the children's progress, independent of the treatment regimes.

The second set of differences were in the therapeutic qualities of the therapists. In a previous publication (Nicol *et al.* 1977) we have reported and examined a variety of measures we used to estimate therapeutic qualities. These included direct observations (made during the senior group therapy sessions) of therapists' accurate empathy, non-possessive warmth and genuineness, and of group qualities of group cohesiveness and openness of discussion. In addition, the supervisors of the project rated the therapists on a series of characteristics it was thought may be important in their effectiveness. A third source of data was the therapists' reports on their subjective reactions to the children and the reports of the children on their subjective reactions to the groups.

A large number of the supervisor-rated therapist qualities, including warmth, empathy, clinical and social judgement, good relations with colleagues and with those in authority, and a positive attitude to therapy, showed a strong positive correlation (i.e. 0.65 to 0.90) with direct ratings of warmth and empathy. Only supervisor-rated neuroticism correlated negatively with these directly rated qualities. There were also correlations between supervisor ratings of assertiveness, positive attitude to therapy, and openness and the direct rating of openness of discussion in the groups. All these inter-correlations seemed to suggest that the ratings were measuring important variables that could be measured in a variety of different ways.

In this section we compare the progress of the children treated by the different therapists. Each therapist was involved in four different treatments, i.e. junior parent counselling-teacher consultation, senior parent counselling-teacher consultation, playgroups, and senior group therapy. For the two junior regimes each therapist worked within one school; the same applied for the two senior regimes. This meant that the school characteristics constituted a confounding variable. In order to try to partial out the effect of the school and get an estimate of which were the effective therapists, we correlated the mean outcome score for each therapist in the different regimes, both in the junior and senior schools. We postulated that if correlations between senior and junior regimes were high then there was justification for thinking that the differences were due to therapist rather than school qualities. If the correlations were low, this would tend to indicate that school characteristics were more important than those of the therapist.

Method

The mean outcome scores for each therapist for every regime were calculated for baseline to first follow-up (eighteen months) and baseline to second follow-up (three years). The six therapists were then ranked according to their relative effectiveness in each regime in each of these follow-ups. These ranks were then intercorrelated using Spearman's rank correlation method between pairs of regimes. The resulting correlations are shown in *Table A4(1)*.

The table shows that at first follow-up three of the six intercorrelations were very high. Two of these three high correlations were between junior and senior regimes, suggesting that the same therapists were effective in junior and senior schools, at least as regards parent counselling-teacher consultation and playgroups. Senior group therapy appeared to be relatively independent.

At the second follow-up the only high correlation was between the two senior regimes so that effects could have been due to school differences as well as therapist differences.

These data are consistent, at least, with the possibility that in the early post-treatment phase therapist effects were strong enough to outweigh school effects, whereas at the three-year follow-up school effects were the most powerful determinants of outcome.

Table A4(1) *Correlations of six therapists' effectiveness in four different treatment regimes*

treatment regime	base to midline follow-up			
	1. junior parent counselling- teacher consultation	2. playgroups	3. senior parent counselling- teacher consultation	4. senior group therapy
regime 2	0.94			
regime 3	0.89	0.77		
regime 4	0.26	0.43	0.43	
	base to final follow-up			
	1.	2.	3.	4.
regime 2	−0.14			
regime 3	0.31	−0.14		
regime 4	0.09	−0.20	0.88	

THERAPEUTIC QUALITIES OF THERAPIST AND OUTCOME

Having established that characteristics of individual therapists may have some importance, at least in the early post-treatment stage, we can go on to ask what the important qualities of the effective therapist are. To examine this the therapeutic quality scores of the therapists, based on supervisor ratings, were ranked and correlated with the ranked outcomes from the different therapists on each of the various treatment regimes. The result was a large number of correlations, and we now give an overview of the findings.

Strong positive correlations occurred between outcome measures and the therapeutic qualities of extroversion, treatment assertiveness, and openness.

Strong negative correlations occurred between some outcome measures and the qualities of empathy, warmth and genuineness, neuroticism, charm, and good relationships.

Apart from neuroticism, these negative correlations were the opposite to what was expected (Truax and Carkhuff 1967). Empathy and warmth, in particular, have been found to correlate positively with outcome in other clinic- and hospital-based outcome studies. We suggest that different therapeutic qualities are required in school intervention than in clinic or inpatient intervention. It seems logical that in the hurly-burly of the school, which, after all, is not primarily designed to provide therapy, a greater degree of assertiveness and extroversion is needed than in the clinic and that the sensitive, empathic therapist may well be overwhelmed in a school setting.

Finally, it should be added that we regard these findings as indicators as to what may be important therapeutic qualities in the school. This is a most important topic which merits further research.

References

Abidin, R. R. (1971) What's Wrong with Behaviour Modification? *Journal of School Psychology* **9**: 38–42.

Abraham, K. A. (1972) The Effectiveness of Structured Sociodrama in Altering Classroom Behavior of 5th Grade Students. *Dissertation Abstracts Int.* **32**A: 3677–778.

Abramowitz, C. V. (1976) The Effectiveness of Group Psychotherapy with Children. *Archives of General Psychiatry* **33**: 320–26.

Abramowitz, C. V., Abramowitz, S. I., Roback, H. B., Jackson, C. (1974) Differential Effectiveness of Directive and Nondirective Group Therapies as a Function of Client Internal-External Control. *Journal of Consulting Clinical Psychology* **42**: 849–53.

Adams, P. L. (1975) Children and Para-services of the Community Mental Health Centers. *Journal of American Academy of Child Psychiatry* **14**(1): 18–31.

Adams, S. (1970) The PICO Project. In N. Johnson, L. Savitz, and M. E. Wolfgang (eds) *The Sociology of Punishment and Correction*. New York: John Wiley.

Alexander, J. F. and Parsons, B. V. (1973) Short-Term Behavioural Intervention with Delinquent Families: Impact on Family Process and Recidivism. *Journal of Abnormal Psychology* **51**: 219–33.

Allen, K. E., Hart, B. M., Buell, J. S., Harris, F. R., and Wolf, M. M. (1964) Effects of Social Reinforcement on Isolate Behavior of a Nursery School Child. *Child Development* **35**: 511–18.

Allen, K. E., Turner, K. D., and Everett, P. M. (1970) A Behavior Modification Classroom for Head Start Children with Behavior Problems. *Exceptional Children* **37**: 119–29.

Allen, R. P., Safer, D. H., Heaton, R., Ward, A., and Barrell, M. (1975) Behavior Therapy for Socially Ineffective Children. *Journal of American Academy of Child Psychiatry* **14**: 500–09.

Allinsmith, W. T. and Goethals, G. W. (1962) *The Role of Schools in Mental Health*. New York: Basic Books.

Altmann, H. A., Conklin, R. C., and Hughes, D. C. (1972) Group Counseling of Underachievers. *Canadian Counselor* **6**: 112–15.

Anderson, R. J. (1974) School Social Work: The Promise of a Team Model. *Child Welfare* **53**(8): 524–30.

Anthony, W. A. and Carkhuff, R. R. (1977) The Functional Professional Therapeutic Agent. In A. S. Gurman and A. M. Razin (eds) *Effective Psychotherapy: A Handbook of Research*. New York: Pergamon Press.

Ashby, J. D., Ford, D. H., Guerney, B. B., and Guerney, L. F. (1957) Effects on Clients of a Reflective and a Leading Type of Therapy. *Psychological Monographs* **71**: 24.

Aspy, D. N. and Roebuck, F. N. (1971) An Investigation of the Relationship Between Student Levels of Cognitive Functioning and the Teacher's Classroom Behavior. *Journal of Educational Research* **65**: 365–68.

Atkeson, B. M. and Forehand, R. (1978) Parents as Behaviour Change Agents with School Related Problems. *Education and Urban Society* **10**: 521–38.

Atkinson, D. R., Davis, J. L., and Sanborn, M. P. (1972) Behavioral Techniques: Effective with Superior High School Students. *School Counselor* **19**: 254–60.

Axline, V. M. (1947a) *Play Therapy*. Boston: Houghton Mifflin.

—— (1947b) Non-Directive Therapy for Poor Readers. *Journal of Consulting Psychology* **11**: 61–9.

Ayllon, T. and Roberts, M. D. (1974) Eliminating Discipline Problems by Strengthening Academic Performance. *Journal of Applied Behavior Analysis* **7**: 71–6.

Ayllon, T., Layman, D., and Burke, S. (1972) Disruptive Behavior and Reinforcement of Academic Performance. *The Psychological Record* **22**: 315–23.

Baer, D. M. and Wolf, M. M. (1972) The Entry into Natural Contingencies of Reinforcement. In R. Ulrick, T. Stachnik, and J. Malony (eds) *Control of Human Behavior*. Glenview, Ill.: Scott, Foresman.

Baer, D. M., Wolf, M. M., and Risley, T. R. (1968) Some Current Dimensions of Applied Behavior Analysis. *Journal of Applied Behavior Analysis* **1**: 91–7.

Barcai, A. and Robinson, E. H. (1969) Conventional Group Therapy with Preadolescent Children. *International Journal of Group Psychotherapy* **19**: 334–45.

Barcai, A., Vinbarger, C., Pierce, T., and Chamberlain, P. (1973) A Comparison of Three Group Approaches to Underachieving Children. *American Journal of Orthopsychiatry* **43**: 133–41.

Barker Lunn, J. C. (1967) Effects of Streaming and Other Forms of Grouping in Junior Schools. *NFER New Research in Education* **1**: 4–45; 46–75.

—— (1969) The Development of Scales to Measure Junior School Children's Attitudes. *British Journal of Educational Psychology* **39**: 64–71.

Barrett, L. C., Hampe, I. E., and Miller, L. C. (1978) Research on Child Psychotherapy. In S. L. Garfield and A. E. Bergin (eds) *Handbook of Psychotherapy and Behavior Change* (2nd edn). New York: John Wiley.

Barrish, H. H., Saunders, M., and Wolf, M. M. (1969) Good Behavior Game: Effects of Individual Contingencies for Group Consequences on Disruptive Behavior in a Classroom. *Journal of Applied Behavior Analysis* **2**: 119–24.

Baymur, F. B. and Patterson, C. H. (1960) Comparison of Three Methods of Assisting Underachieving High School Students. *Journal of Counseling Psychology* **7**: 83–9.

Becker, W. C., Madsen, C. H. Jnr., Arnold, C. R., and Thomas, D. R. (1967) The Contingent Use of Teacher Attention and Praise in Reducing Classroom Behavior Problems. *Journal of Special Education* **1**(3): 287–307.

Bentovim, A. (1977) The Role of Play in Psychotherapeutic Work with Children and Their Families. In B. Tizard and D. Harvey (eds) *Biology of Play*. Clinics in Developmental Medicine No. 62. London: Heinemann Medical Books Ltd (Spastics International Medical Publications).

Bergin, A. E. (1966) Some Implications of Psychotherapy Research for Therapeutic Practice. *Journal of Abnormal Psychology* **71**: 235–46.

—— (1971) The Evaluation of Therapeutic Outcomes. In A. E. Bergin and S. L. Garfield (eds) *Handbook of Psychotherapy and Behavior Change* (1st edn). New York: John Wiley.

Bergin, A. E. and Lambert, M. J. (1978) The Evaluation of Therapeutic Outcomes. In S. L. Garfield and A. E. Bergin (eds) *Handbook of Psychotherapy and Behavior Change* (2nd edn). New York: John Wiley.

Berlin, I. N. (1965) Mental Health Consultation in the Schools: Who can do it and Why. *Community Mental Health Journal* **1**: 19–22.

—— (1967) Preventive Aspects of Mental Health Consultation to Schools. *Mental Hygiene* **51**: 34–40.

Berlin, I. N. (1969) Mental Health Consultation for School Social Workers: A Conceptual Model. *Community Mental Health Journal* **5**(4); 280–88.

Berlyne, D. E. (1969) Laughter, Humor and Play. In G. Lindzey and E. Aronson (eds) *Handbook of Social Psychology*. Reading, Mass.: Addison-Wesley.

Bevins, S. M. C. (1970) A Comparison of the Effectiveness of Individual and Group Counseling in the Improvement of Social Adjustment of 5th and 6th Grade Children. *Dissertation Abstracts Int.* **30**A: 5277.

Biasco, F. (1966) The Effects of Individual Counseling, Multiple Counseling and Teacher Guidance upon Sociometric Status of Children Enrolled in Grades 4, 5 and 6. *Dissertation Abstracts Int.* **27**A: 323.

Biblow, E. (1973) Imaginative Play and the Control of Aggressive Behavior. In J. Singer (ed.) *The Child's World of Make-Believe*. New York: Academic Press.

Bijou, S. W. and Baer, D. M. (1978) *Behavior Analysis of Child Development*. Englewood Cliffs, N.J.: Prentice-Hall.

Birch, H. G. (1945) The Relation of Previous Experience to Insightful Problem Solving. *Journal of Comparative Psychology* **38**: 367.

Birch, H. G. and Gussow, J. D. (1972) *Disadvantaged Children*. New York: Grune and Stratton.

Birnbrauer, J., Wolf, M. M., Kidder, J., and Tague, C. (1965) Classroom Behavior of Retarded Pupils with Token Reinforcement. *Journal of Experimental Child Psychology* **2**: 119–35.

Blanchard, E. B. and Johnson, R. A. (1973) Generalization of Operant Classroom Control Procedures. *Behavior Therapy* **4**: 219–29.

Blom, G. E. (1971) Motivational and Attitudinal Content of First Grade Reading Textbooks: Their Influence on Reading Behavior and Socialization. *Journal of American Academy of Child Psychiatry* **10**(2): 191–203.

Blomfield, J. M. and Douglas, J. W. B. (1956) Bedwetting: Prevalence Among Children 4–7 Years. *Lancet* **1**: 856.

Bolstad, O. D. and Johnson, S. M. (1972) Self-Regulation in the Modification of Disruptive Classroom Behavior. *Journal of Applied Behavior Analysis* **5**: 443–54.

Bower, E. (1969) *Early Identification of Emotionally Handicapped Children in School*. Springfield, Ill.: Charles C. Thomas.

Bowles, P. E. and Nelson, R. O. (1976) Training Teachers as Mediators: Efficacy of a Workshop Versus the Bug-in-the-Ear Technique. *Journal of School Psychology* **14**: 15–26.

Boxall, M. (1973) Multiple Deprivation: An Experiment in Nurture. *British Psychological Society*. Occasional Papers 3.

Braide Report (1969). London: Inner London Education Authority.

Braun, S. J. and Caldwell, B. (1973) Emotional Adjustment of Children in Day Care who Enrolled Prior to or After the Age of Three. *Early Child Development and Care* **2**: 13–21.

Breyer, N. L. and Allen, G. J. (1975) Effects of Implementing a Token Economy on Teacher Attending Behavior. *Journal of Applied Behavior Analysis* **8**: 373–80.

Breyer, N. L., Calchera, D. J., and Cann, C. (1971) Behaviour Consulting From a Distance. *Psychology in the Schools* **8**: 172–76.

Briggs, J. W. (1968) A Comparison of Client-Centred vs Directive Group Counselling with High School Students. *Alberta Journal of Educational Research* **14**: 193–201. (Quoted in Henry and Kilmann.)

Brimer, M. A. and Dunn, L. M. (1962) *English Picture Vocabulary Test*. Bristol: Educational Evaluation Enterprises.

British Association of Social Workers (BASW) (1974) *Social Work in Relation to Schools*. Discussion Paper. Birmingham: British Association of Social Workers.

Broden, M., Hall, R. V., Dunlap, A., and Clark, R. (1970) Effects of Teacher Attention and a Token Reinforcement System in a Junior High School Special Education Class. *Exceptional Children* **36**: 341–49.

Broedel, J., Ohlsen, M., Proff, F., and Southard, C. (1960) The Effects of Group Counselling on Gifted Underachieving Adolescents. *Journal of Counseling Psychology* **7**(3): 163–70.

Bronfenbrenner, U. (1968) When is Infant Stimulation Effective? In D. C. Glass (ed.) *Environmental Influences*. New York: Rockefeller University Press.

—— (1974) *A Report on Longitudinal Evaluation of Preschool Programs*. Washington D.C.: US Department of Health, Education and Welfare; Office of Child Development.

Brophy, J. E. (1972) The Role of Rewards and Reinforcements in Early Education Programmes II Fostering Intrinsic Motivation to Learn. *Journal of School Psychology* **10**: 243–51.

Brophy, J. E. and Good, T. L. (1974) *Teacher-Student Relationships*. New York: Holt, Rinehart and Winston.

Brown, J. C., Montgomery, R., and Barclay, J. (1969) An Example of Psychologist Management of Teacher Reinforcement Procedures in the Elementary Classroom. *Psychology in the Schools* **6**: 336–40.

Brown, P. and Elliott, R. (1965) Control of Aggression in a Nursery School Class. *Journal of Experimental Child Psychology* **2**: 103–07.

Bryan, T. S. (1974) An Observational Analysis of Classroom Behaviors of Children with Learning Disabilities. *Journal of Learning Disabilities* **7**: 34–43.

Buell, J., Stoddard, P., Harris, F. R., and Baer, D. M. (1968) Collateral Social Development Accompanying Reinforcement of Outdoor Play in a Preschool Child. *Journal of Applied Behavior Analysis* **1**: 167–73.

Buros, O. K. (1959) *The Fifth Mental Measurement Yearbook*. Highland Park, New Jersey: Gryphon Press.

Bushell, D., Wrobel, P. A., and Michaelis, M. L. (1968) Applying Group Contingencies to the Classroom Study Behavior of Preschool Children. *Journal of Applied Behavior Analysis* **1**: 55–61.

Buys, C. J. (1972) Effects of Teacher Reinforcement on Elementary School Pupils' Behavior and Attitudes. *Psychology in the Schools* **9**: 278–88.

California Youth Authority (1970) *The Marshall Program – Assessment of a Short-Term Institutional Program II Amenability to Confrontive Peer Group Treatment*. Research Report No. 59. Sacramento, Calif.: California Youth Authority.

Campbell, D. T. and Stanley, J. C. (1966) *Experimental and Quasi-Experimental Designs for Research*. Chicago: Rand McNally.

Caplan, G. (1964) *Principles of Preventive Psychiatry*. London: Tavistock.

—— (1970) *The Theory and Practice of Mental Health Consultation*. New York: Basic Books.

Carkhuff, R. R. (1968) Lay Mental Health Counseling: Prospects and Problems. *Journal of Individual Psychology* **24**: 88–93.

Carlson, C. S., Arnold, C. R., Becker, W. C., and Madsen, C. H. (1968) The Elimination of Tantrum Behavior of a Child in an Elementary Classroom. *Behaviour Research and Therapy* **6**: 117–19.

Carter, B. D. (1975) School Mental Health Consultation: A Clinical Social Work Interventive Technique. *Clinical Social Work Journal* **3**(3): 201–10.

Cattell, R. B. (1952) *Manual for Scales I, II and III* (3rd edn). London: Harrap.

Catterall, C. D. (1970) Taxonomy of Prescriptive Interventions. *Journal of School Psychology* **8**(1): 5–12.

Catterall, C. D. and Gadza, G. M. (1977) *Strategies for Helping Students*. Springfield, Ill.: Charles C. Thomas.

Cave, R. G. (1970) *Partnership for Change – Parents and Schools*. London: Ward Lock Educational.

Chadwick, B. A. and Day, R. C. (1971) Systematic Reinforcement: Academic Performance of Underachieving Students. *Journal of Applied Behavior Analysis* **4**: 311–19.

Chazan, M., Laing, A. F., Cox, T., Jackson, S., and Lloyd, G. (1976) *Studies of Infant School Children: Deprivation and School Progress*. Oxford: Blackwell.

Cheatham, R. B. (1968) A Study of the Effects of Group Counselling on the Self-Concept and on Reading Efficiency of Low Achieving Readers in a Public Intermediate School. *Dissertation Abstracts Int.* **29**B: 2200.

Chilman, C. S. (1973) Programmes for Disadvantaged Parents: Some Major Trends and Related Research. In B. M. Caldwell and H. N. Riccuiti (eds) *Review of Child Development Research* Vol. 3. Chicago: University of Chicago Press.

Clark, M., Lachowicz, I., and Wolf, M. M. (1968) A Pilot Basic Education Program for School Dropouts Incorporating a Token Reinforcement System. *Behavior Research and Therapy* **6**: 183–88.

Clarke, D. B. and Cornish, R. V. G. (1977) *Residential Treatment and its Effects on Delinquency.* Home Office Research Studies 32. London: HMSO.

Clegg, A. and Megson, B. (1968) *Children in Distress.* Harmondsworth: Penguin Books.

Clement, P. W. and Milne, D. O. (1967) Group Play Therapy and Tangible Reinforcers Used to Modify the Behaviour of 8 Year Old Boys. *Behavior Research and Therapy* **5**: 301–12.

Clements, T. H. (1963) A Study to Compare the Effectiveness of Individual and Group Counselling Approaches with Able Underachievers When Counsellor Time is Held Constant. *Dissertation Abstracts Int.* **24**: 1919–920.

Cobb, J. A. (1970) *Survival Skills and First Grade Academic Achievement.* Report No. 1. Eugene, Oreg.: University of Oregon Center for Research and Demonstration in the Early Education of Handicapped Children. Office of Education.

—— (1972) Relationship of Discrete Classroom Behavior to 4th Grade Academic Achievement. *Journal of Educational Psychology* **63**: 74–80.

Cobb, J. A. and Hops, H. (1973) Effects of Academic Survival Skill Training on Low Achieving First Graders. *Journal of Educational Research* **67**: 108–13.

Cochrane, R. and Sobell, M. P. (1976) Myth and Methodology in Behaviour Therapy Research. In P. Feldman and A. Broadhurst (eds) *Theoretical and Experimental Bases of the Behaviour Therapies.* Chichester: John Wiley.

Coleman, J. S. (1966) *Equality of Educational Opportunity.* Washington D.C.: US Dept of Health, Education and Welfare.

Coles, C. (1977) Counselling and Reading Retardation. *Therapeutic Education* **5**: 10–19.

Combs, M. L. and Slaby, D. A. (1977) Social-Skills Training with Children. In B. B. Lahey and A. E. Kazdin (eds) *Advances in Clinical Child Psychology.* New York: Plenum.

Conn, J. H. (1939) The Child Reveals Himself Through Play: The Method of the Play Interview. *Mental Hygiene* **23**: 49–69.

Cooper, B. (1971) Social Work in General Practice: The Derby Scheme. *Lancet* i: 539.

Cooper, M. L., Thomson, C. L., and Baer, D. M. (1970) The Experimental Modification of Teacher Attending Behavior. *Journal of Applied Behavior Analysis* **3**: 153–57.

Copeland, R. and Hall, R. V. (1976) Behavior Modification in the Classroom. In M. Hersen, R. M. Eisler, and P. M. Miller (eds) *Progress in Behavior Modification* Vol. 3. New York: Academic Press.

Cormier, W. H. and Wahler, R. G. (1973) The Application of Social Reinforcement in Six Junior High School Classrooms. In J. Long and R. Williams (eds) *Classroom Management with Adolescents*. New York: MSS Information Corporation.

Cossairt, A., Hall, R. V., and Hopkins, B. L. (1973) The Effect of Experimenter's Instructions, Feedback, and Praise on Teacher Praise and Student Attending Behaviour. *Journal of Applied Behavior Analysis* **6**: 89–100.

Costin, L. B. (1969a) A Historical View of School Social Work. *Social Casework* October: 439–54.

—— (1969b) An Analysis of the Tasks in School Social Work. *Social Services Review* **43**: 274–85.

—— (1975) School Social Work Practice: A New Model. *Social Work* March: 135–39.

Court Report (1976) *Fit for the Future*. Report of the Health and Social Security Committee on Child Health Services. Chairman: Professor S. D. M. Court. London: HMSO.

Cowen, E. L. (1971a) Coping with School Adaptation Problems. *Psychology in the Schools* **8**: 322–39.

—— (1971b) Emergent Directions in School Mental Health. *American Scientist* **59**: 723–33.

—— (1973) Social and Community Interventions. *Annual Review of Psychology* **24:** 423–72. Palo Alto, Calif.: Annual Reviews, Inc.

Cowen, E. L. and Zax, M. (1969) Early Detection and Prevention of Emotional Disorder: Conceptualizations and Programming. In J. W. Carter (ed.) *Research Contributions from Psychology to Community Mental Health*. New York: Behavioral Publications.

Cowen, E. L., Dorr, D. A., and Orgel, A. R. (1971b) Interrelations Among Screening Measures for Early Detection of School Dysfunction. *Psychology in the Schools* **8**: 135–39.

Cowen, E. L., Gardner, E. A., and Zax, M. (1967) *Emergent Approaches to Mental Health Problems*. New York: Appleton-Century-Crofts.

Cowen, E. L., Gesten, E. L., and Wilson, A. B. (1979a) The Primary

Mental Health Project (PMHP): Evaluation of Current Program Effectiveness. *American Journal of Community Psychology* **7**: 293–303.

Cowen, E. L., Zax, M., and Laird, J. D. (1966a) A College Student Volunteer Program in the Elementary School Setting. *Community Mental Health Journal* **2**: 319–28.

Cowen, E. L., Dorr, D., Trost, M. A., and Izzo, L. D. (1972) A Follow-up Study of Maladapting School Children Seen by Non-Professionals. *Journal of Consulting Clinical Psychology* **36**: 235–38.

Cowen, E. L., Orgel, A. R., Gesten, E. L., and Wilson, A. B. (1979b) The Evaluation of an Intervention Program for Young School Children with Acting-Out Problems. *Journal of Abnormal Child Psychology* **7**: 381–96.

Cowen, E. L., Zax, M., Izzo, L. D., and Trost, M. A. (1966b) Prevention of Emotional Disorders in the School Setting: A Further Investigation. *Journal of Consulting Psychology* **30**: 381–87.

Cowen, E. L., Dorr, D., Izzo, L. D., Madonia, A., and Trost, M. A. (1971a) The Primary Mental Health Project: A New Way to Conceptualize and Deliver School Mental Health Service. *Psychology in the Schools* **8**: 216–25.

Cowen, E. L., Lorion, R. P., Dorr, D., Clarfield, S. P., and Wilson, A. B. (1975a) A Preventively Oriented School-Based Mental Health Program. *Psychology in the Schools* **12**: 161–66.

Cowen, E. L., Trost, M. A., Lorion, R. P., Dorr, D., Izzo, L. D., and Isaacson, R. V. (1975b) *New Ways in School Mental Health: Early Detection and Prevention of School Maladaptation*. New York: Human Sciences Press.

Craig, M. M. and Glick, S. J. (1963) Ten Years' Experience with the Glueck Social Prediction Table. *Crime and Delinquency* **9**: 249–61.

Creanage, N. C. (1971) Group Counselling for Underachieving Ninth Graders. *School Counselor* **18**: 279–85.

Crow, M. L. (1971) A Comparison of Three Group Counseling Techniques with Sixth Graders. *Elementary School Guidance Counseling* **6**: 37–42.

Cytryn, L., Gilbert, A., and Eisenberg, L. (1960) The Effectiveness of Tranquilizing Drugs Plus Supportive Psychotherapy in Treating Behavior Disorders of Children: A Double Blind Study of 80 Outpatients. *American Journal of Orthopsychiatry* **30**(1): 113–29.

Davidson, H. H. and Greenberg, J. W. (1967) *School Achievers from a Deprived Background*. Report; Project No. 2805. Washington D.C.: US Department of Health, Education and Welfare.

Davies, B. (1976) Relations Between Social Worker and Teacher. *Social Work Today* **8**(8): 9–11.

Department of Education and Science (DES) (1974) *Circular 3/74*. London: HMSO.

Department of Health and Social Security (DHSS) – Development Group Social Work Service (1977) *Working Together for Children and Their Families*. Report Series.: South Glamorgan County Council and Welsh Office: HMSO.

Deskin, G. (1968) Effects of Differential Treatment Procedures on Reading Ability and Anxiety Level in Children with Learning Difficulties. *Dissertation Abstracts Int.* 28B: 3469–470.

Deutch, M. (1960) *Minority Group and Class Status as Related to Social and Personality Factors in Scholastic Achievement*. Monograph 2. Ithaca, N.Y.: Society for Applied Anthropology.

—— (1971) *Regional Research and Resource Center in Early Childhood: Final Report*. Washington D.C.: US Office of Economic Opportunity.

Devoge, J. T. and Beck, S. (1978) The Therapist-Client Relationship in Behavior Therapy. In M. Hersen, R. M. Eisler, and P. M. Miller (eds) *Progress in Behavior Modification* Vol. 6. London: Academic Press.

Dickenson, W. A. and Truax, C. B. (1966) Group Counselling with College Underachievers. *Personnel Guidance Journal* 45: 243–53.

DiLorenzo, L. T. (1969) *Pre-Kindergarten Programs for Educationally Disadvantaged Children: Final Report*. Washington D.C.: US Office of Education.

Dorfman, E. (1958) Personality Outcomes of Client-Centred Child Therapy. *Psychological Monographs: General and Applied* 72(3): 456.

Dorr, D. and Cowen, E. L. (1972) Teacher's Perception of a School Mental Health Project. *Journal of School Psychology* 10(1): 76–8.

Douglas, J. W. B. (1964) *The Home and the School*. London: MacGibbon and Kee.

Drabman, R. S. (1973) Child- versus Teacher-administered Token Programs in a Psychiatric Hospital School. *Journal of Abnormal Child Psychology* 1: 68–87.

Drabman, R. S., Spitalnik, R., and O'Leary, K. D. (1973) Teaching Self-Control to Disruptive Children. *Journal of Abnormal Psychology* 82: 10–16.

Dunn, L. M. (1959) *Manual for the Peabody Picture Vocabulary Test*. Minneapolis: American Guidance Service.

Dunnett, C. W. (1955) A Multiple Comparison Procedure for Comparing Several Treatments with a Control. *Journal of American Statistical Association* 50: 1096–121.

—— (1964) New Tables for Multiple Comparisons with a Control. *Biometrics* 20: 482–91.

Duthie, J. H. (1970) *Primary School Survey. A Study of the Teacher's Day*. Edinburgh: HMSO.

Eisenberg, L. (1969) The Post-Quarter Century. *American Journal of Orthopsychiatry* **39**: 389–401.

Eisenberg, L., Gilbert, A., Cytryn, L., and Molling, P. A. (1961) The Effectiveness of Psychotherapy Alone and in Conjunction with Perphenazine or Placebo in the Treatment of Neurotic and Hyper-kinetic Children. *American Journal of Psychiatry* **117**: 1088–093.

Elliott, C. D. and Pumfrey, P. D. (1972) The Effects of Non-Directive Play Therapy on Some Maladjusted Boys. *Educational Research* **14**: 157–61.

Emery, R. and Marholin, D. I. (1977) An Applied Behavior Analysis of Delinquency. *American Psychologist* **32**(10): 860–73.

Erikson, E. (1950) *Childhood and Society.* New York: Norton.

Escalona, S. K. (1974) Intervention Programmes for Children at Psychiatric Risk. A Contribution of Child Psychiatry and Development Theory. In E. J. Anthony and C. Koupernik (eds) *The Child in His Family: Children at Psychiatric Risk.* Chichester: John Wiley.

Etaugh, C. (1974) Effects of Maternal Employment on Children: A Review of Recent Research. *Merril-Palmer Quarterly* **20**(2): 69–98.

Evers, W. L. and Schwarz, J. C. (1973) Modifying Social Withdrawal in Preschoolers: The Effects of Filmed Modeling and Teacher Praise. *Journal of Abnormal Child Psychology* **1**: 248–56.

Ewing, T. N. and Gilbert, W. M. (1967) Controlled Study of the Effects of Counseling on the Scholastic Achievements of Students of Superior Ability. *Journal of Counseling Psychology* **14**(3): 235–39.

Eysenck, H. J. (1952) The Effects of Psychotherapy: An Evaluation. *Journal of Consulting Psychology* **16**: 319–24.

—— (1965) The Effects of Psychotherapy. *International Journal of Psychiatry* **1**: 97–178.

Eysenck, S. B. G. (1965) *Manual of the Junior Eysenck Personality Inventory.* London: University of London Press.

Eysenck, S. B. G. and Eysenck, H. J. (1975) *Manual of the Eysenck Personality Questionnaire.* London: Hodder and Stoughton.

Feldhusen, J. F., Thurston, J. R., and Benning, J. J. (1970) Longitudinal Analysis of Classroom Behavior and School Achievement. *Journal of Experimental Education* **38**: 4–10.

Ferritor, D. E., Buckholdt, D., Hamblin, R. L., and Smith, L. (1972) The Noneffects of Contingent Reinforcement for Attending Behavior on Work Accomplished. *Journal of Applied Behavior Analysis* **5**: 7–17.

Fiedler, F. E. (1950) The Concept of an Ideal Therapeutic Relationship. *Journal of Consulting Psychology* **14**: 239–45.

Finer Report (1974) *Report of the Committee on One-Parent Families.* DHSS Cmnd 5629. London: HMSO.

Finlayson, D. J. and Loughran, J. L. (1975) Pupils' Perceptions in Low and High Delinquency Schools. *Educational Research* **18**: 138–45.

Finney, B. C. and Van Dalsem, E. (1969) Group Counseling for Gifted Underachieving High School Students. *Journal of Counseling Psychology* **16**: 87–94.

Fisher, B. (1953) Group Therapy with Retarded Readers. *Journal of Educational Psychology* **6**: 354–60.

Fisher, R. A. (1941) *Statistical Methods for Research Workers* (8th edn). Edinburgh: Oliver and Boyd.

Fitzherbert, K. (1977) School and Social Work. *New Society* **23**(540): 294–95.

Forward, G. E. (1965) Group Therapy for the Emotionally Disturbed Child. (Unpublished.)

Foulds, G. A. (1965) *Personality and Personal Illness*. London: Tavistock.

Fox, R. (1974) Social Agency and the School: Training Educators to Deliver Helping Services. *Child Welfare* **53**(6): 386–93.

Franks, J. D. (1973) *Persuasion and Healing* (2nd edn). Baltimore: Johns Hopkins University Press.

Freeman, J. (1973) Attitudes of Secondary School Teachers Towards Prospective School Counsellors. *British Journal of Guidance and Counselling* **1**(1): 79–84.

Freud, A. (1936) *The Ego and the Mechanisms of Defense*. New York: International Universities Press.

Freud, S. (1911) Formulations on the Two Principles of Mental Functioning. In J. S. Strachey (ed.) (1958) *The Standard Edition of the Complete Psychological Works of Sigmund Freud* Vol. XII. London: Hogarth Press.

—— (1922) *Introductory Lectures in Psychoanalysis*. London: Allen and Unwin.

Freyberg, J. T. (1973) Increasing the Imaginative Play of Urban Disadvantaged Kindergarten Children Through Systematic Training. In J. Singer (ed.) *The Child's World of Make-Believe*. New York: Academic Press.

Friedman, M. L. and Dies, R. R. (1974) Reactions of Internal and External Test Anxious Students to Counselling and Behaviour Therapies. *Journal of Consulting and Clinical Psychology* **42**: 921.

Fundudis, T., Kolvin, I., and Garside, R. F. (1979) *Speech Retarded and Deaf Children: Their Psychological Development*. London: Academic Press.

Gadza, G. M. (1978) *Group Counseling: A Developmental Approach*. Boston: Allyn and Barron.

Garfield, S. L. (1977) In H. Strupp (Chair) *Short-Term Psychotherapy for Whom?* Symposium Presented at the Annual Meeting of the

Society for Psychotherapy. Madison, Wis.
—— (1978) Research on Client Variables in Psychotherapy. In S. L. Garfield and A. E. Bergin (eds) *Handbook of Psychotherapy and Behaviour Change*. (2nd edn). New York: John Wiley.
Garner, J. and Bing, M. (1973) The Elusiveness of Pygmalion and Differences In Teacher-Pupil Contacts. *Interchange* **4**: 34–42.
Garside, R. F., Hulbert, C. M., Kolvin, I., van der Spuy, H. I. J., Wolstenholme, F., and Wrate, R. M. (1973) Evaluation of Psychiatric Services for Children in England and Wales. In J. K. Wing and H. Hafner (eds) *Roots of Evaluation*. Oxford: Oxford University Press (for the Nuffield Provincial Hospitals Trust).
Garside, R. F., Birch, H., Scott, D. McI., Chambers, S., Kolvin, I., Tweddle, E. G., and Barber, L. M. (1975) Dimensions of Temperament in Infant School Children. *Journal of Child Psychology and Psychiatry* **16**: 219–31.
Garvey, C. (1977) *Play*. London: Fontana and Open Books.
Gast, D. L. and Nelson, C. M. (1977) Legal and Ethical Considerations for the Use of Timeout in Special Education Settings. *Journal of Special Education* **11**: 457–67.
Gath, D., Cooper, B., Gattoni, F., and Rockett, D. (1977) *Child Guidance and Delinquency in a London Borough*. Maudsley Monograph No. 24. Oxford: Oxford University Press.
Gaupp, P. G. (1966) Authority, Influence and Control in Consultation. *Community Mental Health Journal* **2**: 205–10.
Gilbreath, S. H. (1967) Group Counseling with Male Underachieving College Volunteers. *American Personnel and Guidance Journal* **45**: 469–76.
Gilmer, B., Miller, J. O., and Gray, S. W. (1970) *Intervention with Mothers and Young Children: Study of Intra-Family Effects*. Nashville, Tenn.: Darcee Demonstration and Research Center for Early Education.
Ginott, H. (1961) *Group Psychotherapy with Children*. New York: McGraw-Hill.
Gitterman, A. (1977) Social Work in the Public School System. *Social Casework* **58**(2): 111–18.
Glass, G. V. and Smith, M. L. (1976) *Meta-Analysis of Psychotherapy Outcome Studies*. Paper presented at meeting of the Society for Psychotherapy Research. San Diego, Calif.
Glavin, J. P. (1974) Behaviorally Oriented Resource Rooms – A Follow-up. *Journal of Special Education* **3**: 337–47.
Glavin, J. P., Quay, H. C., and Werry, J. S. (1971) Behavioral and Academic Gains of Conduct Problem Children in Different Classroom Settings. *Exceptional Children* **37**: 441–46.

Glynn, E. L. (1970) Classroom Application of Self-Determined Reinforcement. *Journal of Applied Behavior Analysis* **3**: 123–32.

Goldberg, D. P. (1972) *The Detection of Psychiatric Illness by Questionnaire*. Maudsley Monographs No. 21. London: Oxford University Press.

Goldstein, A. P. and Simonson, N. R. (1971) Social Psychological Approaches to Psychotherapy Research. In A. E. Bergin and S. L. Garfield (eds) *Handbook of Psychotherapy and Behavior Change* (1st edn). New York: John Wiley.

Goldstein, A. P. and Stein, N. (1976) *Prescriptive Psychotherapies*. Oxford: Pergamon Press.

Gottman, J. (1977) The Effects of a Modeling Film on Social Isolation in Preschool Children: A Methodological Investigation. *Journal of Abnormal Child Psychology* **5**: 69–78.

Gottman, J. and Markman, H. J. (1978) Experimental Designs in Psychotherapy Research. In S. L. Garfield and A. E. Bergin (eds) *Handbook of Psychotherapy and Behavior Change* (2nd edn). New York: John Wiley.

Gottman, J., Gonso, J., and Schuler, P. (1976) Teaching Social Skills to Isolated Children. *Journal of Abnormal Child Psychology* **4**: 179–97.

Graham, P. (1974) Child Psychiatry and Psychotherapy. *Journal of Child Psychology and Psychiatry* **15**: 59–66.

Gray, S. W. and Klaus, R. A. (1970) The Early Training Period: The Seventh-Year Report. *Child Development* **41**: 909–24.

Graziano, A. M. (1977) Parents as Behavior Therapists. In M. Hersen, R. M. Eisler, and P. M. Miller (eds) *Progress in Behavior Modification* Vol. 4. New York: Academic Press.

Greenhouse, S. W. and Geisser, S. (1959) On Methods in the Analysis of Profile Data. *Psychometrika* **24**: 95–111.

Greenwood, C. R., Hops, H., and Walker, H. M. (1977) The Program for Academic Survival Skills (PASS): Effects on Student Behavior and Achievement. *Journal of School Psychology* **15**: 25–35.

Greenwood, C. R., Hops, H., Delquadri, J., and Guild, J. (1974) Group Contingencies for Group Consequences in Classroom Management: A Further Analysis. *Journal of Applied Behavior Analysis* **7**: 413–25.

Gropper, G. L., Kress, G. C., Hughes, R., and Pekich, J. (1968) Training Teachers to Recognise and Manage Social Problems in the Classroom. *Journal of Teacher Education* **19**: 477–85.

Grosser, C., Henry, W. E., and Kelly, J. G. (1969) *Non-Professionals in the Human Services*. San Francisco: Jossey-Bass.

Gurin, G., Veroff, J., and Feld, S. (1960) *Americans View Their Mental Health: A Nationwide Survey*. New York: Basic Books.

Haley, J. (1977) *Problem Solving Therapy – New Strategies for Effective Family Therapy*. San Francisco: Jossey Bass.

Hall, C. S. and Lindzey, G. (1970) *Theories of Personality*. New York: John Wiley.

Hall, R. V. and Copeland, R. E. (1972) The Responsive Teaching Model: A First Step in Shaping School Personnel as Behavior Modification Specialists. In F. W. Clark, D. R. Evans, and L. A. Hamerlynck (eds) *Implementing Behavioral Programs for Schools and Clinics*. Champaign, Ill.: Research Press.

Hall, R. V., Copeland, R., and Clark, M. L. (1976) Management Strategies for Teachers and Parents: Responsive Teaching. In N. G. Harry and R. L. Schiefelbusch (eds) *Teaching Special Children*. New York: McGraw-Hill.

Hall, R. V., Lund, D., and Jackson, D. (1968a) Effects of Teacher Attention on Student Behavior. *Journal of Applied Behavior Analysis* **1**: 1–12.

Hall, R. V., Panyan, M., Robson, D., and Broden, M. (1968b) Instructing Beginning Teachers in Reinforcement Procedures which Improve Classroom Control. *Journal of Applied Behavior Analysis* **1**: 315–22.

Hall, R. V., Fox, R., Willard, D., Goldsmith, L., Emerson, M., Owen, M., Davis, F., and Porcia, E. (1971) The Teacher as Observer and Experimenter in the Modification of Disputing and Talking Out Behaviors. *Journal of Applied Behavior Analysis* **4**: 141–49.

Hansen, J. C., Niland, I. M., and Zani, L. P. (1969) Model Reinforcement in Group Counselling with Elementary School Children. *Personnel and Guidance Journal* **47**: 741–44.

Hare, E. H. and Shaw, G. K. (1965) *Mental Health on a New Housing Estate: A Comparative Study of Health in Two Districts in Croydon*. Maudsley Monograph No. 12. Oxford: Oxford University Press.

Hargrave, G. E. and Hargrave, M. L. (1979) A Peer Group Socialization Therapy Program in the School: An Outcome Investigation. *Psychotherapy in the Schools* **16**: 546–50.

Hargreaves, D. M., Hester, S. K., and Mellor, F. J. (1975) *Deviance in Classrooms*. London: Routledge and Kegan Paul.

Harris, M. R., Kalis, B. L., and Freeman, E. H. (1963) Precipitating Stress: An Approach to Brief Therapy. *American Journal of Psychotherapy* **17**: 465–71.

Harris, V. W. and Sherman, J. A. (1973) Use and Analysis of the 'Good Behavior Game' to Reduce Disruptive Classroom Behavior. *Journal of Applied Behavior Analysis* **6**: 405–17.

Harris, V. W. and Sherman, J. A. (1974) Homework Assignments, Consequences and Classroom Performance in Social Studies and

Mathematics. *Journal of Applied Behavior Analysis* **7**: 505–19.

Hart, B. M., Allen, K. E., Buell, J. S., Harris, F. R., and Wolf, M. M. (1964) Effects of Social Reinforcement on Operant Crying. *Journal of Experimental Child Psychology* **1**: 145–53.

Harvey, L., Kolvin, I., McLaren, M., Nicol, A. R., and Wolstenholme, F. (1977) Introducing a School Social Worker into Schools. *British Journal of Guidance and Counselling* **5**(1): 26–40.

Hays, D. and Grether, J. (1969) *The School Year and Vacation. When do Students Learn?* Paper presented at the Eastern Sociological Convention, New York.

Heaton, R. C., Safer, D. J., Allen, R. P., Spinnato, N. C., and Prumo, F. M. (1976) A Motivational Environment for Behaviorally Deviant Junior High School Students. *Journal of Abnormal Child Psychology* **4**: 263–75.

Heber, R., Garber, H., Harrington, S., and Hoffman, C. (1972) *Rehabilitation of Families at Risk for Mental Retardation.* Madison: University of Wisconsin.

Heinicke, C. M. and Strassman, L. H. (1975) Toward More Effective Research on Child Psychotherapy. *Journal of American Academy of Child Psychiatry* **14**: 561–88.

Heitler, J. B. (1973) Preparation of Lower Class Patients for Expressive Group Therapy. *Journal of Consulting and Clinical Psychology* **41**: 267–81.

Henry, S. E. and Kilmann, P. R. (1979) Student Counseling Groups in Senior High School Settings: An Evaluation of Outcome. *Journal of School Psychology* **17**: 27–46.

Hetznecker, W. and Foreman, M. (1974) *On Behalf of Children.* New York: Grune and Stratton.

Hewett, F. M., Taylor, F. D., and Artuso, A. A. (1969) The Santa Monica Project: Evaluation of an Engineered Classroom Design with Emotionally Disturbed Children. *Exceptional Children* **35**: 523–29.

Hinds, W. C. and Roehike, H. J. (1970) A Learning Theory Approach to Group Counseling in Elementary School Children. *Journal of Counseling Psychology* **11**: 49–55.

Hobbs, N. (1966) Helping Disturbed Children: Psychological and Ecological Strategies. *American Psychologist* **21**: 1105–115.

Hodges, W. L. (1972) The Role of Rewards and Reinforcements in Early Education Programmes. I. External Reinforcement in Early Education. *Journal of School Psychology* **10**(3): 233–41.

Hoehn-Saric, R., Franks, J. D., Imber, S. D., Nash, E. H., Stone, A. R., and Battle, C. L. (1964) Systematic Preparation of Patients for Psychotherapy. 1. Effects on Behaviour and Outcome. *Journal of Psychiatric Research* **2**: 267–81.

Holmes, D. S. and Urie, R. G. (1975) Effects of Preparing Children for Psychotherapy. *Journal of Consulting and Clinical Psychology* **43**: 311–18.

Home Office Research Unit (1966) *Probation Research*. A Preliminary Report. London: HMSO.

Hops, H. and Cobb, J. A. (1973) Survival Behaviors in the Educational Setting: Their Implications for Research and Intervention. In L. A. Hamerlynck, L. C. Handy, and E. J. Mash (eds) *Behaviour Change: Methodology, Concepts and Practice*. Champaign, Ill.: Research Press.

Horn, E. A., Pollock, D., and St. John, B. H. (1969) School Mental Health Services Offered Without Invitation. *Mental Hygiene* **53**: 620–24.

House, R. M. (1971) The Effects of Nondirective Group Play Therapy upon the Sociometric Status and Self-Concept of Selected Second Grade Children. *Dissertation Abstracts Int.* **31**A: 2684.

Hubbert, A. K. (1970) Effect of Group Counselling and Behavior Modification on Attentive Behavior of First Grade Students. *Dissertation Abstracts Int.* **30**A: 3727.

Hugo, M. J. (1970) The Effects of Group Counselling on Self-Concept and Behaviour of Elementary School Children. *Dissertation Abstracts Int.* **30**A: 3728.

Hulbert, C. M., Wolstenholme, F., and Kolvin, I. (1977) A Teacher-aide Programme in Action, Part II. *Special Education: Forward Trends* **4**(1): 27–31.

Hume, K. E. (1967) A Counseling Service Project for Grades One Through Four. *Dissertation Abstracts Int.* **27**A: 4130.

Irwin, E., Levy, P., and Shapiro, M. (1972) Assessment of Drama Therapy in a Child Guidance Setting. *Group Psychotherapy and Psychodrama* **25**: 105–16.

Jeffrey, L. I. H. (1973) Child Psychiatry – The Need for Occupational Therapy. *Occupational Therapy* **36**(8): 429–37.

Jeffrey, L. I. H., Kolvin, I., Robson, M. R., Scott, D. McI., and Tweddle, E. G. (1979) Generic Training in the Psychological Management of Children and Adolescents. *Journal of Associated Workers for Maladjusted Children* **7**(1); 32–43.

Jensen, A. R. (1969) How Much Can We Boost IQ and Scholastic Achievement? *Harvard Educational Review* **39**: 1–123.

Johnson, C. A. and Katz, R. C. (1973) Using Parents as Change Agents for Their Children: A Review. *Journal of Child Psychology and Psychiatry* **14**: 181–200.

Johnson, J. T. (1976) A Truancy Programme: The Child Welfare Agency and the School. *Child Welfare* **55**: 573–800.

Johnson, S. M., Bolstad, O. D., and Lobitz, G. K. (1976) Generalization and Contrast Phenomena in Behavior Modification with Children. In E. J. Mash, L. A. Hamerlynck, and L. C. Handy (eds) *Behavior Modification and Families*. New York: Brunner-Mazel.

Johnston, M. S., Kelley, C. S., Harris, F. R., and Wolf, M. M. (1966) An Application of Reinforcement Principles to Development of Motor Skills of a Young Child. *Child Development* **37**: 379–87.

Jones, R. M. (1972) *Fantasy and Feeling in Education*. Harmondsworth: Penguin Books.

Kadushin, A. (1977) *Consultation in Social Work*. New York: Columbia University Press.

Karnes, M. B., Studley, W. M., Wright, W. R., and Hodgkins, A. S. (1968) An Approach to Working with Mothers of Disadvantaged Pre-School Children. *Merril-Palmer Quarterly* **14**: 174–84.

Kauffman, J. M., Nussen, J. L., and McGee, C. S. (1977) Follow-up in Classroom Behavior Modification: Survey and Discussion. *Journal of School Psychology* **15**: 343–48.

Kaufman, K. F. and O'Leary, K. D. (1972) Reward, Cost and Self-Evaluation Procedures for Disruptive Adolescents in a Psychiatric Hospital School. *Journal of Applied Behavior Analysis* **5**: 293–310.

Kazdin, A. E. (1973) Methodological and Assessment Considerations in Evaluating Reinforcement Programs in Applied Settings. *Journal of Applied Behavior Analysis* **6**: 517–31.

—— (1975) Characteristics and Trends in Applied Behavior Analysis. *Journal of Applied Behavior Analysis* **8**: 332.

Kazdin, A. E. and Bootzin, R. R. (1972) The Token Economy: An Evaluative Review. *Journal of Applied Behavior Analysis* **5**: 343–72.

Kazdin, A. E. and Moyer, W. (1976) Training Teachers to Use Behavior Modification. In S. Yen and R. McIntire (eds) *Teaching Behavior Modification*. Kalamazoo, Mich.: Behavioraelia.

Keeley, S. M., Shemberg, K. M., and Carbonnel, J. (1976) Operant Clinical Interventions: Behavior Management or Beyond? Where are the Data? *Behavior Therapy* **7**: 292–305.

Kelly, E. W. Jnr. and Mathews, D. B. (1971) Group Counseling with Discipline Problem Children at the Elementary School Level. *School Counselor* **18**: 273–78.

Kennedy, K. T. and Duthie, J. H. (1975) *Auxiliaries in the Classroom. A Feasibility Study in Scottish Primary Schools*. Edinburgh: Scottish Education Department: HMSO.

Kent, R. N. and Foster, S. L. (1977) Direct Observational Procedures; Methodological Issues in Naturalistic Settings. In A. R. Ciminero, K. S. Calhoun, and H. E. Adams (Eds) *Handbook of Behavioral Assessment*. New York: John Wiley.

Kent, R. N. and O'Leary, K. D. (1976) A Controlled Evaluation of

Behavior Modification with Conduct Problem Children. *Journal of Consulting and Clinical Psychology* **44**: 586–96.

Kent, R. N., O'Leary, K. D., Diament, C., and Dietz, A. (1974) Expectation Biases in Observational Evaluation of Therapeutic Change. *Journal of Consulting and Clinical Psychology* **42**: 774–80.

Kiesler, D. J. (1971) Experimental Designs in Psychotherapy Research. In A. E. Bergin and S. L. Garfield (eds) *Handbook of Psychotherapy and Behavior Change* (1st edn). New York: John Wiley.

—— (1973) *The Process of Psychotherapy: Empirical Foundations and Systems of Analysis.* Chicago: Aldine.

Kirby, F. D. and Shields, F. (1972) Modification of Arithmetic Response Rate and Attending Behavior in a Seventh-Grade Student. *Journal of Applied Behavior Analysis* **5**: 79–84.

Klein, A. F. (1959) Social Work in Non-Social Work Settings. *Social Work* **4**(4): 92–7.

Klein, M. (1928) *The Psychoanalysis of Children.* London: Hogarth.

Knoblock, P. and Goldstein, A. F. (1971) *The Lonely Teacher.* Boston: Allyn and Bacon.

Kohler, W. (1925) *The Mentality of Apes.* Harmondsworth: Penguin Books.

Kohn, M. and Rossman, B. L. (1972) A Social Competence Scale and Symptom Checklist for the Pre-School Child: Factor Dimensions, Their Cross and Longitudinal Persistence. *Developmental Psychology* **6**: 430–44.

Kolvin, I., MacKeith, R., and Meadow, R. (1973) *Bladder Control and Enuresis.* London: Heinemann.

Kolvin, I., Garside, R. F., Nicol, A. R., Leitch, I. M., Macmillan, A. (1977) Screening School Children for High Risk of Emotional and Educational Disorder. *British Journal of Psychiatry* **131**: 192–206.

Kolvin, I., Garside, R. F., Nicol, A. R., Macmillan, A., and Wolstenholme, F. (1975a) School-Based Action Research. *Proceedings, Sixth European Congress of the Union of Pedopsychiatrists*, Vienna.

Kolvin, I., Garside, R. F., Nicol, A. R., Macmillan, A., and Wolstenholme, F. (1976) Maladjusted Children in Ordinary Schools. *Special Education: Forward Trends* **3**(3): 15–18.

Kolvin, I., Wrate, R. M., Wolstenholme, F., Garside, R. F., Hulbert, C. M., and Leitch, I. M. (1981) *Seriously Troubled Children.* (Under revision.)

Kolvin, I., Wolff, S., Barber, L. M., Tweddle, E. G., Garside, R. F., Scott, D.McI., and Chambers, S. (1975b) Dimensions of Behaviour in Infant School Children. *British Journal of Psychiatry* **126**: 114–26.

Kounin, J. S. (1970) *Discipline and Group Management in Classrooms.* New York: Holt, Rinehart and Winston.

Kounin, J. S. and Obradovic, S. (1968) Managing Emotionally Disturbed Children in Regular Classrooms: A Replication and Extension. *Journal of Special Education* **2**(2): 129–35.

Kounin, J. S., Friesen, W. V., and Norton, E. (1966) Managing Emotionally Disturbed Children in Regular Classrooms. *Journal of Educational Psychology* **57**: 1–13.

Kranzler, G. D., Mayer, G. R., Dyer, C. O., and Munger, P. F. (1966) Counseling with Elementary School Children: An Experimental Study. *Personnel and Guidance Journal* **5**: 944–49.

Kuypers, D. S., Becker, W. C., and O'Leary, K. D. (1968) How to Make a Token System Fail. *Exceptional Children* **11**: 101–08.

Lahaderne, H. M. (1968) Attitudinal and Intellectual Correlates of Attention: A Study of Fourth-Grade Classrooms. *Journal of Educational Psychology* **59**: 320–24.

Lamb, H. R. and Zusman, J. (1979) Primary Prevention in Perspective. *American Journal of Psychiatry* **136**(1): 12–17.

Lambert, M. (1976) Spontaneous Remission in Adult Neurotic Disorders: A Revision and Summary. *Psychological Bulletin* **83**: 107–19.

Lang, P. J., Melamed, B. G., and Hart, J. (1970) A Psychophysiological Analysis of Fear Modification Using an Automated Desensitization Procedure. *Journal of Abnormal Psychology* **76**: 220–34.

Lates, B. J., Egner, A. N., and McKenzie, H. S. (1971) Behavior Analysis of the Academic and Social Behavior of First Grade Children. In E. A. Ramp and B. L. Hopkins (eds) *A New Direction for Educational Behavior Analysis*. Lawrence, Kan.: Support and Development Center for Follow-Thro.

Lawrence, D. (1973) *Improved Reading Through Counselling*. London: Ward Lock.

Lehrman, L. J., Sirluck, H., Black, B. J., and Glick, S. J. (1949) Success and Failure of Treatment of Children in the Child Guidance Clinics of the Jewish Board of Guardians. *Research Monograph* No. 1. New York: Jewish Board of Guardians.

Lennard, H. L. and Bernstein, A. (1960) *Patterns in Human Interaction*. San Francisco: Jossey-Bass.

Levenstein, P. (1970) Cognitive Growth in Pre-Schoolers Through Verbal Interaction with Mothers. *American Journal of Orthopsychiatry* **40**: 426–32.

Levine, F. M. and Fasnacht, G. (1974) Token Rewards May Lead to Token Learning. *American Psychologist* **29**: 816–20.

Levitt, E. E. (1957) The Results of Psychotherapy with Children: An Evaluation. *Journal of Consulting Psychology* **21**: 189–96.

—— (1963) Psychotherapy with Children: A Further Evaluation. *Behaviour Research and Therapy* **60**: 326–29.

—— (1971) Research on Psychotherapy with Children. In A. E. Bergin and S. L. Garfield (eds) *Handbook of Psychotherapy and Behavior Change* (1st edn) New York: John Wiley.

Lewis, M. D. and Lewis, J. A. (1977) The Counselor's Impact on Community Environments. *Personnel and Guidance Journal* **55**: 356–58.

Lieberman, M. A., Yalom, I. D., and Miles, M. B. (1973) *Encounter Groups: First Facts*. New York: Basic Books.

Liebert, R. M., Neale, J. M., and Davidson, E. S. (1973) *The Early Window*. New York: Pergamon.

Light, L. L. and Alexakos, C. E. (1970) Effect of Individual and Group Counselling on Study Habits. *Journal of Educational Research* **63**: 450–54.

Lipinski, O. and Nelson, R. (1974) Problems in the Use of Naturalistic Observation as a Means of Behavioral Assessment. *Behavior Therapy* **5**: 341–51.

Lisle, J. D. (1968) The Comparative Effectiveness of Various Group Procedures Used with Elementary Pupils with Personal-Social Adjustment Problems. *Dissertation Abstracts Int.* **28**A: 4485.

Litow, L. and Pumroy, D. K. (1975) A Brief Review of Classroom Group-Oriented Contingencies. *Journal of Applied Behavior Analysis* **8**: 341–47.

Long, J. L., Morse, C. M., and Newman, R. G. (1971) *Conflict in the Classroom*. Belmont, Calif.: Wadsworth.

Love, L. R. and Kaswan, J.W. (1974) *Troubled Children: Their Families, Schools and Treatments*. New York: John Wiley.

Lovitt, T. C. and Curtiss, K. (1969) Academic Response Rate as a Function of Teacher- and Self-Imposed Contingencies. *Journal of Applied Behavior Analysis* **2**: 49–53.

Luborsky, L. and Spence, D. P. (1978) Quantitative Research and Psychoanalytic Therapy. In S. L. Garfield and A. E. Bergin (eds) *Handbook of Psychotherapy and Behavior Change* (2nd edn). New York: John Wiley.

Luborsky, L., Singer, B., and Luborsky, L. (1975) Comparative Studies of Psychotherapies: Is it True that "Everybody Has Won and All Must Have Prizes?" *Archives of General Psychiatry* **32**: 995–1008.

Luborsky, L., Chandler, M., Auerbach, A. H., Cohen, J., and Bachrach, H. M. (1971) Factors Influencing the Outcome of Psychotherapy. *Psychological Bulletin* **75**: 145–85.

Lyons, K. H. (1973) *Social Work and the School*. London: HMSO.

McAllister, L. W., Stachowiak, J. G., Baer, D. M., and Conderman, L. (1969) The Application of Operant Conditioning Techniques in a Secondary School Classroom. *Journal of Applied Behavior Analysis* **2**: 277–85.

McBrien, R. J. and Nelson, R. I. (1972) Experimental Group Strategies with Primary Grade Children. *Elementary School Guidance and Counseling* **6**: 170–74.

Maccoby, E. E. (1966) Sex Differences in Intellectual Functioning. In E. E. Maccoby (ed.) *The Development of Sex Differences*. Stanford, Calif.: Stanford University Press.

McDonald, S. (1973) The Kibitz Dimension in Teacher Consultation. In R. O. Klein, W. G. Hepbiewiez, and A. H. Roden (eds) *Behavior Modification in Educational Settings*. Springfield, Ill.: Charles C. Thomas.

McKenzie, H. S., Egner, A. N., Knight, M. F., Perelman, P. F., Schneider, B. M., and Garvin, J. S. (1970) Training Consulting Teachers to Assist Elementary Teachers in the Management of Handicapped Children. *Exceptional Children* **37**: 137–43.

McKeown, D., Adams, H. E., and Forehand, R. (1975) Generalization to the Classroom of Principles of Behaviour Modification Taught to Teachers. *Behaviour Research and Therapy* **13**: 85–92.

McLaughlin, T. F. (1975) The Applicability of Token Reinforcement Systems in Public School Systems. *Psychology in the Schools* **12**: 84–89.

MacLennan, B. W. (1977) Modifications of Activity Group Therapy for Children. *International Journal of Group Psychotherapy* XXVII: 85–96.

MacLennan, B. W. and Felsenfeld, N. (1968) *Group Counseling and Psychotherapy with Adolescents*. New York: Columbia University Press.

Macmillan, A. (1976) Behaviour Modification with Disruptive Children. *Journal of the Northern Association for the Advancement of Behavioural Analysis and Change* **1**; 2–13.

Macmillan, A. and Kolvin, I. (1977a) Behaviour Modification in Teaching Strategy: Some Emergent Problems and Suggested Solutions. *Educational Research* **20**(1): 10–21.

Macmillan, A. and Kolvin, I. (1977b) Behaviour Modification in Educational Settings: A Guide for Teachers. *Journal of Association of Workers for Maladjusted Children* **5**(1): 1–13.

Macmillan, A., Kolvin, I., Garside, R. F., Nicol, A. R., and Leitch, I. M. (1980) A Multiple Criterion Screen for Identifying Secondary School Children with Psychiatric Disorder. *Psychological Medicine* **10**: 265–76.

Macmillan, A., Walker, L., Garside, R. F., Kolvin, I., Leitch, I. M., and Nicol, A. R. (1978) The Development and Application of

Sociometric Techniques for the Identification of Isolated and Rejected Children. *Journal of Association of Workers for Maladjusted Children* **6**: 58–74.

Macmillan, D. L., Forness, S. R., and Trumbull, B. M. (1973) The Role of Punishment in the Classroom. *Exceptional Children* **40**: 85–96.

McNamara, J. R. (1971) Teachers and Students as a Source for Behavior Modification in the Classroom. *Behavior Therapy* **2**: 205–13.

—— (1975) Ways by Which Outcome Measures Influence Outcomes in Classroom Behavior Modification Research. *Journal of School Psychology* **13**: 104–13.

Madsen, C. H. and Madsen, C. K. (1973) *Teaching/Discipline: Behavioral Principles Toward a Positive Approach*. Boston: Allyn and Bacon.

Madsen, C. H., Becker, W. C., and Thomas, D. R. (1968b) Rules, Praise and Ignoring: Elements of Elementary Classroom Control. *Journal of Applied Behavior Analysis* **1**: 139–50.

Madsen, C. H., Becker, W. C., Thomas, D. R., Koser, L., and Plager, E. (1968a) An Analysis of the Reinforcing Function of 'Sit-Down' Commands. In R. K. Parker (ed.) *Readings in Educational Psychology*. Boston: Allyn and Bacon.

Madsen, C. H., Madsen, C. K., Saudargas, R. A., Hammond, W. R., Smith, J. B., and Edgar, D. E. (1970) Classroom Raid (Rules, Approval, Ignore, Disapproval): A Co-operative Approach for Professionals and Volunteers. *Journal of School Psychology* **8**(3): 180–85.

Magill, R. S. (1974) The School Social Worker and the Community School. *Social Casework* **55**(4): 224.

Main, G. C. and Munro, B. C. (1975) A Token Reinforcement Program in a Public Junior High School. *Journal of Applied Behavior Analysis* **10**: 93.

Mann, P. H., Barber, J. D., and Jacobson, M. D. (1969) The Effect of Group Counseling on Educable Mentally Retarded Boys' Self-Concepts. *Exceptional Children* **35**: 354–66.

Mannino, F. V. and Shore, M. F. (1970) Consultation Research in Mental Health and Related Fields: A Critical Review of the Literature. *Public Health Monograph* No. 79: 1–55.

—— (1975) The Effects of Consultation: A Review of Empirical Studies. *American Journal of Community Psychology* **3**(1): 1–21.

Marholin, D. I., Siegel, L. J., and Phillips, D. (1976) Treatment and Transfer: A Search for Empirical Procedures. In M. Hersen, R. M. Eisler, and P. M. Miller (eds) *Progress in Behavior Modification* Vol. 3. New York: Academic Press.

Marholin, D. I., Steinman, W. M., McInnis, E. T., and Heads, T. B. (1975) The Effect of a Teacher's Presence on the Classroom Behavior of Conduct-Problem Children. *Journal of Abnormal Child Psychology* **3**: 11–25

Marjoribanks, K. (1979) *Families and Their Learning Environments: An Empircal Analysis*. London: Routledge and Kegan Paul.

Marshall, H. R. (1961) Relations Between Home Experiences and Children's Use of Language in Play Interactions with Peers. *Psychological Monographs* **75**(5): 509.

Marshall, H. R. and Hahn, S. C. (1967) Experimental Modification of Dramatic Play. *Journal of Personality and Social Psychology* **5**: 119–22.

Matarazzo, J. D., Wiens, A. N., Matarazzo, R. G., and Saslow, G. (1968) Speech and Silence Behavior in Clinical Psychotherapy and its Laboratory Correlates. In J. M. Shlien, H. F. Hunt, J. D. Matarazzo, and C. Savage (eds) *Research in Psychotherapy* Vol. III. Washington D.C.: American Psychological Association.

Matarazzo, R. G., Phillips, J. S., Wiens, A. N., and Saslow, G. (1965) Learning the Art of Interviewing: A Study of What Beginning Students Do and Their Pattern of Change. *Psychotherapy: Theory, Research and Practice* **2**: 49–60.

Mayer, E. J. and Timms, N. (1970) *The Client Speaks*. London: Routledge and Kegan Paul.

Meacham, M. L. and Wiesen, A. E. (1974) *Changing Classroom Behavior* (2nd edn). New York: Intext Educational Publishers.

Meares, P. A. (1977) Analysis of Tasks in School Social Work. *Social Work* **22**: 196–201.

Meichenbaum, D. H., Bowers, K., and Ross, R. R. (1968) Modification of Classroom Behavior of Institutionalized Female Adolescent Offenders. *Behavior Research and Therapy* **6**: 343–53.

Mellone, M. E. (1948) *Manual of Instructions for Moray House Picture Intelligence Test I*. London: University of London Press.

Mercatoris, M. and Craighead, W. E. (1974) Effects of Nonparticipant Observation on Teacher and Pupil Classroom Behavior. *Journal of Educational Psychology* **66**: 512–19.

Meyer, J. B., Strowig, W., and Hosford, R. E. (1970) Behavioral-Reinforcement Counseling with Rural High School Youth. *Counseling Psychology* **17**: 127–32.

Meyers, C. E., Atwell, A. A., and Orpet, R. E. (1968) Prediction of Fifth-Grade Achievement from Kindergarten Test and Rating Data. *Educational and Psychological Measurement* **28**: 457–63.

Mezzano, J. (1968) Group Counseling with Low-Motivated Male High School Students – Comparative Effects of Two Uses of Counselor Time. *Journal of Educational Research* **61**: 222–24.

Miller, D. (1964) *Growth to Freedom*. London: Tavistock.

Miller, F. J. W. (1973) Children Who Wet the Bed. In I. Kolvin,

R. MacKeith, and R. Meadow (eds) *Bladder Control and Enuresis*. London: Heinemann.

Miller, F. J. W., Court, S. D. M., Knox, E. G., and Brandon, S. (1974) *The School Years in Newcastle-upon-Tyne*. Oxford: Oxford University Press.

Miller, G. W. (1972) *Educational Opportunity and the Home*. London: Longman.

Miller, L. (1972) School Behavior Check List: An Inventory of Deviant Behavior for Elementary School Children. *Journal of Consulting and Clinical Psychology* **38**: 134–44.

Miller, L. C., Barrett, C. L., Hampe, E., and Noble, H. (1972) Comparison of Reciprocal Inhibition, Psychotherapy and Waiting List Controls For Phobic Children. *Journal of Abnormal Psychology* **79**(3): 269–79.

Minuchin, S. (1974) *Families and Family Therapy*. London: Tavistock.

Mischel, W. (1968) *Personality and Assessment*. New York: John Wiley.

Mitchell, K. M. and Ingham, R. (1970) The Effects of General Anxiety on Group Desensitization of Test Anxiety. *Behavior Research and Therapy* **8**: 69–78.

Mitchell, K. M., Bozarth, J. D., and Krauft, C. C. (1977) A Reappraisal of the Therapeutic Effectiveness of Accurate Empathy, Nonpossessive Warmth and Genuineness. In A. S. Gurman and A. M. Razin (eds) *Effective Psychotherapy: A Handbook of Research*. New York: Pergamon Press.

Montessori, M. (1964) *The Montessori Method*. New York: Schocken Books.

Moore, T. (1966) Difficulties of the Ordinary Child in Adjusting to Primary School. *Journal of Child Psychology and Psychiatry* **7**: 17–38.

Morse, W. C. (1967) Enhancing the Classroom Teacher's Mental Health Function. In E. L. Cowen, E. A. Gardner, and M. Zax (eds) *Emergent Approaches to Mental Health Problems*. New York: Appleton-Century-Croft.

Moulin, E. K. (1970) The Effects of Client-Centered Group Counseling Using Play Media on the Intelligence, Achievement and Psycholinguistic Abilities of Underachieving Primary School Children. *Elementary School Guidance and Counseling* **5**: 85–98.

Mulligan, W., Kaplan, R. D., and Reppucci, N. D. (1973) Changes in Cognitive Variables Among Behavior Problem Elementary School Boys Treated in a Token Economy Special Classroom. In R. D. Rubin, J. P. Brady, and J. D. Henderson (eds) *Advances in Behavior Therapy* Vol. 4. New York: Academic Press.

Mullin, L. (1979) Social Factors and Child Management Within

Schools. MA thesis. University of Newcastle upon Tyne. (Unpublished.)

Myrick, R. D. and Haight, D. A. (1972) Growth Groups: An Encounter with Underachievers. *School Counselor* 20: 115–21.

Natzke, J. H. and Bennett, W. S. Jnr. (1970) Teacher-aide – Use and Role Satisfaction of Inner-City Teachers. *Education and Urban Society* 5: 295–314.

Neligan, G. A., Prudham, D., and Steiner, H. (1974) *The Formative Years: Birth, Family and Development in Newcastle-upon-Tyne*. Oxford: Oxford University Press (for the Nuffield Provincial Hospitals Trust).

Newman, R. G. (1967) *Psychological Consultation in the Schools: A Catalyst for Learning*. New York: Basic Books.

Newsom Report (1963) *Half Our Future*. Report of Central Advisory Council for Education (England). London: HMSO.

Newson, J. and Newson, E. (1976) *Seven-Years-Old in the Home Environment*. London: Allen and Unwin.

—— (1977) *Perspectives on School at Seven-Years-Old*. London: Allen and Unwin.

Nicol, A. R. (1979) Annotation: Psychotherapy and the School. *Journal of Child Psychology and Psychiatry* 20: 81–6.

Nicol, A. R. and Bell, M. (1975) *Group Counselling in Schools*. Paper presented at the *Vth Congress of the Union of European Pedopsychiatrists*, Vienna.

Nicol, A. R. and Parker, J. (1981) Playgroup Therapy in the Junior School. I. Method and General Problems. *British Journal of Guidance and Counselling* 9: 86–93.

Nicol, A. R., Kolvin, I., Garside, R. F., Macmillan, A., Wolstenholme, F., and Leitch, I. M. (1981) A Multiple Criterion Screen for Identifying Secondary School Children with Psychiatric Disorder. II Studies of Validity. (Under revision.)

Nicol, A. R., Kolvin, I., Wolstenholme, F., McLaren, M., Garside, R. F., Macmillan, A., Hulbert, C. M., and Leitch, I. M. (1977) A School Group Counselling Project Assessing Therapeutic Qualities of Staff. In P. J. Graham (ed.) *Epidemiological Approaches in Child Psychiatry*. New York: Academic Press.

Nietzel, M. T., Winett, R. A., McDonald, M. L., and Davidson, W. S. (1977) *Behavioural Approaches to Community Psychology*. London: Pergamon Press.

Nolen, P. A., Kunzelmann, H. P., and Haring, N. G. (1967) Behavioral Modification in a Junior High Learning Disabilities Classroom. *Exceptional Children* 34: 163–68.

O'Connor, R. D. (1972) Relative Efficacy of Modeling, Shaping and the Combined Procedures for Modification of Social Withdrawal. *Journal of Abnormal Psychology* **79**: 327–34.

O'Dell, S. (1974) Training Parents in Behavior Modification: A Review. *Psychological Bulletin* **81**: 418–33.

Ohlsen, M. (1973) *Counseling Children in Groups.* New York: Holt, Rinehart and Winston.

O'Leary, K. D. (1972) The Entree of the Paraprofessional in the Classroom. In S. W. Bijou and E. Ribes-Inesta (eds) *Behaviour Modification: Issues and Extensions.* London: Academic Press.

—— (1978) The Operant and Social Psychology of Token Systems. In A. C. Catania and T. A. Brigham (eds) *Handbook of Applied Behavior Analysis: Social and Instructional Processes.* New York: Halsted Press.

O'Leary, K. D. and Becker, W. C. (1967) Behavior Modification of an Adjustment Class: A Token Reinforcement Program. *Exceptional Children* **33**: 637–42.

—— (1968) The Effects of the Intensity of a Teacher's Reprimands on Children's Behavior. *Journal of School Psychology* **7**: 8–11.

O'Leary, K. D. and Drabman, R. (1971) Token Reinforcement Programmes in the Classroom: A Review. *Psychological Bulletin* **75**(6): 379–98.

O'Leary, K. D. and Kent, R. N. (1973) Behavior Modification for Social Action: Research Tactics and Problems. In L. A. Hamerlynck, L. C. Handy, and E. J. Mash (eds) *Behavior Change: Methodology, Concepts and Practice.* Champaign, Ill.: Research Press.

O'Leary, K. D., Kent, R. M., and Kanowitz, J. (1975) Shaping Data Collection Congruent with Experimental Hypotheses. *Journal of Applied Behavior Analysis* **8**: 43–51.

O'Leary, K. D, Becker, W. C., Evans, M. B., and Saudargas, R. A. (1969) A Token Reinforcement Program in a Public School: A Replication and Systematic Analysis. *Journal of Applied Behavior Analysis* **2**(1): 3–13.

O'Leary, K. D., Kaufman, K. F., Kass, R. E., and Drabman, R. S. (1970) The Effects of Loud and Soft Reprimands on the Behavior of Disruptive Students. *Exceptional Children* **37**: 145–55.

O'Leary, S. G. and O'Leary, K. D. (1976) Behavior Modification in the School. In H. Leitenberg (ed.) *Handbook of Behavior Modification.* Englewood Cliffs, N.J.: Prentice-Hall.

Parker, J. and Nicol, A. R. (1981) Playgroup Therapy in the Junior School. II. The Therapy Process. *British Journal of Guidance and Counselling* **9**: 202–06.

Parloff, M. B., Waskow, I. E., and Wolfe, B. E. (1978) Research on Therapist Variables in Relation to Process and Outcome. In S. L.

Garfield and A. E. Bergin (eds) *Handbook of Psychotherapy and Behaviour Change* (2nd edn). New York: John Wiley.

Parten, M. (1933) Social Play Among Pre-School Children. *Journal of Abnormal and Social Psychology* **28**: 136–47.

Patterson, C. H. (1973) *Theories of Counseling and Psychotherapy*. New York: Harper and Row.

Patterson, G. R. (1972) *Families*. Champaign, Ill.: Research Press.

—— (1974) Interventions for Boys With Conduct Problems: Multiple Settings, Treatments and Criteria. *Journal of Consulting and Clinical Psychology* **42**: 471–80.

Patterson, G. R., Cobb, J. A., and Ray, R. S. (1973) A Social Engineering Technology for Retraining the Families ofAggressive Boys. In H. E. Adams and I. P. Unikel (eds) *Issues and Trends in Behavior Therapy*. Springfield, Ill.: C. C. Thomas.

Patterson, G. R., Shaw, D. A., and Ebner, M. J. (1969) Teachers, Peers and Parents as Agents of Change in the Classroom. In F. A. Benson (ed.) *Modifying Deviant Social Behaviors in Various Classroom Settings*. Eugene, Oreg.: University of Oregon.

Paul, G. (1966) *Effects of Insight, Desensitization and Attention Placebo Treatment of Anxiety*. Stanford, Calif.: Stanford University Press.

Pelham, L. E. (1972) Self-Directive Play Therapy with Socially Immature Kindergarten Students. *Dissertation Abstracts Int.* **32**A: 3798.

Persons, R. W. (1966) Psychological and Behaviour Change in Delinquents Following Psychotherapy. *Journal of Clinical Psychology* **22**: 337–40.

Peterson, R. F., Cox, M. A., and Bijou, S. W. (1971) Training Children to Work Productively in Classroom Groups. *Exceptional Children* **37**: 491–500.

Piaget, J. (1951) *Play, Dreams and Imitation in Childhood*. London: Heinemann.

Pines, N. A. (1967) A Pressure Cooker for Four-Year-Old Minds. *Harpers Magazine* **234**: 55–61.

Plog, S. C. (1974) Effectiveness, Leadership and Consultation. In *In the Workshop of Mental Health Consultation*, pp. 49–69. Washington D.C.: National Technical Information Service: US Department of Commerce.

Plowden, Lady B. (1968) School and the Social Services Department. *Social Work* **25**(4): 33–7.

Plowden Report (1967) *Children and Their Primary Schools*. Report of Central Advisory Council for Education. London: HMSO.

Pope, B. (1977) Research on Therapeutic Style. In A. S. Gurman and A. M. Razin (eds) *Effective Psychotherapy: A Handbook of Research*. New York: Pergamon Press.

Poser, E. (1966) The Effect of Therapists' Training on Group Therapeutic Outcome. *Journal of Consulting Psychology* **30**: 283–89.

Power, M. J., Benn, R. T., and Morris, J. N. (1972) Neighbourhood, School and Juveniles Before the Courts. *British Journal of Criminology* **12**: 111–32.

Power, M. J., Alderson, M. R., Phillipson, C. M., Schoenberg, E., and Morris, J. N. (1967) Delinquent Schools? *New Society* **10**: 542–43.

Powers, E. and Witmer, H. L. (1951) *An Experiment in the Prevention of Delinquency*. New York: Columbia University Press.

Quay, H. C., Glavin, J. P., Annesley, F. R., and Werry, J. S. (1972) The Modification of Problem Behavior and Academic Achievement in a Resource Room. *Journal of School Psychology* **10**: 187–98.

Rachman, S. (1973) The Effects of Psychological Treatment. In H. J. Eysenck (ed.) *Handbook of Abnormal Psychology*. New York: Basic Books.

Radin, N. (1972) Three Degrees of Maternal Involvement in a Pre-School Programme: Impact on Mothers and Children. *Child Development* **43**: 1355–364.

—— (1979) Assessing the Effectiveness of School Social Workers. *Social Work* **14**(2): 132–37.

Ralphs Report (1973) *Report of the Working Party on Training of Educational Welfare Officers*. Local Government Training Board. London: HMSO.

Randolph, D. L. and Hardage, N. C. (1973) Behavioural Consultation and Group Counseling with Potential Dropouts. *Elementary School Guidance and Counseling* **7**: 204–09.

Redl, F. (1949) The Phenomenon of Contagion and 'Shock Effect' in Group Therapy. In K. R. Eissler (ed.) *Searchlights on Delinquency*. London: Imago Publishing.

—— (1959) The Life-Space Interview. *American Journal of Orthopsychiatry* **29**: 1–18.

—— (1966) *When We Deal With Children*. New York: The Free Press.

Registrar-General's Office (1951) *Classification of Occupations*. London: HMSO.

Rehin, G. F. (1972) Child Guidance at the End of the Road. *Social Work Today* **2**(24): 21–4.

Reid, W. J. and Epstein, L. (1972) *Task-Centred Casework*. New York: Columbia University Press.

—— (1977) *Task-Centred Practice*. New York: Columbia University Press.

Reid, W. J. and Shyne, A. W. (1969) *Brief and Extended Casework*. New York, London: Columbia University Press.

Reynolds, D., Jones, D., and St Leger, S. (1976) Schools Do Make a Difference. *New Society* **37**: 321.

Reynolds, P. (1972) Play, Language and Human Evolution. In J. Brimer, A. Jolly, and K. Sylva (eds) *Play: Its Role in Development and Evolution*. Harmondsworth: Penguin Books.

Richman, N. (1977) Short-Term Outcome of Behaviour Problems in 3-Year-Old Children. In P. J. Graham (ed.) *Epidemiological Approaches to Child Psychiatry*. London: Academic Press.

Riessman, F. and Popper, H. I. (1968) *Up From Poverty*. New York: Harper and Row.

Ringer, U. M. J. (1973) The Use of a 'Token Helper' in the Management of Classroom Behavior Problems and in Teacher training. *Journal of Applied Behavior Analysis* **6**: 671–77.

Robbins, P. R. and Spencer, E. C. (1968) A Study of the Consultation Process. *Psychiatry* **31**: 362–68.

Robins, L. N. (1966) *Deviant Children Grown Up*. Baltimore: Williams and Wilkins.

—— (1970) Follow-Up Studies Investigating Childhood Disorders. In E. Hare and J. K. Wing (eds) *Psychiatric Epidemiology*. Oxford: Oxford University Press.

—— (1972) Follow-Up Studies of Behavior Disorders in Children. In H. C. Quay and J. S. Werry (eds) *Psychopathological Disorders of Childhood*. New York: John Wiley.

—— (1973) Evaluation of Psychiatric Services for Children in the United States. In J. K. Wing and H. Hafner (eds) *Roots of Evaluation*. Oxford: Oxford University Press (for the Nuffield Provinical Hospitals Trust).

Robins, L. N., West, P. A., and Herjanic, B. L. (1975) Arrests and Delinquency in Two Generations: A Study of Black Urban Families and Their Children. *Journal of Child Psychology and Psychiatry* **16**: 125–40.

Robinson, M. (1978) *Schools and Social Work*. Library of Social Work series. London: Routledge and Kegan Paul.

Rock, P. (1973) *Deviant Behaviour*. London: Hutchinson.

Roedell, W. C., Slaby, R. G., and Robinson, H. B. (1977) *Social Development in Young Children*. Monterey, Calif.: Brooks/Cole.

Rogers, C. R. (1952) *Client-Centred Therapy*. Boston: Houghton Mifflin.

—— (1959) A Theory of Therapy, Personality and Interpersonal Relationships as Developed in the Client-Centred Framework. In S. Koch (ed.) *Psychology: A Study of a Science* Vol. 3. New York: McGraw-Hill.

Rollins, H. A., McCandless, B. R., Thompson, M., and Brassell,

W. R. (1974) Project Success Environment: An Extended Application of Contingency Management in Inner City Schools. *Journal of Educational Psychology* **66**: 167–78.

Romanczyk, R. G., Kent, R. N., Diament, C., and O'Leary, K. D. (1973) Measuring the Reliability of Observational Data: A Reactive Process. *Journal of Applied Behavior Analysis* **6**: 175–84.

Roper, R. and Hinde, R. A. (1978) Social Behaviour in a Play Group: Consistency and Complexity. *Child Development* **49**: 570–79.

Rose, G. and Marshall, A. M. (1974) *Counselling and School Social Work.* Chichester: John Wiley.

Rose, S. A., Blank, M., and Spalter, I. (1975) Situational Specificity of Behaviour in Young Children. *Child Development* **46**: 464–69.

Rotter, J. B. (1966) Generalized Expectancies for Internal Versus External Control of Reinforcement. *Psychological Monographs* **80**(1): 609.

Rule, S. A. (1972) Comparison of Three Different Types of Feedback on Teachers' Performance. In G. Semb (ed.) *Behavior Analysis and Education.* Lawrence, Kan.: University of Kansas.

Rutter, M. (1965) Classification and Categorisation in Child Psychiatry. *Journal of Child Psychology and Psychiatry* **6**: 71–83.

—— (1966) *Children of Sick Parents*: An Environmental and Psychiatric Study. Maudsley Monograph No. 16. Oxford: Oxford University Press.

—— (1967) A Children's Behaviour Questionnaire for Completion by Teachers: Preliminary Findings. *Journal of Child Psychology and Psychiatry* **8**: 1–11.

—— (1970) Sex Differences in Children's Responses to Family Stress. In E. J. Anthony and C. Koupernik (eds) *The Child and His Family.* Chichester: John Wiley.

—— (1971) Parent-Child Separation: Psychological Effects on the Children. *Journal of Child Psychology and Psychiatry* **12**: 233–60.

Rutter, M. and Madge, N. (1976) *Cycles of Disadvantage: A Review of Research.* London: Heinemann.

Rutter, M., Tizard, J., and Whitmore, K. (1970) *Education, Health and Behaviour.* London: Longman.

Rutter, M., Maughan, B., Mortimore, P., and Ouston, J. (1979) *Fifteen Thousand Hours. Secondary Schools and Their Effects on Children.* London: Open Books.

Rutter, M., Cox, A., Tupling, C., Berger, M., and Yule, W. (1975) Attainment and Adjustment in Two Geographical Areas: I. The Prevalence of Psychiatric Disorder. *British Journal of Psychiatry* **126**: 493–509.

Rycroft, C. (1966) Introduction: Causes and Meaning. In C. Rycroft (ed.) *Psychoanalysis Observed*. London: Constable.

Sainsbury, P. (1975) Evaluation of Community Mental Health Programmes. In M. Guttentag and E. L. Struening (eds) *Handbook of Evaluation Research* Vol. 2. Beverley Hills, Calif.: Sage.

Sandford, N. (1965) The Prevention of Mental Illness. In B. Wolman (ed.) *Handbook of Clinical Psychology*. New York: McGraw-Hill.

Sandler, J., Holder, A., and Dare, C. (1970) Basic Psychoanalytic Concepts. II The Treatment Alliance. *British Journal of Psychiatry* **116**: 555–58.

Santogrossi, D. A., O'Leary, K. D., Romanczyk, R. G., and Kauffman, K. F. (1973) Self-Evaluation by Adolescents in a Psychiatric Hospital School Token Program. *Journal of Applied Behavior Analysis* **6**: 277–87.

Saslow, B. and Peters, A. (1956) A Follow-up of 'Untreated' Patients With Behavior Disorders. *Psychiatric Quarterly* **30**: 283–302.

Saudargas, R. A. (1972) Setting Criterion Rates of Teacher Praise: The Effects of Videotape Feedback in a Behavior Analysis Follow-Through Classroom. In G. Semb (ed.) *Behavior Analysis and Education*. Lawrence, Kan.: University of Kansas.

Saunders, B. T. (1971) The Effect of the Emotionally Disturbed Child in the Public School Classroom. *Psychology in Schools* **8**: 23–6.

Schaefer, C., Baker, E., and Zawel, D. (1975) A Factor Analytic and Reliability Study of the Devereux Elementary School Behavior Rating Scale. *Psychology in the Schools* **12**: 295–300.

Schaefer, E. S. and Aaronson, M. (1972) Infant Education Research Project: Implementation and Implications for a Home Tutoring Project. In R. K. Parker (ed.) *The Pre-School in Action*. Boston: Allyn and Bacon.

Schiffer, A. L. (1966) The Effectiveness of Group Play Therapy as Assessed by Specific Changes in a Child's Peer Relations. *Dissertation Abstracts Int.* **27**B: 972–74.

Schiffer, M. (1971) *The Therapeutic Play Group*. London: Allen and Unwin.

Schild, J. S., Scott, C. B., and Zimmerman, D. J. (1976) The Child Welfare Agency as School Consultant. *Child Welfare* **55**: 491–500.

Schonell, F. J. and Schonell, F. E. (1963) *Diagnostic and Attainment Testing* (8th edn). Edinburgh: Oliver and Boyd.

Schools Council (1968) *Enquiry 1: Young School Leavers* Part 2. London: HMSO.

Schutte, R. C. and Hopkins, B. L. (1970) The Effects of Teacher Attention on Following Instructions in a Kindergarten Class. *Journal of Applied Behavior Analysis* **3**: 117–22.

Sears, R. R., Maccoby, E. E., and Levin, H. (1956) *Patterns of Child-Rearing*. New York: Harper and Row.

Seebohm Committee (1968) *Report of the Committee on Local Authority and Allied Personal Social Services*. London: HMSO.

Seeman, J., Barry, E., and Ellinwood, C. (1964) Interpersonal Assessment of Play Therapy Outcome. *Psychotherapy: Theory, Research and Practice* **1**: 64–6.

Shapiro, R. J. and Budman, S. H. (1973) Defection, Termination and Continuation in Family and Individual Therapy. *Family Process* **12**: 55–68.

Sharrock, A. (1970) *Home-School Relations: Their Importance in Education*. Basic Books in Education Series. London: Macmillan.

Shaw, M. C. (1962) *Group Counseling Fails to Aid Underachievers*. Research Brief No. 4. Sacramento, Calif.: State Department of Education.

Shepherd, M., Oppenheim, A., and Mitchell, S. (1966) Childhood Behaviour Disorders and the Child Guidance Clinic: An Epidemiological Study. *Journal of Child Psychology and Psychiatry* **7**: 39–52.

—— (1971) *Childhood Behaviour and Mental Health*. London: University of London Press.

Sherif, M. and Sherif, C. W. (1969) *Social Psychology*. New York: Harper and Row.

Sherman, J. A. and Bushell, D. (1974) Behavior Modification as an Educational Technique. In F. D. Horowitz (ed.) *Review of Child Development Research* Vol. 4. Chicago: University of Chicago Press.

Sherman, T. M. and Cormier, W. H. (1974) An Investigation of the Influence of Student Behavior on Teacher Behavior. *Journal of Applied Behavior Analysis* **7**: 11–21.

Shouksmith, G. and Taylor, J. W. (1964) The Effect of Counselling on the Achievement of High-Ability Pupils. *British Journal of Educational Psychology* **34**: 51–7.

Siegel, C. L. (1972) Changes in Play Therapy Behaviors Over Time as a Function of Differing Levels of Therapist-Offered Conditions. *Journal of Clinical Psychology* **28**: 235.

Slavson, S. R. and Schiffer, M. (1975) *Group Psychotherapies for Children*. New York: International Universities Press.

Sloane, R. B., Cristol, A. H., Peperink, M. C., and Staples, F. R. (1970) Role Preparation and Expectation of Improvement in Psychotherapy. *Journal of Nervous and Mental Diseases* **150**: 18–26.

Sloane, R. B., Staples, F. R., Cristol, A. H., Yorkston, N. J., and Whipple, K. (1975) *Short-Term Analytically Oriented Psychotherapy*

Versus Behavior Therapy. Cambridge, Mass.: Harvard University Press.

Smethells (1977) In DHSS Developmental Group — Social Work Service. *Working Together for Children and Their Families.* Report series. South Glamorgan County Council and Welsh Office.

Smilansky, S. (1968) *The Effects of Sociodramatic Play on Disadvantaged School Children.* New York: John Wiley.

Smith, M. B. (1968) School and Home: Focus on Achievement. In A. H. Passow (ed.) *Developing Programs for the Educationally Disadvantaged.* New York: Teachers College Press.

Smith, M. L. and Glass, G. V. (1977) Meta-Analysis of Psychotherapy Outcome Studies. *American Psychologist* 32: 752–60.

Smith, P. K. and Connelly, K. (1972) Patterns of Play and Social Interaction in Pre-School Children. In N. Blurton-Jones (ed.) *Ethological Studies in Child Behaviour.* Cambridge: Cambridge University Press.

Snedecor, G. W. and Cochran, W. G. (1967) *Statistical Methods.* (6th edn) Ames, Iowa: Iowa State University Press.

Sobey, F. (1970) *The Non-Professional Revolution in Mental Health.* New York: Columbia University Press.

Solomon, R. W. and Wahler, R. G. (1973) Peer Reinforcement Control of Classroom Problem Behavior. *Journal of Applied Behavior Analysis* 6: 49–56.

Speilberger, C. D., Weitz, H., and Denny, J. P. (1962) Group Counseling and the Academic Performance of Anxious College Freshmen. *Journal of Counseling Psychology* 9: 195–204.

Spivack, G. and Swift, M. (1967) *Devereux Elementary School Behavior Rating Scale Manual.* Devon, Pa.: The Devereux Foundation.

—— (1973) The Classroom Behavior of Children: A Critical Review of Teacher-Administered Rating Scales. *Journal of Special Education* 7: 55–89.

Start, K. B. and Wells, B. K. (1972) *The Trend of Reading Standards.* London: National Foundation for Educational Research.

Stokes, T. F. and Baer, D. M. (1977) An Implicit Technology of Generalization. *Journal of Applied Behavior Analysis* 10: 349–67.

Strain, P., Cooke, T., and Apolloni, T. (1976) *Teaching Exceptional Children: Assessing and Modifying Social Behavior.* New York: Academic Press.

Stromer, R. (1977) Remediating Academic Deficiencies in Learning Disabled Children. *Exceptional Children* 43: 432–40.

Strupp, H. H. (1958) The Psychotherapist's Contribution to the Treatment Process: An Experimental Investigation. *Behavioural Science* 3: 34–67.

—— (1978) Psychotherapy Research and Practice: An Overview. In S. L. Garfield and A. E. Bergin (eds) *Handbook of Psychotherapy and Behavior Change* (2nd edn). New York: John Wiley.

Strupp, H. H. and Bergin, A. E. (1969) Some Empirical and Conceptual Issues for Co-ordinated Research in Psychotherapy: A Critical Review of Issues, Trends and Evidence. *International Journal of Psychiatry* 7: 18–90.

Stuart, R. B. (1970) *Trick or Treatment: How and When Psychotherapy Fails*. Champaign, Ill.: Research Press.

Sullivan, H. S. (1953) *Conceptions of Modern Psychiatry*. New York: W. W. Norton.

—— (1956) *Clinical Studies in Psychiatry*. New York: W. W. Norton.

Sulzer, B., Hunt, S., Ashby, E., Koniarski, C., and Krams, M. (1971) Increasing Rate and Percentage Correct in Reading and Spelling in a 5th Grade Public School Class of Slow Readers by Means of a Token System. In E. Ramp and B. L. Hopkins (eds) *A New Direction for Education: Behavior Analysis*. Lawrence, Kan.: University of Kansas.

Surrat, P. R., Ulrich, R. and Hawkins, R. P. (1969) An Elementary Student as a Behavioural Engineer. *Journal of Applied Behavior Analysis* 2: 85–92.

Swift, M. S. and Spivack, G. (1968) The Assessment of Achievement-Related Classroom Behavior. *Journal of Special Education* 2: 137–53.

—— (1969) Achievement-Related Classroom Behavior of Secondary School Normal and Disturbed Students. *Exceptional Children* 36: 677–84.

Sylva, K. (1977) Play and Learning. In B. Tizard and D. Harvey (eds) *Biology of Play*. Clinics in Developmental Medicine No. 62. London: Heinemann Medical Books Ltd. (Spastics International Medical Publications).

Taplin, P. S. and Reid, J. B. (1973) Effects of Instructional Set and Experimenter Influence on Observer Reliability. *Child Development* 44: 547–54.

Taylor, W. F. and Hoedt, K. (1974) Classroom-Related Behaviour Problems: Counsel Parents, Teachers or Children? *Journal of Counseling Psychology* 21: 3–8.

Tharp, R. G. and Wetzel, R. J. (1969) *Behavior Modification in the Natural Environment*. New York: Academic Press.

Thomas, D. R., Becker, W. C., and Armstrong, M. (1968) Production and Elimination of Disruptive Classroom Behavior by Systematically Varying Teachers' Behavior. *Journal of Applied Behavior Analysis* 1: 35–45.

Thombs, M. R. and Muro, J. J. (1973) Group Counselling and the

Sociometric Status of Second Grade Children. *Elementary School Guidance and Counseling* **7**: 194–97.

Thorndike, R. L. (1963) *Problems of Over- and Under-Achievement*. New York: Teachers College Press.

Tizard, J. (1973) Maladjusted Children and the Child Guidance Service. *London Educational Review* **2**(2): 22–37.

Tolor, A. (1970) The Effectiveness of Various Therapeutic Approaches: A Study of Sub-Professional Therapists. *International Journal of Group Psychotherapy* **20**: 48–62.

Tomlinson, J. R. (1972) Implementing Behavior Modification Programs with Limited Consultation Time. *Journal of School Psychology* **10**: 379–86.

Tonge, W. L., James, D. S., and Hillam, S. M. (1975) *Families Without Hope*: A Controlled Study of 33 Problem Families. Special Publication No. 11. Kent: Royal College of Psychiatrists and Headley Bros. Ltd.

Truax, C. B. and Carkhuff, R. R. (1967) *Toward Effective Counseling and Psychotherapy: Training and Practice*. Chicago: Aldine Press.

Truax, C. B. and Lister, J. L. (1970) Effectiveness of Counselors and Counselor-Aides. *Journal of Counseling Psychology* **17**: 331–34.

Truax, C. B., Altmann, H., Wright, L., and Mitchell, K. M. (1973) Effects of Therapeutic Conditions in Child Therapy. *Journal of Community Psychology* **1**: 313–18.

Turkewitz, H., O'Leary, K. D. and Ironsmith, M. (1976) Generalization and Maintenance of Appropriate Behavior Through Self-Control. *Journal of Consulting and Clinical Psychology* **43**: 577–83.

Twardosz, S. and Sajwaj, T. (1972) Multiple Effects of a Procedure to Increase Sitting in a Hyperactive, Retarded Boy. *Journal of Applied Behavior Analysis* **5**: 73–8.

Vriend, T. J. (1969) High Performing Inner City Adolescents Assist Low-Performing Peers in Counselling Groups. *Personnel and Guidance Journal* **47**: 897–904.

Wahler, R. G. (1969) Setting Generality: Some Specific and General Effects of Child Behavior Therapy. *Journal of Applied Behavior Analysis* **2**: 239–46.

Walker, H. M. and Buckley N. (1968) The Use of Positive Reinforcement in Conditioning Attending Behavior. *Journal of Applied Behavior Analysis* **1**: 245–57.

Walker, H. M. and Hops, H. (1973) The Use of Group and Individual Reinforcement Contingencies in the Modification of Social Withdrawal. In L. A. Hamerlynck, L. C. Handy, and E. J. Mash (eds) *Behavior Change: Methodology, Concepts and Practice*. Champaign, Ill.: Research Press.

—— (1977) Increasing Academic Achievement by Reinforcing Direct

Academic Performance and/or Facilitative Non-Academic Responses. *Journal of Educational Psychology* **68**: 218–25.

Walker, H. M., Hops, H. and Johnson, S. M. (1975) Generalization and Maintenance of Classroom Treatment Effects. *Behavior Therapy* **6**: 188–200.

Wall, W. D. (1973) The Problem Child in Schools. *London Educational Review* **2**(2): 3–21.

Wallin, P. (1954) A Guttman Scale for Measuring Women's Neighbourliness. *American Journal of Sociology* **59**: 243.

Wallston, B. (1973) The Effects of Maternal Employment on Children. *Journal of Child Psychology and Psychiatry* **14**: 81–95.

Ward, J. (1971) Modification of Deviant Classroom Behaviour. *British Journal of Educational Psychology* **41**(3): 304–13.

Ward, M. H. and Baker, B. L. (1968) Reinforcement Therapy in the Classroom. *Journal of Applied Behavior Analysis* **1**: 323–28.

Warner, R. W. (1971) Alienated Students: Six Months After Receiving Behavioral Group Counseling. *Journal of Counseling Psychology* **18**: 426–30.

Warner, R. W. and Hansen, J. C. (1970) Verbal Reinforcement and Model Reinforcement Group Counseling with Alienated Students. *Journal of Counseling Psychology* **17**: 168–72.

Warnock Report (1978) *Special Educational Needs*. Report of the Committee of Enquiry into the Educational Needs of Children and Young People. London: HMSO.

Wasik, B., Senn, K., Welch, R., and Cooper, B. (1969) Behavior Modification with Culturally Deprived School Children. *Journal of Experimental Child Psychology* **2**: 181–94.

Watkins, R. and Derrick, D. (1977) *Co-Operative Care*. Practice and Information Profiles. Manchester: Centre for Information and Advice on Educational Disadvantage.

Watts, A. F. (1948) *The Holborn Reading Scale*. London: Harrap.

Wedge, P. and Prosser, H. (1973) *Born to Fail*. London: Arrow Books.

Wechsler, D. (1949) *The Wechsler Intelligence Scale for Children – Manual*. New York: The Psychological Corporation.

Weikart, D. P., Deloria, D. J., and Lawson, S. (1974) Results of a Pre-School Intervention Project. In *Longitudinal Evaluations*. Washington D.C.: US Department of Health, Education and Welfare; Office of Child Development.

Weinstein, L. (1969) Project Re-Ed: Schools for Emotionally Disturbed Children: Effectiveness as Viewed by Referring Agencies, Parents and Teachers. *Exceptional Children* **35**: 703–11.

Whitaker, D. S. and Lieberman, M. A. (1965) *Psychotherapy Through the Group Process*. London: Tavistock.

White, M. A. (1975) Natural Rates of Teacher Approval and Disapproval in the Classroom. *Journal of Applied Behavior Analysis* **8**: 367–72.

Whiting, B. B. (1963) *Six Cultures: Studies in Child-Rearing*. New York: John Wiley.

Willems, E. P. (1974) Behavioural Technology and Behavioural Ecology. *Journal of Applied Behavior Analysis* **7**: 151–65.

Williams, R. L., Long, J. D., and Yoakley, R. W. (1972) The Utility of Behavior Contracts and Behavior Proclamations with Advantaged Senior High School Students. *Journal of School Psychology* **10**: 329–38.

Willner, A. G., Brankman, C. J., Kirigin, K. A., and Wolf, M. M. (1978) Achievement Place: A Community Treatment Model for Youths in Trouble. In D. Marholin (ed.) *Child Behavior Therapy*. New York: Halsted Press.

Wilson, G. T., Hannon, A. E., and Evans, W. I. M. (1968) Behavior Therapy and the Therapist-Patient Relationship. *Journal of Consulting and Clinical Psychology* **32**: 103–09.

Winer, B. J. (1971) *Statistical Principles in Experimental Design* (2nd edn). New York: McGraw-Hill.

Winett, R. A. and Roach, E. M. (1973) The Effects of Reinforcing Academic Performance on Social Behavior. *Psychological Record* **23**: 391–96.

Winett, R. A. and Winkler, R. C. (1972) Current Behavior Modification in the Classroom: Be Still, Be Quiet, Be Docile. *Journal of Applied Behavior Analysis* **5**: 499–504.

Winkler, R. C., Teigland, J. J., and Munger, P. F. (1965) The Effects of Selected Counselling and Remedial Techniques on Underachieving Elementary School Students. *Journal of Counseling Psychology* **12**: 384–87.

Winn, E. V. (1962) The Influence of Play Therapy on Personality Change and the Consequent Effect on Reading Performance. *Dissertation Abstracts Int.* **22**: 4278–279.

Winnicott, D. W. (1971) *Playing and Reality*. London: Tavistock.

Wolf, M. M., Giles, D. K., and Hall, V. R. (1968) Experiment With Token Reinforcement in a Remedial Classroom. *Behavior, Research and Therapy* **6**: 51–64.

Wolf, M. M., Hanley, E. L., King, L. A., Lachowicz, J., and Giles, D. K. (1970) The Timer-Game: A Variable Interval Contingency for the Management of Out-of-Seat Behavior. *Exceptional Children* **37**: 113–17.

Wolff, A. and Schwartz, E. K. (1971) Psychoanalysis in Groups. In H. I. Kaplan and B. J. Sadock (eds) *Comprehensive Group Psychotherapy*. Baltimore: Williams and Wilkins.

Wolff, S. and Acton, W. P. (1968) Characteristics of Parents of Disturbed Children. *British Journal of Psychiatry* **114**: 599–601.

Wolstenholme, F. and Kolvin, I. (1980) Social Workers in Schools – The Teachers' Response. *British Journal of Guidance and Counselling* **8**: 44–56.

Wolstenholme, F., Hulbert, C. M., and Kolvin, I. (1976) Promoting Mental Health in Schools. *Special Education: Forward Trends* **3**(4): 15–17.

Wrate, R., Nicol, A. R., and Kolvin, I. (1981) Reliability of Clinical Ratings of Psychiatric Disorder From Standard Case Records. (In Preparation.)

Wright, D. M., Moelis, I., and Pollack, L. J. (1976) The Outcome of Individual Psychotherapy: Increments at Follow-up. *Journal of Child Psychology and Psychiatry* **17**: 275–85.

Yalom, I. D. (1975) *The Theory and Practice of Group Psychotherapy.* (2nd edn). New York: Basic Books.

Yalom, I. D. and Rand, K. (1967) Compatibility and Cohesiveness in Theory Groups. *Archives of General Psychiatry* **15**: 267–75.

Yarrow, M. R. (1963) Problems of Methods in Parent-Child Research. *Child Development* **34**: 215–26.

Young, D. (1968) *Manual for the Group Reading Test.* London: University of London Press.

Younghusband Report (1959) *Report on the Working Party on Social Workers in the Local Authority Health and Welfare Services.* London: HMSO.

Yule, W. (1977) Behavioural Approches. In M. Rutter and L. Hersov (eds) *Child Psychiatry: Modern Approaches.* Oxford: Blackwell.

Zax, M., Cowen, E. L., Rappaport, J., Beach, D. R., and Laird, J. D. (1968) Follow-up Study of Children Identified Early as Emotionally Disturbed. *Journal of Consulting and Clinical Psychology* **32**: 369–74.

Zax, M., Cowen, E. L., Izzo, L. D., Madonia, A. J., Merenda, J., and Trost, M. S. (1966) A Teacher-Aide Programme for Preventing Emotional Disturbance in Primary Grade School Children. *Mental Hygiene* **50**: 406–14.

Zimmerman, E. H. and Zimmerman, J. (1962) The Alteration of Behavior in a Special Classroom Situation. *Journal of Experimental Analysis of Behavior* **5**: 59–60.

Zunker, V. G. and Brown, W. F. (1966) Comparative Effectiveness of Student and Professional Counsellors. *Personnel and Guidance Journal* **44**: 738–43.

Name index

Aaronson, M. 23, 416
Abidin, R. R. 104, 385
Abraham, K. A. 226, 261, 385
Abramowitz, C. V. 26, 226, 229, 385
Acton, W. P. 64–5, 423
Adams, H. E. 100, 406
Adams, P. L. 27, 312, 385
Adams, S. 20, 385
Alexakos, C. E. 261, 405
Alexander, J. F. 21, 385
Allen, G. J. 101, 389
Allen, K. E. 87, 97, 385, 400
Allen, R. P. 104, 385, 400
Allinsmith, W. T. 141, 386
Altmann, H. A. 261, 386
Anderson, R. J. 174–75, 178, 181, 386
Anthony, W. A. 27, 386
Apolloni, T. 93, 418
Armstrong, M. 87–8, 419
Artuso, A. A. 91, 400
Ashby, J. D. 26, 386
Aspy, D. N. 28, 386
Atkeson, B. M. 98, 178, 386
Atkinson, D. R. 89, 386
Atwell, A. A. 92, 408
Axline, V. M. 50, 223, 230–31, 303, 386
Ayllon, T. 92–3, 386

Baer, D. M. 94, 97, 100, 102, 386, 388–89,
   392, 406, 418
Baker, B. L. 88, 96, 421
Baker, E. 337, 416
Barber, J. D. 229, 261, 407
Barcai, A. 227–29, 261, 386–87
Barclay, J. 102, 389
Barker Lunn, J. C. 347, 387; see also subject
   index
Barrett, L. C. 22, 307, 387, 409
Barrish, H. H. 90, 387

Barry, E. 261, 417
Baymur, F. B. 229, 261, 387
Beck, S. 119, 394
Becker, W. C. 14–15, 87–90, 110, 155, 387,
   390, 404, 407, 411, 419
Bell, M. 51, 230, 240, 401
Benn, R. T. 325, 413
Bennett, W. S. Jr 144–45, 410
Benning, J. J. 92, 395
Bentovim, A. 223, 387
Bergin, A. E. 7, 30, 32, 118, 178, 307, 309,
   387, 419
Berlin, I. N. 174–75, 178, 387–88
Berlyne, D. E. 222, 388
Bernstein, A. 27, 404
Bevins, S. M. C. 228, 261, 388
Biasco, F. 261, 388
Biblow, E. 225, 388
Bijou, S. W. 88, 388, 412
Bing, M. 41, 397
Birch, H. G. 29, 388, 397
Birnbrauer, J. 95, 388
Blanchard, E. B. 90, 388
Blank, M. 224, 415
Blom, G. E. 118, 388
Blomfield, J. M. 63, 388
Bolstad, O. D. 98, 138, 388, 401
Bootzin, R. R. 94, 402
Bower, E. 5, 39, 141, 328, 388
Bowers, K. 90, 95, 138, 408
Bowles, P. E. 99, 388
Boxall, M. 141, 145–47, 157, 388
Bozarth, J. D. 27, 409
Braun, S. J. 23, 389
Breyer, N. L. 88, 101, 389
Briggs, J. W. 261, 389
Brimer, M. A. 339–40, 389
Broden, M. 88–90, 96, 389
Broedel, J. 229, 261, 389

Bronfenbrenner, U. 22–4, 325, 389
Brophy, J. E. 147, 389
Brough, W. 75
Brown, J. C. 102, 389
Brown, P. 87, 389
Brown, W. F. 28, 423
Bryan, T. S. 92, 389
Buckley, N. 90, 420
Budman, S. H. 31, 417
Buell, J. 87, 104, 390, 400
Burke, S. 92, 386
Buros, O. K. 340–41, 390
Bushell, D. 86, 90, 92, 99, 390, 417
Buys, C. J. 97, 390

Calchera, D. J. 88, 389
Caldwell, B. 23, 388
Campbell, D. T. 30, 390
Cann, C. 88, 389
Caplan, G. 14, 18, 141, 175, 328, 390
Carbonnel, J. 95, 402
Carkhuff, R. R. 26–7, 32, 75, 144, 148, 314,
   383, 386, 390, 420
Carlson, C. S. 90, 390
Carter, B. D. 175, 390
Cattell, R. B. 340–41
Catterall, C. D. 11, 220, 390
Cave, R. G. 178, 180, 390
Chadwick, B. A. 92, 104, 390
Chazan, M. 180, 194, 390
Cheatham, R. B. 261, 391
Chilman, C. S. 99, 391
Clark, M. 91, 99, 100, 328, 391, 399
Clarke, D. B. 20, 391
Clegg, A. 13, 179, 391
Clement, P. W. 226, 261, 391
Clements, T. H. 261, 391
Cobb, J. A. 21, 92, 391, 401, 412
Cochran, W. G. 353, 418
Cochrane, R. 95, 391
Coleman, J. S. 325, 391
Coles, C. 261, 391
Combs, M. L. 93, 391
Conklin, R. C. 261, 386
Conn, J. H. 223, 392
Connelly, K. 224, 418
Cooke, T. 93, 418
Cooper, B. 177, 392
Cooper, M. L. 100, 102, 392
Copeland, R. 99–100, 392, 399
Cormier, W. H. 89, 94, 392, 417
Cornish, R. V. G. 20, 391
Cossairt, A. 101, 392
Costin, L. B. 174–75, 392
Court, S. D. M. vii, 409; see also subject
   index
Cowen, E. L. 141–45, 148, 154, 157, 164,
   170–71, 314, 326, 328, 392–94
Cox, M. A. 88, 412
Craig, M. M. 326, 393
Craighead, W. E. 129, 408

Creanage, N. C. 261, 393
Crow, M. L. 229, 261, 393
Curtiss, K. 90, 405
Cytryn, L. 19, 393, 395

Dare, C. 221, 416
Davidson, H. H. 92, 393
Davies, B. 173, 176, 393
Davis, J. L. 89, 386
Day, R. C. 92, 104, 390
Deloria, D. J. 23, 421
Denny, J. P. 261, 418
Derrick, D. 173–74, 195, 421
Deskin, G. 227, 261, 394
Deutch, M. 23, 145, 394
Devoge, J. T. 119, 394
Dickenson, W. A. 261, 394
Dies, R. R. 26, 396
DiLorenzo, L. T. 23, 394
Dorfman, E. 226, 229, 261, 394
Dorr, D. 142–43, 164, 392–94
Douglas, J. W. B. 63, 177, 325, 341, 388, 394
Drabman, R. S. 90, 94, 98, 113, 178, 394,
   411
Dunn, L. M. 339–40, 389, 394
Dunnett, C. W. 354–55, 394
Duthie, J. H. 144–45, 149–50, 394, 402

Egner, A. N. 88, 404
Eisenberg, L. 7, 19, 393, 395
Ellinwood, C. 261, 417
Elliott, C. D. 261, 395
Elliott, R. 87, 389
Emery, R. 92, 395
Epstein, L. 187, 413
Erikson, E. 221, 225, 395
Escalona, S. K. 18, 395
Etaugh, C. 69, 395
Evans, W. I. M. 119, 422
Everett, P. M. 87, 385
Evers, W. L. 93, 395
Ewing, T. N. 227, 261, 395
Eysenck, H. J. 17, 30, 307, 309, 336, 395
Eysenck, S. B. G. 336, 395

Fasnacht, G. 113, 395, 404
Feld, S. 144, 398
Feldhusen, J. F. 92, 395
Felsenfeld, N. 242–43, 406
Ferritor, D. E. 90, 92, 395
Fieldler, F. E. 25, 395
Finlayson, D. J. 9, 396
Finney, B. C. 261, 396
Fisher, B. 227, 261, 396
Fisher, R. A. 121, 158, 396
Fitzherbert, K. 173, 196, 396
Forehand, R. 98, 100, 178, 386, 406
Forness, S. R. 91, 407
Forward, G. E. 231, 396
Foster, S. L. 129, 402
Foulds, G. A. 65, 396

Fox, R. 175, 396
Franks, J. D. 314, 396
Freeman, E. H. 28, 399
Freeman, J. 196, 396
Freud, A. 225, 396
Freud, S. 13, 218, 224, 325, 396
Freyberg, J. T. 225, 396
Friedman, M. L. 26, 396
Friesen, W. V. 11, 404
Fundudis, T. 63, 396

Garfield, S. L. 28, 396
Garner, J. 41, 397
Garside, R. F. 7–8, 51, 63, 71, 187, 339,
   396–97, 403, 406, 410
Garvey, C. 222, 397
Gast, D. L. 91, 397
Gath, D. 174, 397
Gazda, M. 220, 390, 396
Geisser, S. 348–49, 398
Gesten, E. 170, 392–93
Gilbert, A. 19, 393, 395
Gilbert, W. M. 227, 261, 395
Gilbreath, S. H. 261, 397
Giles, D. K. 91, 422
Gilmer, B. 23, 397
Ginott, H. 14, 50, 220, 231, 233, 397
Gitterman, A. 174, 397
Glass, G. V. 18, 310–11, 397, 418
Glavin, J. P. 96, 397, 413
Glick, S. J. 326, 393, 397, 404
Glynn, E. L. 92, 398
Goethals, G. W. 141, 386
Goldberg, D. P. 65, 398
Goldstein, A. F. 8, 403
Goldstein, A. P. 220, 311, 398
Gonso, J. 93, 398
Good, T. L. 118, 389
Gottmann, J. 18, 93, 398
Graham, P. 13, 398
Gray, S. W. 23, 397–98
Graziano, A. M. 99, 398
Greenberg, J. W. 92, 393
Greenhouse, S. W. 348–49, 398
Greenwood, C. R. 98, 398
Grether, J. 23, 400
Gropper, G. L. 10, 398
Grosser, C. 143, 149, 398
Gurin, G. 144, 398
Gussow, J. D. 29, 388

Hahn, S. C. 225, 408
Haight, D. A. 261, 410
Haley, J. 178, 399
Hall, C. S. 230, 399
Hall, R. V. 87–8, 99–101, 110, 389, 392, 399
Hall, V. R. 91, 422
Hampe, I. E. 22, 307, 387, 409
Hannon, A. E. 119, 422
Hansen, J. C. 220, 226, 228, 261, 399, 421
Hardage, N. C. 226, 228, 261, 413

Hare, E. H. 65, 399
Hargrave, G. E. 261, 399
Hargreaves, D. M. 13, 399
Haring, N. G. 90, 410
Harris, M. R. 28, 399
Harris, V. W. 90, 92, 399
Hart, B. M. 87, 400
Hart, J. 119, 404
Harvey, L. 51, 177–78, 400
Hawkins, R. P. 129, 419
Hays, D. 23, 400
Heaton, R. C. 90, 103, 385, 400
Heber, R. 24, 400
Heinicke, C. M. 29, 400
Heitler, J. B. 235, 400
Henry, S. E. 226, 400
Henry, W. E. 143, 149, 398
Herjanic, B. L. 13, 414
Hester, S. K. 13, 399
Hewett, F. M. 91, 400
Hillam, S. M. 194, 420
Hinde, R. A. 224, 415
Hinds, W. C. 226, 228, 261, 400
Hobbs, N. 8, 400
Hodges, W. L. 147, 400
Hoedt, K. 229, 261, 419
Hoehn-Saric, R. 235, 400
Holder, A. 221, 400, 416
Holmes, D. S. 8, 235–36, 401
Hopkins, B. L. 101, 392
Hops, H. 92, 94, 97–8, 391, 398, 401, 420
Hosford, R. E. 261, 408
House, R. M. 228, 261, 401
Hubbert, A. K. 226, 228, 261, 401
Hughes, D. C. 261, 386
Hugo, M. J. 229, 261, 401
Hulbert, C. M. 8, 15, 51, 145–46, 158, 177,
   397, 401, 403, 423
Hume, K. E. 229, 261, 401

Ingham, R. 30, 409
Ironsmith, M. 98, 104, 420
Irwin, E. 229, 261, 401

Jacobson, M. D. 229, 261, 407
James, D. S. 194, 420
Jeffrey, L. I. H. 11, 232, 234, 401
Jensen, A. R. 325, 401
Johnson, C. A. 99, 178, 401
Johnson, R. A. 90, 388
Johnson, S. M. 97–8, 113, 138, 388, 401
Johnston, M. S. 87, 402
Jones, D. 9, 29, 414
Jones, R. M. 220, 402

Kadushin, A. 175, 402
Kalis, B. L. 28, 399
Kanowitz, J. 129, 411
Kaplan, R. D. 104, 409
Kaswan, J. W. 325–26, 405
Katz, R. C. 99, 178, 401

Kauffman, J. M. 95, 402
Kaufman, J. M. 91, 402, 411, 416
Kazdin, A. E. 94, 99, 102–03, 402
Keeley, S. M. 95, 402
Kelly, E. W. Jr 226, 261, 402
Kelly, J. G. 143, 149, 398
Kennedy, K. T. 144–45, 402
Kent, R. N. 95, 102–04, 129, 402–03, 411,
    415
Kiesler, D. J. 14, 17–18, 311, 403
Kilmann, P. R. 226, 400–01
Kirby, F. D. 88, 92, 403
Klaus, R. A. 23, 398
Klein, A. F. 181, 403
Klein, M. 223, 403
Knoblock, P. 8, 403
Kohler, W. 224, 403
Kolvin, I. 396–97, 400, 403, 406, 410, 423;
    on behaviour modification 86, 103, 105,
    107, 111, 115, 120, 138; on community
    intervention 8; on conduct disorders
    12–13, 19; on enuresis 63; on families 60,
    62, 65–6, 69, 71, 177; on group therapy
    247; on parent counselling-teacher
    programme 201; on screening 4, 38, 40,
    52, 54, 187, 301, 335; on theoretical
    problems 51; on teacher-aides 15
Kounin, J. S. 10–11, 89, 184, 403–04
Kranzler, G. D. 228, 261, 404
Krauft, C. C. 27, 409
Kuypers, D. S. 90, 95–6, 404

Lachowicz, I. 91, 328, 391
Lahaderne, H. M. 92, 404
Lamb, H. R. 141, 404
Lambert, M. 30, 118, 306–07, 309, 387, 404
Lang, P. J. 119, 404
Lates, B. J. 88, 404
Lawrence, D. 226, 228, 261, 404
Lawson, S. 23, 421
Layman, D. 92, 386
Lehrman, L. J. 307, 404
Leitch, I. M. 349, 403, 406, 410
Lennard, H. L. 27, 404
Levenstein, P. 23, 404
Levine, F. M. 113, 404
Levitt, E. E. 7, 17, 22, 31, 227, 230, 307–09,
    316, 404
Levy, P. 229, 261, 401
Lewis, M. D. and J. A. 261, 405
Lieberman, M. A. 219, 228, 405, 421
Light, L. L. 261, 405
Lindzey, G. 230, 399
Lipinski, O. 129, 405
Lisle, J. D. 261, 405
Litow, L. 94, 405
Lobitz, G. R. 138, 401
Long, J. D. 90, 422
Long, J. L. 6, 184, 405
Loughran, J. L. 9, 396
Love, L. R. 325–26, 405

Lovitt, T. C. 90, 405
Luborsky, L. 25, 28, 314–15, 405
Lund, D. 88, 399
Lyons, K. H. 173–74, 405

McAllister, L. W. 88–9, 110, 405
McBrien, R. J. 261, 406
Maccoby, E. E. 118, 406
McDonald, S. 101, 406
McGee, C. S. 95, 402
MacKeith, R. 63, 403
McKenzie, H. S. 88, 99, 404, 406
McKeown, D. 100, 406
McLaughlin, T. F. 90, 406
McLennan, B. W. 232, 242–43, 406
Macmillan, A. 403, 406–07, 410; on
    behaviour modification 86, 103, 105,
    107, 111, 120, 138; on screening 4, 41–2,
    54, 301, 335; on sociometry 39, 93; on
    teacher-aides 15
Macmillan, D. L. 91, 407
McNamara, J. R. 96, 101, 407
Madge, N. 66, 415
Madsen, C. H. 86–8, 105, 110–12, 390, 407
Magill, R. S. 174
Main, G. C. 90, 407
Mann, P. H. 229, 261, 407
Mannino, F. V. 175–76, 407
Marholin, D. L. 92, 94, 395, 407
Markman, H. J. 18, 398
Marjoribanks, K. 177, 408
Marshall, A. M. 173–74, 197, 415
Marshall, H. R. 225, 408
Matarazzo, R. G. and J. D. 27, 408
Mathews, D. B. 226, 261, 402
Meacham, M. L. 86, 408
Meadow, R. 63, 403
Meares, O. A. 174, 408
Megson, B. 13, 179, 391
Meichenbaum, D. H. 90, 95, 138, 408
Melamed, B. G. 119, 404
Mellor, F. J. 13, 399
Mercatoris, M. 129, 408
Meyer, J. B. 261, 408
Meyers, C. E. 92, 408
Mezzano, J. 230, 261, 408
Michaelis, M. L. 90, 390
Miles, M. B. 228, 405
Miller, D. 21, 408
Miller, F. J. W. vii, 63, 69, 408–09
Miller, J. O. 23, 397
Miller, L. 20, 22, 29, 177, 307, 309, 311, 409
Milne, D. O. 226, 261, 391
Minuchin, S. 178, 409
Mischel, W. 96, 409
Mitchell, K. M. 27, 30, 409
Mitchell, S. 7, 41, 227, 230, 328
Moelis, I. 29, 230, 316, 423
Montessori, M. 147, 409
Montgomery, R. 102, 389
Moore, T. 178, 409

Morse, C. M. 184, 405
Morse, W. C. 6, 174, 409
Moulin, E. K. 227, 261, 409
Moyer, W. 99, 101, 402
Mulligan, W. 104, 409
Mullin, L. 59, 317, 381, 409
Munger, P. F. 261, 404, 422
Munro, B. C. 90, 407
Munro, J. J. 228, 261, 419
Myrick, R. D. 261, 410

Natzke, J. H. 144, 410
Neligan, G. A. 38, 63, 410
Nelson, C. M. 91, 397
Nelson, R. I. 261, 406
Nelson, R. O. 99, 129, 388, 405
Newman, R. G. 184, 405, 410
Newson, J. and E. 177, 179, 224, 410
Nicol, A. R. 400, 403, 406, 410–11, 423; on
    community intervention 8; on family 60,
    62, 65–6, 69, 71, 187; on group therapy
    235, 240, 247, 259; on psychotherapy
    221, 229–30; on screening 335; on
    theoretical problems 51; on therapists
    75–6, 259, 381
Nietzel, M. T. 86, 94, 410
Niland, I. M. 220, 226, 228, 399
Nolen, P. A. 90, 410
Norton, E. 11, 404
Nussen, J. L. 95, 402

Obradovic, S. 184, 404
O'Connor, R. D. 93, 410
O'Dell, S. 99, 411
Ohlsen, M. 14, 389, 411
O'Leary, K. D. 402–04, 411, 415–16, 420;
    on behaviour modification 86, 88–91,
    95–6, 98, 102–04, 112, 129; on parents
    178; on teacher-aides 145
Oppenheim, A. 7, 115, 227, 230, 328, 417
Orgel, A. R. 142–43, 392–93
Orpet, R. E. 92, 408

Parker, J. 230, 238, 410–11
Parloff, M. B. 119, 411
Parsons, B. V. 21, 385
Parten, M. 224, 412
Patterson, C. H. 221, 229, 261, 387, 412
Patterson, G. R. 14–15, 21, 86, 104, 412
Paul, G. 31, 412
Pelham, L. E. 261, 412
Persons, R. W. 229, 261, 412
Peters, A. 30, 416
Peterson, R. F. 88, 412
Phillips, D. 94, 407
Piaget, J. 222, 412
Pines, N. A. 147, 412
Pollack, L. J. 29, 230, 316, 423
Pope, B. 26, 412
Popper, H. I. 149, 414

Poser, E. 28, 413
Power, M. J. 5, 9, 325, 413
Powers, E. 20, 413
Prosser, H. 61–2, 179, 421
Prudham, D. 38, 63, 410
Pumphrey, P. D. 261, 395
Pumroy, D. K. 94, 405

Quay, H. C. 24, 96, 396, 413

Rachman, S. 118, 307, 413
Radin, N. 23, 173, 175, 413
Rand, K. 235, 423
Randolph, D. L. 226, 228, 261, 413
Ray, R. S. 21, 412
Redl, F. 11, 184, 413
Rehin, G. F. 6, 413
Reid, J. B. 129, 419
Reid, W. J. 187, 413
Reppucci, N. D. 104, 409
Reynolds, D. 9, 29, 414
Reynolds, P. 223, 414
Riessman, F. 149, 414
Risley, T. R. 97, 386
Roach, E. M. 93, 422
Roberts, M. D. 93, 386
Robins, L. N. 7–8, 13–14, 20, 115, 414
Robinson, E. M. 228, 261, 386
Robinson, M. B. 93, 173–74, 414
Rock, P. 13, 414
Roebuck, F. N. 28, 386
Roedell, W. C. 93, 414
Roehike, H. J. 226, 228, 261, 400
Rogers, C. R. 25, 50, 230–32, 303, 314, 414
Rollins, H. A. 90, 102, 105, 414
Romanczyk, R. G. 129, 415–16
Roper, R. 224, 415
Rose, G. 173–74, 197, 415
Rose, S. A. 224, 415
Ross, R. R. 90, 95, 138, 408
Rotter, J. B. 26, 415
Rule, S. A. 101, 415
Rutter, M. 380, 415; on disorders 11, 13; on
    families 29, 64–6, 325; on results 319; on
    school types 9, 309; on screening 4–5,
    39–44; on social workers 174; see also
    subject index
Rycroft, C. 223, 416

Sainsbury, P. 51, 247, 267, 342–43, 416
St Leger, S. 9, 29, 420
Sajwaj, T. 96, 414
Sanborn, M. P. 89, 386
Sandford, N. 141, 416
Sandler, J. 221, 416
Santogrossi, D. A. 98, 416
Saslow, B. 30, 416
Saudargas, R. A. 101, 408, 416
Saunders, B. T. 327, 416
Saunders, M. 90, 387
Schaefer, C. 337, 416

Schaefer, E. S. 23, 416
Schiffer, A. L. 228, 416
Schiffer, M. 223, 232–34, 261, 416–17
Schild, J. S. 175, 416
Schonell, F. J. and F. E. 340, 416
Schuler, P. 93, 398
Schutte, R. C. 88, 416
Schwarz, J. C. 93, 395
Scott, C. B. 175, 416
Seeman, J. 261, 417
Shapiro, M. 229, 261, 401
Shapiro, R. J. 31, 417
Sharrock, A. 179, 417
Shaw, G. K. 65, 399
Shaw, M. C. 261, 417
Shemberg, K. M. 95, 402
Shepherd, M. 7, 115, 227, 230, 328, 417
Sherif, M. and C. W. 218, 417
Sherman, J. A. 86, 90, 92, 99, 399, 417
Sherman, T. M. 99, 417
Shields, F. 88, 92, 403
Shore, M. F. 175–76, 407
Shouksmith, G. 227, 261, 417
Shyne, A. W. 187, 413
Siegel, C. L. 27, 417
Siegel, L. J. 94, 407
Simonson, N. R. 220, 398
Singer, B. 28, 314–15, 405
Slaby, D. A. 93, 391
Slaby, R. G. 93, 414
Slavson, S. R. 223, 232, 417
Sloane, R. B. 235, 314, 417
Smilansky, S. 225, 418
Smith, M. B. 24, 418
Smith, M. L. 18, 310–11, 397, 418
Smith, P. K. 224, 418
Snedecor, G. W. 353, 418
Sobell, M. P. 95, 391
Sobey, F. 143–44, 418
Solomon, R. W. 94, 418
Spalter, I. 224, 415
Speilberger, C. D. 261, 418
Spence, J. vii
Spitalnik, R. 98, 394
Spivack, G. 92, 134, 337, 418–19
Stanley, J. C. 30, 390
Start, K. D. 341, 418
Stein, M. 311, 398
Steiner, M. 38, 63, 410
Stokes, T. F. 94, 418
Strain, P. 93, 418
Strassman, L. M. 29, 400
Stromer, R. 91, 418
Strowig, W. 261, 408
Strupp, H. H. 7, 25, 28, 314–15, 418–19
Stuart, R. B. 115, 419
Sullivan, H. S. 25, 419
Sulzer, B. 90, 419
Surrat, P. R. 129, 419
Swift, M. S. 92, 134, 337, 418–19
Sylva, K. 224–25, 419

Taplin, P. S. 129, 419
Taylor, F. D. 91, 400
Taylor, J. W. 227, 261, 417
Taylor, W. F. 228, 261, 419
Teigland, J. J. 261, 422
Tharp, R. G. 114, 419
Thomas, D. R. 87–8, 407, 419
Thombs, M. R. 228, 261, 419
Thomson, C. L. 100, 102, 392
Thorndike, R. L. 227, 420
Thurston, J. R. 92, 395
Tizard, J. 4, 11, 39–44, 328, 336, 415, 420
Tolor, A. 229, 261, 420
Tomlinson, J. R. 105, 420
Tonge, W. L. 194, 420
Truax, C. B. 26, 28, 32, 75, 144, 261, 314, 383, 394, 420
Trumbull, B. M. 91, 407
Turkewitz, H. 98, 104, 420
Turner, K. D. 87, 385
Twardosz, S. 96, 420

Ulrich, R. 129, 419
Urie, R. C. 8, 235–36, 401

Van Dalsen, E. 261, 396
Veroff, J. 144, 398
Vriend, T. J. 227, 261, 420

Wahler, R. G. 89, 94, 96, 392, 418, 420
Walker, H. M. 90, 92, 94, 97–8, 113, 398, 420–21
Wall, W. D. 325, 421
Wallston, B. 69, 421
Walton, W. S. vii
Ward, M. H. 87–8, 96, 421
Warner, R. W. 226, 230, 261, 421
Wasik, B. 88, 421
Waskow, I. E. 119, 411
Watkins, R. 173–74, 195, 421
Wedge, P. 61–2, 179, 421
Weikart, D. P. 23, 421
Weinstein, L. 24, 421
Weitz, H. 261, 418
Wells, B. K. 341, 418
Werry, J. S. 96, 397, 413
West, P. A. 13, 414
Wetzel, R. J. 114, 419
White, M. A. 86, 422
Whitmore, K. 4, 11, 39–40, 42–4, 336, 415
Whittaker, D. S. 219, 421
Wiesen, A. E. 86, 408
Willems, E. P. 104, 422
Williams, R. L. 90, 422
Willner, A. G. 22, 422
Wilson, G. T. 119, 170, 422
Winer, B. J. 127, 345–46, 349, 422
Winett, R. A. 92–3, 410, 422
Winkler, R. C. 92, 261, 422
Winn, E. V. 226, 229, 261, 422
Winnicott, D. W. 223, 422

Witmer, H. L. 20, 413
Wolf, M. M. 90–1, 95, 97, 328, 386–88, 391, 400, 402, 422
Wolfe, B. E. 119, 411
Wolff, S. 64–5, 403, 423
Wolstenholme, F. 8, 15, 51, 145–46, 158, 177, 201, 397, 401, 403, 410, 423
Wrate, R. 247, 397, 403, 423
Wright, D. M. 29, 230, 316, 423
Wrobel, P. A. 90, 390

Yalom, I. D. 219, 227–28, 242–43, 405, 423
Yarrow, M. R. 63, 423

Yoakley, R. W. 90, 422
Young, D. 40, 423
Yule, W. 109, 415, 423

Zani, L. P. 220, 226, 228, 261, 399
Zawel, D. 337, 416
Zax, M. 142, 144, 154, 164, 168, 392–93, 423
Zimmerman, D. J. 175, 416
Zimmerman, E. H. and J. 88, 423
Zunker, V. G. 28, 423
Zusman, J. 141, 404

Subject index

ability 74
absenteeism 41, 56–7, 73, 238; *see also*
    attendance
academic performance 92, 117–18, 170,
    227, 251–53, 257, 279, 305, 326–27
Achievement Place Project 21–2
additional assessments 45
adolescents *see* senior schools
advice-giving 26
age: of child 20, 24–5, 37–8; of teachers
    56–7
aggregate measures 347–48
aggression 238–39
aims and method of research 35–53
alcohol problems 67
allocation to groups 45–7
alternative management methods 198
altruism 220
analysis: covariance 51, 130–01, 135, 344–45,
    361; final 265–98; poor 229–30;
    regression 32, 351–52, 361
antisocial behaviour 12–13, 20–2, 73, 76–9;
    in juniors 167, 169, 171, 207, 249, 270,
    281–83; outcome and improvement
    115–17, 133–35, 211, 255, 267–70, 273,
    283; in seniors 132, 211, 255
anxiety 72, 244
application of techniques 110–13
Asian families 62
assessment: of behaviour modification
    114–19; of group therapy 245–46, 258; of
    nurturing approach 158–68
assumptions and ideas about group
    therapy 218–26
atmosphere of groups 258–59
at-risk children 19, 36, 39, 46–7, 357
attendance 55, 57, 238, 240; *see also*
    absenteeism
attention-placebo control groups 239, 241

attention-seeking behaviour 239, 241
autism 12

background to research 4–6
back-up services 189, 329–30
Barker Lunn Children's Attitude Scale 74,
    135, 257, 274–77, 295–96, 337, 347–79
    passim
behaviour: adjustment and academic
    progress 326–27; contract system
    112–13; interviews 72; scale 40; –shaping
    139, 146–48; teacher 86–91; transfer
    96–9; *see also* antisocial; changes;
    improvement; neurotic; outcome
behaviour modification 21–2, 36–7, 46,
    48–9, 78, 83–138; assessment of 114–19;
    improvement after 114–17, 121–23,
    130–38; literature on 86–103; methods
    used 103–14; observational measures
    122–38; summary of 299–332 *passim*; and
    teachers 119–22
between-schools controls 46
bias 118–19, 317–18
birth problems 62–3
boys *see* sex of child
Braide Report *1969* 173, 389

case histories 190–93
catharsis 221
Cattell Intelligence Test 340–41
changes, behavioural 96–7, 101, 104,
    136–38, 175–76, 301, 348–49; *see also*
    improvement; outcome
children: characteristics of 18–25, 54–79;
    numbers studied 35, 52–3, 104, 301; *see
    also* families
class, social 38, 67–8, 149, 178–79
classroom *see* behaviour; observation
clinical ratings 74–5, 114–15, 318, 327–29,
    342–43

cognitive improvement *see* academic
    performance
cohesiveness, group 220, 243–44
communication problems 154–55
community 7–9, 71
comparisons of regimes 287–88, 290,
    295–96, 310–11, 346
compensation 145
compensatory: education 177; stimulation
    23
composition of groups 233
concentration, lack of 72
conclusions and summary 299–332
conduct disorders *see* antisocial behaviour
confidentiality 236–37
consistency 186
consultation 174–76, 181–85
Consulting Teacher Model 99
contagion 11
contamination, control groups 31, 306
content of group therapy 240–43
continuity of contact 155
contract system 112–13
control groups 30–2, 36–7, 45–8, 131–34,
    306
cost effectiveness 323–25
counselling 20–1, 221; *see also* parent
    counselling-teacher programme
Court Report *1976* 6, 392
covariance analysis 130–35, 344–45, 361
curriculum, individualization of 185
cut-offs 42–4

data 44–5, 52–3, 335–41; *see also* analysis;
    re-analysis
deafness 64
death of parent 66, 190–91
delinquency 20–2, 229
dependency 72
DESB *see* Devereux etc.
developmental history of child 63
Devereux Elementary School Behaviour
    rating 74, 265, 270–74, 278, 287–88, 295,
    337; and behaviour modification 131,
    137; and group therapy 251–52, 257;
    results 347–79 *passim*; and teacher-aides
    168–70
deviations, quantitative 12–13
diagnostic categories *see* behaviour
differences: between regimes 353–55;
    significant 364–65, 370–72; in teachers
    155
direct therapy 14, 312
directive therapy 26
disability 64
disapproval, teacher 86–8
discipline, family 69–70
disorders, types of 11–15, 19–25, 73; *see also*
    antisocial behaviour; neurotic
divided authority 154
Draw a Person Tests 96

drug treatment 19
dual loyalties 154
Dunnett's tables 354–55
duration *see* time
dynamic group theories 243–45

education: philosophy of 9–10; policy and
    research 331–32; problems 22–5; process
    177; *see also* schools
Educational Priority Area 173
Educational Welfare Officer 173
effectiveness of treatment 306, 310–11, 317
effects of treatment 50–3; *see also*
    improvement; outcome
emotional: development 224–25; health
    64–5; problems 191
employment of parents 67–9
English Picture Vocabulary Test 339–40,
    351
enuresis 12, 63
environment, social 8; *see also* families
EPVT *see* English Picture etc.
errors in observation 129–30; *see also* bias
ethical issues 320
evaluation 16–32, 50–3, 130–38, 168–71,
    206–16, 267–68, 335–41; *see also*
    improvement; outcome
exclusion from school 55–6
existential factors 221
experimental design in behaviour
    modification 103
extra-curricular activities 186

families of children studied 60–71, 188–89,
    191, 195, 205–06, 216, 322; *see also*
    parents
family group in therapy 220
fantasy in play 225
fathers 154, 193; *see also* parents
feasibility of special help 321–22
feedback 100–01, 198, 200
financial difficulties 55, 57, 191; *see also*
    cost-effectiveness
findings of research 301–06
Finer Report *1974* 61, 395
flow chart of study 47–8
follow-ups 29, 104, 217, 257, 259, 278, 301,
    316
Foulds Hostility Scale 65
free school meals 55, 57
frequency: of consultations 184; of contact
    29
future of programmes 157, 201

General Ability Test 341
general disturbance *see* severity, overall
generalization 94–5
germophobia 11
girls, improvement in 117–18, 128, 266; *see
    also* sex of child
global reports 252–53, 257–58

goals of behaviour modification 108–09
Goldberg Health Questionnaire 65
group: behaviour modification 90;
    consultation 183; defined 218–21
group therapy 36–7, 46, 48, 50, 79, 217–61,
    303–04; assessment of 245–46, 258;
    assumptions about 218–26; atmosphere
    of 258–59; content of 240–43; in
    Newcastle upon Tyne 230–45; outcome
    and improvements 246–58; previous
    studies 226–30; summary 299–332
    passim; see also playgroups

handicapped children 9–10
head injury 64
Head Start 22–4, 145, 170
health 62–5, 190
here-and-now interaction 241–43
heterogeneity of regression 361
Holborn Test 44, 74
home 135–38, 177; –school linking 186,
    194–95; *see also* family; parents
Home Office Research Unit 180, 401
homogeneity of regression 351–53
hope, installation of 219
housing 69
hypotheses: and aims 36–8; confirmation
    of 302–05

ideas *see* assumptions
identification of disturbed children 15,
    18–19; *see also* screening
ignoring inappropriate behaviour 87–8,
    147, 155
imitation 220
improvement 51–2, 136, 251–52, 267–68,
    278–79, 344–45, 350–57; after behaviour
    modification 114–17, 121–23, 130–38; in
    context 307–10; and disorder type 37,
    115–17, 269–70, 278–79, 283, 355–56;
    after group therapy 246–58; in junior
    schools 251–53, 267–72, 283–86, 298,
    362–63, 373–74, 377; after parent
    counselling-teacher programme 214–16;
    after teacher-aide scheme 140, 170; of
    teacher-aide scheme 157; results 357–79;
    in senior schools 253–58, 268, 273–77,
    289–94, 366–69, 374–76, 378–79; and sex
    of child 37–8, 115–18, 128, 266, 278–79,
    305, 356–57, 377–79; summary of
    299–332 *passim*
independent evaluation *see* evaluation
indirect therapy 8–9, 14–15, 312
individual children, plans for 185–86
ineffective treatment 322–23
information, imparting of 219–20
instructional methods in teacher training
    99–100
intact families 61
intelligence tests 74, 96–7, 340–1, 351
intensity of therapy 315

interaction 241–43, 279–80, 345, 355, 357,
    373
interpersonal learning 220
intervention 86–94
interviews 72, 187, 338
introduction of workers into schools
    151–2, 180
irritability 72
Isle of Wight study 39–40
isolation: as punishment 91; sociometric
    39, 44, 74, 94, 136, 139

JEPI *see* Junior Eysenck etc.
Junior Eysenck Personality Inventory
    42–4, 74, 336, 348–79 *passim*; in
    behaviour modification 109, 135–36; in
    final analysis 274–78, 295–96; in group
    therapy 257
junior schools: antisocial behaviour in 167,
    169, 171, 207, 249, 270, 282, 289;
    characteristics of 36, 47–50, 59–71;
    evaluation in 335–37, 339–41;
    improvement in 251–53, 267–70, 283–86,
    298, 362–63, 373–74, 377; outcome in
    165–67, 207–09, 248–50, 267–69, 281–83,
    287–88, 359; parent counselling-teacher
    programmes in 206–10; playgroups
    230–31, 233–35, 238–39; psychiatrists'
    assessments in 247–50; results in 357–65,
    373–74, 377; summary 299–332 *passim*
'labelling' 319
learning and play 224
limit-setting 231, 238, 245
literature 385–423; on behaviour
    modification 86–103; on group therapy
    226–30, 261; on nurturing approach
    141–45; on parent counselling-teacher
    programme 173–80; *see also* name index
long-term effects 170; *see also* follow-ups

maintenance in behaviour modification
    95, 97–9, 113
maladjusted child 42, 270, 327; *see also*
    antisocial; neurotic
marriages of parents 61, 70, 192
married teachers 56–7
measurement 73–4, 122–33; *see also*
    evaluation; results
mediator, teacher as 114
Mental Health Consultation 175
methods of research 35–53, 103–14,
    184–85, 342–49
mild disorders 19
model, 'good' child as 111–12
modelling 93, 102
modification, behaviour 83–138; *see also*
    improvement
monopolization of group 243–44
Moray House Picture Intelligence Test 74,
    340

434 Help Starts Here

mothers 153–54; *see also* family; parents
motivation, teacher 119–22
moving school 55–7
multiple criterion screen 39–42

National Child Development Study 61–2,
257, 295, 341, 352, 371–79 *passim*
National Foundation for Educational
Research Sentence Reading Test 40, 337
National Health Service Reorganization
Act 1973 6
national origin of families 61–2
NCDS *see* National Child Development
etc.
Neale's Analysis of Reading Ability 40
negative intervention 86–9
neighbourhood support 56–8
neurotic disorders 12–13, 19–20, 43–4, 73,
76–9, 109–10; after behaviour
modification 115–17, 130–35;
improvement in 269, 283; in junior
schools 166, 169, 208, 248, 269, 282, 283;
outcome 208, 212, 248, 254, 267–68, 273,
282; in senior schools 133, 135, 212, 254
Newcastle upon Tyne 5, 38, 46
Newman-Keuls technique 346, 354
Newsom Report 1963 177, 410
NFER *see* National Foundation etc.
non-directive therapy 25
non-professionals 27–8, 314; *see also*
teacher-aides
non-volunteers, teachers as 118, 120
Northways House 21
numbers: of children 4, 9, 35, 38, 41, 52–3,
104, 301; of schools 36, 38; of teachers
104, 182–83, 237
nurturing programme 139–71, 299–332
passim; see also teacher-aides

observation of behaviour modification
122–38
'observer drift' 129
ordinal position of child 62
ordinary school 9–10
origins of teacher-aide programme 142–43
outcome 267, 280, 350; clinical measures of
342–43; in context 307–10; and disorder
type 130–35, 208, 211–12, 248, 254–55,
267–68, 270, 273, 277, 282; in junior
schools 165–67, 207–09, 248–50,
267–69, 282, 287–88, 281–83, 359; school
and therapist effects on 380–83; in senior
schools 130–34, 211–13, 254–56, 268,
272–73, 289–90, 295–97, 360; and sex of
child 266, 277–79; results 357–79;
summary 299–332 *passim*
overactivity 72
overcrowding 71

parents 14–15; age of 62; and behaviour
modification 21, 98–9, 114; -child

relationships 69–70, 192–93; counselling
187; education of 23–4; health of 64–5;
and home-based education 23–4;
involvement of 71, 98–9, 114, 153–54,
161, 176–80, 215–16, 325–26; reports by
25, 27, 71, 202–03, 251–52, 257–58, 338–39
(*see also* Rutter A scale); and teacher-aide
programme 153–54, 161; *see also* families
parent counselling-teacher programme
36–7, 46–50, 75–6, 78, 172–216, 303; in
action 180–94; and home-school link
194–95; and improvement 214–16;
independent evaluation of 206–16;
literature on 173–78; parental
involvement in 176–80, 215–16;
perception of programme 195–206;
summary of 299–332 *passim; see also*
social workers
partnership, teacher and social worker
181–86
patterns of behaviour and change 348–49
Peabody Picture Vocabulary Test 339
peer relationships 93, 228, 251, 257–58,
261; *see also* sociometry
perceptions of teacher-aide programme
158–69
personality *see* teacher-aides; therapists
phasing out of treatment 98
philosophy, educational 9–10
phobias 20, 328
physical illness 63–5, 190
plans, treatment 185–86
play, defined 222–26
playgroups 14, 36, 46–7, 50, 77, 230–31,
233–35, 238–39, 247–50, 299–332 *passim;*
see also group therapy
Plowden Report 1967 143, 145, 173, 177,
179–80, 412
points system *see* token procedures
police, involvement with 67
positive intervention 87–9
practical issues in research 321–32
praise 87–8, 91, 147, 155
preparation of children for therapy 235–38
pre-school behaviour modification 87
prevention 22–4, 141–45
problems: definition 11–13, 108–09;
educational 22–5; emotional 191; in
evaluation 16–32; family 188–89, 195,
216, 322; in group therapy 245; patients'
311–12; with teacher-aides 140, 154–57;
of teacher-parent links 178–80
programme design of behaviour
modification 107
progress *see* improvement
Project Re–Ed 22, 24
psychiatric: assessment 247–50, 253; care
64–5; disorders 11–12
psychoanalysis 25, 223, 225
psychodrama 229
psychodynamic therapy 21, 312–13

psychosocial environment 16–17, 29, 317
psychotherapy 221, 311–17; ineffective 7,
    46; problems in 16–32; and time 28–9; *see
    also* group therapy
pupil management 177–78

qualities *see* personality
questionnaires 159–63, 196–98, 202–03

Ralphs Report *1973* 413
rating aspects of teacher motivation
    120–22
reactivity in observation 129
reading tests 34, 39–40, 43–4, 74, 227–28,
    340
Reading Comprehension Test 34
re-analysis of data 200–01, 271–72, 276–77;
    see also analysis
reflective therapy 26
regression, statistical 32, 351–53, 361
reinforcement, social 84–138
rejection 39, 44, 74, 110, 136
relationship with teachers 151–53, 156,
    181–87, 236–37; *see also* parents,
    involvement
reliability checks 125–27, 129
reports *see* parents; self; teachers
research: settings 102–03; techniques
    310–11, 317–20
residential therapy 21–2, 24
resource room 24
Responsive Teaching Model 99–100
results 307–10, 350–79
reversal 94
rewards 21–2, 147; *see also* token
    procedures
Rochester University group 142, 145, 152,
    154
role: -playing 93, 102; of social worker 174,
    203–06; of teacher 10; of teacher-aide
    149–50; of therapist, taken by child 244
rows, family 70
rules 87–8, 147, 186
Rutter A scale (parents) 135, 274, 287,
    295–96, 336–37, 354, 369, 376–79
Rutter B scale (teachers) 40–4, 73, 271–72,
    278, 287–88, 295–96, 335; and behaviour
    modification 109, 135–37; and group
    therapy 251–52, 257; and results 348–79
    passim; and teacher-aide programme
    168–69, 171

sample studies 13
scapegoating 245
schizophrenia 12
Schonell Reading Test 340
schools: attitudes to 253, 257; -based
    measures of improvement 130–35;
    characteristics of 57–60, 317, 330,
    380–81; -home linking 186, 194–95;
    ordinary 9–11; resistance 72; and

therapist 380–83; *see also* junior; parents;
    senior
Schools Council survey of school leavers
    178–80, 416
Scottish Educational Department 145
screening: of children 38–44, 109, 335–38;
    of teacher-aides 149; *see also* testing
secondary prevention 18
Seebohm Committee *1968* 6, 173, 177, 179,
    417
selection *see* screening
self-concepts 229, 261
self-disclosure 244
self-reinforcement 94, 98
self-report 197–201, 253, 257; *see also* Junior
    Eysenck
senior schools 36, 48–50, 59–61, 335–38,
    341; antisocial behaviour in 132, 211,
    255; family situations 60–71; group
    therapy in 231–32, 240–45, 253;
    improvement in 253–58, 268, 273–77,
    289–94, 366–69, 374–76, 378–79; out-
    come in 133–34, 211–13, 254–56, 268,
    272–73, 290, 295–96; parent counselling-
    teacher programmes in 210–14; teachers
    in 182–83, 237; results 360–61, 366–76;
    summary 299–332 *passim*
sensitivity 72, 110
separation 65–6
severity of disorder 18–19, 280
severity, overall: and behaviour therapy
    131; in final analysis 267, 269–70, 273,
    281, 290–92; and group therapy 250, 256;
    and parent counselling-teacher
    programme 209, 213; and teacher-aides
    165
sex of child 73; and conflict 233; and
    disorder type 60, 277–79; and
    improvement 37–8, 115–18, 128, 266,
    305, 356–57, 377–79; and outcome 266,
    277–79; and regime interaction 355
sexual matters 12
shyness 72, 110, 239
siblings 65; *see also* family
single-parent families 61, 70
size of family 62
sleep problems 72
'sleeper' effects 137
Smethells Report *1977* 195, 418
social: climate 8; reinforcement 84–138;
    welfare agencies 67
social workers in schools: role of 174,
    203–06; and teachers 181–87, 198–201;
    training of 180–81; *see also* parent
    counselling-teacher programme
socializing 5, 220, 223
sociometry 39, 42–4, 74, 93–4, 136, 228,
    239, 251, 257–58, 274, 354
somatic symptoms 72–3
space problems 156
special school 10–11

specificity of treatment 317
spontaneous remission 31–2, 307, 316
stages of group therapy 242
Stanford Achievement Test 91
Stanford-Binet Vocabulary 340
statistical analysis *see* analysis
status of traditional approach 6–7
stealing 72
stimulation 23
structure, classroom 185–86
studies, previous 385–423; *see also* literature
style 25–6; *see also* therapist, qualities
sub-group analyses 136
substitution of different behaviour modification programmes 97
summary and conclusions 299–332

tantrums 72
task-relevant behaviour 124, 127–28
teacher-aides 14–15, 36–7, 46–9, 75, 77, 139–71; in action 145–51; in future 157; improvement after 140, 170; improvement of 157; independent evaluation of 168–71; literature on 142–45; parental involvement with 153–54, 161; personality of 144, 148; perceptions of 158–69; problems of 154–57; role of 149–50; selection of 148–49; and teachers 151–53, 156; training of 140, 150–51, 157, 162, 170; summary of 299–332 *passim*
teachers: age 56–7; behaviour 11, 86–91; changes in 101; differences in 155; evaluations and reports by 114–19, 251–52, 257–58, 261 (*see also* Rutter B); expectations 8; motivation 119–22; numbers of 182–83, 237; in parent counselling-teacher programme 196–98; relationships with 151–53, 156, 181–87, 236–37; response in behaviour modification 125–33; role of 10; selection of 105; and social workers 181–87, 198–201; and teacher-aides 152–53, 156; training of 14, 119; *see also* parents, involvement; Rutter B
temperament measurement 72, 339
termination of therapy 245
terminator controls 31
testing 116–19; *see also* Barker Lunn; Cattell; Devereux; Draw a Person; English Picture Vocabulary; General Ability; Holborn; intelligence; Junior Eysenck; Moray House; National Child; National Foundation; Neale's; Peabody; reading; Rutter
theoretical issues 306–11
therapeutic qualities 280, 314–15; *see also* therapist, qualities

therapist 75–9; qualities 25–7, 280, 305, 314–15, 381–83; role taken by child 244; techniques 312–15; training of 232–33; variables 119
therapy *see* group therapy; psychotherapy
time 37–8, 315–16; of assessments 46; of consultation 104, 106; and effectiveness 300, 302, 305, 315; and psychotherapy 28–9; for training 104–05; *see also* follow-ups
timetabling problems 156
token procedures 89–92, 96, 101–02, 112–13
toy selection 233–34
traditional approach 6–7
training: in group therapy 232–33; of social workers 180–81; of teacher-aides 140, 150–51, 157, 162, 170; of teachers 14, 99–107, 119
transfer of behaviour 96–9
'trap', behavioural 97
treatment groups, allocation to 45–7
trends in data 73
truancy 193

underprivilege index 56–8
unemployment 67–8
United States: Head Start programmes in 22–4, 145, 170; disorders in 328; psychotherapy in 6, 17, 22, 46; school type 325; social workers in 173–75; teacher-aides in 142–43, 145, 152, 154, 157, 164; teachers in 86; tests 339; token procedure in 90–1, 96
universality 219

valence concept 233–34
vandalism 55, 57
Vernon's Graded Word Reading Test 40
visual problems 63

waiting list control groups 31
Warnock Report *1978* 6, 9, 177, 421
Watts Vernon Test 341
Wechsler Intelligence Scale for Children 96, 340
Weightings, assigning 42–4
WISC *see* Wechsler etc.
withdrawal 110; from class 164, 319
within-school controls 46
Woodberry Down Child Guidance Clinic 145–46
work analysis 193

Young Group Reading Test 40, 44, 74
Younghusband Report *1959* 173, 423